A COMPARATIVE EXAMINATION OF MULTI-PARTY ACTIONS

This monograph addresses the phenomenon of mass harm and how it may be resolved through collective redress. It examines particularly how such redress may be achieved through mechanisms such as multi-party actions (MPAs). In order to do this an analytical framework is created against which to evaluate various multi-party procedures. This is illustrated through the experience of a selection of common law jurisdictions in dealing with mass harm, namely that of England and Wales, Canada, Australia and the United States, as well as that of EU collective redress. It examines multi-party action laws benchmarked against the objectives identified in the analytical framework. The phenomenon of environmental mass harm in particular is explored as a case study, as it illustrates some of the difficulties that may arise in mass harm litigation. Also, this work explores where the best solutions for mass harm redress may lie in the future—perhaps in collective actions or through alternatives such as regulation and alternative dispute resolution or a combination of these. Finally, the experience of mass harm litigation in Ireland is examined, as currently this jurisdiction does not have an effective mechanism for dealing with mass harm.

Volume 4 in the series Civil Justice Systems

Civil Justice Systems

Series General Editor, Christopher Hodges, Director, Swiss Re/CMS Research Programme, Centre for Socio-Legal Studies, University of Oxford

This series covers new theoretical and empirical research on the mechanisms for resolution of civil disputes, including courts, tribunals, arbitration, compensation schemes, ombudsmen, codes of practice, complaint mechanisms, mediation, and various forms of Alternative Dispute Resolution. It examines frameworks for dispute resolution that comprise combinations of the above mechanisms, and the parameters and conditions for selecting certain types of techniques and procedures rather than others. It also evaluates individual techniques, against parameters such as cost, duration, accessibility, and delivery of desired outcomes, and illuminates how legal rights and obligations are operated in practice.

Volume 1: *The Costs and Funding of Civil Litigation: A Comparative Perspective* edited by Christopher Hodges, Stefan Vogenauer and Magdalena Tulibacka

Volume 2: *Consumer ADR in Europe* by Christopher Hodges, Iris Benöhr and Naomi Creutzfeldt-Banda

Volume 3: *Law and Corporate Behaviour: Integrating Theories of Regulation, Enforcement, Compliance and Ethics* by Christopher Hodges

A Comparative Examination of Multi-Party Actions

The Case of Environmental Mass Harm

Joanne Blennerhassett

·HART·
PUBLISHING
OXFORD AND PORTLAND, OREGON
2016

Hart Publishing
An imprint of Bloomsbury Publishing Plc

Hart Publishing Ltd
Kemp House
Chawley Park
Cumnor Hill
Oxford OX2 9PH
UK

Bloomsbury Publishing Plc
50 Bedford Square
London
WC1B 3DP
UK

www.hartpub.co.uk
www.bloomsbury.com

Published in North America (US and Canada) by
Hart Publishing
c/o International Specialized Book Services
920 NE 58th Avenue, Suite 300
Portland, OR 97213-3786
USA

www.isbs.com

First published 2016

British Library Cataloguing-in-Publication Data
A catalogue record for this book is available from the British Library.

ISBN:	HB:	978-1-50990-529-4	(Hart Publishing)
	HB:	978-3-406-703-62-1	(Verlag CH Beck)
	ePDF:	978-1-50990-530-0	
	ePub:	978-1-50990-531-7	

Library of Congress Cataloging-in-Publication Data

Names: Blennerhassett, Joanne, author.

Title: A comparative examination of multi-party actions : the case of environmental mass harm / Joanne Blennerhassett.

Description: Oxford ; Portland, Oregon : Hart Publishing, 2016. | Series: Civil justice systems ; volume 4 | Includes bibliographical references and index.

Identifiers: LCCN 2016019865 (print) | LCCN 2016020006 (ebook) | ISBN 9781509905294 (hardback) | ISBN 9781509905317 (Epub)

Subjects: LCSH: Class actions (Civil procedure) | Joinder of actions. | Liability for environmental damages.

Classification: LCC K2243 .B54 2016 (print) | LCC K2243 (ebook) | DDC 344.04/6—dc23

LC record available at https://lccn.loc.gov/2016019865

Series: Civil Justice Systems, volume 4

Typeset by Compuscript Ltd, Shanno n

To my family, my Doctors of Love.

FOREWORD

The perennial question of how to deliver collective redress is complex and multifarious. It is one that continues to vex policymakers and lawyers. The reality of the way in which modern life operates has led to an increase in 'massification' on many levels, such as mass production and mass consumption. Unfortunately the occurrence of mass harm is also increasingly evident in our time.

We are familiar with the broad spectrum of types of harm that may occur, ranging from mass injuries caused by defective products or environmental exposure to toxic chemicals, to mass financial losses resulting, inter alia, from violations of consumer law or competition law. In almost every part of the world, unfortunately, such harm may occur and the need for redress becomes a key question. Where do the solutions to providing collective redress to mass harm lie? The answer may be found in an array of approaches such as through regulation or dispute resolution. The appropriate response varies and it is clear that there is no 'one size fits all' answer to the phenomenon of mass harm. The issue of access to justice for those who suffer mass harm is a concomitant question. In appropriate circumstances, where legal proceedings result, groups of victims may wish to aggregate their legal proceedings in order to try to surmount some of the obstacles that they may face in pursuing a legal action individually. One of the procedural mechanisms that has evolved as a response is that of the multi-party action (MPA).

The author, Dr Blennerhassett, as an expert in tort law and dispute resolution, examines the issues surrounding mass harm, collective redress and MPAs in a broad and practical way to address these questions. She has scrutinised the experience of a selection of common law jurisdictions and analyses how they have dealt with MPAs and alternative tools in the pursuit of collective redress. The US, as a forerunner in multi-party actions, teaches broad lessons and evidences many of the positives and perceived ills of mass litigation. England and Wales have adopted a much more conservative approach to such litigation. Dr Blennerhassett's expertise in EU law helps the reader to engage with EU policy and EU Member State experience in addressing the challenges of mass harm, as many Member States have faced similar difficulties in responding to such harm. She appraises whether and to what extent MPAs may improve access to justice and empower those harmed with a route to collective redress. Dr Blennerhassett has created an excellent analytical framework of MPA objectives and uses these as benchmarks to assess how and whether MPAs may assist in the pursuit of collective redress. This is a unique and valuable contribution to scholarship in the field of dispute resolution. As an environmental law specialist, Dr Blennerhassett invokes the phenomenon of environmental mass harm as a case study to illustrate some of the challenges and complexities that mass harm litigation can present.

Having a background and training as a practitioner, Dr Blennerhassett recognises the need to explore the very real challenges facing those dealing with mass harm and she was strongly motivated by the practical law reform aspect of this research. The results of this work are both informative and compelling. It is clear from her research that jurisdictions without some form of procedural mechanism are impeding access to justice for those who have suffered mass harm.

Dr Blennerhassett concludes that MPAs are not the panacea to mass harm litigation. Instead, they only form part of a suite of solutions that may enable access to justice and collective redress. She advocates a holisitic approach to such redress, highlighting the use of regulatory solutions and alternative dispute resolution techniques as complementary tools in this range of solutions. It is clear that MPAs have a crucial role as management mechanisms for dealing with cases of mass harm. While MPA methods may vary from jurisdiction to jurisdiction, their objective does not. The methods invoked reflect the realities of the different legal systems. The question of which MPA mechanism may best suit each jurisdiction is a policy decision based on these realities. All of the jurisdictions examined are endeavouring to achieve the same output of managing collective redress, the overriding need being that of procedural justice. This conclusion is supported by the author's analytical framework which clarifies that the fundamental reason for the need for MPAs is to enable the efficient management of mass harm litigation so as to maximise just outcomes; that they are an invaluable procedural tool to assist in 'managing the unmanageable'.

Ireland is an example of a jurisdiction that has clearly experienced many large instances of mass harm, often resulting in costly, unmanageable, inefficient litigation or compensation tribunals. A few examples include: the army deafness cases against the State; the blood contamination caused by Hepatitis C; the pyrite construction damage that resulted in the longest-running case in the history of the High Court. Despite a clear procedural need for managing mass harm redress, Ireland still does not have an effective MPA procedure. Moreover, MPAs appear to be actively discouraged. Instead, the courts invoke a confusing array of alternative methods where MPAs might have played a more obvious role. In 2005, the Irish Law Reform Commission (LRC) recommended the introduction of an MPA procedure as an additional procedural mechanism to assist with mass harm litigation for use in cases where there is a clear need. Despite this recommendation, more than 10 years later there has still been no change. Dr Blennerhassett raises a number of critical questions in this work that need to be urgently addressed and resolved. These questions include: why a jurisdiction such as Ireland, despite having experienced many cases of mass harm and litigation, remains reluctant to introduce MPAs? Why has it not yet taken steps to adopt a procedural mechanism that will enhance access to justice for those who need it? More than 10 years after the Law Reform Commission recommendations, why have these questions not been resolved?

One may speculate that there are policy reasons behind this stagnation as there seems to be an almost de facto prohibition on such a mechanism. Perhaps it is because the State is likely to be a regular defendant in cases of mass tort and personal injury litigation. It is also likely that a fear exists of opening the cliched floodgates of litigation if such a procedure were to be introduced without adequate controls. The LRC, however, recommended the introduction of a procedure designed to minimize such risk. Due the lack of appropriate mechanism, those with cases that would be suited to MPA must pursue them in another way. It is evident that great injustices and inefficiencies would result from these improvisations. Claims that the introduction of an MPA procedure would encourage a 'compensation culture' are erroneous, because, in suitable cases, MPAs can assist the efficient management of such cases. While MPAs are not a metaphorical silver bullet that will resolve all the challenges of delivering effective collective redress, they are a necessary procedural mechanism that ought to be in the legal armoury of any jurisdiction in order to assist in providing access to procedural justice. Dr Blennerhassett offers a keen insight into the nature and necessity of MPAs as a response to the modern phenomenon of mass harm. She explores why Ireland, in particular, not only requires but also deserves this legal mechanism in order to protect its people from those who have caused mass harm. This book will provide invaluable guidance to judges, lawyers, academics and policymakers who inevitably face the modern challenge of managing mass harm litigation.

Peter Sutherland SC

CONTENTS

ACKNOWLEDGEMENTS

With heartfelt thanks to Dr Owen McIntyre, Professor Christopher Hodges, Professor Steve Hedley, Peter Sutherland SC, Erin Brockovich, Professor Colin Scott, Professor Joe McMahon, Professor Imelda Maher, Professor Deborah Hensler, Professor Vince Morabito, Professor Stefaan Voet, Professor Allan Kanner, Professor Itzchak Kornfeld, Professor Jasminka Kalajdzic, Mark Tynan, Caroline Fine, Dr David McFadden, Veronica Calnan, Pat Rice, Sinead Moloney, Mel Hamill, Robert Crossley, Tom Adams, Emma Platt and all at Hart Publishing. Special thanks to Rowland, Veronica, Rowley and Geoff Blennerhassett for giving me solace and safe haven. Also to all my dear friends for their kindness. Lastly, to Sully, Chloe and Jamie, without whom I would never have managed to do this—thank you for all your love and for keeping me going—it's been an emotional odyssey.

AUTHOR BIOGRAPHY

Dr Joanne Blennerhassett is a graduate of Trinity College Dublin, Université Paris 2 Panthéon-Assas, University College Dublin, the Law Society of Ireland and University College Cork. She is a College Lecturer in the Sutherland School of Law, University College Dublin, where she has lectured since 2003, specialising in Environmental Law, Tort Law, and Dispute Resolution. She has a background as a practitioner having practiced as a solicitor. She is also a qualified mediator and arbitrator. She was recently awarded a PhD in collective redress which formed the background research for this monograph.

Part I

Collective Redress, Mass Harm, Multi-party Actions and Environmental Mass Harm

1

Introduction

1. Background

The origins of this research project can be traced to a 2007 conference in Dublin where a question raised by a guest speaker in relation to collective redress mechanisms ignited my curiosity. This led me to explore further the theme of collective redress and underlying questions about the role of Multi-Party Actions (MPAs) and how these may help to deliver the outcome of collective redress for those injured by widespread harm.

Ireland is an example of a common law jurisdiction that, at present, has no formal statutory or judge-made rules for MPAs, save for restricted representative actions. These representative actions are rarely invoked because they are of very limited use. Collective action, a common form of MPA, is not yet permitted. This sets Ireland apart from common law jurisdictions that have such MPA mechanisms and is a gap in the Irish legal framework. Under the existing statutory framework, MPAs seem to be actively discouraged. This is despite the fact that the Irish Law Reform Commission (LRC), Ireland's principal public body for the investigation of law reform, has recognised the procedural gap that results from the absence of MPAs. In a major study in 2005 and subsequent LRC report, it explored the prospects for MPAs in Ireland and recommended their introduction.[1] While Ireland does not yet have a mechanism for MPAs as such, occasionally, the courts use a confusing array of alternative methods in cases where MPAs would have played an obvious role. In recent years there have been a number of cases of mass harm, including contaminated blood products, army deafness and asbestos-related ill health. Such cases usually draw widespread public interest owing to the nature of the claims involved, the scale of the potential class or the prospect of State liability. Normally, however, owing to the lack of an appropriate mechanism, those with cases potentially suited to an MPA must pursue them in another way. Great injustices and inefficiencies have resulted from these improvisations, yet, despite the LRC recommendations, there have not yet been any proposals for change in Ireland. This raises the question of why Ireland appears to be reluctant to adopt such an MPA procedure when it is has clearly experienced many cases of mass harm.

This suggests the need for an examination of the issues surrounding mass harm, collective redress and MPAs in a broad way and to undertake a comparative analysis of how other jurisdictions, in particular a selection of common law jurisdictions, use MPAs to try to achieve collective redress. One of the key themes arising in this research is the need for procedural justice and of managerial mechanisms to help deal with mass harm. It appears that MPAs play an important role in response to this need.

[1] Irish Law Reform Commission, *Consultation Paper on Multi-Party Litigation* (LRC CP 25-2003) 14.

2. Aims, Original Contribution, Anticipatory Findings

Surprisingly few commentators have attempted to evaluate whether or to what extent MPAs have, in fact, improved access to justice.[2] This research examines the use of MPAs as a remedy for mass harm and addresses how they might empower those harmed and provide them with a route to collective redress. It examines what roles MPAs may play in enhancing access to justice. In order to do so, this work creates an analytical framework that establishes a series of MPA objectives in order to evaluate the extent to which MPAs may deliver collective redress. This framework highlights the fundamental aims of MPA procedures, comprising the following: (1) access to justice; (2) judicial and procedural economy; (3) fairness (including proportionality, balancing individual rights and personal autonomy, and non-abuse); (4) predictability; (5) deterrence; (6) compensation. This framework is then used to provide benchmarks against which to assess the use of MPAs and the extent to which MPAs may assist in the achievement of effective collective redress. This framework provides touchstones against which to examine the use of MPAs as redress mechanisms for mass harm generally and environmental mass harm in particular.

The area of environmental mass harm illustrates how challenging mass harm can be. It demonstrates the complexities and difficulties that can be involved this type of litigation, particularly for its victims. For this reason it is used as a case study of mass harm. It is used as an example to illustrate the findings in relation to MPAs and collective redress generally. It is touched upon within the examination of the jurisdictions in this research, where appropriate.

The areas of tort law, mass harm, environmental mass harm and collective redress are specific fields in which there is considerable scholarship and literature. It appears, however, that there has not been much research on their interaction. It seems that there has been little research in the area of collective redress for environmental mass harm to date and, therefore, a great need for further studies in this increasingly important area. Much of the environmental mass harm literature focuses on toxic torts, particularly in the United States (US).[3] Despite the lack of literature on the area of environmental mass harm, it provides a good case study against which to test the findings of this study.[4] This work is informed by the experience of a selection of common law jurisdictions in dealing with mass harm through MPAs. It also examines the emerging European Union (EU) solutions to collective redress to assess what role MPAs may play in the future pursuit of collective redress. This work also explores, as a corollary, alternative tools to litigation that appear to be growing in popularity, particularly in EU Member States.

MPA procedures form part of a range of remedies required to achieve collective redress for mass harm. It appears that MPAs are needed in order to surmount some of the challenges and difficulties presented by mass harm litigation. For example, it is clear that the collective nature of MPAs may assist plaintiffs to overcome some of the difficulties that may

[2] J Kalajdzic, 'Accessing Justice' ('Class Actions' Conference, University of Windsor, Canada, 2011).

[3] See eg G Boston and S Madden, *Law of Environmental and Toxic Tort Cases: Cases, Materials and Problems* (West Academic Publishing, Boston 2005).

[4] This is because it illustrates the difficulties that can be involved in mass harm litigation, eg those involving evidential complexity and proving causation.

be encountered in taking legal action because their greater combined resources may enable them to 'pool their resources' and deal with these challenges collectively. In an apparent paradox, it is possible that mass treatment, whether by judges or other bodies involved in collective redress, can sometimes achieve a more effective remedy for individuals either through the courts or by using other procedures that are evolving for the resolution of mass torts, such as ADR and ombudsmen. MPAs can also aid enforcement.

When each of the MPA objectives is explored against the practical experience of the various modes of collective redress in the selected common law jurisdictions, the common theme of management emerges. The findings of this work will demonstrate that MPAs make an important contribution to the effective management of mass harm litigation. It appears that the idea of MPAs as managerial mechanisms is the overarching value informing each of the MPA objectives. This suggests that the essence of each of the criteria reflects the need for effective management of mass harm litigation. When these MPA objectives are achieved, they are indicative of procedural justice. The *Oxford English Dictionary* defines 'management' as: 'the process of dealing with or controlling things or people'. For the purposes of this research, management in this context alludes to the ways in which MPAs, to the extent that they help to achieve the MPA objectives, can assist those involved in the process of mass harm litigation. Logistics and case management are elements of this but it comprises other issues, congruent with the MPA objectives. These encompass the ideas that are omnipresent around issues such as access to justice, judicial and procedural economy, and fairness, while ensuring that individual needs are met. This work does not focus on management techniques within MPAs as these relate to the procedural and technical managerial aspects of mass harm litigation.[5] Instead, this study examines the objectives of MPAs and how these are indicators of the effectiveness of MPAs as managerial mechanisms that can help achieve procedural justice in mass harm litigation.

The administration of civil litigation is in crisis almost worldwide, due to the workload of courts. Therefore the challenges experienced in managing this crisis are common to many jurisdictions. With typical judicial clarity, Lord Woolf, in his *Access to Justice* report, highlights the need for MPA mechanisms as one of the solutions to help manage this crisis. He recognised that there are inherent difficulties with multi-party procedures and that his report was not a panacea to this.

> In this area of litigation more than any other, my examination of the problems does not pretend to present the final answer but merely to try to be the next step forward in a lively debate within which the parties and judges are hammering out better ways of managing the unmanageable.[6]

Lord Woolf acknowledged that MPAs are not without their flaws and are not the end solution in order to ensure collective redress. He highlights, however, that they can act as mechanisms to assist with the managerial difficulties by surmounting some of multiple logistical challenges that mass harm presents. This suggests that he recognises that the key question around collective redress is of efficient management of scarce judicial and other legal resources so as to maximise the delivery of just outcomes to the victims of mass harm. This

[5] For detail on management techniques, see further C Hodges, *Multi-Party Actions* (Oxford University Press, 2001) 15. eg pt I of this book examines 2 competing managerial models for multi-party litigation, that of the 'generic model' and that of the 'individual case model'.

[6] Lord Woolf, *Access to Justice: Final Report* (1996) ch 17 [6].

supports the notion that MPAs play an important role as managerial mechanisms to assist with the litigation of mass harm.

The LRC Report advocated that principles for reform in MPA litigation should ensure procedural fairness and practicality, procedural efficiency and access to justice.[7] It suggested that, ideally, a multi-party procedure should render the system as efficient for the collective group as the demands for individual fairness will allow. The LRC acknowledged that the need for procedural fairness is the core element in any multi-party litigation. The LRC supported the objectives for multi-party litigation procedure advocated by Hodges in his discussion of Group Litigation Orders (GLOs) in England and Wales and cited his opinion that:

> The claims, which are managed in a co-ordinated fashion under a GLO, remain no more than a collection of individual claims, each of which must ultimately be resolved. The objective is to dispose of all the claims as effectively and swiftly as possible. In deciding on a managerial mechanism to move forward resolution of all the individual claims, the paramount consideration is that the court must be satisfied that the selected approach will be *dispositive* of as many cases or issues as possible in as efficient and proportionate a manner as possible.[8]

In this statement, Hodges has crucially captured the essence of the role of MPAs, which is that of 'managerial mechanisms' that can enable procedural justice. This theme is visible throughout the MPA mechanisms evaluated in each of the common law jurisdictions in this research.

3. Approach

The identification of the analytical framework of MPA objectives in this work provides a functional analysis of MPAs. As one point of this entire study is to question the basis for the use of MPAs, the objectives that the framework identifies help to assess what MPAs are intended to do. Also, this research has a practical law reform perspective and may help to inform jurisdictions such as Ireland about the use of MPAs as a route to collective redress. This work also refers to the alternatives to MPAs that will help decide future directions for mass harm and collective redress developments. This study explores a range of different solutions employed in several jurisdictions. The only way to engage meaningfully in comparative analysis of these is to use such a functional analytical framework. This helps to demonstrate how the law is responding to the challenges presented by mass harm. Throughout this work, it is important to return to these objectives and to use them as benchmarks against which to assess MPA mechanisms. In identifying these considerations, it becomes clear that the need to address issues of mass justice in collective redress presents particular practical problems and challenges to legal systems, lawmakers and lawyers. Such challenges include interpreting new demands in civil claims and making policy choices rise to the challenges of these demands, for example the question of how to resolve issues of mass environmental harm.

[7] Irish Law Reform Commission, *Report on Multi-party Litigation* (LRC 76-2005) 18.

[8] Ibid 19 [1.53] citing Hodges, *Multi-Party Actions* (n 5) 68, ch 5 [11].

Following the examination of the concept of mass harm in general, the MPA as one of the various means of collective redress for such mass harm, and its treatment in a selection of common law jurisdictions, is then evaluated. In order to produce sound and meaningful research results, it is essential to adopt a logical and consistent method in any comparative study. A comparative study of MPAs in different jurisdictions is complex. First, while the aim is to identify similarities and differences in the design of procedures, there must be some fundamental common denominators to ensure that the comparison is relevant. Subject jurisdictions are studied to identify similarities and differences in the civil procedure mechanisms whose function is to enable management of mass claims. The definitions and purposes of MPAs, as well as the safeguards that the underlying norms require, vary by necessity. Furthermore, depending on the constitutional context, laws are interpreted and applied in different ways. For this reason, some division of jurisdictions into comparator groups is necessary and this study focuses on common law jurisdictions. There are important differences in civil procedure within these groups. For example, England and Wales is a common law jurisdiction that does not have a written constitution. It is also subject to EU laws in many areas. For these reasons it is not easy to compare it to the US, which has a written constitution and a federal system of laws. These factors limit some aspects of the comparative study, but such a study is still informative.

The comparative research focus in this study examines the resolution of mass torts in five selected common law jurisdictions in particular, as well as the EU approach to collective redress. There are also some references to various civil law jurisdictions' regimes for the purposes of illustration and comparison. This work is illustrated by examples of environmental mass harm and its remediation through collective redress and MPAs in each jurisdiction. It will not focus in extensive detail on procedural rules and safeguards. This study particularly examines three common law jurisdictions that have established collective action statutory regimes: the US (the federal class action rule), Australia (the representative proceedings regime) and Canada (the class action regime). Outside of the US, Australia and Canada are the two most notable jurisdictions that have adopted legislative changes to facilitate mass harm through collective action procedures for cases of mass torts. It is beyond the scope of this research to look at the class action regime throughout all of these jurisdictions in detail. In Canada, therefore, it examines procedures at federal level and also in two provinces in particular, Ontario and British Columbia. This is because these are legally important common law jurisdictions for reasons of population and the volume of litigation. It also examines one province that is heavily influenced by the civil code tradition, Quebec. As for the Australian examination, owing to the scope and scale of this research, discussion will focus on the federal system and that of the states of Victoria and New South Wales. This is because these states have the most highly developed legislative and judicial systems for MPAs, so they will be taken as the best examples for discussion. The comparative study of England and Wales provides an example of a jurisdiction where other forms of MPA have evolved, such as the group action, and also where alternatives to litigation are being embraced as viable routes to collective redress. The English and Welsh examination includes a detailed combined case study of two landmark cases of environmental mass harm and demonstrates two contrasting management approaches that may be used in such cases, that of the GLO and also that of case management. The cases are *The Corby Group Litigation*, which was resolved using a GLO, and the *Buncefield Oil Disaster*, which was resolved through case management. England and Wales is the closest comparator jurisdiction to Ireland and so its

MPA experience can practically inform the debate about what procedures may be adopted in Ireland. The EU approach to collective redress is examined, both at Member State and at EU level, in order to assess what methods of collective redress are being used in practice and what direction EU policy advocates that collective redress should proceed in the future. Finally, Ireland will be discussed as an example of a common law jurisdiction that does not have an effective MPA mechanism. There are lessons that a jurisdiction such as Ireland may learn from the experience of other regimes in this field. The MPA experience of other, non-common law jurisdictions is also referred to, where appropriate, for the purposes of illustration. For example, Sweden[9] and Brazil[10] have developed an official doctrine of collective actions within their civil law systems. This is notwithstanding the view that some consider the collective action as 'a procedural mechanism whose peculiarities elude the formally defined structure of traditional civil litigation'.[11] In addition to an evaluation of the MPA mechanisms in each jurisdiction, there is an examination of the background legal context, for example the constitutional structure and legal system.

It was necessary to carry out a comparative study of these jurisdictions' experience of MPAs. This is because comparative studies are informative where similar problems are being faced in many jurisdictions. This research evaluates the experience of these jurisdictions in redressing mass harm through the mechanism of MPAs in an effort to ensure justice. As Markesinis propounds, the complete advantage of legal systems arises where a comparison of 'like with like' is possible.[12] Numerous jurisdictions' law reform agencies have analysed comparative multi-party reform with the aim of 'comparing approaches in different countries in the hope that all might learn from experience elsewhere'.[13] The experience that has originated from the much longer-established class action regime in the US is of helpful guidance and a source of cross-fertilisation of ideas by judges in charge of the adoption of class action systems in Australia and Canada. While jurisdictions will vary in areas such as drafting, the procedures will be broadly similar. This comparative study of existing MPA regimes will also be helpful to jurisdictions that do not, as yet, have such mechanisms. For example, when Lord Woolf was making his litigation reform recommendations in England, he referred to a study of overseas regimes with particular reference to the US. Since the growth of the jurisprudence in these countries has now reached a sizeable scale it

[9] Sweden introduced a class action that may be brought in a general court by a member of a group, or by an organisation, or an administrative agency (eg the Consumer Ombudsman) allowing claims for both injunctive relief and individual damages for group members. This mechanism was introduced by the Group Proceedings Act, which entered into force on 1 January 2003. For further detail on class actions in Sweden, see generally H Lindblom in D Hensler, C Hodges and M Tulibacka (eds), *The Globalization of Class Actions* (2009) 622 The Annals of the American Academy of Political and Social Science 231.

[10] Brazil has led the development of collective rights in Ibero-American States and this has grown from consumer origins through a general procedure on 'public civil actions' largely brought by the Attorney General. These have a 2-stage process involving a declaration on general liability, followed by individuals bringing personal compensation claims. For further details, see generally A Gidi, 'Class Actions in Brazil—A Model for Civil Law Countries' (2003) 51 *Am J Comp L* 311; and A Pellegrini Grinover, 'Brazil' in Hensler and others, *The Globalization of Class Actions* (n 9) 63.

[11] R Dreyfuss, 'Class Action Judgment Enforcement in Italy: Procedural "Due Process" Requirements' (2002) 19 *Tulane J Int'l and Comp L* 5. For similar reservations, see also T Rowe, 'Debates over Group Litigation in a Comparative Perspective: What Can We Learn From Each Other?' (2001) 11 *Duke J Comp Group Litigation and Int'l L* 160.

[12] B Markesinis, *Always on the Same Path* (Hart Publishing, 2001) 306. See also by same author, *Foreign Law and Comparative Methodology* (Hart Publishing, 1997).

[13] Rowe, 'Debates over Group Litigation in Comparative Perspective' (n 11) 160.

has become invaluable for comparative use. While there is a body of scholarship around the concept of transplant in comparative law, it is beyond the scope of this research to examine this idea.[14] In summary, comparative analysis aids MPA introduction, implementation and reform in legal systems, with inspiration from the valuable experience of the US federal approach and selected other common law MPA regimes. However, as Gidi has opined:

> Importing class action law does not necessarily mean importing American-style litigation. The transplant can be 'surgically controlled'. There is no reason to believe that the whole 'Yankee package' would invade a foreign system through the window opened by class action device. Contrary to the traditional myth, class actions can succeed in the absence of discovery, contingency fees, the American cost rule, an entrepreneurial bar, and powerful and active judges, at least as effectively as can traditional individual litigation.[15]

4. Structure

This work is set out in two parts. Part I comprises chapters two to four and examines collective redress, mass harm and environmental mass harm. Part II sets out the comparative study, in chapters five to ten.

A. Part I

Chapter two explores the phenomenon of mass harm and the challenges that it presents. It begins with an explanation of the commonly used terminology in this study. The use of collective redress mechanisms as a remedy for such harm is then discussed, in particular that of the MPA and the sectors in which it may be invoked. The history and background of mass torts are explained together with the legal responses to mass harm, ranging from private law (tort law) to public law and regulation. This chapter sets out the context in which collective redress arises. It then gives an introductory overview of the MPA procedures used in each of the jurisdictions examined in this study in order to give readers an explanation of how these procedures operate before they are discussed in more detail. Chapter three sets out the MPA analytical framework of the MPA objectives that is used throughout this research to evaluate the MPA mechanisms. The background to and elements of this framework are examined in detail. It becomes apparent that each of these objectives has an overarching theme, which is that of facilitating the management of mass harm litigation. The role of MPAs as 'management mechanisms' is therefore explored. Chapter four discusses environmental mass harm as a case study, as this area is an example of the difficulties that mass harm can present. It is a practical area in which to test the use of MPAs as mechanisms for collective redress. There is an explanation of how the enforcement of environmental mass harm through tort law can play a regulatory role. The distinctive features

[14] Examples of prominent scholars and their work in this field include: A Watson, *Legal Transplants: An Approach to Comparative Law* (University of Georgia Press, 1974); A Watson, 'Legal Transplants and Law Reform' (1976) 92 *LQR* 79; O Kahn-Freund, 'On Uses and Misuses of Comparative Law' (1974) 37 *MLR* 1–27; W Ewald, 'Comparative Jurisprudence II: The Logic of Legal Transplants' (1995) 43 *Am J Comp L* 489–510.

[15] Gidi, 'Class Actions in Brazil' (n 10) 322.

of environmental mass harm litigation and responses to these are then explored in detail, including issues such as toxic torts, causation and evidential complexity, latency and environmental justice issues. There is also an evaluation of novel remedies for mass harm. This chapter illustrates how MPAs, by collectively dealing with mass harm litigation, particularly through the use as management mechanisms, can help to overcome the difficulties encountered in mass harm litigation.

B. Part II

Chapters five, six, seven, eight, nine and ten comprise the comparative element of this research and these chapters evaluate the experience of selected other common law jurisdictions and their varying collective redress MPA mechanisms as well as the EU approach to collective redress. Chapter five examines the US experience of mass harm litigation. As it is the forerunner in this area, the US MPA experience teaches broad lessons about such litigation. Chapter six examines the Canadian class action regime and chapter seven examines the MPA experience of Australia. Chapter eight examines MPAs and collective redress in England and Wales. It examines two contrasting case studies of landmark English mass environmental harm cases, through a combined case study: the *Corby Group Litigation*, which was resolved using a GLO, and the *Buncefield Oil Disaster*. These cases illustrate the importance of management mechanisms in delivering collective redress. Chapter nine examines the EU approach to collective redress. It traces the evolution of EU collective redress both at Member State and at EU level. It considers the European Commission's 2013 collective redress proposals in order to assess how EU collective redress may proceed in the future. Chapter ten discusses collective redress for mass harm in Ireland, with a particular focus in parts on mass environmental harm. Ireland is an example of a common law jurisdiction without an effective MPA procedure and this sets it apart from the other common law jurisdictions examined in this research. There may be lessons for Ireland to learn from the MPA experience of these jurisdictions. These lessons may help to inform the metaphysical question of whether Ireland ought to adopt such a MPA procedure.

In conclusion, chapter eleven considers the findings of this study, particularly the theme that has been identified regarding the management mechanism role that MPAs may play and the need for such mechanisms where litigation is necessary as a last resort in order to deliver collective redress. Even though the MPA methods of collective redress may vary, the objective does not. The different methods of collective redress adopted simply reflect the realities of the legal structures and systems in each national jurisdiction. The question of which MPA mechanism to adopt is a policy decision based on these realities. All of these methods are trying to achieve the same output of managing collective redress and they are informed by the overriding need for procedural justice. The analytical framework of MPA objectives supports this argument. This work argues that the efficient management of mass harm litigation so as to maximise just outcomes is one of the fundamental reasons for the need for MPAs. The conclusions also reflect on whether the findings for environmental mass harm seem to be (or are) very different from other mass harms and how these findings relate to the monograph as a whole.

2

Collective Redress and Mass Harm

1. Overview

This study examines and evaluates various methods of collective redress as a response to the phenomenon of mass harm, which is severe or widespread damage. There is a vast range of solutions to such harm ranging from court-based remedies, to non-litigious collective redress options. Mass torts are one of the means of seeking redress for mass harm and this study shall deal with some of the routes to seeking collective redress that victims of mass torts pursue in selected common law jurisdictions. The focus of this work will be on tortious remedies for mass harm. This study will examine and appraise MPAs in particular as a route to achieving collective redress for such harm. It will then focus especially on the use of MPAs as a solution to mass environmental harm as this provides examples of a complex area in which there are many difficulties in achieving collective redress, and so these will be highlighted where relevant. If this study were to deal with mass harm in depth it would have to extend to areas such as consumer law, which is beyond the scope of this work but such areas may be mentioned for the purposes of analogy. This work examines whether litigation through MPAs, and particularly the use of collective actions, a common form of MPA, achieves the results for which such actions are intended and confers the benefits attributable to them or whether different solutions to mass harm may be more appropriate. Factors that influence the answer to this question will depend on the legal architecture and enforcement strategy of the jurisdiction in question and how it deals with mass harm. We will see a stark contrast between the approach of the United States (US) and the European Union (EU) in particular. In some countries, such as the US, tort claims usually offer the only possibility of compensation. Fleming claims that this is due to the absence of widespread publicly funded social security and that, as a result, the US has been at the forefront of such litigation.[1] Private actions can be an alternative form of public enforcement. What becomes clear from this examination is that mass harm raises managerial issues due to the volume and complexity of the harm that may result and that MPAs or case management solutions are required to deal with this challenge. Initially, a brief background will be provided before a more detailed exploration.

It is important to note that while mass disasters often cause injury and loss on a vast scale, resulting in mass harm, they may not always result in legal consequences. One reason for this may be that the disaster is of natural origin (for example, flooding or earthquake). Another reason may be that access to justice is denied to victims due to their impoverished

[1] J Fleming, 'Mass Torts' (1994) 42 *Am J of Comp Law* 508.

state, ignorance of the law or underdeveloped legal mechanisms. However, this is changing. First, owing to increased technology there has been an alarming increase in man-made hazards that can cause vast harm. Secondly, there is now a greater ethos of social accountability and this has evolved towards victims, both public and private, which is resulting in a greater need for collective redress.

2. Terminology

An examination of mass harm and methods for its redress needs to begin with an explanation of what the commonly used terminology in this area means. This is a complex area and the language used often makes it even more confusing, so such an explanation will help to clarify what is being discussed. This study will begin by immediately addressing and explaining its components.

A. Mass Harm

Discourse on mass harm is bedevilled by a lack of clarity in terminology, which varies from jurisdiction to jurisdiction. For the purposes of this study 'mass harm' includes:

> Mass injuries caused by defective products or environmental exposure to toxic chemicals, mass financial losses resulting from violations of competition law, securities law, consumer protection statutes, and contemporaneous civil rights and human rights abuses.[2]

It is injury suffered by multiple parties and can take many forms. If one is a victim of such harm then, where possible, it is natural that redress will be sought for injury. Where others share in similar injury collective redress may be needed.

B. Collective Redress

This is the attainment of a remedy for mass harm. There are many different types of routes used to try to deliver this ranging from those sought before the courts to alternatives to litigation, including alternative dispute resolution (ADR), regulation and public enforcement. For the purposes of this research, the collective redress methods examined will concentrate on procedural mechanisms that allow many single claims relating to the same incident to be grouped together using MPAs through multi-party litigation. There are many objectives behind such litigation, including providing procedural economy.[3] It is a broad concept that includes injunctive relief and compensatory relief. The legal contexts in which collective redress for mass harm can be sought through multi-party litigation are various and

[2] D Hensler, C Hodges and M Tulibacka (eds), *The Globalization of Class Actions* (2009) 622 The Annals of the American Academy of Political and Social Science 7.

[3] These will be discussed in detail in ch 3.

the possible defendants may be State or private actors. Collective redress procedures have been introduced in many legal jurisdictions but these procedures vary widely as well as the terminology and complex rules.

C. Multi-party Actions

MPAs[4] are one form of collective redress procedure that may lead to a remedy or broaden access to a remedy for mass harm.[5] They are court-based mechanisms and can take many guises. One of these is the 'collective action' or 'representative action', which is often used for civil litigation seeking to secure collective redress.[6] These are cases involving multiple plaintiffs[7] with similar claims against the same defendant or defendants.[8] Although the terms are sometimes used interchangeably, there are technical differences between them when applied in the context of a specific jurisdiction. For example, a US class action is a particular phenomenon and is different from a Canadian class action. In some cases these mechanisms are actions in which a representative of one or more members of a group sues on behalf of the entire group[9] but without all the members of the class being identified in court.[10] In the US, class action use is relatively common due to the American system of legal enforcement. Also 'US style' class action is different from the collective action procedure being espoused by the European Commission in its 2013 collective redress policy.[11] There are other forms of group litigation procedures that need to be distinguished from collective actions as the claimants' cases remain separate and distinct but are grouped together for collective management, such as the English and Welsh tool of the Group Litigation Order (GLO).

[4] Under the UK Funding Code a multi-party action is defined as 'Any action or actions in which a number of clients have causes of action which involve common issues of fact or law arising out of the same cause or event'. It states that MPAs cover a wide variety of different circumstances, but most can be divided into either:

1. Instant disasters—ie where a large number of people have been affected, usually suffering from personal injury, by a sudden event such as a major transport disaster;
2. Creeping disasters—ie where a large number of people have been harmed by a common cause such as an allegedly harmful product or form of treatment.

See further detail at: www.legalservices.gov.uk/.../Funding_Code_-_Chapter_15_-_Multi_Party_Actions_-_April_2010.pdf.

[5] For further detail, see C Hodges, *Multi-Party Actions* (Oxford University Press, 2001) 3.

[6] Definition extracted from House of Commons Briefing Paper, 'Collective or Class Actions', available at: www.parliament.uk/briefing-papers/SN05240.pdf.

[7] The term 'plaintiff' and 'claimant' are used interchangeably throughout this work. In England and Wales, please note that the term 'claimant' replaced 'plaintiff' in the Civil Procedure Rules 1998. In relation to the use of the term 'plaintiff' in that jurisdiction, therefore, in specific cases the appropriate term to be used depends on the year. When not referring to actual cases, but speaking more generally, the term 'plaintiff' is used.

[8] Irish Law Reform Commission, *Consultation Paper on Multi-Party Litigation* (LRC CP 25-2003) 1.

[9] In such a situation, a representative body or person (also sometimes known as an ideological claimant) has the right to bring an action on behalf of a class or group of which it is not itself a member. The term can also apply to representative party actions where 1 member of a class can pursue an action on behalf of others, who are not before the court but who share this common interest, as under CPR, r 19.6 in England and Wales.

[10] Definition extracted from *House of Commons Briefing Paper* (n 6).

[11] Each of the US class action system and the EU collective redress policy will be discussed in detail in separate chapters.

As it is beyond the scope of this research to examine all possible collective redress mechanisms, although they will be referred to generally, this work will examine MPAs as a form of collective redress in particular. The terms 'collective action', 'class action', 'representative action' and 'aggregate proceedings' or 'group action' shall be known collectively as MPAs and for reference purposes the term MPA is used in the wide sense to mean any form of actual or potential litigation involving multiple parties.[12] It is notable that MPAs in general only became a recognisable phenomenon in a small number of jurisdictions in the last quarter of the twentieth century.[13]

D. Mass Torts

Mass torts are defined as the 'medical and other losses associated with personal injuries'.[14] Mass torts could, of course, be seen more broadly as encompassing harm such as some environmental losses where these cause personal injury or damage to property.[15] The term came into use in the 1980s to describe large numbers of similar legal actions against one or a few defendants arising out of the same circumstances and claiming compensation for personal injury or damage to property.[16] Litigation categorised as mass torts includes mass disaster torts, mass toxic torts (such as for harm caused by asbestos), product liability torts, environmental pollution claims (such as the Gulf oil spill) and claims for physical and psychological abuse. According to Hensler, the term 'mass tort' is a term of art, not a legal category.[17] Mass torts are a common route to collective redress for mass harm and what distinguishes them from other tort claims is their aggregated treatment by parties, lawyers and judges. In some jurisdictions, in order to provide a legal remedy, redress for mass harm is frequently sought through mass tort actions but in others this is not necessarily the case. Law firms often use the mass media to reach potential claimants, as this is the best way to make possible claimants aware of a potential legal action. Class actions for mass torts, along with class actions on behalf of consumers for relatively small monetary losses are two types of class action that have attracted particular criticism in the US in recent years. Since the adoption of the modern class action rule in the US (Federal Rules of Procedure, Rule 23),[18] courts have generally ruled that because mass tort plaintiffs' injury claims are

[12] It is noteworthy that defendant class actions are possible for cases involving multiple defendants. These are far more infrequent than plaintiff actions and usually less complex. This research will focus on class actions brought on behalf of multiple plaintiffs as these are more numerous and relevant to MPAs and mass harm.

[13] See Hodges, *Multi-Party Actions* (n 5).

[14] See Hensler and others, *The Globalization of Class Actions* (n 2) 6. However, this definition is perhaps best suited to the US context as it only deals with personal injury and does not deal with harm other than personal injury.

[15] The reference to property is included in several definitions of mass torts by commentators in this area. An example of where harm has occurred to property without necessarily causing personal injury is seen in the Fukushima nuclear disaster. Residents in the vicinity had to evacuate their homes in the immediate aftermath of the accident and they were unable to return to live there afterwards due to nuclear contamination, which rendered their homes uninhabitable.

[16] See D Hensler, 'The Socio-Economics of Mass Torts: What We Know, Don't Know and Should Know' in J Arden (ed), *Research Handbook on the Economics of Torts* (Edward Elgar, 2013) 279.

[17] Ibid.

[18] Civil actions in the US state courts are governed by state-adopted versions of this class action rule.

usually somewhat different in significant ways, mass torts do not satisfy the formal requirements for class certification.[19] Therefore, judges use other forms of aggregation that do not require court inquiry into such differences.[20]

When dealing with mass torts it is necessary to categorise such damage. Fleming says that mass torts are principally concerned with three types of disaster:[21]

1. single-event occurrences, which simultaneously inflict injury on many individuals, like aeroplane crashes or nuclear explosions;
2. serial injuries ('creeping disasters') caused by the same product to numerous victims over a period of time, like asbestos and pharmaceuticals; and
3. toxic damage affecting persons or property over a given area.

In relation to the categories above and their treatment in the US legal system, Fleming propounds that the first (single events) poses least problems to traditional tort remedies. In most cases, causation is straightforward and contributory negligence is seldom a factor. For these reasons, it is easy to consolidate claims as they all concern the same operative facts. He notes that categories (2) and (3) are often combined as 'mass exposure' cases. The second category (creeping disasters), he asserts, is vastly more challenging to legal process. In addition to the hurdles in the first category, there are added issues of causation (including possibly multiple causes), as well as possible consumer misuse of the product and often latency of injuries. These require individualised handling for each separate claimant, which does not facilitate aggregative resolution. The third category (toxic or environmental torts) is beleaguered by even more problems.[22] They can be refuted by 'background risks' that could equally have contributed to the damage, especially where the fallout covers a large area.[23] In the US, standard of proof issues arise and will call for more than a balance of probability. There are further requirements such as technical scientific evidence. The threat of action being excluded through the Statute of Limitations combined with latency of claims exacerbates the claimant's low chances of success. A further complication is that the basis of liability is typically negligence, whereas, under US law, the other categories often impose strict liability, such as liability for defective products and for nuclear accidents (again in the US). Similar difficulties arise if the damage stems from multiple-cause accidents, where a single cause cannot be identified with certainty. Issues of foreseeability of damage may also occur.

It would appear that Fleming's identification of three categories is unnecessary. The evidence suggests that it is unwarranted to distinguish between (2) and (3). Instead, more general categories could be used. This could be restricted to two categories, with two subcategories within a 'mass exposure' category. The reason for this is that, in reality, the similarities between these categories lead them to be best treated together and that there is not enough convincing reason for dealing with them separately. Instead, they could be

[19] See Hensler, 'The Socio-Economics of Mass Torts: What We Know, Don't Know and Should Know' (n 16) 279.

[20] See Hensler and others (n 2) 6. For further analysis of the economics of mass torts, see Hensler (n 16) 280.

[21] Fleming, 'Mass Torts' (n 1) 508.

[22] Difficulties encountered in environmental mass harm and toxic torts are discussed in ch 4.

[23] Fleming (n 1) 507. He also notes foreign terminology for mass torts such as 'délits à grande échelle, Massendelikte'.

regrouped into one category named 'chronic exposure' with perhaps the subclasses given. If this were the case, the categories may be summarised as:

1. Single-event occurrences, such as nuclear explosions or plane crashes, which simultaneously inflict injury on many individuals.[24]
2. 'Mass exposure' cases dealing with:
   a. serial injuries ('creeping disasters') which take a perhaps less spectacular, more chronic form, caused by the same product to many victims over a period of time, such as pharmaceuticals and asbestos; and[25]
   b. toxic damage affecting people or property in a certain area (toxic or environmental torts).[26]

Each of these types of occurrence has resulted in legal claims by their victims, for either personal injuries or property losses. Claims for such redress have created challenges for legal systems and there have been varied responses. These will be explored in this examination of collective redress for mass harm, in particular mass environmental harm as it frequently exhibits many of the difficulties listed here. Several chapters will deal with selected common law jurisdictions' experience of resolving such harm through MPAs.[27]

3. Typology and Sectoral Coverage of MPA Collective Redress

This section will look at some of the different types of MPAs as well as the different sectors where they are commonly used. It is not a definitive examination, rather an exploration of the most common forms of MPA. There are many types of collective redress and the key characteristics of these can vary. In numerous jurisdictions, individuals, non-governmental organisations (NGOs) and public representatives are resorting to the courts for redress for mass harms. In some such cases, public officials, on behalf of private citizens, may initiate litigation. However, it appears that an increasing amount of this is civil litigation being brought by private entities using MPAs, as well as through other collective redress mechanisms such as ADR. Looking at the various types of MPA collective redress procedure, there are two main forms of such MPA that will first be summarised: (A) collective actions; and (B) joinder or aggregate litigation proceedings.[28] Following this, section C looks at examples of sectors in which MPAs are used and these will be explored briefly: (i) consumer law collective redress; (ii) competition law collective redress; and (iii) collective redress for environmental mass harm (which will be examined in more detail in a specific chapter

[24] An environmental example would be Seveso-type situations, eg the Bhopal Disaster.

[25] An environmental example would perhaps be a leak from a single source contaminating water, eg Erin Brockovich mass water contamination experience (note asbestos is more likely to be an occupational injury due to smaller injury numbers, such as in the Irish case of *Fletcher v Commissioner of Public Works* [2003] IESC 13. This was not a mass tort case although other cases could perhaps have been joined in this action).

[26] eg marine oil pollution such as that seen in the wake of the BP oil spill in the Gulf of Mexico following the explosion of the Deepwater Horizon Rig in April 2010.

[27] It is beyond the scope of this research to examine further complications that arise in cases of harm arising from transnational litigation. Instead, suffice it to say that uncertainly as to applicable law, forum-shopping etc further complicate and exacerbate the risks and problems surrounding such litigation.

[28] These will be examined in further jurisdiction-specific analysis in the chapters dealing with each of the selected common law jurisdictions.

dealing with this). Finally, collective redress in the EU will be discussed as this ranges across the previous three sectors.

A. Class Actions (also Known as Collective or Representative Actions)

The term 'class action' is a synonym for collective or representative action and is most commonly used to describe such actions in the US system. These mechanisms enable a large group of people who share a common interest to collectively bring a claim to court. It is most apt to describe actions brought on behalf of a defined class, but without all members of the class being identified to the court. As shown, diverse terminology is used in different legal jurisdictions and varying complex rules can apply. These mechanisms are generally used where harms have been perpetrated on a group with similar concerns, but not all of whom may be identifiable when litigation is commenced and the action is initiated by someone who asserts to represent the group in a representative action.[29] Depending on the rules established in any particular jurisdiction, it may be possible for class members to opt in or to opt out and to bring separate actions, or class membership may be compulsory. Any judgment or settlement will bind all the members of the class. It can take many different forms and vary widely. One definition of a class action is as follows:

> A class action is a legal procedure which enables the claims (or part of the claims) of a number of persons against the same defendant to be determined in one suit. In a class action, one or more persons ('representative plaintiff') may sue on his or her own behalf and on behalf of a number of other persons ('the class') who have a claim to a remedy for the same or similar alleged wrong to that alleged by the representative plaintiff, and who have claims that share questions of law or fact in common with those of the representative plaintiff ('common issues'). Only the representative plaintiff is party to the action. The class members are not usually identified as individual parties but are merely described. The class members are bound by the outcome of the litigation on the common issues, whether favourable or adverse to the class, although they do not, for the most part, take any active part in that litigation.[30]

Mulheron comments that, notwithstanding the simplicity of the above definition, class actions *are* complicated, sometimes controversial and are a concomitant of a complex society. She opines that this has manifested in two particular respects: by a strongly held opinion for and against their introduction, and by frequent appellate review.[31]

In class actions, most, if not all, of the class members are not in attendance in court and the class representative and class lawyer (also sometimes referred to as class counsel) are formally assigned control of the litigation by the courts.[32] The concept of representative

[29] eg consumers, employees, indigenous peoples etc.

[30] R Mulheron, *The Class Action in Common Law Legal Systems: A Comparative Perspective* (Hart Publishing, 2004) 3.

[31] Ibid.

[32] A class representative is a person (or multiple persons) similarly situated to the other members of the class. The class representative's interests are typical of the rest of the class, and can fairly and adequately represent all the other members of the class. Since not all members of the class are named in the proceedings the class representative stands in for all those allegedly harmed by the defendant. Typically, it is a concerned consumer who is one of the first to contact a lawyer regarding their complaints or problems with a defendant that ends up being named as the class representative of a lawsuit. However, it is the court that ultimately approves who can be the class representative for a given class action.

civil litigation has existed for quite some time in the form of public officials taking civil legal actions on their citizens' behalf to enforce laws. For example, in Ireland, action by the Attorney General falls into this category for public nuisance or charitable trusts. In France, the Procureur de la République exercises this role. Such lawsuits do not normally provide individual redress. Instead, their aim is declaratory or injunctive relief and sanctions, such as fines, against defendants.[33] What is relatively new is to permit private actors (individuals and organisations) to take civil actions on behalf of sizeable numbers of identifiable but absent individuals.[34] The US has been a forerunner in multi-party litigation developments, especially in the class action domain. In examining various methods of mass harm resolution, a large part of any discussion will reflect strongly on the US experience of class actions. This is because the US has had more extensive and longer experience of mass procedures than any other similar mechanism used in any other jurisdiction, and also because the US influence has been significant internationally.

Some jurisdictions have introduced procedures based on the US model, for example Canada and Australia.[35] In the last decade, varying models are emerging in several jurisdictions that are either adopting some elements of the US model[36] or are trying to avoid some of the perceived negative aspects of the US approach. 'US style class action' is a term commonly used for regimes with features similar to that of the US. This includes trans-substantive application of the procedure, meaning that it can cover a variety of types of harm traditionally across a range of sectors, such as environmental, consumer and personal injury; as well as the standing (*locus standi*) of private actors to represent a class; the availability of monetary damages; and opt-out rather than opt-in procedures for monetary damage class actions. According to a study on class action developments worldwide undertaken by Hensler and others, by March 2009, at least 18 countries globally had adopted some form of class action that meets the definition above.[37] Several more, including the EU, were debating adopting such procedures.[38] Some countries that have adopted a type of class action are considering altering or enhancing this procedure to a kind that would possibly improve access to the courts for groups of citizens, consumers and investors but the majority of these developments have been relatively recent.[39] It was shown in the global study that only six countries at that time had class action mechanisms similar to the US style: Australia, Canada, Indonesia, Israel Portugal and Norway.[40] All of these, except the

[33] In some jurisdictions such as Germany and Switzerland private associations have been able to sue for injunctive relief on behalf of various 'social interests'. See further detail in Hensler and others (n 2).

[34] Such individuals who would have standing to bring their own actions but are not officially in attendance. Ibid 7.

[35] The Canadian and Australian regimes will each be discussed in a separate chapter.

[36] eg a common attitude to aggregation.

[37] Hensler and others (n 2).

[38] According to Hensler and others (n 2) 13, this comprised Argentina; Australia, Brazil, Canada, Chile, China, Denmark, Finland, Indonesia, Israel, the Netherlands, Norway, Portugal, South Africa, Spain, Sweden, Taiwan and the US. At least 4 more, as well as the EU, were said to be debating the adoption of such procedure at that time: Austria; England and Wales; France and Poland. Italy adopted class action legislation that became effective in January 2010 (following the implementation of Law no.99/2009); in 2014 France introduced limited class action legislation (when French Parliament adopted the Consumer Law Bill (also known as the "Harmon Act"); in 2015 England and Wales introduced a limited form of collective action for competition claims; Austria has yet to introduce any form of class action legislation.

[39] Hensler and others (n 2) 13.

[40] Ibid.

US, have been adopted since 1990. It is worthwhile examining the key features of class actions in summary:

The issue of who has standing to bring an action varies widely. It may be confined to government-approved associations (approved for the purposes of bringing representative actions) or designated public officials.[41] In many jurisdictions, private individuals—such as investors, consumers, businesses and other private parties—have standing to represent a class of similarly situated absent parties in at least some circumstances. None of these jurisdictions allows a party a monopoly over representative litigation, but those seeking to represent a class must show the judge that they can adequately and fairly represent it. They may, however, do so without the worry that their decision to pursue certain cases may offend the government in power.[42] There is great variation as to the scope and relief available in relation to class actions. In more than half of the countries that have implemented some type of class action the procedure can be used for a range of different legal claims.[43] The remainder of these countries restrict their use to securities, competition, consumer fraud, constitutional rights claims or a combination of these. Most of the countries allow monetary damages as relief.[44] Some jurisdictions impose conditions that restrict the real effect of class actions.[45] It is perhaps noteworthy that many jurisdictions prohibit punitive damages.[46] Studies of various legal systems show that once a class action mechanism has been introduced, it can evolve to new uses and be invoked in innovative ways by parties and lawyers, so its range of potential can expand.[47] Similarly, however, class action statutes may be restricted by court decisions and practice.

A crucial feature of class action litigation procedure is the question of whether it should be opt-in or opt-out. Class actions, by definition, allow one or a few parties to act on behalf of many other similarly situated individuals who are absent from court. This is an extraordinary practice for most modern legal systems, which safeguard individual independence and control of one's legal rights.[48] If the class action succeeds, those in the class share in the rewards but if their action is unsuccessful, their rights to redress may be extinguished.

[41] Where action is brought by either it presumably exerts pressure that such actor will not act in a way that is inconsistent with government policies.

[42] See Hensler and others (n 2) 14. However, in China, it seems that class counsel are 'supervised' by public officials, which would indicate some restrictions.

[43] This comprises 10 out of 18 of the countries examined by Hensler and others. Also, the procedure is 'trans-substantive', according to D Hensler and others, *Class Action Dilemmas: Pursuing Private Goals for Public Gain* (RAND, 2001) 14.

[44] This occurs in 16 out of the 18 country studies. In some jurisdictions, however, further litigation may be required to obtain this.

[45] See Hensler and others (n 2) 22. eg Israel's trans-substantive rule provides special protection, although limited, for State agencies and 'sensitive' economic sectors. Chile requires that class actions can only arise from a breach of contractual duty and it also denies pain and suffering damages. In the US, the 1966 rule-drafters advised federal district court judges that Federal Rules of Procedure, r 23(b)(3) (which provides for monetary damage class actions) would not usually be suitable for mass accident cases. See also D Hensler, 'Has the Fat Lady Sung: The Future of Mass Toxic Torts' (2007) 26 *Rev of Litig* 883. As a result, apart from a brief spell in the early-1990s, federal judges have mainly refused to apply the rule to mass injury cases, including those involving defective products.

[46] At present, punitive, 'pain-and-suffering', emotional distress and other types of non-economic damages are largely unavailable to plaintiffs outside the US and in recent years, the US has been taking a more restrictive approach in this area, esp with respect to punitive damages awards.

[47] eg Israel's legislature included provisions for class actions in statutes for environmental risks, consumer protection, work equality, disability rights etc between 1988 and 2005. In 2006, it introduced a trans-substantive class action statute to replace this regime.

[48] Hensler and others (n 2) 15.

Those in a class action are bound by settlements, whether they feel that they are fair or not. Opt-out regimes require that class members (meaning all those who meet the criteria that define the class) must be notified that representative litigation is proceeding and they must be given the opportunity to leave themselves out of this litigation. This means that they will be excluded from the remit of any judgment or settlement if they 'opt out'. They then remain free to litigate on their own behalf. All other class members are bound by the result of the litigation. Opt-in regimes are the converse—all those who meet the class criteria must positively show that they wish to participate in the litigation. So far, countries that allow representative litigation by private actors are equally divided on the opt-in opt-out issue.[49] Some commentators feel that opt-out class actions breach due process, as those who do not know about the proceedings and who may have chosen not to participate or do not understand the repercussions are bound by the results. Other commentators believe that opt-in regimes limit the deterrence potential of class litigation as defendants face diminished liability exposure, due to lack of information or interest from some putative class members.

B. Joinder or Aggregate (also Known as Group) Litigation Procedures

This is the term used for procedures that allow for similar cases to be combined (joined) for litigation purposes. In some countries, aggregated procedures for mass claims have been adopted in addition to, or perhaps instead of, class action litigation.[50] It is notable that virtually all of the legal jurisdictions mentioned so far also have some form of joinder procedure. It has been seen in some cases recently that this joinder procedure has been used for mass litigation. However, the term 'group litigation' is best used to describe procedures to deal principally with aggregated mass litigation. This involves numerous individuals or bodies, comparably situated, who have combined their individual proceedings. In these cases, the parties are formally before the court and in control of their own legal actions. While these terms are sometimes used interchangeably, there are important technical differences between the terms when applied in the context of a specific jurisdiction. Note, by definition, all aggregate litigation procedures are opt-in. Some jurisdictions have particular procedures to aggregate mass damage claims that are too numerous for traditional joinder. England and Wales provides a clear example because group litigation was introduced there in the last few years. It has mechanisms for group action but does not have class actions. It has a number of different procedural mechanisms that can be used to manage multi-party litigation. These are: the test case; consolidation and single trial of multiple actions; the Group Litigation Order (GLO); and the representative action. The GLO is a relatively new mechanism as it was introduced in 1999. It provides for a registry of individual claims that arise from the same factual circumstances.[51] With the GLO mechanism, where a number of

[49] 8 out of 16 have chosen an opt-out regime, 4 have chosen an opt-in regime and 2 have chosen a default opt-in regime with an opt-out variant in certain circumstances; Hensler and others (n 2) 16.

[50] At least 6 countries have done this: England and Wales, Finland, Germany, Japan, Switzerland and the US (note Germany's procedure is more a hybrid form—more like a means of consolidating aggregate claims than a true representative action). In Japan and Switzerland, these procedures are based on contractual agreements rather than court rules or judge-made orders.

[51] This will be discussed in detail in ch 8.

claims are similar, usually involving the same issue or product and or the same defendants, they are formally coordinated and administered by the same judge.

Similarly, the US Multidistrict Litigation (MDL) procedure enables diffuse federal court claims that arise from the same facts to be collected for pre-trial management.[52] After this pre-trial stage, the MDL statute dictates that mass claims are to be disaggregated and returned to the courts where they were initiated. In practice, in both English and US courts, once mass claims are aggregated they are nearly always resolved through summary disposition or group settlements.

C. Examples of MPA Sectors

i. Consumer Law Collective Redress

There has been growing international recognition that collective redress is an important and necessary legal procedure, especially to enhance consumer rights. The OECD has reflected this by recommending that Member States provide consumers with access to different means of redress, including collective redress mechanisms.[53] A model has been emerging in many jurisdictions of a representative action procedure that is restricted to enforcing certain aspects of consumer law, such as protection against unfair advertising or unfair contract terms.[54] These models have a number of noticeable features. First, it is noteworthy that these models do not apply to other types of claims.[55] Secondly, a 'representative' model is commonly used, often with a consumer association acting as a representative intermediary. There are often restrictions on the bodies that are allowed to act as representatives; for example, they may be required to be a public body with sufficient standing, permanence and assets.[56] The most active intermediaries are public enforcement bodies.[57] Thirdly, most of the procedures being debated are limited to giving injunctive relief.[58] Currently, a controversial question involves whether the relief available should be extended to damages claims. This raises questions of who should initiate, control, be bound by and pay for such claims, as well as the question of the purpose of this—or any—type of representative procedure and asks whether it is to address enforcement or whether it ought

[52] This will be discussed in detail in ch 5.

[53] Commission (EC) 'Consumer Collective Redress' (Green Paper) COM(2008) 794.

[54] Such models are seen in many EU Member States.

[55] C Hodges, 'What are People Trying to Do in Resolving Mass Issue, How is it Going, and Where are We Headed?' in S Vogenauer and C Hodges (eds) *Civil Justice Systems in Europe: Implications for Choice of Forum and Choice of Contract Law* (Hart Publishing, January 2013). Hodges notes that 'this is a vertical solution, not a generic one'.

[56] eg in England a public representative action may be taken under the Competition Act 1998, s 47B for such consumer harm. However, claims can only be brought by a 'specified body' as an 'ideological claimant' acting as a representative claimant, not by a directly affected consumer as a representative claimant. Consumer bodies need government approval to bring such actions and the only 'specified body' that has been licensed to take such action so far is the national consumers' association 'Which?', under the Specified Body (Consumer Claims) Order 2005, SI 2005/2365. This will be discussed in further detail in ch 8.

[57] Hodges, 'What are People Trying to Do in Resolving Mass Issue, How is it Going, and Where are We Headed?' (n 55) 79. Hodges further cites the examples of what was previously known as the UK Office of Fair Trading (now the CMA), the Brazilian Attorney General and the Australian Competition and Consumer Commission.

[58] This avoids the difficult issue in the US experience of FRCP, r 23(b)(2) of defining the class, as the model is essentially non-opt-out.

to be extended to damages claims.[59] Using any of these procedures, remedies have been limited to declaratory or injunctive relief up until recently. Some jurisdictions, however, are beginning to include claims for damages. Under EU policy, Member States are encouraged to provide representative procedures for the enforcement of certain consumer protection provisions[60] and EU legislation requires action by consumer organisations in numerous areas.[61] This usually occurs through consumer organisations empowered to bring cases on behalf of consumer interests. Many Member States already have similar mechanisms in their national law and this does not affect their national approaches.[62] For example, in some States, only consumer associations are permitted to bring representative proceedings. However, in other States, such proceedings can be taken by regulators acting to defend the public interest. Examples of this are the Director of Consumer Affairs in Ireland, or the Competition and Markets Authority (CMA) in England and Wales. For consumer organisations to bring representative claims, this can only be done where funding for such action is available to cover the potential risk of liability for opponents' costs if the case is unsuccessful.

As court proceedings are expensive and slow they are not necessarily the best way to achieve collective redress. Other options to litigation, including various ADR-type mechanisms that try to achieve fast and economical results, are being used for consumer redress in many EU States. These procedures may be stand-alone or may be included in judicial procedures. Examples of this include the use of ombudsmen and dispute resolution schemes. There is, however, little scope to examine these mechanisms in detail in this work. It appears that some of these are highly effective in some circumstances; for example, the combination of a regulator's redress power and an ombudsman system has proved to be highly effective for many financial services claims, and to obviate any need for a class action procedure. There is increasing evidence that these can be successful in preventing large numbers of unmeritorious claims and in avoiding litigation where voluntary settlement may be possible instead.[63] There is, however, a need for further detailed empirical examination of the advantages and disadvantages of all such alternative mechanisms before definitive conclusions may be drawn. According to the European Commission, 'mediation or arbitration schemes can provide consumers with easy and affordable redress'.[64] For example, Spain has a comprehensive system of consumer arbitration and Nordic countries have no-fault compensation schemes for medical and drug injuries and, as a result, very few such court actions occur.[65] Consumer associations may assist negotiated settlements, as seen in Italy, Portugal and Poland.[66] From a funding point of view, it is interesting that in Portugal the

[59] See further Hodges (n 55).

[60] This will be discussed in detail in ch 9.

[61] Such as misleading advertising in Directive 84/450 EEC; unfair terms in contracts with consumers by sellers or suppliers in Directive 93/13/EEC; and unfair commercial practices in Directive 2005/29/EC.

[62] Commission (EC), 'Access of Consumers to Justice and the Settlement of Consumer Disputes in the Single Market' (Green Paper) COM(93) 576, 64 noted that of the then 12 Member States, 8 gave consumer organisations a right to bring claims for the protection of the collective interests of consumers. One of these States (Belgium) permitted such actions to be undertaken by both consumer organisations and by an administrative authority, and 3 other States protected consumer collective interests through an independent administrative authority (this role was previously exercised by the Office of Fair Trading in the United Kingdom and is now undertaken by the CMA, the Consumer Ombudsman in Denmark and the Director of Consumer Affairs in Ireland).

[63] C Hodges, 'Nordic Compensation Schemes for Drug Injuries' (2006) 29 *J Consum Policy* 142.

[64] European Commission, MEMO/08/741, 27 November 2008, 2.

[65] Hodges, 'Nordic Compensation Schemes for Drug Injuries' (n 63) 143.

[66] Hensler and others (n 2) explain that both Poland and Portugal have Offices of Consumer Protection.

consumer organisation DECO (which is independent and has charity status) is exempted from legal costs except where it loses a case, in which case it pays between one-tenth and one-half of the normal cost.[67]

ii. Competition Law Collective Redress

There are varying forms of collective redress for competition law, particularly between EU Member States. A large part of this stems from EU initiatives such as the Green Paper on damages for breaches of competition law adopted by the European Commission in 2005[68] and the White Paper in 2008,[69] both of which include a chapter on collective redress. It is beyond the scope of this work to examine competition law but it is important to note one of the most recent EU policy developments in this area. In June 2013, the Commission adopted a proposal for a Directive on antitrust damages actions under national law for breaches of EU competition law.[70] This proposed Directive aims to harmonise procedural law issues relating to private enforcement in Member States. It leaves it to Member States to decide whether or not to introduce collective actions in the context of private enforcement of competition law.[71]

iii. Collective Redress for Environmental Harm

This area will be examined in chapter four, which deals specifically with environmental mass harm. It is becoming clear that MPAs may have an important role as a managerial tool where environmental mass harm is litigated. This can be seen particularly in toxic torts.[72] For example, in such cases claimants can have many technical difficulties trying to prove causation due to problems of dealing with serious scientific evidence, and this can make it very difficult to establish facts. Where these issues are dealt with collectively, there can be advantages to individual claimants, as difficulties that may otherwise confound them if they were acting individually, may be surmounted as a group. Where victims have suffered similar injuries, some type of managerial tool, such as MPAs, may enable them to overcome these difficulties and to deal with such issues collectively.

iv. EU Approach to Collective Redress

There is ongoing debate in the EU about the introduction of collective procedures for monetary damages due to concerns about controls on excess and abuse. It seems that although the US model might allow such claims for consumers and investors, there are huge problems such as the cost, conflicts of interest between representatives, lawyers and claimants and unjust settlements.[73] A solution may be to refine the US model by adding controls

[67] Ibid.

[68] Commission (EC), 'Damages Actions for Breach of the EC Antitrust Rules' (Green Paper) COM(2005) 672.

[69] Commission (EC), 'Damages Actions for Breach of the EC Antitrust Rules' (White Paper) COM(2008) 165.

[70] Commission (EC), 'Proposal for a Directive on Anti-trust Damages Actions' COM(2013) 404.

[71] This will be discussed in detail in ch 9.

[72] These are injuries caused by toxic substances and will be explained in detail in ch 4.

[73] G Miller, 'Group Litigation in the Enforcement of Tort Law' in Arden (ed), *Research Handbook on the Economics of Torts* (n 16) 267.

against abuse into the procedure or instead to introduce alternative means of dealing with the fundamental issues. The EU collective redress proposals for collective action endeavour to achieve this as they contain many safeguards to avoid the perceived problems resulting from the excesses of US style class action. Many jurisdictions have introduced anti-abuse controls in their legislation.[74] It is unclear, as yet, whether these controls work. It is important, when analysing EU collective redress, to highlight the approach that underlies enforcement of law in the EU. The European Commission enforces EU law as a public authority and guardian of the EU treaties. In parallel, individuals, business and entities representing interests of different groups can seek enforcement of their rights under EU law in national courts. The violation of EU law may, in some cases, trigger multiple individual lawsuits. Collective redress in such cases may complement public enforcement. EU law currently provides for the possibility of injunctions for those pursuing collective actions for consumer law but there is great variation among national legal systems in relation to environmental protection, competition, financial markets and other areas of law. There is even more diversity among Member States when numerous consumers or businesses wish to seek damages in the same case.

The European Commission has worked for several years on developing standards of collective redress in the field of consumer and competition law. As mentioned in section (ii) on competition law collective redress, the Commission adopted a Green Paper on antitrust damages in 2005[75] and a White Paper in 2008,[76] both of which include a chapter on collective redress. In 2011, the Commission carried out a broad public consultation to assess whether and how a European approach to collective redress could help European citizens and businesses.[77] It also took into account the European Parliament's Resolution 'Towards a Coherent European Approach to Collective Redress' asking for a horizontal framework for collective redress.[78] The consultation replies showed divergent views among stakeholders and a need for balanced solutions.[79] In June 2013, the European Commission made a Recommendation that set out a series of non-binding principles for collective redress mechanisms in Member States so that citizens and companies can enforce their EU law rights where these have been infringed.[80] It aims to ensure a coherent horizontal approach to collective redress in the European Union without harmonising Member States' legal systems and advocates that national redress mechanisms should be available in different areas where EU law grants rights to citizens and companies, notably in consumer protection, competition, environmental protection and financial services. By recommending to Member States that they put in place national collective redress mechanisms, the Commission aims to improve access to justice, while ensuring appropriate procedural guarantees

[74] The US system controls include the requirements of adequacy of representation, numerosity, superiority and predominance. Other jurisdictions have controls such as the 'loser pays costs' rule and provisions on representation and settlement.

[75] Commission (EC), 'Damages Actions for Breach of the EC Antitrust Rules' (Green Paper) (n 68).

[76] Commission (EC), 'Damages Actions for Breach of the EC Antitrust Rules' (White Paper) (n 69).

[77] http://ec.europa.eu/dgs/health_consumer/dgs_consultations/ca/docs/cr_consultation_paper_en.pdf.

[78] www.europarl.europa.eu/sides/getDoc.do?type=TA&language=EN&reference=P7-TA-2012-21.

[79] http://ec.europa.eu/dgs/health_consumer/dgs_consultations/ca/replies_collective_redress_consultation_en.htm.

[80] Commission (EC) Recommendation of 11 June 2013 on Common Principles for Injunctive and Compensatory Collective Redress Mechanisms in the Member States concerning violations of rights granted under Union Law (2013/396/EU).

to avoid abusive litigation. Also in June 2013, as previously mentioned, the Commission adopted a proposal for a Directive on competition damages actions under national law for breaches of EU competition law.[81] The Recommendation complements this proposed Directive. While the Recommendation calls on Member States to put in place collective redress mechanisms, the Directive leaves it up to Member States to decide whether or not to introduce collective redress mechanisms in the context of private enforcement of competition law. These recent developments will be discussed in detail in chapter nine in order to assess whether they are indeed going to deliver their promised aim of collective redress.

4. The History and Background of Mass Torts

The US has been at the forefront of modern aggregate litigation developments, although class actions trace their beginning to group proceedings in the English common law of equity as early as the year 1199. The earliest example is the case of *Master Martin Rector of Barkway v Parishioners of Nuthampstead*.[82] This concerned a dispute between the parishioners of the chapel and their rector. The chapel had once been an independent chapel. By the time the dispute arose, however, the chapel had become a member of the church of Barkway. The witnesses on both sides of the dispute agreed that the rector was to receive the tithes from the chapel and to supply a minister for the chapel. The dispute appears to have been over whether the rector had to supply a chaplain for Nuthampstead every day or just three days a week. Viewed through a modern lens, this case looks like a religious consumer class action, with the parishioners arguing for a full-time, full-service chaplain and the rector arguing for the cheaper part-time alternative. These class action roots, almost a millennium old, date back to when Chancery heard cases with a remarkable similarity to the modern consumer class action. For certain types of groups (here villages and parishes) litigation by representatives on behalf of the group was well established in England by the twelfth century.[83]

These group proceedings were brought to the US as part of common law. Any discussion of 'mass torts' inevitably turns its attention to the US and its distinctive 'class action'[84] regime—whether as a model that other jurisdictions may wish to follow or as an example of the dangers that can attach to the 'massification' of civil claims.[85] As previously mentioned, a very important factor that has influenced the need for class actions in the US is the lack of availability of comprehensive welfare systems there.[86] This void has increased the need

[81] Commission (EC), 'Proposal for a Directive on Anti-trust Damages Actions' (n 70).

[82] This case dates from c 1199. All that remains of *Martin v Parishioners* are records of depositions, which are reported in 95 Seld Society 8 (No 210) (1981).

[83] S Spence, 'Looking Back … In a Collective Way: A Short History of Class Action Law' (2002) 11 *ABA Business Law* 6.

[84] The US class action is deeply controversial, even in its homeland, and its development will be explored in further detail in ch 5.

[85] Cappelletti coined the term 'massification' to describe a modern phenomenon. As commerce has globalised, mass transnational markets have emerged; a single negligent act may potentially harm thousands or millions of individuals. See further detail in M Cappelletti, 'Social and Political Aspects of Civil Procedure- Reforms and Trends in Western and Eastern Europe' (1971) 69 *Mich L Rev* 847.

[86] Fleming (n 1) 508.

for compensation for harm suffered and class action mechanisms have helped to deliver this. Also, as will be explained fully in chapter five, the US legal architecture relies on private enforcement as a form of alternative public enforcement. Legislation for class actions in the US began in 1938 with the adoption of Rule 23 of the Federal Rules of Civil Procedure (FRCP) and later matured into the powerful tool available as a result of amendments to that rule adopted in 1966.[87] Class actions, as we think of them today, stem from this revision of the US federal class action rule in 1966, through amendments to FRCP, Rule 23.[88] These changes relaxed class action procedures and modern class actions were born.

Under the original version of Rule 23, class members were often required to affirmatively 'opt in' to the litigation in order to be bound by any settlement, trial verdict or other resolution of the case, thus placing practical limits on the ultimate sizes of these classes. The 1966 amendments greatly expanded the scope of US class actions by allowing judges to certify certain types of classes in which participation would now be presumed for every potential member unless the individual or entity formally excused themselves out of the class. This change facilitated the creation of classes with memberships numbering in the hundreds of thousands. As a result of these revisions, it became much easier for individuals to take action on behalf of large groups of similarly situated individuals and to be granted remedies, including damages.[89] It is this version of class actions—the very Americanised version of class actions that has evolved out of those 1966 amendments—that constitutes today's understanding of what a class action is.

With the US 1970s 'rights revolution', the American legislature introduced a legislative framework for the affirmation of civil rights through the mechanism of the class action. This has been invoked for the compensation of injury from anti-consumer business behaviour and for protection against environmental harms.[90] At first, public interest lawyers used the procedure in order to get injunctive relief from the government.[91] Lawyers in the private sector used such litigation as a route to compensation for injuries from defective products, environmental damage, breaches of securities regulations and consumer fraud. Some commentators, such as Hensler, are of the opinion that lawyers who engaged in such work became entrepreneurial (given the huge potential fees involved and the practice of engaging in contingent fee arrangements) in their approach to litigation and this caused a surge in the growth of class actions for monetary damages.[92] This practice thrived in an increasingly media-centric mass culture, presumably due to the publicity generated by mass harm events and increased awareness of the use of class actions as a mechanism for

[87] In 1966, the scope of the class action was again clarified and expanded when FRCP, r 23 was amended to provide that unnamed parties to a class action were bound by the final judgment in the action so long as their interests were adequately represented.

[88] This was soon replicated by state courts also.

[89] Hensler and others, *Class Action Dilemmas* (n 43) 13.

[90] A Miller, 'Of Frankenstein Monsters and Shining Knights: Myth, Reality, and the "Class Action Problem"' (1979) 92 *Harv L Rev* 664.

[91] It was used as a tool against racial and other discriminatory practices as well as reform in welfare, education, prison and other areas.

[92] For a discussion of the causal dynamics of mass tort litigation in the US, see D Hensler and M Peterson, 'Understanding Mass Personal Injury Litigation: A Socio-Legal Analysis' (1993) 59 *Brooklyn L Rev* 961.

the pursuit of compensation, as seen through the internet and advertising by lawyers.[93] Mass personal injury litigation in the US emerged in the 1980s. By the end of that decade, formal aggregative procedures, collectively known as MPAs, such as class actions, multidistrict litigation and consolidation were being used to resolve massive numbers of claims that would otherwise result in increasing backlogs.

It can be problematic to accommodate the litigation of mass harm within a legal system's procedural facilities and resources. An example of this is the asbestos litigation in the US in which claims number hundreds of thousands. Similarly, more than two million actions by Vietnam veterans in the *Agent Orange* dioxin defoliation cases have been consolidated in New York.[94] These exemplify an enormous body of mass litigation, which has congested US courts for years. These are surely the antithesis of conventional individual dispute resolution, which is based on a model of individual adversarial litigation between a very limited numbers of multiple parties, where the client's own lawyer controls the case and the judge has a passive, not managerial, role—especially in common law jurisdictions. However, where numerous multiple claimants are involved, logistical constraints, including legal costs, as well as the need to ensure fairness between numerous claimants, have required extensive modification of traditional processes. This has forced the evolution of alternative mechanisms to deal with mass harm litigation, most spectacularly exemplified by the experience of the US legal system. This is because mass litigation levels there have been enormous and have certainly proved a challenge to judicial creativity, with minimal legislative intervention.

In order to deliver collective redress for mass harm there are numerous challenging legal obstacles and the responses of different jurisdictions vary, as will be evidenced in this research. A reason for this may perhaps be that some countries have yet to experience major human-caused disasters and so have not needed to modify their legal procedures but this is unlikely in modern society. Another reason could be the enthusiasm of defendants to afford redress to victims outside of the court process. Perhaps the use of test cases is also a factor. The countries examined all champion the right to individual justice and this can only be forfeited where it is unavoidable in order to ensure justice to all victims, by delivering judicious and effective compensation. So far it is really only the US that has had vast experience of mass litigation, and while there are no doubt systemic limitations and its procedures are far from ideal, it does teach broad lessons in the equitable resolution of mass torts.[95]

As will be seen when examining EU collective redress, European approaches to mass claiming are generally at a different stage of evolution when compared to the US. European legal systems hold differing views on the suitability of various methods of litigating 'massified claims'. The European approach to collective redress is undergoing much change at present and this will be discussed in a separate section of this work.[96]

[93] Hensler and others (n 2) 8.

[94] Major American mass torts between 1960 and 1992 are listed and described by Hensler and Peterson, 'Understanding Mass Personal Injury Litigation' (n 92).

[95] For detail, see T Rowe, 'Debates over Group Litigation in a Comparative Perspective: What Can We Learn From Each Other?' (2001) 11 *Duke J of Comp Group Litigation and Int'l L* 157.

[96] This will be discussed in detail in ch 9.

5. Legal Responses to Mass Harm: Private Law (Tort Law) versus Public Law and Regulation

Quite a large portion of the discussion on collective redress for mass harm is viewed from the perspective of defending private rights, but there is often a public law element to mass accidents. Where public bodies are involved in such incidents, it is common that public inquiries are subsequently established to investigate.[97] Examples of this are often seen where a public body has allegedly contributed to this harm, for example the Irish social welfare equality cases of *Cotter and McDermott v Minister for Social Welfare and Attorney General*,[98] which resulted from the failure by Ireland to implement the 1978 Directive on Equal Treatment in Social Welfare,[99] and also the Irish army deafness claims.[100] The private aspect to such cases commonly involves the assessment of harm suffered by individuals.

Sometimes these are followed by settlement through compensation schemes that often obviate the need for private litigation, and inquiries commonly publish recommendations to prevent the recurrence of such incidents. Where criminal negligence has caused injury there are often criminal proceedings (for example in France[101] and Germany).[102] In the Bhopal disaster, during the action against Union Carbide (the US owners of the plant), the Indian Government interceded as *parens patriae* before the US courts and later obtained a settlement for victims.[103] So it is clear that the solution to achieving mass harm redress may lie in private law, through mass torts, or in public law through regulation, or through a combination of these, which will depend on the approach of the legal system in question. This will be exemplified in the contrasting approaches of the US and EU to be considered shortly. The utility of MPAs as a form of collective redress is conditioned by the availability of effective public mechanisms of enforcement and redress. Where there is effective public

[97] Ireland eg has had numerous such inquiries. These will be discussed in more detail in ch 10.

[98] Case 286/85 *Cotter and McDermott v Minister for Social Welfare (No 1)* [1987] ECR 1453 and Case 377/89 *Cotter and McDermott v Minister for Social Welfare (No 2)* [1991] 1 ECR 1155. These cases arose from the fact that until 1986 Ireland's social welfare policy had discriminated against married women. Married men were the automatic recipients of child benefit and received higher rates of welfare payment based on a presumption that their wives were dependent on them. For married women to receive these payments, they had to prove that their spouses were incapable of supporting themselves. In 1984, a Directive obliged Ireland to remove these practices of sex discrimination, but it did not do so until 1986. The Free Legal Advice Centre (FLAC) (a pro bono NGO) took a case arguing the entitlement of married women to back-payments during the 2-year period when Ireland's discriminatory policy was in breach of EU law. Their victory had far-reaching consequences, making it possible for 69,000 women to claim their entitlement.

[99] Council Directive (EC) 79/7/EEC of 19 December 1978 on the progressive implementation of the principle of equal treatment for men and women in matters of social security OJ 1979 L 6/24.

[100] All of these cases are discussed in detail in ch 10.

[101] In France, an estimated 4,000 people, many haemophiliacs, were given blood infected with HIV. A former Health Minister was convicted for failing to adequately screen the blood, leading to the deaths of 5 people from AIDS, and the contamination of 2 others during a key period in 1985. 2 other government officials who continued to use the old unheated stock in 1985, when a heated product was available, were sent to prison. Allegedly, all 3 politicians delayed the introduction of US blood-screening test in France until a rival French product was ready to be sold on the market.

[102] eg in Germany the prosecution of the Thalidomide manufacturers in Aachen which, as the consequence of a settlement arrangement with the State, resulted in the establishment of a compensation fund for victims. The Aachen Court approved the settlement and suspended the criminal prosecution; see *LG Aachen*, JZ 1971, 517.

[103] See L Hawkes, 'Parens Patriae and the Union Carbide Case' (1998) 21 *Cornell Int'l LJ* 181.

enforcement such as in the EU, MPAs are less necessary. Where such public remedies are not available, as seen in the US, there is a need for private mechanisms of enforcement. Even where there is effective public enforcement, as there is in England and Wales, tort law helps to fill in the gaps for regulation and so both public and private enforcement can play complementary roles. Looking at the US, some consider that tort law and its processes are best left to deal with one-to-one relations that exist in everyday life.[104] This could apply where it may be appropriate to have mass tort class actions, for example where a polluted site is in a neighbourhood or where a dangerous product has been sold to numerous consumers.[105] It is strongly debated however, whether certain ways of adjudicating mass torts and the case management problems this can entail, may undermine the advantages of tort, so this requires careful consideration.[106] Perhaps, therefore, a case management tool may assist in dealing with these problems, rather than full-blown collective action. It would appear that MPAs could help in this management role. Much of this debate about the limitations of tort is being ignored in favour of administrative solutions. In England and Wales, for example, regulators prefer to act in response to a problem rather than leaving it to be resolved through common law. In the US, however, as we have seen, tort law is used as a method of regulation, through deterrence and punishment. The US, until recently almost exclusively in the world, intentionally chose policies that have a very different balance between public and private enforcement.[107] It deliberately emphasises private enforcement in place of public enforcement as a means of behaviour control. This rather unique and fundamental aspect to US public governance in both civil rights and environmental legislation means that policies are often written in a way that seems to encourage litigation so as to implement policy goals.[108]

There is obviously enormous public interest in the aftermath of mass harm and it is often focused on how victims can get justice against the perpetrators of the damage. MPAs may be regarded as performing a 'public function' and some commentators argue that mass accidents are particularly amenable to a 'public law' approach in the US, even to an extent that justifies modifications of the traditional private law standards in relation to proof and remedies.[109] This requires that justice be accessible to many using aggregative procedures such as class actions in order to achieve settlements and that the principles of individual litigation be subordinated to this goal. The US legal system has a number of high-profile public regulatory bodies possessing powerful enforcement powers.[110] In 1941, there was a seminal scholarly analysis by Kalven and Rosenfield that profoundly influenced the development of US policy.[111] They acknowledged the theoretical notion of empowering the

[104] See A Kanner 'Toxic Tort Litigation in a Regulatory World' (2002) 41 *Washburn L J* 535.

[105] eg in *re Asbestos Ach. Litigation*, 104 FRD 422 (ED Pa 1984).

[106] G Robinson and K Abraham, 'Collective Justice in Tort Law' (1992) 78 *Va L Rev* 1481.

[107] This is seen in relation to business-to-consumer relations and corporate relations. See H Kalven and M Rosenfield, 'The Contemporary Function of the Class Suit' (1941) *U Chicago L Rev* 684.

[108] See C Hodges, 'Objectives, Mechanisms and Policy Choices in Collective Enforcement and Redress' in J Steele and W van Boom (eds), *Mass Justice: Challenges of Representation and Distribution* (Edward Elgar, 2011).

[109] See D Rosenberg, 'Mandatory-Litigation Class Action: The Only Option for Mass Tort Cases' (2002) 115 *Harv L Rev* 831. For further discussion of this public law approach in detail, see D Rosenberg, 'The Causal Connection in Mass Exposure Cases: A "Public Law" Vision of the Tort System' (1984) 97 *Harv L Rev* 849.

[110] eg the Department of Justice (also at state level, led by Attorneys General for each state), the Food and Drug Administration and the Office of Safety and Health Administration.

[111] Hodges, 'Objectives, Mechanisms and Policy Choices in Collective Enforcement and Redress' (n 108) 105.

then newly created public agencies to deliver enforcement and behaviour control. They opined, however, that because there were 'many fields in which administrative bodies have not made an appearance ... private litigation must still police large areas of modern law and provide exclusive remedy for may large-scale group injuries'.[112] There is a striking balance between these two pillars of private and public enforcement in the US. There is pervasive criticism of the effectiveness of regulators and the existing agencies there, which some consider to be beholden to the political forces that govern them and also by the community that they are intended to regulate. Therefore, Kalven and Rosenfield further explained that class litigation could serve a regulatory function, with plaintiff attorneys acting privately as the equivalent of private attorneys general.[113] Instead, private litigation is extensively used as a means of public enforcement and can be an efficient and attractive form of public regulation.[114] Private individuals are incentivised to take action to remedy breaches of law and, in this way, often create a by-product of public enforcement. The right of citizens to bring suits is a crucial feature of many environmental regulations.[115] As a result, litigants act as 'private attorneys general' enforcing their rights as private citizens. This phenomenon is quite particular to the US and the use of private litigation there as a form of public enforcement. This is also a key aim of the US environmental justice movement—the concept of access to justice—and this will be discussed in more detail in chapter four. There are three recognised incentives for this private enforcement.[116] First, the US Government prefers this practice as it shifts the cost of policy enforcement from them to individuals (the cost shifting incentive). Activists prefer this approach as it gives them control over achieving policy aims, rather than this being in the hands of government (the control incentive) and it also insulates policy from the risk of unfair influence by wealthy pressure groups (the insulation incentive). Some commentators believe that these suits are a more efficient way of remedying environmental harm than regulatory action by the EPA.[117] In the US, mass environmental harms are very expensive cases to litigate one-on-one. However, most of these class action cases settle before coming to trial and therefore there is little in the way of documentation in the public sphere.[118]

Bearing these features in mind, it is important to remember some other essential features of private law enforcement in the US. Contingency fees are available and this means that the plaintiff does not have to fund the action. There is no cost shifting, so the claimant has no risk. One-way cost shifting may perhaps be allowed in cases where enforcement is positively encouraged.[119] Procedural rules give powerful mechanisms for private parties to investigate

[112] Kalven and Rosenfield, 'The Contemporary Function of the Class Suit' (n 107) 684.

[113] Hodges (n 108) 105.

[114] Rosenberg 'The Causal Connection in Mass Exposure Cases' (n 109).

[115] eg CERCLA legislation provides for citizen suit as does the Endangered Species Act which permits a private citizen to sue for injunctive relief against another private citizen who may have breached the Act by destroying a listed species' habitat.

[116] T Burke, *Lawyers, Lawsuits and Legal Rights* (Univ of California Press, 2002).

[117] R Baker and M Markoff, 'By-Products Liability: Using Common Law Private Actions to Clean Up Hazardous Waste Sites' (1986) 10 *Harv Env'l L Rev* 99–134.

[118] Miller, 'Group Litigation in the Enforcement of Tort Law' (n 73) 262.

[119] This is essentially a device in civil litigation funding that bars a defendant from recovering its costs from a claimant who is unsuccessful. Farhang analysed how, in new legislation, Congress adopted a one-way cost shift to encourage private enforcement; see S Farhang, *The Litigation State: Public Regulation and Private Lawsuits in the U.S.* (Princeton University Press, 2010).

whether wrongdoing has occurred, and therefore extensive depositions and discovery of evidence are possible. A key feature is that juries decide on the awarding of damages. This gives a reflection of prevailing public sentiment. Damages are generally higher than Europe and this, in part, reflects the absence of comprehensive healthcare. Finally, very importantly, punitive damages are possible.[120]

In the US, Rosenberg believes that the traditional 'private law' process results in the tort systems' exclusion of most mass exposure claims and that the claims that do manage to gain access to the system are 'redundantly adjudicated at a disproportionately high cost to plaintiff attorneys'.[121] While tort law has responded in many ways to modern needs by using this private process, he claims that this reflects a disjointed perception of the causes and consequences of accidents. However, in traditional public law areas such as civil rights, consumer and competition law and environmental enforcement, courts have adopted an aggregative approach to make the most of the advantages of MPA mechanisms.[122] This has occurred most notably through the use of the class action mechanism, which some claim is the 'keystone of the public law process' there.[123] In public law claims, MPAs can play a public role as the interests of the victims of the defendant's misconduct are, by their nature, intrinsically collective but it is only where a critical mass of victims take a claim for compensation that the wrongdoer is faced with the threat of liability that is strong enough to deter it from reoffending in the future. In such cases in the US, judges have adopted an aggressive managerial role in public litigation and use procedures to increase access for claims and the efficiency of the process. Public law cases are considered to be collective, whereas personal injury claims are perceived as being individualistic. In order to achieve the optimum balance of both, Rosenberg advocates using the mechanism of class actions as a key tool of the public law process in the US. He believes that, together with the managerial role adopted by the judiciary used in class action procedure, this would enhance the use of the court system and that by enabling courts to exploit the aggregative nature of mass exposure claims, that public law procedures would fulfil both the utilitarian goals of the tort system and also the system's rights-based objectives.[124] Obviously, class actions can deliver some economies of scale in litigation by combining claims into one action and these advantages can help towards resolving mass exposure claims, both in numerical terms and in delivering compensation and deterrence. Despite this, courts in the US are often reluctant to certify class actions, even where they obviously constitute public law litigation. A reason for this is the fear is that class actions do not adequately recognise differences among claimants but this apprehension is mostly misplaced according to some who believe that, from a rights-oriented perspective, potential mass exposure

[120] This will be discussed in detail in ch 5.

[121] Rosenberg, 'The Causal Connection in Mass Exposure Cases' (n 109) 905.

[122] eg *Ouellette v International Paper Co*, 86 FRD 476(D Vt 1980) where it was held that common questions would justify class action against the defendant polluter for loss of property value and loss of the use and enjoyment of property, but not for personal injury because of the opportunity for 'particularised defences'); see also *Biechele v Norfolk & W Ry*, 309 F Supp 354 (ND Ohio 1969) which allowed a nuisance class action for injunctive relief and damages to abate and redress injuries to the plaintiffs' persons and property.

[123] Rosenberg, 'The Causal Connection in Mass Exposure Cases' (n 109) 907.

[124] Ibid.

victims have a collective interest in preserving the value of their entitlements by deterring tortious conduct.[125] It will be shown in chapter four that it is often only through combining their evidence that victims of mass environmental harm can win their cases. Also, the class action may enable a victim's loss to be assessed more easily.[126] It seems, paradoxically, that in the US, class actions may provide the prospect of individualised treatment that traditional case-by-case litigation does not.

6. Context in which Collective Redress Arises

According to Steele, our legal world is one of growing 'massification'.[127] For example, mass torts either from disasters or defective products can involve many victims and often multiple wrongdoers. An example of this is how environmental problems can affect whole communities and can have diffuse effects. Another example is the use of standard form contracts, which can affect multiple customers. This massification can be intensified by difficulties such as the financial cost for claimants of taking individual legal actions, especially considering that many defendants benefit from economies of scale. Conversely, civil liability can achieve deterrence. If these objectives were combined through MPAs, in some cases, this could lead to such action having a regulatory effect as the boundaries between public law and private law overlap. Under order to deliver 'mass' civil justice there are novel challenges for legal systems and there is clearly a need for solutions. Examples of these challenges are questions of access and civil procedure, such as issues of costs, representation and procedure as well as the balance between the public and private goals of civil law.[128] Modern legal systems must grapple with the challenge of how the law should react in cases where a larger number of parties are involved. These and other issues of mass justice can arise in diverse legal contexts, in spheres ranging from environmental to consumer litigation to personal injury.

Examining the roles of the traditional participants in a civil action, these are the plaintiffs, the defendants and the legal representatives. The courts' role is to administer justice as efficiently and speedily as possible while balancing individual access to justice by safeguarding crucial standards such as transparency. The role of the legislature is to prescribe the rules of justice and this often requires them to balance both individual and the collective interests. Some legislatures are more receptive to mass justice needs and are willing to provide specific mass justice procedures. Other legal systems, in contrast, believe in individual adjudication and such systems can be averse to massification of procedures and claims.

[125] Ibid.

[126] K Dam, 'Class Actions: Efficiency, Compensation, Deterrence and Conflict of Interest' (1975) 4 *J Legal Stud* 59.

[127] Presumably this term was borrowed from Cappelletti, 'Social and Political Aspects of Civil Procedure-Reforms and Trends in Western and Eastern Europe' (n 85); Steele and Van Boom, *Mass Justice* (n 108) 1.

[128] In the US, it has been suggested that the study of doctrinal detail has declined and the study of civil procedure has grown, showing an inversion of the current hierarchy of attention in the UK at least. Mass claims and mass representation are undoubtedly implicated in any such change in emphasis. See C Saiman, 'Faith in Legal Doctrine: An Anglo-American Comparison' ('Obligations V Rights and Private Law Conference', University of Oxford, July 2010).

These varying approaches will be explored in the examination of selected jurisdictions' experience of MPA collective redress.

7. Outline of Common Law MPA Procedures

The discussion and examination of MPA procedures in this study is illustrated through a comparative approach that makes frequent references to the MPA procedures of the five selected common law jurisdictions as well as the approach of the EU to MPAs. These MPA procedures and the legal systems of these jurisdictions will be discussed in detail in subsequent jurisdiction-specific chapters. As readers may not yet be familiar with the MPA procedures of these jurisdictions, a summary overview is given below, by way of introduction, in order briefly to explain the core situation of MPAs in these jurisdictions. The MPA analytical framework that is created and is invoked throughout this work is based on the objectives of MPAs. There are two main forms of such MPA that will be described in particular, collective actions and aggregate litigation proceedings (joinder and consolidation).[129]

A. United States

The US has a broad range of representative and group litigation procedures. The formal and informal procedures for aggregating similar claims include: joinder; consolidation; multidistrict litigation (MDL) transfer of distinct but related claims into a single action; US bankruptcy proceedings for corporate reorganisation; attorney 'inventories'; representative litigation by associations—'private attorneys general litigation'; representative litigation through government-initiated actions; class actions. The two main forms of aggregative procedure are consolidation and class actions. These are governed by the Federal Rules of Civil Procedure (FRCP). Generally these are replicated in the states' legal systems.[130]

i. Consolidation

When separate actions that involve common questions of law or fact are pending before the court, the judge may order that they be consolidated.[131] Proceedings may be consolidated for various stages of the action, for only for the pre-trial stage of discovery, or for the trial stage.[132] As will be discussed in chapter five, there is a clear judicial preference for consolidation as a means of resolving mass tort litigation in the US.

[129] As discussed above, these will be examined in further jurisdiction-specific analysis in the chapters dealing with each of the selected common law jurisdictions.

[130] States determine their own rules, which apply in state courts, though most states have adopted rules that are based on the FRCP. Note also that the FRCP were most recently revised in 2006 with practical changes to discovery rules to make it easier for courts and litigating parties to manage electronic records.

[131] A procedure provided by federal statute: The Multidistrict Litigation Statute (28 USCA § 1407).

[132] FRCP, r 42 sets out the rules for consolidation and similar rules exist in most states although courts can tailor consolidated trials as they see appropriate; eg by dividing plaintiffs into smaller groups; holding 'bellwether' trials with small groups of related plaintiffs; or bifurcating the trial into 2 parts with a liability phase for common questions of law and fact and a subsequent causation/damages phase either for questions common to all plaintiffs or each individual plaintiff.

ii. Class Actions

Class actions are brought under Rule 23 of the FRCP. This provides for representative litigation by individuals who voluntarily participate in a lawsuit. The US is the only jurisdiction with long-established experience of class actions. The more liberal class action standing rules of the 1970s and 1980s have been eroded significantly in recent years by a series of seminal decisions. Rule 23 is long and complex, reflecting in part types of class action that are now largely historical.

A 1966 revision of the Rule removed some of the more technical provisions of its operation. This revision also clarified the scope of the class action and Rule 23 was amended to provide that unnamed parties to a class action were bound by the final judgment in the action so long as their interests were adequately represented. A Rule 23 class action is essentially 'party neutral', and accordingly, defendant class actions are possible although they are quite rare in practice. Groups cannot file class action lawsuits unless a court recognises their legal standing to file a complaint and this is then certified. This requires an order certifying the proceedings as a class action and is called a *motion for class certification*, describing the proposed class and requesting the judge to review the class definition and the relief sought, with the aim of formally certifying a plaintiff class. The proposed class must consist of a group of individuals or business entities that have suffered a common injury, typically resulting from an action on the part of a business, or product defect or policy, which applied to all proposed class members in a uniform manner. If a class is certified, one or more of the plaintiffs' attorneys will be named as class counsel. Any subsequent resolutions that bring about a settlement or verdict at trial will apply to the claims of all class members. In certain categories of certified class actions ('opt-out' class actions), for example those where principally monetary damages are sought, the class members are given notice (perhaps indirectly through published advertisements or directly through the post) of the fact that certification has occurred and they are notified of a timeframe within which they have the opportunity to opt out of the case if they do not wish to participate. If they decide to opt out, they can still take their own individual action against the defendants. If they do not opt out, or neglect to do so either wittingly or unwittingly, then they will be bound by the outcome of the case and they cannot file their own individual lawsuits for similar claims against the same defendant. In other types of class actions, mainly those involving civil rights or those in pursuit of injunctive relief, there is no notice of certification nor is there an opportunity given to opt out. If the case goes to trial the verdict will apply to all class members. More commonly, a settlement is negotiated and this agreement is delivered to the judge to decide whether the terms are fair, reasonable and adequate. In terms of the comparative element of this research, it is notable that the US class action categorisation approach, which will be explained shortly, was expressly rejected by the law reform agencies in Australia and Ontario. For this reason, it is the category of Rule 23(b)(3) (which encompasses damages claims) that comprises the main focus of this research.

Rule 23 governs the procedure and conduct of class action suits brought in federal courts. It is a complex rule with numerous subcategories. In assessing the US class action requirements, Rule 23 provides that class actions can only be maintained if all its prerequisites in Rule 23(a) are met and the proposed class falls into one of four subcategories listed under Rule 23(b). First, looking at the Rule 23(a) prerequisites, these are the requirements of numerosity, commonality, typicality and adequacy of representation. These are the four prerequisites of any class action. They are designed to ensure that class treatment is both necessary and desirable in the circumstances, having regard also to the interests of the absent class members of the potential class. Numerosity requires that a judge must, first, find that the class is 'so numerous that joinder of all members is impracticable'.[133] This means that it is logistically inconvenient or problematic to name each individual class member as a separate party to the lawsuit. Numerosity is met when there are 40 or more plaintiffs. Commonality requires there must be 'questions of law or fact common to the class'. This is most likely the most difficult of Rule 23's requirements. The plaintiffs must highlight one or more issues of law or fact that affect every class member.[134] Typicality requires that the claims or defences of the representative parties are typical of the claims and defences of the class. This requires that class members' and the representative plaintiffs' common claims need to be based on the same issues of liability and arise from the same events or practices.[135] Adequacy of representation requires that the class representatives will 'fairly and adequately protect the interests of the class'. The court will look at several factors to ensure that that the representative plaintiffs' interests would not be in conflict of interest with those of the class members.[136]

Once these four prerequisites above are satisfied, Rule 23(b) must also be satisfied. This imposes further requirements related to judicial economy. A class action may be certified if the court is shown that the action falls into one of the categories listed. It defines three kinds of class actions. These are set out in Rule 23(b)(1) or (b)(2) or (b)(3). These categories are 'functional in that they sort class actions according to the class's particular objectives'.[137] For the sake of simplicity, these can be grouped into those with 'mandatory classes' and those with 'opt-out classes'. Mandatory class cases are certified under Rule 23(b)(1)(A), Rule 23(b)(1)(B) or Rule 23(b)(2). These are often cases involving civil rights or seeking social change. In these cases judges are not required to give absent class members notice of certification or of the option to exclude themselves from the litigation. These cases mainly seek injunctions or declaratory judgments rather than monetary damages. Because this kind of equitable relief is indivisible and is for the benefit of all who fall within the class definition, arguably it does not make any difference whether they know they are class

[133] See R Roth, 'Mass Tort Malignancy: In the Search for a Cure, Courts Should Continue to Certify Mandatory, Settlement-Only Class Actions' (1999) 79 *BUL Rev* 577.

[134] The US Supreme Court has made this requirement even more restrictive since *Wal-Mart Stores v Dukes* (20 June 2011, No 10-277) in 2011. This was a decision in one of the largest class action lawsuits ever made. Betsy Dukes and approximately 1.5 million current and former female Wal-Mart employees brought a suit for discrimination against women in Wal-Mart's promotion and pay policies. The US Supreme Court ruled against class certification in a decision that has significantly changed the legal landscape for large-scale federal class action lawsuits. It held that, for a potential class action lawsuit to be certified by federal courts, the lead plaintiffs must produce 'significant proof' that their claims share such strong commonality with those of the general class members that the determination of the validity of each claim can be resolved in one class-wide stroke. The Court also made it clear that claims for individualised monetary relief such as back-pay cannot be certified under the r 23(b)(2) 'injunctive-type' lawsuits; instead, suits involving *any* type of individualised monetary claims can now only be brought as a r 23(b)(3) 'damages-type' lawsuit irrespective of whether the injunctive or monetary relief predominates.

[135] If the matter goes to trial, the class representative's individual claims would be decided by the judge or jury and the outcome would be effectively applied to the whole class.

[136] eg that their lawyers are sufficiently qualified, experienced, unconflicted and have adequate financial means to robustly prosecute the litigation.

[137] Roth,' Mass Tort Malignancy' (n 133) 583.

members or exclude themselves from the class. Other good reasons for mandatory classes include the potential that the defendants might be faced with conflicting judgments of the issue if opt-outs were permitted and circumstances where a very limited amount of funds is available to pay all claimants.

The final category of opt-out classes under Rule 23(b)(3) is known as 'money damage' cases. This is because often the principal aim of these Rule 23(b)(3) cases is to seek restitution or monetary damages that can include claims involving mass torts, employment, competition law, securities and shareholders, or various consumer issues.[138] This category of cases has two extra requirements that must be established for certification. These are the *predominance* test and the *superiority* test, which impose further requirements: that the common questions of law or fact common to the members predominate over any individual questions affecting only individual members; and that a class action is superior to other methods of adjudication.[139] These requirements indicate a requirement that a class action suit is a more efficient means to resolve a dispute and that the court is mindful of judicial and other economy, particularly procedural economy. There is a requirement that notice be given to all potential class members that a class has been certified and that they have the choice of excluding themselves from any proceedings. Courts have held that due process requires that absent class members under Rule 23(b)(3) class actions be given adequate notice, adequate representation and adequate opportunity to opt out, before they can be bound by a final judgment in the suit.[140] If there is a settlement proposal, notice of this must be sent to all members of the certified class. If class members do not opt out within the specified time period they will be bound by any judgment or court-approved settlement. This notification requirement can be difficult and expensive to satisfy but is a necessary concomitant of the MPA objective fairness. This burdensome requirement is not necessary for class actions brought under Rule (b)(1) and (b)(2). Litigants frequently decide to sidestep the Rule 23(b)(3) notice requirements by instead proceeding under Rule 23(b)(2). If this is done, claims for damages can be added on to claims for injunctive relief under this rule. This prompted the Advisory Committee in 1966 to discourage the use of class actions in tort cases and they have also been cited as reasons for declining certification.

To sum up the US experience of class actions, it is very important to stress that, despite the common misperception, especially held abroad, class actions have rarely been certified for mass tort claims.[141] This is perhaps due to confusion with the practice of consolidation or because a few exceptional high-profile cases may have led to this impression. The fact that it can be increasingly difficult to get certification and that there has been a major shift to arbitration and class arbitration have reduced the number of class actions being brought in the US.

[138] Note, while FRCP, r 23 provides the foundation for securities-related class action litigation, such cases operate under a very different set of rules from other opt-out money damage class actions. The Federal Private Securities Litigation Reform Act 1995 and the Federal Securities Litigation Uniform Standards Act 1998 are instrumental in how these cases are litigated.

[139] These 2 further requirements for r (b)(3) class actions were added in 1966 by the Rules Advisory Committee; see Rules Advisory Committee, 'Notes to 1966 Amendments to Rule 23'(1966) 39 FRD 69, 102–03.

[140] *Phillips Petroleum Co v Shutts*, 472 US 797, 105 S Ct 2965, 86 L Ed 2d 628 [1985].

[141] eg class or multidistrict actions have been repeatedly rejected for asbestos claims.

B. Canada

Outside of the US, not many common law countries have adopted legislative changes to facilitate mass harm through collective redress procedures. Australia and Canada provide exceptions to this as both have introduced class actions for cases of mass torts.[142] Both of these jurisdictions eschew the US categorisation approach to class actions as this was expressly rejected by the law reform agencies in Australia and Ontario. It is also remarkable that the Canadian and Australian class action regimes stand apart from the US rule in that they *expressly* contemplate claims for damages for mass tort cases, whereas the US Rules do not refer to damages.[143]

Canada's civil procedure rules allow joinder or consolidation of multiple claims in all provinces, as well as class actions.[144] The current class action procedures are broadly based on the Uniform Class Proceedings Act[145] and Rule 23 of the US Federal Rules of Procedure. The requirements arising under Canadian legislation for class action proceedings and certification are not quite as arduous as those of the US in Rule 23. However, all the class action legislation requires that leave to proceed with the litigation as a class is obtained from the court by way of a motion to certify the proceedings as a class action. In general for the action to be certified, the promoter of the class proceedings is required to satisfy five criteria. These require that:

1. the pleadings disclose a cause of action;
2. there exists an identifiable class;
3. there are common issues among the claims of the class members ('common issues');
4. a class action would be the preferable procedure for resolving these common issues ('preferability'); and
5. the class representative will fairly and adequately represent the interests of the class on the basis of a workable trial plan.[146]

The tests for certification vary slightly in each state's legislation. The requirement that a class be 'identifiable' merely means that it ought to be possible to determine that a person is a class member but the identity and quantity of individual class members need not be definite. While the 'common issues' requirement is a critical element of the certification, neither the Ontario nor the British Columbia legislation dictates that the common issues must

[142] In Canada, class actions were first introduced in Quebec in 1978 by Lois Que 1978 c 8; Code of Civil Procedure (CCP), Arts 999–1051, followed in 1992 by Ontario with its Class Proceeding Act 1992 (c 6). In Australia, both the federal system and the 2 states of Victoria and New South Wales have introduced representative or group proceedings regimes which are similar to US style class actions. These Australian procedures have been available in the Federal Court since 4 March 1992, in Victoria since January 2000 and in New South Wales since 4 March 2011. In each instance, those regimes have been established by the passage of legislation. The federal procedures were introduced under the Federal Court of Australia Amendment Act 1991 in the form of pt IVA, an amendment to the Federal Court of Australia Act 1976 (Cth). The state procedures were introduced through pt 4A of the Supreme Court Act 1986 (Vic) and pt 10 of the Civil Procedure Act 2005 (NSW). However, owing to the limited scope of federal jurisdiction, this is more or less limited to product liability.

[143] Fleming (n 1).

[144] See eg Ontario Rules of Civil Procedure, RRO 1990, reg 994, rr 5 and 6.

[145] Adopted by the Uniform Law Conference of Canada in 1996.

[146] The representative must be appropriate. See LRC, *Consultation Paper on Multi-Party Litigation* (n 8) 38.

'predominate'. Also, a representative plaintiff does not need to be typical of the putative class once he does not have a conflict of interest and can show that he will progress the class claims fairly and effectively. Even though it may seem that the threshold set by these requirements is quite easy to establish, certification can still be as difficult to attain as in the US. However, in Ontario, class action certification is considered easier to obtain than in the US, especially after the passage of the US Class Action Fairness Act 2005.[147]

A defining trait of all the relevant legislation is that it aims to protect the interests of class members. This protection generally requires the court to use the mechanisms available to it in the legislation to make sure that class members are treated justly all the time. The Canadian approach is largely opt-out,[148] although there are exceptions to this. British Columbia, for example, while it operates an opt-out regime, obliges class members who are not resident in the province to opt in.[149] Class members must usually be notified of certification; however, the court may decide to abolish notice entirely.[150] The content of the notice is prescribed by the legislation and it must be court-approved. If a class is certified, then any decision of court or settlement will bind members of the class unless they opt out within a specified time after certification. Canadian law explicitly provides the possibility of bifurcating common issues and individual issues within a single procedural agenda. This means that once an action has been certified and notice has been given, a court will usually deal with the issues common to the class, followed by those common to any subclass, then any issues relating to individual members of a class.[151]

One of the most remarkable traits of the Canadian class action regime is the way in which class actions are funded. Most class actions are funded through the use of contingency fee agreements with class counsel. In such agreements counsel undertake to fund the litigation and recoup fees. The representative plaintiff will only have to pay these fees if the litigation outcome is successful, either because of settlement or at trial. Such agreements are normally for 20 to 40 per cent of the award. Class counsel sometimes arrange for a consortium of third-party investors to finance the litigation by giving a loan to the representative plaintiffs that is repayable only in the event of a successful outcome to the litigation.[152] The use of contingency fees or funding arrangement is common because, in the jurisdictions where cost awards can be obtained, court-ordered costs will, by themselves, be insufficient financial incentive to entice counsel to act in the proceedings.[153] Court approval is required for any fee agreement between a lawyer and representative plaintiff, whether contingent or not and the fee has to be justified by the class counsel. Ontario and Quebec have government funds to which representative plaintiffs may apply for litigation funding. The Ontario Law Society also operates a Class Proceedings Fund, which is a highly original mechanism.[154] This provides funding for disbursements only. The Class Proceedings Fund

[147] Pub L No 109-2, 119 Stat 4 (codified in scattered sections of 28 USC).

[148] Ontario Class Proceedings Act 1992, SO 1992, c 6, s 9.

[149] British Columbia Class Proceedings Act, RSBC 1996, s 16(1).

[150] Ontario CPA (n 148) s 17(2).

[151] eg in a class action for damages in tort, liability might be established through the resolution of common issues. The court would then proceed to make an aggregate award of damages in favour of the class or to conduct further proceedings leading to individualised assessments.

[152] See *Toronto Star*, 'Investors Betting Lawsuits Will Bring Big Payoffs' (22 February 1998).

[153] This refers to what is known as 'party and party costs', which will include the successful party's reasonable disbursements.

[154] It is administered by their Class Proceedings Committee.

was created in order to alleviate potential hardship of the losing class representative and it provides two things. First, the representative may apply for funding towards expenses of the proceedings.[155] Secondly, where the representative sought funding and this was awarded but the class action then failed, the Fund will absolve the representative plaintiff of liability for the defendant's costs. As a *quid pro quo* for this facility, a levy is imposed by the Fund on beneficiaries who consequently win their cases.[156] While this innovative approach hypothetically shows potential, the reality is that, in practice, the Fund has only achieved moderate success owing to its failure to attract representative plaintiffs, especially in the large, successful class actions.[157] The small numbers who have sought funding and the smaller still numbers of those who have been given it has meant that the levy is effectively a redundant way of financing the Fund.[158]

As for litigation costs, the extent and nature of the plaintiff's liability differs in each of the provinces, although in Canadian litigation generally the rule for costs is that the losing party must pay the costs of the winning party as 'costs follow the event'. This applies equally to class actions, but astoundingly it is only the representative plaintiff who is liable for the costs of the other side in the event the class action is defeated. Some of the provinces have adopted a no costs rule, by which litigants usually bear their own costs and some provinces retain a two-way costs rule whereby the loser pays. In Ontario, a representative plaintiff will only escape liability for costs if the court feels that the action was a test case, or raised a novel point of law or involved a matter of public interest. To offset this disincentive to litigate, Ontario law expressly exempts class actions from the province's general prohibition on contingent fees in civil proceedings. Apart from funding difficulties that putative plaintiffs face there is also the additional obstacle of the risk of an adverse costs award if the defendants succeed (in provinces with the two-way costs rule). The Canadian courts have been generally very aware of the risks that large costs pose to class action viability. They have recognised the role played by class actions in increasing access to justice in the legal system and have stated that 'large cost awards against unsuccessful plaintiffs will have a chilling effect and likely discourage meritorious class actions'.[159] Despite this statement, there have been some sizeable costs awards made against unsuccessful plaintiffs and some commentators believe that the courts are becoming less protective towards plaintiffs.[160] This situation might appear either intentionally or by accident to create an incentive for the use of the 'man of straw' as a plaintiff, as has been seen in both Ireland and Australia, in

[155] They apply to the committee and funding is awarded based on several factors, eg the merits of the class action, the representative's ability to raise funds elsewhere and the existence of financial controls to make certain that the monies are spent suitably.

[156] Where a plaintiff who had received funding succeeds in the class action, 10% of the damages award must be given to the Fund.

[157] eg *Nantais v Telectronics Proprietary (Canada) Ltd.* [1995] 129 DLR (4th) 110 (Ont Gen Div) (Can), *prob juris noted* 127 DLR (4th) 552 (Can$23.1m settlement in heart pacemakers); *Serwaczek v Medical Engineering Corp* [1996] 3 CPC (4th) 386 (Gen Div) (Can$29.1m settlement in breast implants case); *Dabbs v Sun Life Assurance Co of Canada* [1998] 40 OR (3d) 776 (Gen Div) (Can) (multi-million dollar settlement in a fraudulent life assurance case).

[158] In 2007, only 3 applications for funding were made and 2 of these were approved. The total amount awarded to applicants in 2007 was Can$257,209.

[159] *Pauli v Ace INA Insurance Co*, [2004] AJ No 883, [31] (CA) (QL).

[160] As a result of the Supreme Court decision in *Kerr v Danier Leather* 2007 SCC 44.

order to avoid potentially crippling costs awards. Courts are involved in case management of class actions in order to avoid this complicated type of litigation becoming unmanageable and to safeguard class members' interests.[161]

As for the determination of class actions, there may be settlement or trial. If there is a settlement, this must be approved by the court.[162] Some commentators have noted that Canadian judges, when scrutinising settlements, are more demanding than their US equivalents.[163] The vast majority of class actions are settled and it appears that less than 5 per cent of all class actions go to trial.[164] Class actions offer a wide range of remedies to class members. While there is generally no limit on the type of relief that may be sought or by whom, once the proposed representative plaintiff satisfies the prescribed requirements, some jurisdictions do impose limitations on corporations and other non-natural persons acting as representative plaintiffs.[165] The majority of representative plaintiffs are, however, individuals seeking monetary relief. There are detailed provisions including provisions concerning the participation of individual class members for the determination of their own particular issues.[166] Other possibilities include the assessment of aggregate awards[167] and the distribution of judgments, including a form of *cy pres*.[168] In the context of class actions, this refers to the application of an aggregate award or settlement in a way which may reasonably be expected 'to compensate or benefit class members, where actual division and distribution of the award among the class members is impossible or impracticable'.[169] Precise Canadian class action statistics are not available[170] but research has shown that there has been a significant increase in class action proceedings in recent years.[171]

C. Australia

Until 1992, class action type procedures did not form part of the Australian legal landscape. There was much debate in this area including a report published in 1988 by the Australian Law Reform Commission (ALRC).[172] The rules of the various Australian courts

[161] See eg opinion of Winkler J, 'Advocacy in Class Proceedings Litigation' (2000) 19 *Advocates' Soc J* 6, where he commented that case management judges have a 'weighty responsibility' and a 'broad discretion' in overseeing class actions.

[162] As being fair and reasonable and in the best interests of the class.

[163] eg in *Parsons v Canadian Red Cross Society* [1999] 40 CPC (4th) 151 (Ont S C), 101 ACWS (3d) 694 (Can), the trial judge refused to approve an initial settlement proposal for a Can$1.5bn settlement of a class claim in relation to Hepatitis C-contaminated blood.

[164] Settlements can happen either before or after certification or the common issues trial.

[165] eg Quebec CCP (n 142) Arts 999 and 1048.

[166] Ontario CPA (n 148) s 25.

[167] Ibid ss 23 and 24.

[168] Ibid s 25.

[169] See generally Mulheron, *The Class Action in Common Law Legal Systems* (n 30).

[170] For Canadian 2012 statistics, see http://harrisonpensa.com/wp-content/uploads/2012/07/Summary-of-Common-Issues-Trial-Activity-Across-Canada-Jul-11-12-FINAL-Read-Only.pdf.

[171] K Baert and A Guindon, 'Class Proceedings in Ontario: that Growing Risk of Adverse Costs Awards Against Representative Plaintiffs' ('5th Annual Symposium on Class Actions', Toronto, April 2008).

[172] Australian Law Reform Commission (ALRC), *Grouped Proceedings in the Federal Court*, Report no 46 (Sydney, Australia, 1988) para 1. 11 years were spent preparing this report. The ALRC subsequently recommended numerous enhancements to the FCA in 2000 and advised the Federal Government to order a review of the operation of pt IV; see further ALRC, *Managing Justice—A Review of the Federal Civil Justice System*, Report no 89 (Sydney, Australia, 1994) para 7.128.

did, however, provide for what were known as 'representative actions'. These were based on common law and the old English rules. These were of comparatively limited application and they were generally considered to have no useful application in modern society. They still exist and their particular weakness is the prerequisite that the parties have the 'same interest' in the proceedings. This requirement restricts the availability of the representative action procedure and has been narrowly interpreted by Australian judges.[173] Therefore, until relatively recently, multi-party litigation was limited to this common law representative action. This changed in 1992, when the Federal Parliament amended the Federal Court of Australia Act 1976 (the FCA) to introduce to the federal court system what are referred to in that legislation as 'representative proceedings'.[174] These are, in essence, analogous to US class actions. Most 'class actions' in Australia are commenced under this mechanism.[175] However, owing to the limited scope of federal jurisdiction, this is more or less limited to product liability. In 1994, an advisory committee made a recommendation that 'fair and efficient [class] action procedures should be available in all Australian jurisdictions.[176] As a result, in November 2000, the State of Victoria also introduced a class action regime that is almost the same as the federal regime, followed by New South Wales in March 2011.[177] In June 2013, there were proposals by the Western Australian Law Reform Commission (WALRC), supported by the Law Council, that Western Australia (WA) adopt legislation to create a scheme allowing representative proceedings on substantially similar terms to Part IVA of the FCA.[178]

The 1992 amendments to the FCA formed part of a package of reforms that included amendments to the Trade Practices Act[179] that established a new product liability regime based on strict liability. At the same time as these changes were made by the Federal Parliament the various state and territory legislatures amended the rules governing the practice of law in Australia so as to remove the longstanding restrictions on lawyers advertising for

[173] This requirement is set out in the Federal Rules of Court, Ord 6, r 13. See, for an example of judicial interpretation, *Markt and Co Ltd v Knight Steamship Co Ltd* [1910] 2 KB 1021 (CA), where the English Court of Appeal held that the 'same interest' requirement, under the traditional representative action procedure, meant that the procedure was unavailable in actions where separate and individual contracts were involved or in cases where damages were claimed.

[174] The Representative Group Proceedings Act 1991 provided for this and introduced it through the addition of a new pt IVA to the Federal Court of Australia Act 1976, as inserted by the Federal Court of Australia Amendment Act 1991 (No 181 of 1991), s 3. P IVA provided for representative proceedings. Under this regime, proceedings can be commenced if 3 threshold requirements are met: (1) 7 or more persons have claims against the same respondent; (2) the claims of all those persons are in respect of, or arise out of, the same, similar, or related circumstances; and (3) the claims of all those persons give rise to a substantial common issue of law or fact.

[175] These Australian 'representative proceedings' procedures have been available in the Federal Court since 4 March 1992, in Victoria since January 2000 and in New South Wales since 4 March 2011. In each instance those regimes have been established by the passage of legislation.

[176] Advice of a committee established by the Federal Parliament: Access to Justice Advisory Committee, *Access to Justice—An Action Plan* (Canberra, Australia, 1994) para. 2.105.

[177] The state procedures were introduced through pt 4A of the Supreme Court Act 1986 (Vic) and pt 10 of the Civil Procedure Act 2005 (NSW). A regime similar to the federal regime's pt IVA took effect from 1 January 2000 through the inclusion of pt 4A of the Supreme Court Act 1986 in Victoria. This followed a Supreme Court challenge to the court rules for their introduction. See report by V Morabito, 'Class Actions, Group Litigation and Other Forms of Collective Litigation: National Report Australia'.

[178] This resulted from the WA Law Reform Commission Discussion Paper 2009—Project No 103. Details of this may be found in Bogart W and Matthews I in D Hensler, C Hodges and M Tulibacka (eds), *The Globalization of Class Actions* (2009) 622 The Annals of the American Academy of Political and Social Science 41, pp 320–327.

[179] Trade Practices Act 1974.

clients.[180] Contingency fees are prohibited in Australia so lawyers are not permitted to take a proportion of clients' awards but they can use 'no win no fee' agreements to incorporate a success fee. Taken as a whole, these changes significantly increased the level of litigation in Australia. Lawyers began to advertise in the media offering to act for plaintiffs on a no win no fee basis. This led to the emergence of a number of prominent law firms specialising in large-scale litigation on behalf of plaintiffs. In many instances, this litigation is attempted to advance claims in Australia that were identical with proceedings being run by their associates in the US. The reforms of the early-1990s contributed to the public liability crisis that came to prominence in 2002. This led to the Federal Government establishing a review of key areas of the law of negligence and resulted in the subsequent passage by all state and territory governments of civil liability reform legislation.[181] In the last few years, there has been a transformation in the Australian legal system and it is now a commonly held perception that, apart from the US, Australia is the most likely place for a plaintiff to bring class action type proceedings.[182] In terms of resolution of class actions, most class actions are settled. This is a reflection of the fact that the risks associated with class action litigation are too high for both defendants and the class. It is also not unusual for class actions to be settled even before they are filed.

i. Joinder, Test Cases and Consolidation

Where neither representative proceedings nor representative action procedures are available or are not used, there are three other options for dealing with disputes that involve multiple claimants.[183] One option is to join all of the plaintiffs with a common claim in one action through use of a joinder procedure. In this way, for example, two or more persons may be joined as plaintiffs in any proceeding.[184] Another option is to commence separate actions for each claimant, and then try 'test cases' to resolve the common issues. The third option is to consolidate existing non-group proceedings that relate to the same dispute with respect to the same defendants.[185]

ii. Representative Proceedings

These are effectively class actions and are provided for under Part IV of the FCA.[186] One of the main features of Australian representative proceedings is that there is *no* requirement that the proceedings are judicially certified under either regime, unlike the US and

[180] eg in 1993 the New South Wales Parliament inserted s 38J into the Legal Profession Act 1987 which entitled a barrister or solicitor to advertise in any way that he or she thought fit.

[181] Ipp Committee Report (October 2002).

[182] See generally J Kellam and S Stuart Clark, 'Multi-Party Actions in Australia' in C Hodges, *Multi-Party Actions* (Oxford University Press, 2001) ch 15; and also S Stuart Clark and C Harris, 'Multi-Plaintiff Litigation in Australia: A Comparative Perspective' (2001) 11 *Duke J Comp & Int'l L* 289.

[183] V Morabito, 'Australasia' in Hensler, Hodges and Tulibacka (eds), *The Globalization of Class Actions* (n 2).

[184] This is an example of how the joinder of parties procedure operates in Australia under r 9.02 of Victoria's Supreme Court (General Civil Procedure) Rules 1986.

[185] The rules in the State of Victoria are a good example of how this procedure may be used. r 9.12 provides that where several proceedings are pending, the court may order those proceedings to be consolidated, or tried at the same time, or tried one immediately after another, or may order them to be stayed until the determination of any of them. This power may only be exercised where it appears to the court: that some common questions of law or fact arise in both or all of them; that the rights to relief claimed therein are in respect of, or arise out of, the same transaction or series of transactions; or that for some other reason it is desirable to make an order under the rule.

[186] See Mulheron (n 30) 481–90.

Canadian systems. A representative plaintiff may commence class action proceedings under Part IVA of the FCA once three threshold requirements are met:

1. the class comprises at least seven persons;
2. the claims of the class members arise out of the same, similar or related circumstances; and
3. the claims give rise to at least one substantial common issue of law or fact.[187]

The mechanism has been described as a 'sophisticated and improved version' of the representative action procedure.[188] This indicates that it has overcome the shortcomings of the representative action, which was the motivation for the introduction of the representative procedure in the first place. The drafters of both the federal and Victorian class action regimes favoured an opt-out system. For this regime to function, it is provided that an application to begin proceedings need not 'name, or specify the number of, the group members'[189] unless they opt out of the proceedings.[190] The Australian rules empower the court with a broad discretion to direct the way in which the group members are to be notified of the proceedings[191] and they also allow any member to opt out by giving written notice within a specified period.[192] However, the court has the power to not require group member notice where the relief the class is seeking does not include damages.[193] Otherwise, the court must approve the content and form of the notice and it may also decide who is to bear the cost of the notice distribution.[194] The action must only describe the class in general terms. The group can be defined by a list of names or a set of criteria. It may however, be defined in a way that effectively requires members to opt in to the class, including for example by entering into a retainer with a particular law firm or an arrangement with a particular litigation funder. The claim is brought on behalf of all group members by one, or a small number of, representative plaintiffs. The representatives are the only group members to be parties to the proceedings. There is no requirement that the claims of the representative parties should be typical of those of the class nor that the common issues predominate over the individual issue. This is in stark contrast to the US Rule 23. The system in Australia provides for the consideration of individual issues as well as common issues and provides for the use of subclasses if necessary. FCA, section 33C(2)(a) provides that a class may be commenced whether or not the relief sought is, or includes, equitable relief or damages; or includes claims that may require individual assessment; or is the same for each person represented. FCA, section 33C(2)(b) provides that proceedings may be brought regardless of whether they concern separate transactions, acts or omissions between the defendant and individual group members. Once the proceedings have been commenced all members of the group are bound by the outcome of the proceedings unless they opt out. In order to take that step the group member must give written notice to the court of their intention to opt out. Once the class action has been initiated, the court may terminate proceedings

[187] FCA, pt IVA, s 33C(1).

[188] Scottish Law Commission, *Multi-Party Actions* (Rep no 154, 1996) para 6.1. See generally R Mulheron, 'From Representative Rule to Class Action: Steps Rather than Leaps' (2005) 24 *Civil Justice Q* 424.

[189] FCA, pt IVA, s 33H(2); and pt 4A, s 33H(2).

[190] Ibid s 33H.

[191] Ibid ss 22X and 33Y.

[192] Ibid s 33J. Notice must be given to class members of commencement of the proceeding and of their right to opt out of the group prior to the date the court has fixed.

[193] Ibid pt IVA, s 33X(2); and pt 4A, s 33X(2).

[194] Ibid IVA, s 33Y(2); and pt 4A, s 33Y(2).

as a class proceeding, if, upon application by the defendant, it is satisfied that the litigation does not satisfy the threshold requirements. The onus is on the defendant to persuade the trial court that the proceedings should be concluded.[195] Even where the judge holds that the requirements have been met, the court can discontinue the class proceedings in certain circumstances. The most important of these is FCA, section 33 N(1), which allows the court to order that the action no longer constitutes a class proceeding because it is in the interests of justice to do so. Under the opt-out system in both regimes all class members are bound by any judgment of the court.[196] Crucially, a class action may not be ceased or settled without court approval.[197]

As regards damages, the court has a wide discretion and if the class action is successful it may award damages to the class as a whole, to any subclass or to individual members.[198] As regards costs, Australia has a similar system to Canada in that it uses the traditional rule that costs follow the event, but it has a narrow interpretation in terms of who is liable if the plaintiff is unsuccessful. If a class action is defeated, only the representative plaintiffs and not the individual group members will be liable for costs. This is because, as previously mentioned, group members are bound by the outcome of representative proceedings without being formal parties to the litigation.[199] Effectively this confers them with immunity from adverse costs awards. Without fee and retainer agreements between individual group members and the lawyers that the class representatives have employed, group members are not liable for the costs and fees involved in organising the proceeding for the plaintiffs.[200] As a result, group members are often described as 'free riders'. Increasingly, solicitors acting for class representatives have begun effectively to fund many Australian representative proceedings by entering into no win no fee agreements with representatives. Also, litigation funders often finance these proceedings and their fee can comprise up to 40 per cent of an award. In these cases, an essential part of their involvement is that the representative group is restricted to those claimants who are prepared to enter into funder agreements with litigation funders and also to enter fee agreements with the lawyers for the class representatives.[201] Commercial third-party litigation funders have been operating in Australia

[195] eg according to FCA s 33C and s 33N, on the ground that the action is frivolous or oppressive or that the procedure is not the most efficient and effective means of disposing of the claims in question.

[196] FCA, s 33Z provides that a judgment delivered in a class proceeding 'binds all such persons [described or otherwise identified in the judgment] other than any person who has opted out of the proceeding.' ie those who fall within the class description who have not opted out in writing.

[197] Ibid pt IVA, s 33V(1). 'Contingency fees are prohibited in Australia so lawyers are not permitted to take a proportion of clients' awards but they can use 'no win no fee' agreements to charge a loading for successful outcomes'.

[198] Damages may consist of specified amounts, amounts calculated in a particular manner or an average amount to be divided among class members.

[199] *Johnson Tiles Pty Ltd v Esso Australia Ltd* (1999) 166 ALR 731, 738 (per Merkel J).

[200] This is expressly stated by s 43(1)(A) of pt IVA and s 33ZD of pt 4A.

[201] The Victoria Law Reform Commission (VLRC), *Civil Justice Review Draft Proposals* (Melbourne, Australia, 2007) 49–50 stated that: 'Some commercial funders are prepared to finance the litigation, meet any obligations to provide security for costs and provide an indemnity in respect of any adverse costs order. This is usually in consideration of an agreement by the assisted parties to pay to the litigation funder a specified percentage of the amount recovered if the litigation is successful. However, such agreement cannot be entered into by the representative party on behalf of the class. Thus, in order to secure a legal entitlement to share in the amount recovered by class members litigation funders usually endeavour to get individual class members to enter into contractual litigation finance arrangements. Moreover, litigation funders are usually only agreeable to fund litigation on behalf of those individual class members who have agreed to enter into litigation finance agreements. These commercial considerations have led to a proliferation of class actions where the defined classes are limited to persons who have agreed to enter into litigation funding arrangements with commercial litigation entities'.

since the 1990s.[202] Their presence has been the most important factor in the development of the Australian MPA landscape in recent times, with more than three times the number of representative proceedings being commenced in the three years since these third-party litigation funders began to operate.[203] Now it is highly unusual for such proceedings to be pursued without third-party funding. A crucial detail in relation to third-party funding in Australia is the requirement that third-party funders need to have contracts with all group members so as to recover their fee and to exclude 'free riders', and to therefore maximise the group membership. This requirement has led to a *reversal* of the initial opt-out model into a de facto opt-in model. This obviously has had huge implications for the Australian regime.

D. England and Wales

MPAs can trace their origins to England, as discussed previously.[204] However, such actions were very rare in the following centuries and the group action was a phenomenon that only began properly in the 1980s due to the availability of legal aid and a core group of lawyers who had explored the techniques in managing US class actions. Significantly, this movement was launched by a series of disasters, such as the Piper Alpha fire. Subsequently, there were a number of cases resulting from 'creeping disasters'. Examples of these include the following: those resulting from allegations of defective medical products such as the Dalkon Shield; defective pharmaceutical products; defective blood products supplied by the NHS which caused hepatitis or HIV infection. Many English lawyers learned MPA skills in these cases and developed ways of working together and with the courts that could be applied in new areas to facilitate mass harm litigation. A recent growth area is that of financial actions. There have been considerable reforms since 1999 that have introduced much greater judicial control through case management and that have eased funding difficulties. Courts have the power to limit the number of expert witnesses, the amount of documentary evidence and oral argument admitted in litigation, and settlement through mediation is encouraged. It is very rare that punitive damages are awarded.[205]

England and Wales have been more cautious than the US in relation to fully embracing formal collective action mechanisms, with both England and Wales and Ireland being notable exceptions to the selected common law regimes in this study that have fully adopted such procedures. This situation is currently changing in England and Wales following significant developments whereby, in 2013, the Government published plans for reforming the regime for private competition law actions. This includes the creation of a new opt-out collective action for competition law on behalf of both consumers and businesses in the Competition Appeal Tribunal (CAT).

England and Wales have several kinds of MPA mechanisms. The first is for those based on statutes that have a mainly regulatory nature, particularly for consumer protection,

[202] In insolvency cases.

[203] V Morabito, 'An Empirical Study of Australia's Class Action Regimes—First Report: Class Action Facts and Figures' (Department of Business Law and Taxation, Monash University, December 2009).

[204] As discussed in section 4 of this chapter, the earliest trace of group litigation was an action brought on behalf of an entire parish against their rector who was alleged to have failed to provide their church with appropriate financial support in the case of *Master Martin Rector of Barkway v Parishioners of Nuthampstead*. See further S Yeazell, *From Medieval Group Litigation to The Modern Class Action* (Yale University Press, 1987) 54.

[205] *Kuddus v Chief Constable* [2002] 2 AC 122 (HL).

and these are commonly based on EU provisions.[206] These are known as public representative procedures and they are limited to injunctive relief, although some claims for damages are now possible. The second form of collective relief is based on procedural rules of court that can be used for any sort of individual claim. There has been significant concern over the introduction of collective damages cases because of the perils of promoting litigation, especially in the scattered damages scenario where claims are of limited financial value but may result in large costs, as this could endanger economic competitiveness. The Government's policy has been to promote public authorities' supervision of restitutional payments as part of their regulatory enforcement activities. It is also encouraging fast and economical settlement and good behaviour through alternative collective redress avenues, such as ombudsmen,[207] mediation, sectoral schemes[208] and compensation schemes.[209]

i. Consolidation, Joinder and Test Cases

While the English legal system, until very recently, did not contain any private collective action mechanism like those seen in the US, Canada or Australia, the occurrence of multi-party litigation is well established there. This has traditionally been carried out by the combination of some of the methods also used in Ireland such as the representative procedure, joint proceedings, consolidated proceedings, test cases and the allocation of several similar cases to a specific judge. As for joinder and consolidation of individual claims, the court has general powers to combine a number of individual proceedings into one action and can order that two or more claims be tried together. Both of these can result in efficiencies of cost and other economies but they do not result in a decision that binds all parties.

ii. Representative Actions

A new system for conducting MPAs was introduced as part of a comprehensive reform of England and Wales's Civil Procedure Rules 1998 (CPR). The amendments to these rules came into effect in 1999 and include various procedures for multi-party litigation. There are four additional procedures, including a procedure for representative actions, particularly where a single representative party may represent all the parties that have the same interest.[210] These new rules came about as a result of the Woolf Report in 1996 that made

[206] Public representative procedures are commonly used for consumer protection and competition law enforcement, often based on EU legislation that provides for representative claims in this area. These include powers for consumer organisations to bring claims that are usually limited to injunctive relief.

[207] eg the Financial Services Ombudsman and the Local Government Ombudsman.

[208] eg the medical injury scheme proposed under the NHS Redress Act 2005.

[209] There are various disparate compensation schemes in the UK: see forthcoming book by Macleod and Hodges on compensation schemes.

[210] In addition to the normal tools of joinder or consolidation of individual actions, CPR, pt 19.II, specifies 4 different mechanisms:

1. representative parties with the same interest (r 19.6);
2. representation of persons who cannot be ascertained in relation to the estate of a deceased person (r 19.7);
3. representation of a person who has died (r 19.8); or
4. a claim by one or more members of a company, body or trade union … to be given a remedy to open it (a 'derivative claim': r 19.9).

recommendations for litigation reform.[211] They aimed to encourage swifter and more cost-effective dispute resolution.

Representative actions, in their English and Welsh form, are the closest equivalent to collective actions. They comprise a legal action in which one or a few members of a class sue on behalf of themselves and other members of the same class. They are the oldest procedure for obtaining collective redress in English law.[212] By using a representative action, claims can be pursued where one representative claimant or defendant acts on behalf of a class of individuals. Pursuant to Rule 19.6 of the CPR, representative actions may be brought 'by or against one or more persons who have the same interest' in a claim 'as representatives of any other persons who have that interest'. Any judgment or order given is then binding on all persons represented, but can only be enforced by or against a person who is not a party to the claim with the permission of the court. This 'same interest' requirement is designed to ensure that the interests of all bound by the action are adequately represented. It aims to avoid risks that may arise where a representative party may not pursue aspects of the case in which he has no direct interest. It also aims to avoid conflicts of interest between class members where the representative party may advance a case that undermines the interests of the other class members. Court permission is not required for representative action proceedings, nor is consent needed from the represented person. Therefore a party may appoint himself as representative of others in legal proceedings—and thus make them potentially liable—regardless of whether he has been authorised to do so, and without any review by the court.[213] For these reasons, the court has interpreted the representative action requirements very narrowly, in particular the requirement that all persons in the representative class have the 'same interest'.[214] Historically, this procedure was not available if the action was for damages, because group members would be likely to be entitled to different damages.[215]

iii. Group Litigation Orders

The Woolf Report, referred to above, suggested that MPAs ought to be facilitated in England and Wales. There were fears that this could lead to US style class actions because, at the time, there were no specific rules in England and Wales for MPAs. Instead, procedures developed to a large extent as cases proceeded, often increasing costs. Lord Woolf's recommendation was to devise a new scheme for proceedings that require collective treatment. In 1999, as a result of these reforms, the Group Litigation Order (GLO) was introduced as a means of case management.[216]

Apart from the representative action, the Group Litigation Order is the other principal mechanism for collective redress litigation in England and Wales. Under the rules,[217] a court can make a GLO when numerous claims 'give rise to common or related issues of fact

[211] As discussed in ch 3, Lord Woolf: *Access to Justice: Final Report* (1996).

[212] See J Sorabji, 'The Hidden Class action in English Civil Procedure' (2009) 28 *Civil Justice Q* 498.

[213] *Independent Ltd v Music Trading On-Line (HK) Ltd* [2003] EWHC 470 (Ch); *Howells v Dominion Insurance Co Ltd* [2005] EWHC 552 (QB).

[214] J Seymour, 'Representative Procedures and the Future of Multi-Party Actions' (1999) 62 *MLR* 564.

[215] *Markt v Knight* (n 173).

[216] Court Rules on Co-ordinated Management of Multiple Claims through Litigation.

[217] CPR, r 19.11.

or law'. This procedure provides that a number of similar claims can be officially organised and coordinated, then managed and adjudicated by the same judge.[218] It arose out of a practice that had developed spontaneously to enable a series of large pharmaceutical multi-party cases to be managed by the courts in the 1980s and 1990s.[219] GLOs are regulated by their own specific regime.[220] A new 'codified' approach reflecting this practice was included in the new CPR. These adopted general rules for managing individual litigation that were suitable for managing groups of similar claims.

The fundamental difference between a GLO and a collective action is that a GLO comprises multiple distinct suits that are administered together, rather than a single suit. A GLO may be applied for by either a plaintiff or by a defendant, or the court on its own initiative may order a GLO.[221]

In a GLO, a managing judge is appointed with overall responsibility for the group litigation.[222] He has wide-ranging discretion to give case management directions[223] and may decide what issues and evidence are necessary or unnecessary. He may require parties to state their estimated costs and also order reductions or caps on costs. He may call Case Management Conferences to manage and control the litigation effectively. Unviable cases may be struck out and also parties may be encouraged to mediate or settle cases. The judge's goal is always to resolve cases with minimal delay, at a low and proportionate cost, usually by agreement of the parties outside of the court. The judge will normally select one or more individual cases to try as test or lead cases and the resolution of these should shed light on how many others may be resolved or settled. The managing judge has a general power to direct trial of common issues and/or individual issues.[224] A judgment or order on a GLO is binding on all parties on the register at the time the judgment or order is made.[225] A party who is negatively affected by a judgment or order may seek leave to appeal. The outcome of a test claim will be binding on all similar claims on the register.[226] The overall effect of a GLO is that all those subject to it will be bound by a judgment on the common (GLO) issues. The GLO procedure gives the court maximum flexibility to use the appropriate management techniques tailored to each case and these can be innovative where necessary.[227]

As regards costs in a group litigation situation, the general rule is that costs will follow the event, so the normal rules on civil litigation costs apply. Therefore, group litigants will be liable for the other side's costs if the group loses the action as 'loser pays winner's costs'.

[218] See generally Hodges (n 5) chs 2–8; N Andrews 'Multi-Party Proceedings in England: Representative and Group Actions' (2001) 11 *Duke J Int'l & Comp L* 249.

[219] Further details of this history can be found in Hodges (n 5) 218.

[220] Rules, practice directions and subordinate legislation, ie s III of the Civil Procedure Rules, rr 19.0.10–19.15; Practice Direction 19B—Group Litigation.

[221] *sua sponte.*

[222] He may be assisted by a master or district court to deal with procedural issues and also by a costs judge.

[223] LRC (n 8) 40 [2.40] states that this includes: varying the GLO issues; providing for one or more claims on the register to proceed as test claims; applying the results of the settlement of a test claim to other claims; appointing a solicitor as the lead solicitor for the parties on either side; setting a cut-off date for the entry of additional claims on the register; and removing a party from the register.

[224] Practice Direction 19B—Group Litigation, cl. 5.

[225] This is unless the court orders otherwise. The court may also extend any judgment or order to any late claimants.

[226] It will also be binding on any subsequent claims if the court so directs.

[227] A Higgins and A Zuckerman, 'Class Actions in England? Efficacy, Autonomy and Proportionality in Collective Redress' (2013) University of Oxford Legal Research Paper Series 12.

Group litigants will usually be given an order for common costs which will entail each group litigant being severally liable for an equal share of the common costs. Individual group litigants will be liable for costs relating to their own individual claims. Complex arrangements may be required for funding GLOs and a cost/risk analysis of individual group members may be undertaken in order to determine common costs. Some argue that the complexity and size of costs create a barrier to group cases.

Surprisingly, the GLO has not been invoked as often as might have been expected and it has been eschewed in cases in which it may have appeared an obvious solution, for example in the *Buncefield* disaster, which is discussed in detail in a case study in chapter eight. The court may refuse a GLO where insufficient consideration has been given to following a more cost-effective way of resolving the dispute, by using test cases or consolidating individual actions, as well as failure to identify a 'group litigation issue'. There is ongoing debate about potential reform, in which the Government is endeavoring to balance the challenges of improving access to justice while preventing the growth of a 'compensation culture'.[228] It is trying to achieve this by pursuing a new approach that involves public authorities supervising restitution as part of regulatory enforcement.[229]

E. Ireland

Ireland is a common law jurisdiction that does not yet have an effective mechanism for multi-party litigation. This fact distinguishes Ireland from other common law jurisdictions with MPA mechanisms and appears to be a gap in the Irish legal framework. This is despite recommendations by the Irish Law Reform Commission (LRC), Ireland's principal public body for the investigation of law reform, for the introduction of a new litigation procedure in the form of a multi-party action.[230] In a major study in 2005, it explored the prospects for MPAs in Ireland and recommended their introduction.[231] Despite the LRC recommendations, there have not yet been any such legislative proposals for change in Ireland. At present, there are still no formal statutory or court rules for MPAs, so neither multi-party nor specifically collective action is yet permitted, save for very limited representative actions. These possibilities are rarely invoked because they are of such restricted use. Under the existing statutory framework MPAs seem to be actively discouraged. Instead, occasionally the courts use a confusing array of alternative methods in cases where MPAs would have played an obvious role. In recent years there have been a number of cases of mass harm, including contaminated blood products, army deafness and asbestos-related ill health. Such cases usually draw widespread public interest due to the nature of their claims, the scale of

[228] See Department of Constitutional Affairs, *Tackling the 'Compensation Culture': Government Response to Better Regulation Task Force Report 'Better Routes to Redress'* (2005).

[229] Hodges (n 5).

[230] The Law Reform Commission was established by the Law Reform Commission Act 1975 as an independent statutory body whose main aim is to keep the law under review and to make practical proposals for its reform. It has published over 100 documents containing proposals for law reform which are available online at http://www.lawreform.ie. The LRC usually publishes in 2 stages: first, a Consultation Paper and then a Report. This occurred with the *Multi-Party Litigation* recommendations. The Consultation Paper is intended to form the basis for discussion and its recommendations, conclusions and suggestions are therefore provisional. The LRC *Consultation Paper on Multi-Party Litigation* was published in 2003 and its *Report on Multi-Party Litigation* was published in 2005.

[231] Irish Law Reform Commission, *Report on Multi-party Litigation* (LRC 76-2005).

the potential class or the prospect of State liability. Normally, however, owing to the lack of an appropriate mechanism, those with cases potentially suited to an MPA must pursue them in another way. Great injustices and inefficiencies have resulted from these improvisations.

Multi-party litigation in Ireland can arise in a variety of situations. First, public actions comprise a category of actions whereby certain public officials are empowered to institute litigation on behalf of a wide group of affected individuals. Secondly, it may be possible for certain organisations to institute proceedings that could otherwise be taken by a number of individuals (these are known as organisation actions). Such organisations are often public interest groups or pressure groups that are deemed to have a sufficient interest in the case to qualify for standing. In this way an action by an appropriate organisation could effectively dispose of multiple potential individual cases.[232] However, the issue of *locus standi* could operate as an obstacle and also the possibility of damages does not exist, as only declaratory or injunctive relief may be given.[233]

Occasionally it may be best to deal with a group of individual actions together in a way that avoids litigation and to facilitate a remedy in a more sensitive and efficient way, particularly where a question of public interest is involved. An obvious example of this is the special mechanisms such as statutory no-fault compensation schemes that deal with mass cases of personal injury (for example, injuries arising from infected blood products supplied by State bodies,[234] and injuries suffered by those who had been in residential institutional care).[235] In situations of serious injury or widespread mismanagement, usually for which there is some State accountability, there have been cases in which a public inquiry is necessitated, for example the recently established State inquiry into banking malpractice. The aim of a public inquiry is to determine facts relating to a particular incident or series of incidents of public interest and to ascertain whether a wrong has been committed against society or the public interest. Its aim is *not* to deliver judgment on legal rights. Depending on the results of such inquiry this may lead to claims for compensation by victims or their relatives, such as occurred with the Hepatitis C Tribunal and the Institutional Redress Board under the no-fault compensation schemes discussed above. Other methods of litigation avoidance, which have been used particularly in consumer actions, include the use of ADR and prevention through regulation (which will both be discussed in detail later in this work). The influence of effective regulatory mechanisms will often function to prevent the wrong arising in the first place and therefore preclude the need for any type of multi-party litigation.[236] There is an important background role played by certain Irish regulatory and standards agencies in this area, for example the Office of the Director of Consumer Affairs. Also, the State Claims Agency is charged with the function of identifying risks that could lead to future claims against public bodies. It is empowered to liaise with these bodies to

[232] An example of this is the case of *Irish Penal Reform Trust v Minister for Justice, Equality and Law Reform* [2005] IEHC 305.

[233] This may be a deterrent to such actions being used in environment-related cases. It is notable, however, that in the case of actions to enforce the Environmental Impact Assessment (EIA) Directive (Council Directive 85/337/EEC on the assessment of effects of certain public and private projects on the environment, OJ L 175 1985) or Directive 2008/1/EC of the European Parliament and of the Council of 15 January 2008 concerning Integrated Pollution Prevention and Control (the IPPC Directive), OJ L 24, 2008. The fact that environmental NGOs enjoy automatic standing avoids some of these difficulties). See Directive (EC) 2003/35 OJ 2002 L 156/17, amending the EIA Directive to implement the Aarhus Convention.

[234] See Hepatitis C Compensation Tribunal Act 1997 (No 34/1997).

[235] See Residential Institutions Redress Act 2002 (No 13/2002).

[236] *LRC Report* (n 231).

ensure that these foreseeable risks are managed and controlled appropriately. In this way it carries out an important preventative role.

Private actions refer to procedures that enable a group of individuals to institute proceedings to deal with that group collectively. Unlike the public action or organisation action, in private litigation the decision to pursue an action rests solely with the group of individuals. As mentioned at the outset, Ireland has a confusing array of mechanisms that have occasionally been used for cases of mass harm. These are rarely invoked and are private multi-party procedures that currently fall short of MPAs. They comprise the following four mechanisms.

i. Representative Actions

Irish courts have taken a very restrictive attitude towards these: they are permitted in very limited circumstances in which parties have the same interest and where certain prerequisites are met.[237] They cannot be used for tort claims[238] and it is not possible to get damages. It is not possible to get legal aid for these cases. This type of representative action is a long way from the US class action procedure.

ii. Joinder

As discussed in relation to other common law jurisdictions, these can be helpful tools to assist with mass harm litigation. Joinder is a process whereby the court can simply join additional litigants to an action where it is necessary in the interests of justice and in this way it can hear related cases together. The joinder system is used regularly to combine actions involving two or more parties and can, on occasion, broaden to actions involving many parties.[239]

iii. Consolidation

As an alternative to joinder, consolidation may occur. In such cases, the court rules that disputes must be tried or consolidated together by a plaintiff uniting several causes of action in the same proceedings.[240] The Irish rule for consolidation further provides that where such causes of action cannot be tried together conveniently, the court may order separate trials or make such other order as may be necessary or expedient to dispose of the matters.[241] Where a plaintiff does not take steps to unite several causes of action in the same

[237] This 'same interest' has been examined in representative proceedings in other common law jurisdictions, such as those in England and Wales.

[238] Ord 6, r 10 of the Circuit Court Rules 2001 expressly excludes representative actions founded on tort. No further explanation can be found of why this is so but this was also stated by the Supreme Court in *Moore v Attorney General (No 2)* [1930] IR 471.

[239] See eg *Abrahamson v Law Society* [1996] 1 IR 403 (Law students challenged the Law Society's decision to deny them exemption from the entrance examination to the Law Society. Their individual actions were combined in a single action before the High Court as the plaintiffs were a defined group with identical claims for declaratory and injunctive relief, represented by one legal team.)

[240] Ord 18, r 1 of the Irish Rules of the Superior Courts (RSC) provides that a plaintiff may unite several causes of action together in the same proceedings.

[241] Ibid ord 18, r 9 provides that where it appears to the court that causes of action are such that they cannot all be conveniently disposed of together, the court may order any of such causes of action to be excluded and consequential amendments to be made to such order as to costs may be just.

proceedings, matters pending in the High Court may be consolidated by order of the court on the application of any party and regardless of whether or not all the parties consent to the order.[242] Aside from the provisions in the Rules, the court has an inherent jurisdiction to order that cases be heard simultaneously.[243] The difference between joinder and consolidation is that consolidation does *not* involve making all the claimants parties to a single set of proceedings. Instead, the plaintiff litigates the consolidated claims on the premise that he represents the other litigants. Any judgment is deemed to be binding on the other litigants (the plaintiffs in the parallel proceedings, with which his claim has been consolidated). In this way, consolidation resembles the representative action and is a less flexible system for managing large class claims.

iv. Test Cases

Test cases are a commonly used mechanism. They are currently used in Ireland as the favoured means of dealing with mass harm litigation. Quite often a plaintiff proceeds on an individual basis. The test case establishes a benchmark and, while subsequent actions by other litigants are not bound by the result, the test case outcome gives an indicator of the outcome of future litigation both in terms of formal precedent and the similarity of subsequent proceedings.[244] This is uncomplicated where the test case pronounces an administrative or legislative action unconstitutional,[245] but is less straightforward where an individual assessment of damages is necessary. Test cases were used to deal with the many army deafness claims taken against the State and also in private actions.[246] These are unduly costly and result in procedural inefficiencies as well as unnecessary duplication.

F. European Union

As previously outlined, there has been much debate in the European Commission about how best to address collective redress in the EU in order to deal with mass harm and about whether a collective action or some other approach is appropriate for Member States. What becomes clear from the examination of MPA procedures in various common law jurisdictions is that litigation through MPAs is only one of a suite of possible remedies for mass harm, and therefore for collective redress. Other remedies lie in public enforcement, regulatory law and ADR. In terms of the EU, it is important to remember that its raison d'être is the creation of the internal market and maintaining competitiveness, particularly by enhancing competition and consumer protection. It is essential to recognise that European traditions do not include the American approach of 'private enforcement', but are based on the primacy of public enforcement.[247] The EU uses regulatory law and public enforcement as its principal tools to protect these core objectives. Options for EU collective redress mechanisms must be tailored to reflect the reality of the different enforcement approaches

[242] Ibid ord 4, r 6; *Duffy v News Group Newspapers Ltd* [1992] 2 IR 369.

[243] *O'Neill v Ryanair Ltd* [1992] 1 IR 160.

[244] G Whyte, *Social Inclusion and the Legal System* (Institute of Public Administration, 2002) 104.

[245] See G Hogan and G Whyte, *Kelly: Irish Constitution* (4th edn, Butterworths, 2003) 487–97 (such a declaration nullifies the impugned act or legislation in all situations including those where litigation is pending).

[246] See eg *Gough v Neary* [2003] 3 IR 92, [2003] IESC 39 (successful negligence claim against an obstetrician for an unnecessary hysterectomy during childbirth, in advance of a further 65 similar cases pending against him).

[247] See C Hodges, 'European Union Legislation' in Hensler, Hodges and Tulibacka (n 2) 81.

between the US and EU. For a long time there was no clear EU consensus on what method of enforcement is the best solution to incidents of mass harm, as the history of EU collective redress policy indicates.

According to the principle of subsidiarity the EU is under an obligation to respect Member States' national systems.[248] This principle recognises that although the EU's aim is to establish an area of freedom, justice and security, it must respect the different legal systems of the Member States. Therefore, the experience of Member States is clearly key in informing the development of EU policy. For this reason it is important to examine this experience in order to help us understand why EU policy developed in the way that it has. An early informer of Commission policy was the Stuyck Report empirical study.[249] This showed that evidence does not demonstrate any unanimity about the cost-benefit justification of collective actions,[250] that potential advantages may be propounded, but so can risks and disadvantages,[251] as is particularly shown in the literature on US class actions.[252] We have seen ADR and various other methods of enforcement through public law and regulation already mentioned as viable alternatives to litigation. The reasons why a wider, holistic approach is the most sensible way for the EU to proceed with collective redress are two-fold: first, because of the fundamental difference between the US and EU enforcement 'architecture' and legal traditions; secondly, because of this empirical evidence and support for the use of ADR and other techniques.

DG SANCO has been pioneering in the Commission in its endorsement of an ADR approach. In a 2009 study for DG SANCO, 750 national ADR systems in the EU were identified, which have compliance rates by businesses averaging 99 per cent.[253] This was

[248] TFEU, Art 67(1) states that the Union shall constitute an area of freedom, security and justice with respect for fundamental rights and the different legal systems and the traditions of the Member States.

[249] J Stuyck and others, *Commission Study on Alternative Means of Consumer Redress other than Redress Through Ordinary Judicial Proceedings* (Catholic University of Leuven, 2007).

[250] Hodges, 'European Union Legislation' (n 247) 82 cites, as an example, the significant precedent in the case of the French consumer organisation UFC Que Choisir? It invested €500,000 in a damages case for overcharging against mobile phone operators but only 12,500 consumers (0.6%) opted to join and bring claims.

[251] Stuyck and others, *Commission Study on Alternative Means of Consumer Redress other than Redress Through Ordinary Judicial Proceedings* (n 249) identified eg a significant concern for consumers of the potential for 1 party to achieve additional advantages at the expense of another, especially in the case of legal counsel: para 377. For business, there is the concern about unmeritorious claims, pressure on businesses to settle even bad claims, as well as the risk of bankruptcy. The report claims that mechanisms can be provided to prevent unmeritorious claims, such as having judges assess the claims at an early stage. It later notes that in Sweden, a judge applies a cost-efficiency test at an early stage, and Australia requires that the award should exceed the costs: para 393. It dismisses the bankruptcy risk, citing it is business' failure to adhere to proper standards of conduct that drives bankruptcy, and no bankruptcies having occurred in Canada: para 378. For the legal system, the report dismisses the risk that courts would be overwhelmed, as this has not happened in Sweden, Canada or Australia. The report does not, however, note the crucial influence of local funding systems and cost rules on the incidence of claims, as cited by Hodges (n 247) 82.

[252] It noted that in 2004, 31.7% of federal class actions were civil rights cases, and 20.3% were securities actions.

[253] Civic Consulting, *Study on the Use of Alternative Dispute Resolution in the European Union* (16 October 2009). According to this the numbers were Germany (247), Italy (129), UK (43) and France (35). The study said that ADR is more relevant in Belgium, UK, Spain, Sweden, Austria, Ireland, Netherland and Denmark than elsewhere. The highest number of cases for any individual scheme was the UK with the FOS often dealing with over 100,000 per annum—most other large schemes deal with 5,000 to 20,000 per annum. The total number of cases in the EU in 2008 was 530,000, increased from 410,000 in 2006. (As cited by C Hodges, 'Collective Redress: A Breakthrough or Damp Squibb? (2014) 37 *J Consum Policy* 70.) Subsequent research, however, showed that the number of substantial ADR bodies was far lower and that some were dealing with large numbers of cases and mass issues; see C Hodges, 'A Market-Based Competition Enforcement Policy' (2011) 22(3) *Eur Bus L Rev* 261–91; C Hodges, 'European Competition Enforcement Policy: Integrating Restitution and Behaviour Control' (2011) *World Competition* 385–96.

brought to life with DG SANCO's 'three-pillar' approach, as shown in its 2009 Green Paper and follow-on consultation,[254] and it also advocated that ADR techniques had yet to reach their full potential.[255] The European Parliament has been supportive of this concept also, highlighting the need for alternatives to the US litigation approach.[256] The empirical evidence and studies showed that an ADR and three-pillar approach was reducing the pressure on litigation mechanisms and that the most efficient way of dealing with mass harm was through alternative methods to judicial proceedings.[257] Also, there was a subtle change in terminology being used in the EU collective redress debate moving away from that of collective action and towards collective redress. Coupled with this evidence was the collaboration between the three DGs—DG COMP, DG SANCO and DG JUST—in an effort to adopt a unified and holistic approach to collective redress. In addition to this, a Directive was adopted in 2013 that obliges Member States to provide full ADR facilities within two years and requires businesses to comply with ADR schemes.[258] There has also been the introduction of a pan-EU online dispute resolution (ODR) facility to promote the resolution of national and cross-border ADR disputes.[259] All of these signs strongly indicate that efforts were being made at EU level to keep collective redress out of the courts where possible.

Debate in EU Member States about facilitating collective actions for damages has heightened during the past decade and a half. By 2007, 16 of the then 27 EU Member States had collective redress schemes that allowed for damages: Austria, Bulgaria, Denmark, Finland, France, Germany, Greece, Hungary, Italy, Lithuania, the Netherlands, Poland, Portugal, Spain, Sweden and England and Wales). These procedures vary greatly and have different results.[260] Evidence shows that, despite these mechanisms, there has been low usage of collective procedures in most Member States.[261] Studies and consultations by the Commission show that:

> The vast majority of the existing collective redress mechanisms tend to have some elements that work and some that do not. Almost all existing collective redress mechanisms have some added value compared to individual judicial redress and alternative dispute resolution schemes. But their efficiency and effectiveness could be improved. The mechanisms have been applied in relatively few cases.[262]

In terms of Member State collective redress mechanisms generally, most approaches are the antithesis of the US private enforcement of public law approach. This is perhaps because of

[254] eg Commission (EC), 'Consumer Collective Redress' (Green Paper) COM(2008) 794; 'Consultation Paper for Discussion on the Follow-up to the Green Paper on Consumer Collective Redress' 15.

[255] Commission (EC), 'Consultation paper on the use of Alternative Dispute Resolution as a means to resolve disputes related to commercial transactions and practices in the European Union' (January 2011).

[256] European Parliament Resolution of 2 February 2012 'Towards a Coherent European Approach to Collective Redress' 2011/2089(INI), see chapter on EU collective redress for a detailed discussion of this.

[257] Stuyck and others (n 249); C Hodges, *The Reform of Class and Representative Actions in European Legal Systems: A New Framework for Collective Redress in Europe* (Hart Publishing, 2008). As cited by Hodges, 'Collective Redress: A Breakthrough or Damp Squibb? (n 253).

[258] Directive 2013/11/EU of the European Parliament and of the Council on Alternative Dispute Resolution for Consumer Disputes and amending Regulation (EC) No 2006/2004 and Directive 2009/22/EC (Directive on Consumer ADR) OJ, L 165, 18 June 2013.

[259] Regulation (EU) No 524/2013 on online dispute resolution for consumer disputes (Regulation on Consumer ODR) OJ L 165, 18 June 2013.

[260] Stuyck and others (n 249).

[261] Commission (EC). 'Consumer Collective Redress' (Green Paper) (n 254) para 12.

[262] Ibid.

a fear that policymakers have that private enforcement will only reach a significant level of activity if it is encouraged by considerable financial incentives and that these are associated with 'excess and abuse'.[263] This is generally the reason why most EU States do not have opt-out class actions. It is also a factor in why decisions on liability and quantum are not made by juries, nor are there high success fees for legal advisers. High damages are influenced by the possible availability of vast punitive damages, which, even if they are rarely awarded, have an inflationary effect on settlements.[264] When we look at examples of the various collective redress mechanisms in some of these Member States in practice, we can get an idea of why so few class action cases are occurring, although there are of course different reasons for this in each Member State. A fundamental reason is because better alternative options to litigation exist and are now operating well, particularly consumer ADR, with some States having effectively adopted new regulatory powers.[265] This compounds the European approach of consciously discouraging litigation and also preferring public to private enforcement—the opposite of the US approach. However, both public and private enforcement exist throughout the EU. There is also a question of difference in litigation cultures. Overall, policymakers are questioning whether litigation is the best mechanism for the resolution of mass torts or whether other tools, broadly termed ADR and regulatory techniques, would be faster, more economical and better at controlling misbehaviour, particularly that of a corporate nature. Obviously, a further reason is that some jurisdictions' national rules on costs and funding create obstacles to mass litigation.[266] Examining the legal systems of the Member States, the majority of these use the 'loser pays costs' rule.[267] Also most EU Member States prohibit contingency fees and do not have juries or punitive damages in civil cases. Some EU countries have been innovative in encouraging public authorities to participate in delivering collective redress by way of private compensation in several ways. One way is through a public authority being empowered to bring a collective damages claim on behalf of multiple consumers, as evidenced in Denmark, Sweden, Norway and Finland. While private individuals or consumer associations may have the power to take damages claims, the costs and loser pays rule are prohibitive, making action by public authorities preferable.[268] Throughout Europe, experience reflects low usage of collective actions. The evidence shows that class cases are slow, contrasting poorly with the faster, more efficient, less expensive solutions that can be achieved through the use of tools such as consumer ADR and regulatory schemes.[269] As a result, ADR and other techniques have filled the role of collective redress in many EU Member States. There are various examples of different collective redress systems in Europe. While some Member

[263] C Hodges, 'Collective Redress: A Breakthrough or Damp Squibb?' (2014) 37 *Journal of Consumer Policy* 70.

[264] Ibid.

[265] Hodges (n 5) 81.

[266] Such as the 'loser pays' rules on costs and restrictions on obtaining funding. Although there are changes being seen in some jurisdictions such as those seen when the UK Government announced in March 2011 the introduction of contingency fees and qualified one way cost shifting for personal injury cases: Ministry of Justice, *Reforming Civil Litigation Funding and Costs in England and Wales—Implementation of Lord Justice Jackson's Recommendations: The Government Response* (2011).

[267] C Hodges, S Vogenauer and M Tulibacka, 'Costs and Funding of Civil Litigation: A Comparative Study' (2009) Oxford Legal Studies Research Paper No 55, available at: http://papers.ssrn.com/sol3/papers.cfm?abstract_id=1511714##.

[268] As seen in the England and Wales with the GLO as well as in Denmark, Sweden and Norway.

[269] Hodges (n 263) 81.

States have been enthusiastic about introducing collective procedures, such as Norway,[270] Italy[271] and Poland,[272] their use in practice has been inhibited by the ability of plaintiffs to meet certification requirements in many cases.[273] From this brief examination, it is becoming clear that litigation is not the preferred means of ensuring mass harm redress both at EU policy level and at Member State level and that the future for dispute resolution lies in invoking other mechanisms such as ADR. In June 2013, the European Commission published its policy on collective redress. This comprised a set of three documents. These were a Recommendation[274] and an accompanying Communication[275] on collective redress in Member States, alongside a proposal for a Directive on rules governing actions for damages under national law for infringements of EU competition law.[276] These will be discussed in detail in chapter nine. In essence, the European collective redress debate questions:

> Whether private damages claims should be enlisted as supplementary mechanisms for regulatory enforcement and whether it is possible to balance civil procedures and funding systems for multiple claims to avoid excessive litigation and cost.[277]

What becomes clear from the analysis of the history of EU collective redress is that there is no single solution to the problems that mass harm presents, as it appears that remedies lie in a combination of techniques, including ADR.[278]

The MPA experience and approaches of all of the above jurisdictions will be discussed in further detail in the forthcoming chapters. There will naturally be some unavoidable repetition in order to fully describe the situation in each of the jurisdictions previously briefly explained.

8. Summary

This chapter examined the components of and the interplay between the elements of mass harm and collective redress. It then explored some of the MPA mechanisms for dealing with

[270] Norway has seen the greatest class action activity of any of the Nordic States, with 38 cases started from 2008 to the end of 2011. This may possibly because the court may decide to apply opt-out instead of opt-in, according to A Nordby, Danish Presidency, 'Copenhagen Conference on Collective Redress in a European Perspective' (Copenhagen 22–23 March 2012) cited by Hodges (n 263) 80.

[271] Ibid. Italy introduced class actions in 2010, following the adoption of Law of 12 December 2007 No 224, Art 2, para 446, and a considerable number of claims have since been filed but many, approximately 50%, were not certified.

[272] Class action procedures were introduced in Poland in 2010 with many cases following, approx 60 actions in 2 years, although many failed to be certified. In Hodges' opinion the class action procedure there has highlighted rather than solved underlying problems with the civil justice system; Hodges (n 263) 80.

[273] It has been suggested that this may be reflective of either a 'valiant crusading zeal and the satisfactory operation of the certification safeguard by the courts, or, on the other hand, evidence of a worryingly aggressive compensation culture that needs strenuous control'; Hodges (n 263) 81.

[274] Commission Recommendation (n 80). The legal basis for this Recommendation is Art 292 of the Treaty on the Functioning of the European Union.

[275] Commission (EC) Communication 'Towards a European Horizontal Framework for Collective Redress' COM(2013) 401/2.

[276] Commission (EC), 'Proposal for a Directive on Anti-trust Damages Actions' (n 70).

[277] Hodges (n 247) 82.

[278] Hodges,'Collective Redress: A Breakthrough or Damp Squibb? (n 253).

mass torts, their background and the various sectors in which they may operate. From this examination it is clear that litigation is not the only solution by which collective redress may be achieved; it is one of a number of collective redress options. What route is best at delivering this will depend on the enforcement landscape in the jurisdiction and the balance between private and public law and whether other tools such as ADR and regulation may be invoked as part of a holistic collective redress approach. This balance dictates the role that MPAs are intended to play, and whether they are a managerial tool or something more. It also ought to depend on the comparative advantages of the various collective redress options, such as cost, duration, quality and number of outcomes, which are other key criteria in the selection of MPA mechanisms. Finally, an introductory overview of the various MPA procedures used in the jurisdictions examined in this study was given in order to give readers some background information before these procedures are examined in more jurisdiction-specific detail. It is now time to look at the rationale behind MPAs and then to evaluate whether they achieve these aims in a selection of common law jurisdictions in which they operate.

3

Objectives of MPAs

1. Overview

This chapter will examine the underlying aims of MPAs and what they endeavour to achieve as a route to collective redress. In jurisdictions across the world there is ongoing debate about MPA procedures. It is important to identify a number of criteria in order to assess what the use of MPAs endeavours to accomplish having regard to the difficulties of mass harm. In order to do this, an analytical framework is created against which to evaluate various multi-party procedures. These criteria should assist debate about whether to introduce MPAs and will be enlightened by the experience of a number of jurisdictions in dealing with mass harm. It is illustrated in particular through a comparative approach by the experience of a selection of five common law jurisdictions, namely those of England and Wales, Ireland, Canada, Australia and the United States, as well as that of EU collective redress. The experience of mass harm litigation in Ireland is also discussed, as currently this jurisdiction does not have an effective mechanism for dealing with mass harm. This comparative approach will make frequent reference to these jurisdictions, all of which were discussed in the previous chapter. It will also make reference to the experience of other common law and civil law jurisdictions, where necessary, for the purposes of illustration.

The purpose of identifying a series of MPA objectives is to provide an analytical framework against which the effectiveness of MPA mechanisms can be assessed. The functions that are clearly attributable to tort or tort-type breaches or harms provide us with very important benchmarks of what MPAs try to achieve. There will, of course, be overlap between objectives, but they are mutually reinforcing. It is useful to set out each of these grounds, even if there is duplication because each gives a different viewpoint of aspects of the same objective. One point of this entire study is to question the basis of the use of MPAs. It would appear that, overall, MPAs have an important role as management mechanisms. Each of the MPA objectives identified in the framework analysis is a component of this overriding managerial function. We can gain insight into the underlying objectives of MPAs by referring to five leading, expert studies in this area, across a range of jurisdictions.

2. Expert Studies

A. Access to Justice Study by Lord Woolf MR

First, the *Access to Justice Study* by Lord Woolf MR, which is one of the most comprehensive appraisals of the British legal system to date. In his *Final Report on Access to Justice*, published in 1996, Lord Woolf identified three fundamental objectives that the multi-party litigation regime in England and Wales ought to achieve.[1] According to him, the rules for handling multi-party proceedings should:[2]

1. provide access to justice where large numbers of people have been affected by another's conduct, but individual loss is so small that it makes an individual action economically unviable;
2. provide expeditious, effective and proportionate methods of resolving cases, where individual damages are large enough to justify individual action but where the number of claimants and the nature of the issues involved mean that the cases cannot be managed satisfactorily in accordance with normal procedure; and
3. achieve a balance between the normal rights of claimants and defendants, to pursue and defend cases individually, and the interests of a group of parties to litigate the action as a whole in an effective manner.[3]

The first of these objectives concerns access to justice where individual claims are numerous but the damage suffered by individuals is so small that individual actions are not economically viable. These are known as 'scattered damages' type cases. Examples of such cases include recurrent disputes over inexpensive but widely sold defective consumer products or small but widespread mistakes in calculating benefit payments or fees.[4] In such instances, consumers may not individually feel the impact of wrongdoing to a large extent, but in the absence of enforcement, they would eventually suffer the consequences of widespread breaches, because of incentives to rule-break. Where such small losses may be uneconomic for individuals (or groups such as consumer associations) to pursue, especially where the loser pays rule applies, the eventual harm might be widespread. The cost and low return for private actors may be too small to incentivise any action if they do not have the option of pursuing MPA procedures. Furthermore, most multi-party disputes concern individual claimants taking action against one or more commercial or governmental defendants, who have the advantage of being collective entities. This often gives them substantial resources, economies of scale and easy access to information and expertise. Individual claimants may achieve similar benefits by taking action as a group and sharing their resources.[5] As Zuckerman explains, without such procedures, such claimants would have a *theoretical*

[1] Lord Woolf, *Access to Justice: Final Report* (1996).
[2] Ibid ch 17 [2].
[3] Following this report in 2000, the Civil Procedure Rules 1998 (CPR) were amended by the introduction of CPR, r 19.4. CPR, pt 19 sets out the rules governing multi-party disputes, including representative party actions and Group Litigation Orders (GLOs).
[4] See eg *Eisen v Carlisle & Jaquelin* 391 F 2d 555 (2nd Cir 1968) (alleged social security miscalculation affecting 6 million claimants, who were likely to recover on average US$3.90).
[5] S Hedley, 'Group Personal Injury Litigation and Public Opinion' (1994) 14 *LS* 70, 73.

right to bring actions, but no practical means of gaining access to courts due to the prohibitive and disproportionate cost of litigation.[6] Also, they may also gain a sense of solidarity, enhanced negotiating strength and greater publicity by combining their actions.[7] It is important to note, however, that litigation may still be uneconomic, even if aggregated under the private enforcement system, but at least the existence of such a procedure can have a deterrent effect.[8]

Lord Woolf's second objective is to provide expeditious, effective and proportionate methods to resolve cases that cannot be satisfactorily managed individually. The basis for this objective is the desire to conserve judicial and party resources.[9] He includes principles of procedural economy, proportionality and speedy resolution of claims under this aim. He stipulates that 'methods' for resolving claims should be available in order to achieve this objective and so he advocates the use of multi-party procedures.

The third objective identified by Lord Woolf entails providing a balance between individual rights and group interests. This recognises that, inevitably, the rights of an individual to participate and to have procedural autonomy will have to be compromised in order to provide collective resolution of multiple claims. For example, individuals may not have the normal freedom to choose and instruct their lawyers or they may not have much input on issues such as evidence submitted or settlement negotiation. In this sense, overall, individual rights may have to be sacrificed to some extent for the greater collective good.[10]

In his *Final Report*, Lord Woolf observed that there are inherent difficulties with multi-party procedures and that his report was not a panacea to this.

> In this area of litigation more than any other, my examination of the problems does not pretend to present the final answer but merely to try to be the next step forward in a lively debate within which the parties and judges are hammering out better ways of managing the unmanageable.[11]

Lord Woolf, therefore, acknowledged that MPAs are not without their flaws and are not the end solution in order to ensure collective redress but that they can be mechanisms to help with the difficulties, not least of a managerial nature, of trying to deliver this redress by surmounting some of the multiple logistical challenges that mass harm presents. This suggests that MPAs play an important role as managerial mechanisms to assist with the litigation of mass harm.

B. Irish Law Reform Commission Report on Multi-party Litigation 2005

The second expert study examined is the 2005 Irish Law Reform Commission (hereafter referred to as the LRC) *Report on Multi-party Litigation*. The LRC is an independent

[6] A Zuckerman, *Zuckerman on Civil Procedure* (Sweet and Maxwell, 2006) 12 [38].

[7] S Gibbons, 'Group Litigation, Class Actions and Lord Woolf's Three Objectives—A Critical Analysis' (2008) 27 *Civil Justice Q* 208, 212.

[8] See C Hodges, 'Objectives, Mechanisms and Policy Choices in Collective Enforcement and Redress' in J Steele and W van Boom (eds), *Mass Justice* (Edward Elgar, 2011) 107.

[9] Gibbons, 'Group Litigation, Class Actions and Lord Woolf's Three Objectives' (n 7) 218.

[10] This objective is further detailed in R Mulheron, 'The Objectives of Class Action Regimes' in *The Class Action in Common Law Legal Systems—A Comparative Perspective* (Hart Publishing, 2004) ch 3.

[11] *Woolf, Access to Justice: Final Report* (n 1) 17 [6].

statutory body, established by the Law Reform Commission Act 1975.[12] Its role is to examine areas of the law and make authoritative recommendations for law reform in Ireland. The Taoiseach,[13] in consultation with the Attorney General, nominates Commission members, comprising of senior members of the judiciary, leading academics and practitioners. Most of the recommendations by the LRC have resulted in the enactment of legislation effecting reforms. The 2005 Report advocated that principles for reform in this area should ensure procedural fairness and practicality, procedural efficiency and access to justice.[14] The LRC recognised that it is a challenge for litigation to find an appropriate balance between procedural efficiency and broad procedural fairness.[15] It opined that, ideally, a multi-party procedure should render the system as efficient for the collective group as the demands for individual fairness will allow. The LRC acknowledged that the need for procedural fairness is the core element in any multi-party litigation. In its view, any multi-party procedure should facilitate and not hinder the resolution of individual actions. It recommended that, while a single procedural structure under the management of a designated judge may be capable of dealing with the multi-party action, it is important to divide the various elements of a case into convenient categories that lend themselves to collective resolution. Procedural fairness is also important from the perspective of the defendant and the LRC recommended that this should entail transparency in terms of the future potential scope of the litigation and result in an appropriate reduction in associated costs. Procedural efficiency relates to savings that may be made without impacting on the central issue of procedural fairness and practicality as discussed above. This efficiency should affect each individual within the group. An example given by the LRC is that of defendant liability and the ways in which multi-party treatment may save costs. These resemble the 'economies of scale' factors discussed by Woolf above. First, the outlay in monetary or other resources necessary to litigate the consolidated generic issue may be much less than if conducted on an individual basis because the more frequently the same work is repeated on an individual case basis, the higher the final costs will be throughout the collective group. Secondly, whether or not the issue reaches court, the cost of representation as well as the lesser issue of administrative court costs may be reduced considerably where a single representative acts on behalf of the group. These savings, of course, depend on the consolidation of both the generic issue and also the legal representation.[16] The LRC supported the objectives for multi-party litigation procedure advocated by Hodges in his discussion of Group Litigation Orders (GLOs) in England and Wales and cited his opinion that:

> The claims that are managed in a co-ordinated fashion under a GLO remain no more than a collection of individual claims, each of which must ultimately be resolved. The objective is to dispose of all the claims as effectively and swiftly as possible. In deciding on a managerial mechanism to move

[12] The LRC's main aim is to keep the law under review and to make practical proposals for its reform. It has published over 100 documents containing proposals for law reform which are available at http://www.lawreform.ie. The LRC usually publishes in 2 stages: first, a Consultation Paper and then a Report. This occurred with the Multi-party Litigation recommendations. The Consultation Paper is intended to form the basis for discussion and its recommendations, conclusions and suggestions are therefore provisional. The LRC *Consultation Paper on Multi-party Litigation* was published in 2003 and its *Report on Multi-party Litigation* was published in 2005.

[13] The Irish Prime Minister.

[14] Irish Law Reform Commission, *Report on Multi-party Litigation* (LRC 76-2005).

[15] Ibid 18.

[16] Ibid 19.

forward resolution of all the individual claims, the paramount consideration is that the court must be satisfied that the selected approach will be *dispositive* of as many cases or issues as possible in as efficient and proportionate a manner as possible.[17]

In this statement, Hodges has crucially captured the essence of the role of MPAs, which is that of managerial mechanisms that can enable procedural justice. This theme is visible throughout the MPA mechanisms evaluated in each of the common law jurisdictions examined in this research. It will be discussed in further detail at the end of this chapter and highlighted throughout this research.

In discussing access to justice, the LRC stated that this has traditionally formed a central rationale behind the introduction of multi-party procedures. Under individual litigation (or within the test case model used in Ireland), costs are calculated for the entirety of the case on an individual level. With this approach, the potential exposure to costs orders may present a real disincentive to the institution of proceedings in the first place.[18] By contrast, where the cost of litigating the generic issue is calculated on the basis of a single incident and divided among a group of members, there will be substantial savings to be made at an individual level.[19] While considering access to justice as a laudable principle, the LRC was, however, wary to avoid inferring unrealistic guarantees from its status as a constitutional slogan.[20] It stated that the constitutional right of access, recognised in *Macauley v Minister for Posts and Telegraphs*,[21] has never been considered absolute. It has operated, to date, to prevent unreasonable impediments being placed in the way of individuals wishing to litigate. The LRC qualified this by adding that this did not mean that a clear and unrestricted path needed to be provided for the litigant, as certain obstacles are necessary in the interest of the smooth operation of the judicial process and for the vindication of the rights of the other parties to the litigation.[22] It illustrated this point by reference to an example of a court striking out an action as frivolous or out of time.[23] In the LRC's opinion, so long as these impediments are not unreasonable, they are compatible with the constitutional principle of access to the courts. It viewed the issue of access to justice in the context of multi-party litigation in light of this backdrop and considered that a careful balance between the avoidance of undue impediments to legitimate litigation and the filtration from the system of frivolous actions is required.[24] Access to justice itself, therefore, does not seem to have been the primary objective of the LRC. While savings will be made on an individual basis as a result of the consolidation of the group action, naturally there remains an element of risk and potential financial exposure that exists in all litigation. Despite this, the LRC propounded that savings resulting from the efficiencies of multi-party procedures ensure that meaningful access to justice will be strengthened.[25] The LRC was mindful of developments

[17] Ibid 19 [1.53] 19, citing C Hodges, *Multi-Party Actions* (Oxford University Press, 2001) 68, ch 5 [11].
[18] See the discussion by the LRC on deferred payment of fees, the limitations of civil legal aid and legal expenses in LRC (n 14) ch 3.
[19] Ibid 20.
[20] Ibid 20.
[21] [1966] IR 345.
[22] LRC (n 14) 20.
[23] The Statute of Limitations aims to strike the appropriate balance between the right to litigate, the interests of certainty and protection against outdated, historical claims.
[24] LRC (n 14) 21.
[25] Ibid 21.

in case management of litigation generally and the reforms recommended in England and Wales which were intended to reduce the cost of such litigation by such means as the use of judicial management.[26] Essentially, this entails the promotion of active judicial involvement in the litigation process so as to encourage appropriate resolution as quickly as possible, either through a court hearing or by settlement.[27] The Working Group on a Courts Commission accepted this principle.[28] The Committee on Court Practice and Procedure (CCPP) recommended in 2003 that any further Rules of Court should enable the development of case management.[29] This general trend of case management for all litigation is enshrined in the LRC's approach to multi-party litigation. The LRC recommended that three principles be the basis for multi-party litigation reform: procedural fairness for the plaintiff and defendant; procedural efficiency in terms of resources and time saving; and promotion of access to justice.

C. Civil Justice Council Report

The third key report examined in this study is that of the Civil Justice Council of England and Wales (CJC), an English public body that advises the Lord Chancellor on civil justice and civil procedure in England and Wales, on the state of collective redress in England and Wales in 2008.[30] This report echoed the reference by Lord Woolf and the Irish LRC to access to justice as being one of the three key principles that should underpin a system of collective redress for England and Wales. The CJC Report suggested that the principles that should form the foundation for the introduction of a collective system would include the following:

A civil justice system:

1. Should be just in the results it and they deliver;
2. Should be fair and be seen to be fair;
3. Should ensure litigants have an equal opportunity, regardless of their resources, to assert or defend their legal rights;

[26] In 2 reports on civil procedure in the mid-1990s by Lord Woolf (see Lord Woolf, *Access to Justice Interim Report* (1995) and Lord Woolf, *Access to Justice Final Report* (1996)), which led to the enactment of the Civil Procedure Act 1997 and the Civil Procedure Rules 1998 (CPR).

[27] LRC (n 14) 21.

[28] The Minister for Justice established the Working Group on a Courts Commission in 1997. Its functions include reviewing the operation of the courts system, having regard to the level and quality of service provided to the public, staffing, information technology, etc; its financing; any other aspect of the operation of the courts system which the Group considers appropriate; and to have investigative, advisory and recommendatory functions and to make any interim reports and recommendations as it sees fit to the Minister for Justice. See eg Working Group on a Courts Commission, *Second Report: Case Management and Court Management* (1996).

[29] This is a committee appointed by the Minister for Justice since 1962. Its role includes enquiring into the operation of the courts and considering whether the costs of litigation could be reduced and whether the convenience of the public and the efficient dispatch of civil and criminal business be more effectively secured by amending the law in relation to the jurisdiction of the courts and by making changes in practice and procedure. It may make reports on any matter warranting attention and make recommendations on such matters, including the law, as the Minister may request the Committee to examine; eg the Committee on Court Practice and Procedure, *28th Interim Report: The Court Rules Committees* (2003) 51.

[30] CJC, *Improving Access to Justice through Collective Actions: Developing a More Efficient and Effective Procedure for Collective Actions* (December 2008).

4. Should ensure that every litigant has an adequate opportunity to state his or her own case and to answer their opponent's;
5. Should treat like cases alike (and conversely treat different cases differently);
6. Should deal with cases efficiently and economically, in a way that is comprehensible to those using the civil justice system and which provides litigants with as much certainly as the litigation permits; and do so within a system best organised to realise these principles

It is these principles, which reflect Lord Woolf's commitment to procedural justice now being as important as substantive justice, which guide the Civil Justice Council in making its recommendation [for collective redress reform].[31]

D. Mulheron Global Comparative Study

The fourth expert analysis referred to is that of one of the leading academic commentators in this area, Professor Rachael Mulheron, who has undertaken a detailed global comparative study of the objectives of class action regimes in the US, Australia, Canada and England and Wales.[32] Her authoritative and comprehensive research states that there are six key objectives of group litigation in England and Wales: (1) proportionality; (2) predictability; (3) access to justice; (4) judicial and wider economy; (5) (to a lesser extent) deterrence; and (6) fairness.[33] In assessing class action objectives in common law jurisdictions internationally, she identifies that there are universally applicable general objectives of the class action procedure that are often repeated by both law reformers and judiciary, and which can be applied regardless of the type of litigious scenario.[34] These common objectives evidenced by common law jurisdictions internationally vary slightly from the aims above as the objective of fairness appears to be replaced by the aim of balancing judicial activism and personal autonomy.[35]

E. European Commission Analysis

The fifth expert analysis of collective redress is that contributed by the European Commission. Over the past decade it has examined existing collective redress procedures in order to assess what measures offer the most appropriate solutions. The history of this is detailed in chapter nine and is set out in very brief summary below. The Commission has engaged in much debate with expert commentators, Member States, stakeholders, lawyers and legislators about the features of mechanisms necessary in order to achieve optimum collective redress. As a result of their input, policy in these areas has eventually begun to acknowledge that the solution to mass harm redress does not lie in litigation alone, but rather in a holistic approach involving a combination of tools. It has also taken practical steps to attempt to bring these to fruition. This has occurred in two sectors in particular, competition law and

[31] Ibid 12–13.
[32] Mulheron, 'The Objectives of Class Action Regimes' (n 10).
[33] R Mulheron, 'Cultural Dimensions of Group Litigation' ('International Association of Procedural Law' Conference, Moscow, 2012).
[34] Mulheron (n 10) 47.
[35] All other objectives appear to be the same.

consumer law. There has been considerable apprehension in the European Commission of what are perceived to be the grave disadvantages of the US class action system, especially involving excessive litigation and severe costs for litigants and business. These disadvantages, in turn, burden the economy and impede progress.[36] One of the most important early informers of EU collective redress policy was an empirical study on alternative means of consumer redress other than through ordinary judicial proceedings, the Stuyck Report.[37] This was published in 2007, before the Commission policy began to take its current shape. This study included reports on the variety of alternative means of consumer redress mechanisms from all EU Member States as well as the US, Canada and Australia. It highlighted the important growth in ADR mechanisms, stemming from a desire to avoid the costs and delays of litigation processes. This resulted in the adoption of new techniques involving ADR and ombudsman mechanisms. This strong academic opinion suggests that the fastest and most economical way of achieving collective redress was through the use of voluntary ADR, in particular ombudsmen, and the use of regulatory techniques. In comparison to these methods, litigation was slower and more expensive.[38] This report discredits litigation as the sole solution to mass harm redress and advocated instead how methods including ADR could be more effective. Subsequent DG SANCO and DG COMP developments[39] explored and evaluated options for collective redress.[40] The Commission at this time realised that there was a problem with collective redress, particularly the difficulties associated with US Style class actions. It became aware that it was necessary to distance itself from the US approach to private enforcement, as this was the antithesis of the EU approach to collective redress. Following further deliberation[41] a consensus emerged that a combination of several techniques was the best solution to collective redress. As a consequence of this, and other developments in relation to ADR,[42] EU consumer law is now enforced by a combination of public authorities, self-regulatory or co-regulatory bodies, private enforcement through litigation, and also through consumer ADR bodies.[43] In concurrent developments in the competition law sector, while the EU had traditionally relied on public enforcement

[36] See European Justice Forum, 'Lessons from the United States, Australia and the United Kingdom' (2006) available at: www.europeanjusticeforum.org.

[37] J Stuyck and others, *Commission Study on Alternative Means of Consumer Redress other than Redress through Ordinary Judicial Proceedings* (Catholic University of Leuven, 2007).

[38] C Hodges, 'Collective Redress: A Breakthrough or Damp Squibb? (2014) 37 *J Consum Policy* 72.

[39] It carried out a consultation on benchmarks. See http://ec.europa.eu/consumers/redress_cons/collective_redress_en.htm#Benchmarks. There was criticism that the benchmarks used were based on the assumption that the only remedy was a judicial solution. The Commission privately accepted this criticism; see further C Hodges, 'Towards Parameters for EU Civil Justice Systems' in S Vogenauer and C Hodges (eds), *Civil Justice Systems in Europe: Implications for Choice of Forum and Choice of Contract Law* (Hart Publishing, 2014).

[40] eg Commission (EC), 'Consumer Collective Redress' (Green Paper) COM(2008) 794. This was published together with 2 studies by external consultants. The first was a Problem Study, by Civil Consulting and Oxford Economics (2008), which examined the problems faced by consumers in obtaining redress for infringements of consumer protection legislation, and the economic consequences of such problems. The second was an Evaluation Study, which evaluated the performance and efficacy of the existing collective redress mechanisms in the EU: Civic Consulting and Van Dijk Management Consultants, *Study on the Evaluation of the Effectiveness and efficiency of CR mechanisms in the European Union* (2008).

[41] DG SANCO issued a further consultation paper in 2009 and held a public hearing to gauge responses to this; available at: http://ec.europa.eu/consumers/redress_cons/docs/consultation_paper2009.pdf.

[42] Such as Directive 2013/11/EU of the European Parliament and of the Council on Alternative Dispute Resolution for Consumer Disputes and amending Regulation (EC) No 2006/2004 and Directive 2009/22/EC (Directive on Consumer ADR).

[43] Hodges, 'Collective Redress' (n 38) 70.

in this area, there were signs that the Commission was beginning to move away from this.[44] There were also discussions in the Stuyck Report on possible solutions, especially the development of policy for competition enforcement that would integrate private and public consequences.[45] Extensive debate followed about what collective redress mechanisms were best suited to use for EU collective redress[46] and whether this should include the introduction of private damages claims through collective actions.[47]

All of these developments have helped the Commission to identify key criteria for MPA mechanisms and ways to achieve optimum collective redress. After much deliberation, this culminated in the publication of the Commission's collective redress policy in 2013. In this, the Commission has identified and developed its own criteria for collective redress mechanisms, particularly for collective actions. As these criteria represent the most recent policy on EU collective redress and as they are the result of protracted interaction with the creators and consumers of collective redress mechanisms, these can be used to inform MPA objectives on a broad scale. It is vital that these be integrated into the analytical framework of MPA objectives in this study in order to assess what is the best possible approach to achieve collective redress.

The aim behind the 2013 policy is not to harmonise the legal systems of Member States but to give some non-binding, common principles for Member States to take into account when creating collective redress mechanisms. The Commission stated that its goal was to improve access to justice, to curb illegal activity and to make it possible for those who suffer mass harm to get compensation, while also avoiding abusive litigation by providing appropriate procedural safeguards.[48] In order to achieve the twin aims of economic growth and access to justice, four policy criteria for any European collective redress solution were set out by the Commission so that it should:

— Be capable of effectively resolving a large number of individual claims for compensation of damage, thereby promoting judicial economy;
— Be capable of delivering legally certain and fair outcomes within a reasonable timeframe, while respecting the rights of all parties involved;
— Provide for robust safeguards against abusive litigation; and
— Avoid economic incentives to bring speculative claims.[49]

[44] This was seen December 2005 when it published a Green Paper on damages for breaches of competition law, COM(2005) 672.

[45] Hodges (n 38) 73.

[46] These greatly informed the strong views of the European Parliament in its resolution of 2 February 2012 on 'Towards a Coherent European Approach to Collective Redress' 2011/2089(INI).

[47] Earlier proposals resulted in the Commission (EC) damages actions for breach of EC antitrust rules (White Paper) COM(2008) 165. This explored multiple reforms to enable private damages claims, particularly through a collective procedure, but this was not well received by Member States. It included proposals as to whether an opt-in or opt-out model should be adopted and whether punitive damages should be permitted. Commission Staff Working Paper accompanying the White Paper on damages actions for breach of the EC antitrust rules, SEC(2008)404; Commission Staff Working Document accompanying the White Paper on damages actions for breach of the EC antitrust rules: Impact Assessment, SEC(2008) 405, 'Making antitrust damages actions more effective in the EU: welfare impact and potential scenarios', final report submitted to the Commission on 21 December 2007.

[48] Commission (EC) Recommendation on Common Principles for Injunctive and Compensatory Collective Redress Mechanisms in the Member States concerning violations of rights granted under Union Law (2013/396/EU) Art 1.

[49] Commission (EC) Communication 'Towards a European Horizontal Framework for Collective Redress' COM(2013) 401/2, [3].

In summary, the Commission's proposals set out a number of objectives that comprise (1) access to justice; (2) judicial and procedural economy; (3) fairness; (4) predictability; (5) non-abuse—particularly no economic incentives for speculative claims,[50] (6) deterrence and (7) compensation.[51]

In establishing the context of these proposals at the outset, the Communication stated that the objective was:

> For the Commission, any measures for judicial redress need to be appropriate and effective and bring balanced solutions supporting European growth while ensuring effective access to justice. Therefore, they must not attract abusive litigation or have effects detrimental to respondents regardless of the results of the proceedings. Examples of such adverse effects can be seen in particular in 'class actions' as known in the United States. The European approach to collective redress must thus give proper thought to preventing these negative effects and devising adequate safeguards against them.[52]

Already from this, it is clear that a primary objective of the proposals is access to justice, echoing that of the MPA objectives that have been identified. This access however, is to be tempered by appropriate safeguards to avoid the perceived 'excess and abuse' encountered with US class actions. This is to be achieved through the proposal's stringent requirements in relation to aspects of collective redress such as funding and admissibility requirements on standing. The proposals clearly identify a compensation and deterrence function in their objective of curbing illegal activity and make it possible for those who suffer mass harm to get compensation.[53] In order to do this it provides for both injunctive and compensatory redress. The Recommendation advises that Member States should have a collective redress system that allows private individuals and entities to obtain court orders to deliver payment of damages through compensation where a large number of persons or entities have been harmed by the same illegal practice.[54] Also, compensation and deterrence are known concomitants and results of effective collective redress.

3. MPA Objectives—Analytical Framework

From an analysis of all of the expert studies outlined above, it is clear that there are numerous objectives underpinning collective redress models. These can be combined to compile a set of criteria for an analytical framework by means of which different models of MPAs can be evaluated. This study explores a range of different solutions in several jurisdictions and the only way to meaningfully engage in comparative analysis of these is to use such a functional analytical framework. These criteria provide such a framework and will help demonstrate how the law is responding to these new challenges. It will be useful to return to these

50 Hodges (n 38) 79.
51 Compensation is mentioned in the Recommendation (n 48) Art 112.
52 Communication (n 49) [1.1].
53 Recommendation (n 48) Art 1.
54 Recommendation (n 48) 1.

benchmarks throughout this study and to use them as touchstones against which to assess MPA mechanisms. The following are the criteria that comprise the analytical framework:

A. Access to Justice
B. Judicial and Procedural Economy
C. Fairness (including proportionality, balancing individual rights and personal autonomy, and non-abuse)
D. Predictability
E. Deterrence
F. Compensation

In identifying these considerations, it becomes clear that the need to address issues of mass justice in collective redress presents particular practical problems and challenges. Such challenges include interpreting new demands in civil claims and making policy choices that rise to the challenges of these demands, for example the question of how to resolve issues of mass environmental harm. It is notable that only one of the studies, the Commission's proposals, specifically addresses the objective of compensation, but perhaps this is because it is implicit in the notion of access to justice. This chapter will focus on compensation as a further objective because it clearly merits discussion separately. On the basis of the expert opinions above, it is possible to identify six key criteria in total. On close examination of the selected common law jurisdictions, it is apparent that in practice, the criterion of fairness includes the objectives of proportionality, balancing individual rights and personal autonomy and non-abuse, so these objectives are subsumed within the objective of fairness.

As closely related to the cardinal issue of access to justice, the MPA objective indicators listed above are each elements of this holistic notion. This section will comprise a full discussion of each of these individually, beginning with access to justice. It is, however, beyond the scope of this study to unpack the somewhat nebulous concept of what 'justice' entails.[55] Instead, the focus of this research is on the more substantive notion of access to justice in terms of MPAs. While MPA objectives have been discussed generally by the studies highlighted, they are now dealt with in more detail in the analysis that follows below, with some unavoidable repetition where there is overlap between objectives. Clearly these objectives are not stand-alone and are not mutually exclusive. Each has a significant link to and bearing upon at least one of the others, for example procedural justice and access to justice, but each gives a unique perspective on the functioning of MPAs, notwithstanding obvious overlap.

It is important to clarify that the criteria underlying the MPA objectives in this research are identified from analysis of the above reports from jurisdictions *before* class actions were introduced (or not), rather than extensive *after-the-event* empirical evidence. Also, the evaluation of these criteria is based on an analysis of written materials (such as the class action rules themselves, plus various scholarly and academic statements). It is not an evaluation based on empirical analysis. It is important to make this clear, since a complete analysis of the criteria could only be undertaken on the basis of empirical analysis and this is beyond the scope of this research since this data is very difficult to identify and is not comprehensively

[55] This in itself is an immense discussion. Academic debate about the role of justice often cites the view of John Rawls that principles of justice provide 'an Archimedean point for appraising existing institutions as well as the desires and aspirations they generate'; J Rawls, *A Theory of Justice* (Oxford University Press, 972) 520.

available. The analysis undertaken in this research is limited to this extent, and for this reason, is limited in this way. It is, therefore, to some extent provisional, although it is entirely valid on its own terms. It is also important to recognise that a fundamental limitation to be drawn from this MPA analysis is the lack of reliable statistics. This makes it difficult to assess the extent to which the MPA objectives have been achieved. This limitation applies to all the jurisdictions examined in this work. As a result, the analysis undertaken is against the MPA objectives that are those *claimed* as being *intended* for class actions, but the analysis is restricted to a *theoretical* evaluation of whether the particular architecture of different techniques, rules and safeguards is *likely* to have achieved satisfaction of the criteria. This is not an analysis in which there could be an evaluation of whether *in fact* the various national systems have satisfied the criteria, since that would require empirical data.

A. Access to Justice

Judge Iacobucci defines access to justice generally as including two components: (1) to provide claimants with an opportunity to pursue their claims in court; and (2) to obtain an appropriate restorative result, where warranted.[56] Baron Neuberger, President of the English Supreme Court, expressed his views on contemporary access to justice. In his opinion

> Access to justice has a number of components. First, a competent and impartial judiciary; secondly, accessible courts; thirdly, properly administered courts; fourthly, a competent and honest legal profession; fifthly, an effective procedure for getting a case before the court; sixthly, an effective legal process; seventhly effective execution; eighthly, affordable justice.[57]

Elements of his opinion resonate with the rationales established in this chapter as a framework for evaluating collective redress mechanisms. It appears that access to justice is the overall goal that is delivered once these various criteria are in place. As such, the components above are gauges of access to justice. A third example of the judicial endorsement of the principle of access to justice, this time through MPAs, is seen in *Afrika v Cape plc*,[58] where Lord Justice Longmore remarked that:

> Multi-party actions are a comparatively novel feature of English litigation and the courts have attempted over recent years to fashion new types of order to enable viable actions to be brought in situations where a single individual would find it prohibitively expensive to bring proceedings on his or her own … These actions are difficult, as well as expensive, to run and impose great burdens on the practitioners who conduct them and the judges who try them. They can, however, be a service to many who suffer severe injuries and it is the policy of the courts to facilitate such actions in appropriate cases and adapt traditional procedures accordingly.[59]

The main purpose of collective redress is to maximise or provide access to justice.[60] In order to evaluate whether or to what extent MPAs improve access to justice, one must first

[56] F Iacobucci, 'What is Access to Justice in the Context of Class Actions' in J Kalajdzic (ed), *Accessing Justice, Appraising Class Actions: Ten Years after Dutton Hollick and Rumley* (LexisNexis, 2011) 20.
[57] Quote from a lecture by D Neuberger, President of the UK Supreme Court, 'Justice in an Age of Austerity' (Freshfields LLP, London, October 2013).
[58] [2001] EWCA Civ 2017, [1].
[59] Ibid.
[60] J Peysner, 'Access to Justice in Multi-party Actions' in *Global Governance and the Quest for Civil Society* vol 3 (Hart Publishing, 2008) 103–15.

ask, what is access to justice and how can MPAs provide it? There are numerous differing views of what access to justice means. Kalajdzic canvasses many of these in relation to class actions.[61] Most definitions of access to justice relate to the ability to institute legal proceedings and to have it reach a resolution.[62] It may include the opportunity to obtain legal representation for one's claim.[63] Many commentators have recognised that it does not always amount to having one's day in court and that some wrongs cannot be put right by the court system.[64] Access to justice is clearly a general policy aim, as espoused by both Lord Woolf and the LRC. The notion of access to justice is widely considered to be central to good governance concepts and is a broadly held societal value. It is also a core element identified by proponents of the global administrative law phenomenon as a means of exploring the increasing normativisation of good governance standards and values.[65]

There is an ethos of the importance of access to justice particularly in the environmental policy area, which is a central concern of this study. For example, the Aarhus Convention and subsequent developments in EU law place great significance on access to justice.[66] Essentially the focus is on procedural aspects, such as issues of costs and timeliness, as these are key determinants of access to justice. This has recently been seen in Ireland in the reforms in relation to costs in environmental law cases.[67] It is also evident in the *Edwards* case where the UK Supreme Court referred to the European Court of Justice the question of what test is to be applied to ensure that review proceedings concerning certain environmental matters are not 'prohibitively expensive' as required under EU Directive 85/337, Article 10a and Directive 96/61, Article 15a.[68]

There may be circumstances where individual claims are not taken or may not be able to be processed without collective redress. This, according to Hodges, is a denial of justice and an inefficiency that 'can undermine a society's core reliance on observance of the rule of law and of justice'.[69] From this perspective, combining legal actions is recognised as a powerful means of increasing the efficiency in terms of workload of the legal system as it enables claims to be brought in the first place. In this way, such actions can result in liability for claims that would never, otherwise, have been pursued by individuals.[70] This may be critical in challenging corporations or governmental agencies that have considerable resources. Policymakers may naturally be concerned that collective redress could produce a litigation culture or compensation culture. In the context of the US system, however, Phair stresses that the aim of the US class action was to provide greater access to the courts,

[61] J Kalajdzic, *Access to Justice for the Masses? A Critical and Empirical Analysis of Class Actions* (UBC Press, forthcoming).

[62] Iacobucci, 'What is Access to Justice in the Context of Class Actions' (n 56) 20.

[63] J Kalajdzic (ed), *Accessing Justice, Appraising Class Actions: Ten Years after Dutton Hollick and Rumley* (LexisNexis, 2011) 19.

[64] Kalajdzic, *Access to Justice for the Masses?* (n 61) 43.

[65] See eg B Kingsbury, N Krisch, RB Stewart and JB Wiener, 'Global Governance as Administration—National and Transnational Approaches to Global Administrative Law' (2005) 68(3) and (4) *Law and Contemporary Problems* 1, 2; B Kingsbury, 'The Concept of "Law" in Global Administrative Law' (2009) 20(1) *Eur J Int'l L* 23, 25; C Harlow, 'Global Administrative Law: the Quest for Principles and Values' (2006) 17(1) *Eur J Int'l L* 187–214, 187.

[66] UNECE Convention on access to information, public participation in decision-making and access to justice in environmental matters, 38 ILM (1999) 517 (Aarhus, 25 June 1998).

[67] Planning and Development Act 2000, s 50, which amended rules on costs in relation to judicial review of applications, appeals, referrals and other matters.

[68] *R (on the application of Edwards & Anor) v Environment Agency & Ors* [2010] UKSC 57.

[69] C Hodges, 'Multi-Party Actions: A European Approach' (2001) 11 *Duke J of Comp and Int'l L* 349.

[70] W Bogart, 'Questioning Litigation's Role—Courts and Class Actions in Canada' (1986) 62 *Ind LJ* 665, 691.

particularly for those who 'individually would be without effective strength to bring their opponents to court at all'.[71] Commentators state that access to justice is the 'cornerstone of class proceedings'[72] and that their most important benefit is to provide 'a meaningful remedy to large numbers of otherwise disenfranchised victims of breached obligations.'[73] Access to justice has been widely cited to justify class actions; for example, in Australia, one of the goals behind the amendment of a class action statute was to 'provide a real remedy' to those in the community who individually had uneconomically viable claims, but where overall the total amount at issue was significant. This is a further endorsement of the 'scattered damages' scenarios discussed previously.[74] This is the theoretical proposition that aggregating cases ought to enable cases of small value to be brought. That is by increasing the cost-proportionality of individual cases by sharing generic costs. MPAs can help to spread costs among a range of parties and the US Supreme Court emphasised this in stating that one of the justifications that led to the development of the modern class action was to facilitate spreading litigation costs among numerous litigants with similar claims (once again, the 'economies of scale' identified by the LRC and Lord Woolf).[75] It is also highly important that a key economic factor is that the claimant's power is significantly enhanced through combining cases—especially where defendants cannot recover costs, particularly if they lose.

A crucial factor in access to justice is the issue of funding. The specific funding challenges where they are discussed in the context of each jurisdiction examined will give further evidence of this. For example, claims cannot be brought in the US without contingency fees and the fact that there is no cost shifting. This is also the case in Canada were it not for contingency fees, consortia of funders, costs only being enforceable against representative claimants and the use of the device of 'men of straw' to defeat cost shifting.[76] In Australia, the difficulties of funding have largely been alleviated by the introduction of third-party funding, with representative plaintiffs being 'men of straw'. Historically, funding has been a very large stumbling block in England and Wales and an ongoing problem in Ireland due to the lack of legal aid. Overall, funding of MPAs is absolutely critical and is closely affected by the prevailing costs regime. Ultimate private funding in a loser pays system that has no or limited legal aid can only be through lawyers (through contingency fees) or through other funding intermediaries (such as insurers or investors). So this research identifies that there is a policy choice between allowing funding by intermediaries and the risk that it will lead to conflicts of interest and potential threat of abuse that is too great. If MPAs are to be encouraged, then liberal funding conditions must exist but then abuse must be expected and safeguards will be necessary to prevent it. If there are too many safeguards then the MPA mechanism will be restricted. Hodges believes that it is not possible to calibrate safeguards so as to have just enough access to justice and not too much abuse.[77]

[71] R Phair, 'Resolving the "Choice-of-Law Problem" in Rule 23(b) (3) Nationwide Class Actions' (2000) 67 *University of Chicago L Rev* 835, 839.

[72] J Camp and S Matthews, 'Actions Brought Under the Class Proceedings Act, RSBC, 1995, c 50' in CLE Society of BC, *Torts—1998 Update* (1998) 23.

[73] M Davis, 'Towards the Proper Role for Mass Tort Class Actions' (1998) 77 *Oregon L Rev* 157, 169.

[74] Extracted from the speech of the then Attorney General at the second reading of the Federal Court of Australia Amendment Bill 1991, referring to the new pt IVA of the Act. *Parliamentary Debates*, Senate, 14 November 1991, 3174 (Mr Duffy).

[75] *US Parole Comm v Geraghty*, 445 US 388, 402, 100 S Ct 1202 (1980), cited in re *General Motors Corp Pick-up Truck Fuel Tank Prods Liab Litig*, 55F 3d 768, 784 (3d Cir 1995).

[76] See further ch 6, s 2.

[77] Hodges (n 38).

For this reason, it would appear that Gidi's opinion that 'class actions can succeed in the absence of discovery, contingency fees, the American cost rule, an entrepreneurial bar, and powerful and active judges, at least as effectively as can traditional individual litigation' is clearly misplaced.[78] So this dilemma is a real 'catch 22'. Ultimately, the US has decided that it is in favour of private enforcement, but the EU does not prioritise private enforcement, and uses it in a much more restricted role, certainly in relation to 'deterrence' (ie regulation), so this explains the difference between the opposing US and EU positions. Australia and Canada have clearly chosen to follow the US model. For these reasons, it would appear that funding and costs rules are far more important than detailed procedural aspects.

There can be psychological barriers to accessing justice; for example, if victims are uneducated about the justice system they may be unaware that they can seek legal redress for the harm they have experienced.[79] Similarly, a lack of information may prevent them from identifying who is responsible in order to take legal action against the wrongdoer.[80] Also, where plaintiffs experience long-term psychological and economic side-effects as a result of the harm that they have suffered this may cause them difficulty in asserting their rights. Even where the wrongdoer can be identified and plaintiffs can engage with the legal system to seek redress, the individual litigation process can be traumatic. MPAs can help victims overcome some of these psychological barriers to access to justice because representative plaintiffs may be able to act on their behalf and may afford anonymity to other plaintiffs. In the US, one commentator has described the class action's ability to level the balance of power as 'the new equity'.[81] This is because class actions can give strength to victims of mass harm.[82] However, it is not just MPAs that can have this attribute, as regulation is just one other example of additional means of achieving this.[83] Thus, it is underlined in this research that litigation through MPAs is not the only way of delivering collective redress. Further evidence of this will be demonstrated particularly in the debate surrounding EU collective redress policy.

It is clear that access to justice must contain both procedural and substantive elements because providing injured parties with a mechanism to pursue a claim cannot be separated from the need to ensure that the ultimate remedy provides substantive justice, where necessary.[84] Mulheron states that there are four particular aspects to the objective of 'access to justice'. The first of these is that MPAs can 'provide the substantive law with teeth'.[85] Prichard succinctly states the relationship between class actions and the law as follows:

> In the absence of effective procedural mechanisms for pursuing legitimate and legally cognizable claims, the full meaning of our substantive law can never be known. Thus, both common law and statutory statements of our legal rights are often illusory in that they may generate high expectations that are subsequently dashed on the rocks of procedural barriers.[86]

[78] A Gidi, 'Class Actions in Brazil—A Model for Civil Law Countries' (2003) 51 *Am J Comp L* 322.

[79] Iacobucci (n 56) 24.

[80] Kalajdzic (n 61) 40.

[81] S Finn, 'In a Class All its Own: The Advent of the Modern Class Action and Its Changing Legal and Social Mission' (2005) 2 *Can Class Action Rev* 333, 371.

[82] Such as the consumer who has been injured by a widespread corporate malpractice.

[83] Iacobucci (n 56) 27.

[84] Ibid 20.

[85] Mulheron (n 10) 53.

[86] J Prichard, 'Class Action Reform: Some General Comments' (1984) 9 *Can Bus LJ* 309, 322–23.

Mulheron states that the second aspect of this objective is to 'overcome cost-related barriers which consist not only of the repetitive costs incurred if the same issues have to be heard and decided separately, but also the interaction between the damage claimed and the legal costs'.[87] Chief Justice Winkler opined succinctly that access to justice means people are able to resolve conflicts fairly, affordably and quickly through a court process.[88] This definition endorses the 'economies of scale' aspect of MPAs as a means of improving access to justice.[89] From the perspective of defendants, MPAs can provide a fair and efficient dispute resolution tool because of the certainty associated with collective claims resolution, particularly where this results from a class action with an opt-out process.[90] Some commentators emphasise the facilitative nature of MPAs, as they may encourage action by claimants who have suffered harm and who would not otherwise have sufficient incentive to enforce their rights.[91] Improved access is especially important where the plaintiffs' claims 'might have merit, but the legal cost of proceedings are disproportionate to the amount of each claim (the 'scattered damages' scenario once again)'.[92] In the US, Canada and Australia, case law regularly shows the 'overriding principle that providing sufficient incentive to get at small claims is an important goal of class litigation'.[93]

A third and related element, in Mulheron's opinion, is to ensure that 'the parties are on equal footing'.[94] Newberg opines that class members

> gain a more powerful adversarial posture than they would have through individual litigation … which serves to balance a currently imbalanced adversarial structure, in which large defendants with sufficient economic means are able to enjoy an overwhelming advantage against parties with small individual claims.[95]

Mulheron's fourth and final facet of access to justice is 'timeliness of commencement, conduct, trial or settlement' because, in her opinion, 'there are three things that are off-putting about litigation: costs, risks and delays'.[96] Litigation 'takes too long and costs too much'.[97] This idea of timeliness has been endorsed in some modern procedural regimes[98] and has been recognised in class action jurisprudence.[99] It is important to note, however, that some

[87] Mulheron (n 10) 53.

[88] Kalajdzic (n 61) 52.

[89] As they can make matters easier for plaintiffs by spreading the costs of litigation across a larger group and resolving multiple claims by way of a single procedure.

[90] Finn, 'In a Class All its Own' (n 82) 371.

[91] *Dell Computer Corp v Union des Consommateurs*, [2007] SCJ No 34, 2007 SCC 34, [106].

[92] Definition provided in *Hollick v Metropolitan Toronto (Municipality)* (1998), 18 CPC (4th) 394 (Ont Gen Div) [19] (Jenkins J).

[93] Mulheron (n 10) 54.

[94] Ibid. Mulheron notes that this is expressly encompassed within the English Civil Procedure Rules, CPR, r 1.1(2)(a). The court must also have regard to the financial position of each party in that jurisdiction when interpreting the rules: CPR, r 1.1(2)(c)(iv).

[95] H Newberg and A Conte, *Newberg on Class Actions* (3rd edn, McGraw-Hill Inc, 1992) § 5.57, 478.

[96] Mulheron (n 10) 55. She suggests that for a discussion of this triumvirate as a reason for supporting multi-party actions, see eg *McKrow v Manufacturers Life Ins Co* (1998), 28 CPC (4th)104 (Gen Div) [10]; *Carnie v Esanda Finance Corp Ltd* (1996) 38 NSWLR 465 (SC) 468 (Young J).

[97] Manitoba Civil Justice Litigation Committee, *Civil Justice Review Task Force Report* (1996) 7.

[98] eg the English CPR explicitly state this as an overriding objective of civil procedure there: CPR, r 1.1(2)(d): 'ensuring that [the case] is dealt with expeditiously and fairly'.

[99] Davis, 'Towards the Proper Role for Mass Tort Class Actions' (n 73) 232 ('timely and meaningful vindication of rights and enforcement of responsibilities').

class actions can proceed at a 'glacial pace'[100] and that this encumbers the goal of judicial economy that class action legislation aims to achieve but certain class action features (such as the requirement to consider all dispute resolution methods or the use of judicial devices to manage non-common issues) reflect the principle that timeliness of the decision for class members is as important as the right decision, as well as timeliness for plaintiffs and defendants.[101] Devices such as 'tolling' of class actions may help to ameliorate the harsh elements of the statute of limitations in some circumstances, for example in the US. Tolling refers to a situation or circumstances in which the statute of limitations will be extended beyond the limit named in the state statute. This is applicable in cases of mental incompetency, infancy and cases where the defendant absconds from the state. In the US, the Statute of Limitations applicable to a class action lawsuit is determined by the cause of action named in the lawsuit. Thus, a personal injury class action will carry the Statute of Limitations applicable to negligence law, which varies by state.

In qualifying the aim of access to justice, Mulheron advises that it is important to be mindful of two caveats. First, the objectives discussed in this section may not always co-exist in the same litigation and they may even act as 'competing themes'.[102] This is seen especially in the example of small, uneconomic claims. These place an increased burden on court resources by resulting in claims that would otherwise perhaps not have resulted in litigation.[103] There is a debate about whether class actions reduce litigation by providing consolidation of numerous actions, or whether they enable litigation that would otherwise be problematic to bring.[104] In response to this debate it is argued that 'stirring up' valid litigation is, in fact, one of the goals of class action legislation.[105] In Tur's opinion, if it were the case that only those willing to take legal action should be the ones to benefit, and, if a class action gives gratuitous redress to those not actively seeking it, then the law-breaker obtains unjust enrichment where individuals do not assert their rights by way of litigation.[106] If legally enforceable rights are not asserted or enforced, then illegal activity is enabled because the defendant continues the illegal activity without incurring costs of either prevention or compensation.[107] While there can be a trade-off between access to justice and judicial economy, some judicial opinion suggests that access to justice should take precedence.[108]

[100] J Kleefeld, 'Class Actions as Alternative Dispute Resolution' (2001) 39 *Osgoode Hall LJ* 817.

[101] Mulheron (n 10) 55.

[102] S Yeazell 'From Group Litigation to Class Action, Pt 2' (1980) 27 *U of California at Los Angeles L Rev* 1067, 1100.

[103] Mulheron (n 10) 56.

[104] See P Lindbloom and G Watson, 'Complex Litigation—A Comparative Perspective: a "Two-edged Sword"' (1993) 12 *Civil Justice Q* 33, 5.

[105] B Kaplan, 'A Prefatory Note' (1969) 10 *BC Indust & Comm L Rev* 497 ('the dual missions of the class action device: (1) to reduce units of litigation by bringing under one umbrella what might otherwise be many disparate but duplicating actions; (2) even at the expense of increasing litigation, to providing a means of vindicating the rights of groups of people who individually would be without effective strength to bring their opponents to court at all'.

[106] R Tur, 'Litigation and the Consumer Interest: The Class Action and Beyond' (1982) 2 *LS* 135, 159.

[107] Acknowledged by the Australian Law Reform Commission (ALRC), *Managing Justice* (Rep No 89, 1999) 7.90.

[108] Cases showing examples of this include: *Magic Menu Systems Pty Ltd v AFA Facilitation Pty Ltd* (1997) 72 FCR 261 (Full FCA) 267; *Nantais v Telectronics Proprietary (Can) Ltd* (1995); *Bendall v McGhan Medical Corp* (1994), 106 DLR (4th) 339, 14 OR (3d) 734 (Gen Div).

The second caveat Mulheron suggests is that 'access to justice is a "two-way street": class action jurisprudence must also seek to ensure that a defendant is protected from unmeritorious claims, and understands, and can plead a defence to, the case brought against it'.[109] It is intended that class action statutes only create a procedural mechanism, not that they create a new cause of action to confront the defendant.[110] However, a very notable positive result of the use of the class action mechanism is that defendants are protected from inconsistent obligations that are created by varying results in different courts. Furthermore, 'the procedural balance must not be tipped to far on the side of the plaintiffs', meaning that the defendants should not have to spend money or face adverse publicity as a result of unfounded claims brought against them.[111]

These expert studies suggest that access to justice is the key goal of MPAs. Traditional national civil justice systems are not designed to provide effective access to justice for mass harm events. Cappelletti saw access to justice evolving in three successive, but overlapping, 'waves' to accommodate mass claims: state funding (legal aid); introduction of class or collective action procedures; and mediation and ADR techniques for collective redress.[112] Is Cappelletti correct to state that access to justice proceeds in three waves? It does appear that this is the direction of policy at EU level. If so, does this mean that collective actions will be replaced by ADR? The evolution of civil justice in the European context is seeing those three stages of evolution.[113] Cappelletti's concept is, however, essentially procedural. The fundamental substantive norms are those identified in the analytical framework of the MPA objectives, such as access to justice.

In terms of access to justice in the EU collective redress proposals, this objective was one of the Commission's foremost concerns. At the launch of the package, while recognising the diversity of Member States' legal systems, the EU's Justice Commissioner stated that the aim of the Recommendation was to improve access to justice, while at the same time safeguarding against the risks that can be inherent in class actions:

> Member States have very different legal traditions in collective redress and the Commission wants to respect these. Our initiative aims to bring more coherence when EU law is at stake ... This Recommendation is a balanced approach to improve access to justice for citizens while avoiding a US-Style system of class actions and the risk of frivolous claims and abusive litigation.

The EU Consumer Policy Commissioner Borg added that this is

> An important step towards an EU framework for collective redress ... inviting all EU Member States to equip EU consumers with the tools to enforce their rights and obtain compensation for the harm caused by violations of EU law. Member States should ensure that the collective redress procedures are fair, timely and not prohibitively expensive.

In an increasingly globalised world, those involved in dispute resolution may not be on equal terms when it comes to their resources, for example their financial means. Hopefully,

[109] Mulheron (n 10) 57.

[110] Ibid.

[111] For further detail please see law reform summary, 'Courts Practice and Procedure' (2000), Issue 2, 26 *Commonwealth L Bulletin* 958, 970.

[112] R Money-Kryle, 'The Origins and Roles of Class Action Laws across the World: What Types of Problem do they Deal with, and What Safeguards do they Have?' ('Building Effective Markets—the Role of an Integrated Legal System' Conference, Zurich, January 2013).

[113] Ibid.

they will have access to lawyers and to the appropriate legal dispute resolution machinery. Inequality of resources is commonly seen, for example, in product liability or competition law disputes, where large, financially powerful multinational companies may be in dispute with individuals or smaller companies that do not possess the same deep pockets as they do. Increasingly, individuals find their rights or health collectively affected by a single defendant. This collective interest in the same legal issues is key to all MPA procedures.

Traditionally, MPAs have related to 'instant' disasters, such as industrial accidents, or to 'creeping' disasters such as pharmaceutical cases. The outcome for claimants has been varied in some jurisdictions, with the legal costs far outweighing the damages. Depending on the sector, other justifications may arise for using MPAs. A good example is found in the area of environmental mass harm litigation for toxic torts. There can be difficulties associated with technical evidence in such cases that can create a barrier to justice where the circumstances of a case may make proving a claim particularly difficult. Individual claimants can encounter problems when dealing with issues such as proving causation and dealing with such technical scientific evidence. For example, specialist scientific expert testimony may be required to establish causation and it can be very difficult to establish facts, as seen in *Graham and Graham v Rechem*.[114] The collective nature of MPAs may assist plaintiffs to overcome such difficulties because their greater combined means may enable them to access sophisticated, experienced witnesses and lawyers. By using some form of collective redress, plaintiffs may be able to 'pool their resources' and deal with these challenges collectively.[115] This will be examined in more detail in the chapter dealing with environmental mass harm.

B. Judicial and Procedural Economy

In reviewing many opinions on the justification for class actions, it would appear that the original motivation for aggregated procedures such as MPAs is the delivery of judicial economy.[116] Collective redress aims to avoid the unnecessary delay, inconvenience and expense that the individual pursuit of similar claims can impose on litigants, courts and lawyers. The need for a judicially effective mechanism is important so that the legal system can 'free itself from the individual approach to the granting of legal remedies'.[117] This is especially so as 'we become an increasingly mass producing and mass consuming society, one product or service with a flaw has the potential to injure or cause loss to more and more people'.[118] Trebilcock comments that

> Individually tailored lawsuits for consumers are often as much of an anachronism as the concept that all cars that are put on the market should be handcrafted…economies of scale now dictate mass procedures for consumers prejudiced by a common legal wrong.[119]

[114] [1996] Env LR. This case will be discussed in detail in ch 4.
[115] eg the GLO.
[116] R Bernstein 'Judicial Economy and Class Actions' (1978) 4 *J Legal Stud* 349.
[117] ALRC Report (n 107) 7.90.
[118] R Alkadamani, 'The Beginnings of "Class Actions"?' (1992) 8 *Aust Bar Rev* 271, 275.
[119] M Trebilcock, *A Study on Consumer Misleading and Unfair Trade Practices* (Ottawa, Information Canada, 1976) vol 1 270, and cited with approval in the ALRC Report (n 107) [58].

Lord Woolf identified judicial economy as being important when he dictated that any new procedure should 'provide expeditious, effective and proportionate methods of resolving cases'.[120] It has also been noted already that part of the objectives of the Civil Procedure Rules (CPR) (which are the rules of civil procedure, including collective redress litigation, used by the Court of Appeal, High Court of Justice, and county courts in civil cases in England and Wales) is the need for efficient and economical use of court resources. The importance of this aim was judicially endorsed in *Emerald Supplies Ltd v British Airways plc*, where it was it was found that whether there was the requisite 'same interest' in that representative litigation 'is determined with a view to promoting the litigation objectives of justice, economy, efficiency and expedition'.[121] It was eventually held there that the representative action was procedurally ineffectual.

There is varying treatment of the objective of judicial economy of MPAs in different jurisdictions. In the US, the Supreme Court has stated that class certification in class actions can promote 'the efficiency and economy of litigation which is the principle purpose of the procedure'.[122] Despite this, it seems that there is no denying that there can be negative aspects to mass tort litigation and this is seen in the US opposition to class actions for mass torts and the demands for procedural safety measures for individual case management in group proceedings. The US class action rules explicitly support the achievement of efficiency. This is seen in the rules that govern civil procedure for civil lawsuits in United States district federal courts, particularly in the use of FRCP 23(b)(3) actions where the court is to have regard to the 'fair and efficient adjudication of the controversy'. In the US there was a criticism that judicial economy was not given the consideration that it ought to have been given in the US asbestos litigation, therefore subsequently causing repetitive trials:

> Why should a defendant or group of defendants be entitled to thousands of chances to convince thousands of jurors that one identical set of facts does not give rise to liability? This is what happened in the asbestos litigation that consensus says has been a dismal failure of judicial efficiency and fairness to litigants.[123]

However, in Canadian and Australian class action statutes, the concept of judicial economy is only implicitly included. The Supreme Court of Canada, for example, has held that judicial economy should be considered and evaluated when determining whether the prerequisite of preferability is satisfied by the relevant class action statutes.[124] The Australian Federal Court noted in *Murphy v Overton Investments Pty Ltd* that the question of judicial economy is a direct determinant of whether or not class action proceedings are considered 'inappropriate' under the Federal Court Act, section 33N(1), in which case the proceedings must be discontinued.[125]

It is important to note, however, that MPAs will not always promote the desired judicial efficiencies. They can result in overwhelming caseloads for courts already congested with private litigation and so can counteract judicial economy. According to Mulheron, the

[120] Woolf, *Access to Justice* (n 1) ch 17 [2].
[121] [2010] EWCA Civ 1284, [4].
[122] *General Telephone Co of Southwest v Falcon* 457 US 147, 159, 102 S Ct 2364 (1982).
[123] Davis (n 73) 232.
[124] *Hollick v Metropolitan Toronto (Municipality)* 2001 SCC 68, 205 DLR (4th) 19 (SCC) [15], [27].
[125] [1999] FCA 1123, [69], [87].

limited empirical analysis of class actions[126] suggests that they are far more consumptive of judicial resources than a typical civil case:

> Although caution has been advocated that, were individually recoverable claims to be litigated one by one, the hearings would undoubtedly be duplicative and would cumulatively occupy far more court resources. If the class action is appropriately commenced, then the ultimate knock-on judicial economies which would have been argued are that: few plaintiffs opt out; the vast majority of class actions (like other civil proceedings) settle before trial; and class actions can bring about early settlements.[127]

The objective of judicial economy is normally viewed from the standpoint of class members and the court and the avoidance of re-litigation. Defendants however, can also benefit from class litigation because it can deliver an element of finality for them. This is because the adjudication on the common questions in the class action will be binding on all class members who have not opted out of the litigation. The RAND Institute for Civil Justice has reiterated this view of the resulting class-wide resolution of claims, particularly where there is settlement. It stated that defendants sometimes see it as advantageous if they aim for as wide a definition of the class as possible to bind class members definitely, if it appears to be an efficient means of capping liability exposure.[128] The Alberta Law Reform Institute, in reviewing the US class action regime, has also stated that the opportunity for early closure of claims is a benefit of class action regimes to defendants:

> Rather than waiting for individual claims to pile up, corporate defendants can clean up their liabilities in one proceeding without risking inconsistent decisions or facing multiple lawsuits in numerous jurisdictions.[129]

It is worth noting that the English reform of collective redress views economy and efficiency in a much broader context and that the CJC intended some wider aims in its 'key findings' in its report *Improving Access to Justice Through Collective Actions*:

> Effective collective actions promote competition and market efficiency, consistent with the Government's economic principles and objectives, benefiting individual citizens, businesses and society as a whole. Equally they are effective mechanisms through which individual rights can be upheld. Collective claims can benefit defendants in resolving disputes more economically and efficiently, with greater conclusive certainty than can arise through unitary claims.[130]

These wider objectives were taken into account by the CJC when, in 2008, it proposed a new generic collective action for England and Wales. This recommendation was adopted for the sectoral reform proposed in the Financial Services Bill 2010. From the evidence and discussion of all the factors above which would impact on judicial economy, it is clear that

[126] The following study is frequently cited: T Willging, L Hooper and J Niemic, *Empirical Study of Class Actions in Four Federal District Courts: Final Report to the Advisory Committee on Civil Rules* (University of Michigan Library: 1996). This study was of all class actions (except mass tort class actions) terminated between 1 July 1992 and 30 June 1994 in 4 federal district courts.

[127] Mulheron (n 10) 60.

[128] Hensler and others, *Class Action Dilemmas: Pursuing Private Goals for Public Gain* (RAND Institute, 2000), 402.

[129] Alberta Law Reform Institute Report 'Report on Class Actions, Final Report No 85, Dec 2000' (AltaLRI Report), 122.

[130] CJC Report (n 30), esp key findings number 5 and 6 highlighted in s 2.C of this chapter.

where MPAs can resolve cases speedily and efficiently for parties, then they make a valid contribution to ensuring access to justice.

Miller states that among the principal goals of group litigation is the realisation of litigation efficiencies.[131] In his opinion, the court should ask whether legal claims could be resolved more cheaply with group litigation than with other procedures. He gives the example of the significant savings that can be gained by consolidating proof of facts, so that multiple plaintiffs do not have to re-litigate the issue.[132] He qualifies this by saying that in other situations, however, the circumstances of the putative group may vary, for example claims brought on behalf of victims exposed to asbestos.[133] They may have been exposed in different places, in different amounts, for different lengths of time, their ages may differ and they may have different medical backgrounds and medical histories, for example. Such variations may defeat any economies of scale in proof of facts. Furthermore, even if economies of scale are otherwise present, Miller advises that they may be offset by the complexity that the group litigation introduces, such as problems of manageability.[134] It will be shown in the US examination of environmental mass harm, however, that there are also specific remedies, for example medical monitoring, that can be invoked to overcome issues such as latency that can present themselves in such cases of mass harm. Procedures for group litigation deal with such variations through the use of filters, which are intended to screen out inappropriate cases. The US, for example, will not allow a class action unless it is established that there are common issues of law or fact; the English representative action requires a high degree of overlap between class members' claims, so that even small differences can preclude group litigation status. In contrast, Australia's class action procedure is more liberal than in the US as there is no certification requirement and those seeking class treatment need show only one issue common to the class.[135] The predominance issue can, in theory, be avoided by using 'issue classes', which are class actions limited to proof of certain issues. Australian class actions are effectively all issue classes. US law has not yet gone this far as issue classes, although possible in theory under the rules, are rare.[136] The efficiency of class actions must also be measured in terms of settlements. These are common in US class actions but statistics are difficult to obtain, although it is clear that many class actions are resolved by methods other than settlements, such as voluntary dismissals.[137]

As for the EU collective redress proposals' objectives of judicial and procedural economy, the Communication stated that:

> Any collective redress mechanism should be ... capable of resolving a large number of individual claims that raise the same or common issues and relate to a single infringement of EU law. It should be capable of delivering legally certain and fair outcomes within a reasonable timeframe[138]

[131] See G Miller, 'Group Litigation in the Enforcement of Tort Law' in J Arden (ed), *Research Handbook on the Economics of Torts* (Edward Elgar, 2013) 262.
[132] Ibid.
[133] Ibid 264.
[134] eg class actions might not be manageable, as variations among class members may overtax the court's ability to organise and supervise procedures.
[135] Miller, 'Group Litigation in the Enforcement of Tort Law' (n 131) 264.
[136] Ibid 265.
[137] See N Pace, S Carroll, I Vogelsang and L Zakaras, *Insurance Class Actions in the United States* (RAND Corporation, 2007), which found that negotiated class-wide settlements occurred in only 12% of closed insurance cases filed as class actions.
[138] Communication (n 49) para 2.1.

Clearly procedural efficiency is intricately linked with questions of access to justice, but it is perhaps worth dealing with this briefly again as a separate criterion, despite unavoidable overlap. MPAs can facilitate procedural justice by providing a vehicle for bringing claims to court for those who, for varying reasons, cannot or do not wish to take action individually.[139] This is because claimants will have enhanced strength and bargaining power as a group, resulting in efficiencies and economies of scale, because MPAs can provide cost spreading advantages, in theory at least. In terms of victims' rights, it seems that a key goal of MPAs is the reduction of litigation costs and the availability of compensation.[140] As previously explained, through MPAs claimants can overcome obstacles such as the challenges presented by scientific evidence in individual toxic tort litigation by having such issues resolved collectively.

In the specific context of environmental mass harm, leading commentators have identified and stressed the importance of procedural justice in environmental litigation generally. Shelton's research discerns the procedural dimension of justice such as arrangements for dispute settlement in environmental harm. Steele's research in this area is also concerned with justice as it relates to participation and remedies.[141] She has written widely that participation in environmental law is a key element in access to justice. Spence discusses various methods by which environmental law may be better enforced by citizens and the State in Ireland and assesses weaknesses in current enforcement mechanisms, such as issues of accessibility and cost. These views may support the argument that MPAs have a role to play in providing access to justice for environmental harm. It would appear that MPAs, as mechanisms that help to provide procedural justice, enable access to justice. This arguably suggests that the lack of MPA mechanism in Ireland is a barrier to procedural justice for environmental mass harm.[142]

C. Fairness

(In this section, 'fairness' includes proportionality, balancing individual rights and personal autonomy, and non-abuse)

It is important that a legal system aims to ensure that people get similar awards and that they are treated equally and fairly when taking legal claims. There may be difficulties with this, for example where there are no court procedures for dealing with mass litigation. Without formal aggregation procedures, legal systems must be creative with the traditional devices available. In many jurisdictions it is left to the courts to establish precedent for these, which can be difficult. The reliance on the use of test cases in Ireland is an example

[139] Iacobucci (n 56) 21.

[140] D Rosenberg 'The Causal Connection in Mass Exposure Cases: A "Public Law" Vision of the Tort System' (1984) 97 *Harv L Rev* 905. Rosenberg believes that damages scheduling and other such devices are particularly successful tools for reducing litigation costs and increasing the compensation value of mass exposure class actions.

[141] J Steele, 'Participation and Deliberation in Environmental law: Exploring a Problem-solving Approach' *OJLS* (Oxford University Press, 2001) 415–22; J Steele, 'Remedies and Remediation: Foundational Issues in Environmental Liability' (1995) 58 *MLR* 615–36; T Jewell T and J Steele, *Law in Environmental Decision-Making: National, European, and International Perspectives* (Clarendon Press, 1998).

[142] D Spence in Law Reform Committee of the Law Society of Ireland, *Enforcement of Environmental Law: The Case for Reform* (2007) ch 1, available at: www.lawsociety.ie/Documents/committees/lawreform/Envir%20 Report.pdf

of this. When MPA procedures were examined in practice in this study, it became clear that the criterion of fairness includes the objectives of proportionality, of balancing individual rights and personal autonomy and of non-abuse, so these objectives are subsumed within the meaning of the objective of fairness and will be dealt with under this heading.

The aim of balancing individual rights and personal autonomy was identified by Lord Woolf as his third objective. Mulheron gives further analysis of this and reminds us that one of the main aims of class actions is to protect absent class members. This is reiterated by judges[143] and senior legal advisers[144] alike and has been explicitly recognised by legislators designing class action regimes, for example in their provision of extensive judicial case management powers and the requirement of judicial approval of settlement. As a result of the requirement for court certification, multi-party litigation becomes 'a creation of the court,'[145] and the court must consider the implications of authorising such litigation on behalf of absent class members.[146] Notwithstanding this, Mulheron opines that 'any class litigation scenario will starkly lower individualism in litigation'.[147] She cites the following reasons: first, an opt-out model may cause attendant difficulties in communicating notice to absent class members and in providing them with enough information to make an informed choice as to whether to remain in the class. Secondly, conflicts can arise between class members and these may be overcome by the creation of subclasses, for example. Thirdly, she states that issues such as the selection of the representative plaintiff, the choice of the defendant, the causes of action alleged, the selection of the lawyers, are all issues over which the absent class member largely loses control, but which can have a great influence on the result of the litigation.[148] The loss of individualism pales in significance, however, when compared to the alternative, which is that of no litigation at all if there were no class action. Cooper argues, however, that these concerns about loss of individualism 'are not fully allayed by the justification that class adjudication achieves efficiency, enforces rights … and achieves the social good of enforcing the law'.[149] An example of where individual rights and personal autonomy can be balanced effectively is seen in the Australian regime's representative proceedings. This device provides for the consideration of individual issues and for the use of subclasses if necessary, which further protects individual autonomy. Furthermore, as regards awarding damages there, these can be tailored to individual needs because the court has a wide discretion to award damages to the class as a whole, to any subclass or to individual members. This is a key lever that the court can use in terms of balancing the rights of individuals. A further example of this is seen in Canada's class action regime where some of the compensation provisions allow the participation of individual class members for the determination of their own particular issues.[150] Also, court members are given notice of the hearing at which the proposed settlement will be considered and they have a right to appear at this and to object to the adequacy or fairness of such settlement.

143 eg *US Parole Comm v Geraghty* (n 75).
144 eg *Report of the Civil Rules Advisory Committee* (2001) 122 SCR Ct R-33.
145 In the words of the *Report of the Civil Rules Advisory Committee* (2001) 122 SCR Ct R-47.
146 eg the discussion in AltaLRI Report (n 129) [179] [277].
147 Mulheron (n 10) 62.
148 Ibid.
149 E Cooper, 'Class Action Advice in the Form of Questions' (2001) 11 *Duke J Comp and Int'l L* 223–25, 224.
150 Ontario CPA, s 25.

As previously stated, Lord Woolf, in his review of English civil procedure, emphasised that fairness and balance between litigants was crucial, to the extent that collective redress should 'achieve a balance between the normal rights of claimants and defendants, to pursue and defend cases individually, and the interests of a group of parties to litigate the action as a whole in an effective manner'.[151] In 1998, the Civil Procedure Rules (CPR)[152] included this as part of their overriding objective. They expressly require that, in order to deal with cases justly, this should include, 'as far as is practicable', both 'ensuring that the parties are on an equal footing'[153] and 'ensuring that [the case] is dealt with expeditiously and fairly'.[154] In its report in December 2008, the CJC emphasised that fairness 'remains a valid benchmark' when considering any collective actions reform and design.[155] Lord Woolf's review, in highlighting the need for 'balancing', recognises that individual participation rights and procedural autonomy inevitably must be compromised or curtailed to achieve efficient collective management, and a resolution of multiple similar claims.[156] This may potentially involve significant interferences; for example, under a GLO, individual group members may find that they cannot freely choose or instruct lawyers,[157] or they may be excluded from influencing the pleadings, selection of experts and presentation of evidence. Settlement terms may be negotiated and agreed without their involvement or they may find their cases 'stayed' while other test claims trials proceed. They may be bound by these decisions and also be forced to pay a share of these costs. Furthermore, according to Gibbons, most significantly, not only group members but also group litigants who take entirely separate, parallel proceedings may find that their 'normal' rights are circumscribed in order to give priority to the GLO parties' interests.[158] This, she opines falls within Lord Woolf's broad wording which therefore permits 'balancing' 'not only where conflicts of interest arise between group members, between individual group members and the group as a whole, and also between the group as a whole and individual litigants engaged in other, entirely separate proceedings'.[159]

There is also a need for fairness between plaintiffs themselves as well as between plaintiffs and defendants.[160] According to the LRC the need for procedural fairness forms a core element in any reform of multi-party litigation.[161] From the perspective of plaintiffs, where individual grievances are consolidated in order to achieve administrative efficiency, the boundaries of the procedure will be dictated by the individual cases within the group. In the Commission's view, any devised procedure should facilitate certainty and not hinder the resolution of individual actions. They stated that 'where the process is sidelined into legitimate concerns arising out of a perceived lack of a full hearing of individual issues, the

[151] Woolf, *Access to Justice: Final Report* (n 1) 17 [2].

[152] As stated previously, these are the Civil Procedure Rules (CPR) which apply to all litigation, including collective redress litigation, conducted in England and Wales.

[153] CPR, r 1.1(2)(a).

[154] Ibid r 1.1(2)(d).

[155] CJC Report (n 30) 51.

[156] Gibbons (n 7) 227.

[157] eg where lead solicitors are appointed and a claimants' steering committee is formed to liaise with them.

[158] Gibbons (n 7) 227. She cites the case of *T (formerly H) v Nugent Care Society (formerly Catholic School Services)* [2004] EWCA Civ 51; [2004] 1 WLR 1129 (CA).

[159] Ibid.

[160] Such as multiple individual claims going to different courts, eg for evidential determination esp in toxic tort cases.

[161] LRC Report 2005 (n 14) 1.48, 18.

procedure will no longer serve its purpose'.[162] In terms of assessing the objective of fairness throughout this research, it is important to clarify that, in the absence of empirical evidence, it is not possible to state categorically whether rights are balanced, whether there is fairness between claimants amongst themselves, and that there is no abuse. By comparing different MPA models, one can say that certain models ought or might be more or less fair than others, but this needs to be proved by the outcomes of empirical research.

In relation to the objective of proportionality, multi-party litigation inevitably entails some compromise because of concerns such as time, cost and court resources. Lord Woolf stated in 1996 that 'the effective and economic handling of group actions necessarily requires a diminution, compromise or adjustment of the rights of individual litigants for the greater good of the action as a whole'.[163] He subsequently noted the need to provide 'proportionate methods of resolving [multi-party] cases'.[164] As Zuckerman observed that, whereas once integrity of decision was an overriding value of civil procedure, consideration of timely justice and reasonable costs are now relevant and important factors in the allocation of finite judicial resources.[165] This attitude has been recognised in relation to class actions and, as one US commentator has stated, 'The fact that the class action procedure requires compromises is an insufficient reason to fear and thus reject it'.[166] For example, the principle of proportionality is applied to a cost- benefit analysis of whether a MPA action warrants its commencement at all.[167] As another example, there may be a point at which the costs to class members outweigh the benefit to class members individually, 'a point at which the consumer or person suffering injury must reasonably accept the risk of injury because the cost of providing compensation is too high relative to the benefit'.[168] It has even been noted in US case law that it is possible that individual plaintiffs could recover higher damages if they were to pursue their own claims.[169] Therefore, as Mulheron has stated, 'certifying a class action may well entail the proportionality of lower compensatory awards'.[170] She confirms that

> it is evident that the potentially burdensome field of class litigation has embraced the shift from perfection to proportionality, and reflects the opinion of Scott and Black that, if class litigation is to work at a pragmatic level, the interests of the class must sometimes prevail over individual licence to run litigation as he or she would wish.[171]

In addition to this, Lord Woolf cited a quote by Zander to demonstrate that, 'every system contains a percentage of error; and if by slightly increasing the percentage of error, we can substantially reduce the percentage of cost, it is only the idealist who will revolt'.[172]

[162] Ibid.
[163] Woolf, *Access to Justice* (n 1).
[164] Ibid 17 [2].
[165] A Zuckerman, *Justice in Crisis: Comparative Dimensions of Civil Procedure* (Oxford University Press 1999) 17–18.
[166] Davis (n 73) 232.
[167] Mulheron (n 10) 50.
[168] ALRC Report (n 108) [342].
[169] *Marcarz v Transworld Systems Inc*, 193 FRD 46, 55 (D Conn 2000).
[170] Mulheron (n 10) 51.
[171] Mulheron (n 10) 51, citing C Scott and J Black, *Cranston's Consumers and the Law* (3rd edn, Butterworths, 2000) 122.
[172] M Zander (ed), *What's Wrong with the Law* (BBC, 1970) 76, cited by Woolf (n 1) ch 4, [5].

In England and Wales, all provisions within the CPR, including those concerning collective actions, are subject to the 'overriding objective of dealing with cases justly'[173] and to use proportionality, which relates to 'saving expense' and 'allotting an appropriate share of the court's resources [to the case], while taking into account the need to allot resources to other cases'.[174] The importance of considering the effect of the CPR's overriding objective has also been stated in relation to the Group Litigation Order (GLO)[175] and has been referred to by judges in case law, for example in *Emerald Supplies v British Airways plc*.[176]

In terms of reaching settlements, it is important to be aware that there is a potential conflict of interest for lawyers, particularly in US class actions, between settling an action quickly and achieving maximum compensation. In the opinion of Judge Iacobucci, this inherent conflict of interest raises serious concerns about the efficiency and fairness of class actions.[177]

The aim of non-abuse is a crucial element of the objective of fairness and permeates the aims and procedures of the jurisdictions examined. The US, for example, introduced the Class Action Fairness Act 2005 ostensibly in order to protect against abuse.[178] The objective of non-abuse was a prominent theme in the EU collective redress proposals. It is important to ask what evidence there may be of the existence of safeguards and the extent to which particular safeguards of combinations are effective, or not, as well as evidence of cases that have merit but that cannot be brought. Such questions can only be answered by empirical evidence which does not yet appear to exist. The EU has emphasised the need for safeguards such as procedural safeguards, which are an obvious requirement for MPAs in order to protect against abuse and to ensure access to justice. The methods espoused for EU collective redress include many provisions to protect against abuse. For this reason the Commission's proposals are underlined by features that are designed to prevent abuse. There is great heed paid to avoiding the perceived risks of 'US style class action' and the need for tools that would not impede EU economic progress and for this reason the Communication states that:

> The main concerns voiced against the introduction of collective judicial redress mechanisms were that it would attract abusive litigation or otherwise have a negative impact on the economic activities of EU businesses. Litigation can be considered abusive when it is intentionally targeted against law-abiding businesses in order to cause reputational damage or to inflict an undue financial burden on them.[179]

From this, it is clear that while the primary objective of the proposals is access to justice, this access is to be tempered by appropriate safeguards to avoid the 'excess and abuse' seen with US class actions. This is to be achieved through the proposal's stringent requirements in relation to aspects of collective redress such as funding and admissibility requirements

[173] CPR, r 1.1[1].

[174] Ibid r 1.1(2)(b); r 1.1(2)(e).

[175] eg *Taylor v Nugent Care Society* [2004] EWCA Civ 51, [22].

[176] Where Chancellor Morritt held that the CPR's overriding objective of dealing with the fixed price victim's litigation against airlines fairly would be best achieved by having their recourse to the GLO mechanism rather than the representative action being sought in that case.

[177] Iacobucci (n 56) 29.

[178] Class Action Fairness Act 2005, s 5. This Act was intended to amend the procedures that apply to consideration of inter-state class actions to assure fairer outcomes for class members and defendants, and for other purposes.

[179] Communication (n 49) para 2.2.2.

on standing. How each of these objectives was brought to life in the Commission's collective redress policy will be examined in the chapter on EU collective redress. In the introductory chapter Gidi was cited as stating that a transplant can be 'surgically controlled'[180] and the EU's proposed model specifies a range of safeguards against the risk of abuse. However, it is argued by Hodges that these safeguards are 'porous' and will be ineffectual, and that they cannot be 'calibrated', so there will either be too much or too little mass litigation.[181] It must be questioned whether or how these two opposing arguments can be reconciled.

Overall, procedural fairness is paramount. It is important, however, to ensure that the need for formal, clear and hence inevitably cumbersome requirements does not make MPAs too expensive, and so justice inaccessible. There can be particular difficulties with this if there is inadequate funding. These difficulties would appear to suggest that safeguards should not be reduced in the name of increasing access to justice.

D. Predictability

Conducting MPA litigation can be expensive and intimidating, and therefore, predictability of the outcome and rules are important objectives for those engaged in such action. It is, however, obviously impossible to predict outcomes with certainty in litigation. Both lawyers and claimants require clear rules by which to undertake such complicated litigation in order to avoid procedural and other uncertainty.[182] In the US, it has been stated that the class action 'protects defendants from inconsistent obligations that may be created by varying results in different courts, and similarly, it promotes the equitable principle that similarly situated plaintiffs should receive similar treatment.[183] This might be extended to similar treatment whereby similar cases are heard similarly. Lawyers are the first to advise on the appropriateness of such litigation in the circumstances and their evaluation is a key factor in the eventual allocation of courts' resources and judicial efficiency.[184] In the US, however, there appears to be a strong conflict between courts and regulators. The US tries to maintain the pre-eminence of pre-emptive litigation but whether this is defensible must be questioned, as well as whether this supports predictability.

In England and Wales, the unpredictability and uncertainty surrounding the English bank charges litigation, as well as the inconsistencies in the various litigation strategies that were developed to cope with the volume of claims,[185] appeared to be one of the political motivations behind the proposed reform of collective actions and the introduction of a new collective action in the Financial Services Bill 2010.[186] Another example of unpredictability that can occur in collective redress in England and Wales is that the use of the GLO

[180] Gidi, 'Class Actions in Brazil (n 79).

[181] Hodges (n 38).

[182] P Balen, F Cartwright and H Dickens, 'Group Actions in a Product Liability Context' [1994] 140 *Consumer LJ* 199, 201.

[183] *US Parole Comm v Geraghty* (n 75); Phair (n 71) 837.

[184] ALRC Report (n 107).

[185] In which over 53,000 claims were filed in the English and Welsh County Courts between March 2006 and August 2007.

[186] This was intended to apply to financial services claims and provided for an opt-in or opt-out class action (depending on the judge's choice). This proposal never survived the General Election in May 2010 and was not introduced.

shows how two approaches may be used depending on the circumstances—the test case and generic issues.[187] This makes the use of the GLO mechanism more uncertain. Where class actions have been introduced, calls for further guidance have followed and, in many cases, law reform commissions have responded by recommending the introduction of a developed class action regime.[188] Such reform has had much benefit, as explained by the Supreme Court of Canada:

> While it would have been possible for courts to accommodate moderately complicated class actions by reliance on their own inherent power over procedure, this would have required courts to devise *ad hoc* solutions to procedural complexities on a case-by-case basis … The Class Proceedings Act, 1992, was adopted to ensure that the courts had a procedural rule sufficiently refined to allow them to deal efficiently, and on a principles, rather than an ad hoc basis, with the increasingly complicated cases of the modern era.[189]

E. Deterrence

According to Coffee, another benefit to MPA litigation is its potential to deter wrongful behaviour.[190] Perhaps this deterrence benefit may stem from the capacity of group litigation to overcome the 'scattered damages' issues and economies of scale may make the litigation economically viable. Such potential advantages, however, may not be realised in practice. For example, diffuse interest groups often maintain that group litigation 'over-deters' by creating an unacceptable risk of liability even when the defendant has not done any harm and that, in order to compensate for this, it is claimed that defendants will need to take defensive action, such as charging more for their products, or not undertaking socially beneficial actions that could potentially expose them to litigation.[191] Miller states the argument that class actions can create an unacceptable risk of liability for innocent conduct because class certification results in an overwhelming pressure to reach a settlement, because the prospect of even a small chance of a costly judgment effectively 'blackmails' defendants into settlement.[192] He states that the fact that many class actions do settle does not in itself indicate that defendants are coerced, rather he feels that it is just as plausible to conclude that defendants settle such cases as a cost-effective means of extinguishing their liability.[193] It is important to clarify that the use of the term 'deterrence' has its limitations in this research. Ideally, in order to determine whether deterrence results from MPAs it ought to be evident whether or not a legal technique actually results in changing behaviour. However, the extent

[187] eg the test case approach was used in *Pirelli Cable Holding NV v Revenue and Customs Commrs* [2007] EWHC 583 (Ch) and the generic issues approach was used in *Esso Petroleum Co Ltd v Addison* [2003] EWHC 1860 (QB).

[188] Examples include Ontario Law Reform Commission 'Report on Class Actions, Volume 1' by Ontario Law Reform Commission, Book 112 (1982) (OLRC Report); ALRC Report (n 107); Manitoba Law Reform Commission Report, Class Proceedings, Report number 100 (1999) (ManLRC Report); and AltaLRI Report (n 129).

[189] *Hollick v Metropolitan Toronto (Municipality)* (n 124) [14].

[190] J Coffee, 'Reforming the Securities Class Action: An Essay on Deterrence and Its Implementation' (2006) *Colum L Rev* 106, 1534–86.

[191] Miller (n 131) 266.

[192] These are often referred to as 'blackmail settlements'. See Miller (n 131) 264. Miller refers to further discussion by B Hay and D Rosenberg '"Sweetheart" and "Blackmail" Settlements in Class Actions: Reality and Remedy' (2000) *Notre Dame L Rev* 75, 1377–408.

[193] Miller (n 131) 267.

to which behaviour is actually changed—and by how much—is a point that may be often overlooked and, instead, it is perhaps assumed that if rights are enforced then this qualifies as deterrence. It must be questioned what evidence exists that class actions *in fact* deter, in that they affect future behaviour. Surely whether or not this is true depends on empirical evidence and, unfortunately, such evidence is in fact virtually non-existent.

Mulheron, in her study of a number of common law jurisdictions, has not found any consensus among them that the objective of deterrence and behaviour modification should form an overriding principle of class action litigation.[194] This is despite the possible or potential unjust enrichment of defendants if they are not required to fully compensate the costs of their wrongdoing. Influencing future behaviour is especially important, however, when the effects of the mass harm are widespread and where the payment of damages is ineffective as a deterrent.[195] In Canada, class action regimes aim to change the behaviour of others 'by making it feasible for victims to recover damages from wrongdoers who were previously insulated from having to account for their wrongs because of economic and other barriers to individual proceedings'.[196] In the US, there has been widespread academic acknowledgement of the deterrence function of class litigation, such as its role in 'transforming non-threatening individual claims into mass tort litigation',[197] 'filling the gaps left by regulators'[198] and 'counter-balancing corporate weight'.[199] There is also judicial acknowledgement of this deterrence function.[200] Mulheron reminds us, however, that, as previously explained, the objective of behaviour modification is not always compatible with the previously discussed aims of access to justice and judicial economy, especially where a case involves many small claims.[201]

In the opinion of Hodges, the ultimate goals of enforcement are the delivery of compensation and the influencing of future behaviour.[202] By obliging wrongdoers to pay financial compensation to victims of mass harm, MPAs provide individual deterrence to the future behaviour of the infringer and also some degree of general deterrence in relation to similar future activity by others.[203] As we have seen, the aim of deterrence or enforcement is particularly obvious in cases where the breach is more significant collectively than for individuals, in cases of 'scattered damages'.[204] The widespread nature of dubious activity by commercial or governmental entities raises this important issue of behaviour control.[205] If questionable behaviour goes unchallenged and reaps gains for those perpetrating the harm then it incentivises such behaviour. In terms of the functions of tort law, one of the key indicators is a claim's deterrence value and it is likely that MPAs would have greater deterrent effect in mass exposure cases, compared to individual accident cases.[206] Imposing

194 Mulheron (n 10) 63.

195 See Hodges, 'Objectives, Mechanisms and Policy Choices in Collective Enforcement and Redress' (n 8) 102.

196 *Hollick v Metropolitan Toronto (Municipality)* (1998), 18 CPC (4th) 394 (Ont Gen Div) [19].

197 J Kellam, 'Toxic Torts' (1998) 8 *Aust Product Liability Reporter* 161, 167.

198 D Lennox, 'Building a Class' (2001) 24 *Advocates' Q* 377.

199 C Harlow and R Rawlings, *Pressure through Tort Law* (Routledge, 1992) 113.

200 Examples are *Blackie v Barrack*, 524 F 2d 891, 903 (9th Cir 1975); *In re Gap Stores Securities Litigat*, 79 FRD 283, 295 (ND Cal 1978).

201 Mulheron (n 10) 64.

202 See Hodges (n 8) 102.

203 Ibid.

204 For explanation of this term, see earlier discussion at the beginning of section 2 of this chapter.

205 Hodges (n 8) 107.

206 K Dam, 'Class Actions: Efficiency, Compensation, Deterrence and Conflict of Interest' (1975) 4 *J Legal Stud* 47, 59–60.

pressure on an actor to conform to a State's norms is a well-known function of the law and this is achieved through enforcement. However, MPAs can impose pressures on behaviour that is much greater than individual actions.[207] A large volume of literature, especially from the US, examines the effectiveness of tort law including the use of MPAs and the role of damages in achieving deterrence.[208] It is clear from this that the US class action system has a powerful influence on the behaviour of actual or potential defendants (which are often governmental agencies or large corporations). As we have seen, where there is limited confidence in public regulation, MPAs can provide an important means of potential regulation. Rosenberg opines that:

> Mass exposure cases are frequently products of the deliberate policies of businesses that tailor their safety investments to profit margins. Such risk-taking policies should be especially amenable to control through threats of liability.[209]

In England and Wales, the CJC noted that deterrence is an important ancillary consequence of effective private enforcement:

> Effective enforcement would involve compensatory damage awards that were appropriate according to established substantive law principles of disgorgement of profits. It is a consequence of its primarily compensatory function that effective private enforcement arises, through which it provides a real deterrent effect that such actions are said to have on unlawful conduct. In this context both the OFT and the European Commission have publicly stated that they see private actions by victims in competition law as a necessary complement to their own public enforcement efforts.[210]

The potential for behaviour modification has been considered to be a worthy goal of class action certification in the US but this view is also not unanimously shared by other common law jurisdictions.[211] For example, the Australian Law Reform Commission (ALRC) stated that the objectives of increased access to justice and judicial efficiency did not enhance behaviour modification or deterrence as a goal of its potential class action proceedings.[212] It remarked that whilst 'the expansion of access to legal remedies might lead to greater enforcement of legal liabilities, and, as a result, increase the amount of monetary relief paid' by defendants, that was merely 'incidental' to the primary aim of providing access to the remedy the law prescribed.[213] The EU collective redress proposals specifically refer to 'the need to curb illegal activity' and therefore achieve deterrence.

F. Compensation

At the outset of this chapter, it was noted that none of the studies examined, apart from the EU collective redress policy, specifically addressed the objective of compensation and that this may be because it is implicit in the notion of access to justice. There is obvious overlap

[207] G Schwartz, 'Mixed Theories of Tort Law: Affirming both Deterrence and Corrective Justice' (1997) *Texas L Rev* 75, 1801–34.
[208] eg T Galligan, 'Deterrence: The Legitimate Function of the Public Tort (2001) 58 *Wash & Lee L Rev* 1019.
[209] Rosenberg, 'The Causal Connection in Mass Exposure Cases' (n 140) 929.
[210] CJC Report (n 30) 78–79.
[211] *Scott v TD Waterhouse Investor Services (Can) Inc* (2001), 94, BCLR (3d) 320 (SC) [142].
[212] See ALRC Report (n 107) [2.23].
[213] Ibid [67], [323].

between the notion of compensation and deterrence. It is necessary, however, to address compensation separately as a further objective, because it is important to discuss its role in MPAs and how such litigation can assist those in need of compensation to achieve it.

The EU proposals clearly identify a compensation function in their objective to make it possible for those who suffer mass harm to get compensation.[214] It provides for a route to this through both injunctive and compensatory redress. The Recommendation advises that Member States should have a collective redress system that allows private individuals and entities to obtain court orders to deliver payment of damages through compensation where a large number of persons or entities have been harmed by the same illegal practice.[215]

Miller notes that the provision of compensation for those who have suffered harm from a defendant's tortious acts is another potential advantage of MPAs. He sees such compensation as 'a transfer payment from defendants to plaintiffs without efficiency consequences'.[216] Rosenberg, however, argues that compensation should not even be a goal of MPAs, except insofar as it serves the function of providing implicit insurance for risk-averse parties.[217] He and other commentators note that, on the other hand however, compensation may have efficiency consequences, if plaintiffs are more risk-averse than defendants and cannot easily self-insure, or if defendants have better information or are better able to self-insure or buy insurance.[218] Miller is cognisant that 'the goal of compensation is rarely perfectly achieved' and entails problems such as accurately allocating settlement proceeds among claimants due to difficulties including identifying those who have been harmed.[219]

Conceptually, compensation is the fundamental point of tort law and, according to Hodges, 'it is axiomatic that a primary purpose of tort law and of collective mechanisms in both the US and in Europe is to deliver compensation'.[220] While some collective procedures can provide injunctive relief, these are in the minority. Financial compensation is the traditional remedy for private wrongs and payment of this may provide claimants with substantive justice in some cases. Damages provide individual restorative justice by restoring the position of the injured party's loss by payment by the infringer.[221] However, non-financial compensation may be important for actions that seek to right public wrongs.[222] Obviously, the restorative nature of a remedy can only be judged in light of the individual circumstances of each case.[223] Judge Iacobucci suggests that the courts must consider the plaintiffs, the defendants and the injury and examine questions such as:

1. The plaintiffs: are the victims particularly vulnerable and what would substantively compensate them for their loss?
2. The defendants: is the defendant an individual, a corporation, a governmental agency, an institution or is there a mix of different entities involved?

[214] Recommendation (n 48) Art 1.
[215] Recommendation (n 48) Point 1.
[216] Miller (n 130) 267.
[217] D Rosenberg, 'Decoupling Deterrence and Compensation Functions in Mass Tort Class Actions For Future Loss' (2002) 88 *Va L Rev*, 1871–919.
[218] See generally S Shavell, *Economic Analysis of Accident Law* (Harvard University Press, 1987).
[219] Miller (n 130) 268.
[220] See Hodges (n 8) 102.
[221] Ibid.
[222] Iacobucci (n 56) 21.
[223] Ibid.

3. The injury: what was the effect of the wrong perpetrated? Did the plaintiffs suffer economic loss, physical injury or the kind of emotional and psychological harm that results in enduring effects?[224]

By posing such questions, courts can tailor the remedy that they provide in mass litigation to the individual circumstances of each of the parties involved, ensuring that such remedy is suitable and therefore effective. The amount of compensation, or type of remedy, for example, will depend on the responses to these questions. The need for such compensation is not obvious just because the harm has occurred, as not all harms in society are subject to compensation. Grounds for believing compensation is necessary vary. It may be decided that the injustice of the harm suffered means that liability is required. In some cases this could be on 'corrective justice' grounds, where a tort has been committed. Or it may be for more distributive reasons, for example in the case of strict liability. In cases of mass harm it is important that compensation be broadly available in order to provide restorative justice to victims of such harm. The Scottish Law Commission stated that the 'sole proper object' of a civil action, even a multi-party proceeding, 'is to obtain compensation'.[225] The ALRC agreed but qualified this by stating that whilst 'the expansion of access to legal remedies might lead to greater enforcement of legal liabilities, and as a result, increase the amount of monetary relief paid' by defendants, it did remark, as previously stated, that this was but 'incidental' to the primary goal of providing access to the remedy the law prescribed.[226] MPAs, however, by providing a collective redress procedure, improve the availability of the remedy of compensation. This is not the case, however, where there are difficulties with funding and adverse costs rules. It is, of course, impossible to measure the extent to which the goal of compensation is achieved without empirical evidence. Such evidence would need to demonstrate how much extra compensation has been delivered than was the case before there was an MPA procedure. It is also important to clarify the extent to which compensation actually reaches victims. It is well known in US studies that recoveries are low and fees are significant.[227]

In addition to all of the MPA objectives identified for use in this research's analytical framework, there are further criteria that might also exist as benchmarks for MPA effectiveness. In particular, there are criteria of cost, duration and actual outcomes in relation to the delivery of compensation and changes of behaviour. These criteria are inherent in some of the MPA criteria identified but it is not feasible to include these as individual benchmarks in the framework for analysis due to the lack of comprehensive empirical evidence. Instead they are highlighted explicitly here, briefly. It is important to state, however, that while such important criteria are excluded from this analysis, this is with the caveat that the findings in this research are subject to such wider examination. The criteria of cost and duration are important because several cases show that the 'appalling delay' that can result due to the absence of a class action procedure is not resolved by having such a procedure. Virtually all of the cases examined in this research evidence this, for example, the German *Deutsche Telekom* case took 10 years to reach a finding of no liability.[228] Further examples include the

224 Ibid 22.
225 Scottish Law Commission, *Multi-Party Actions* (1996) [2.23].
226 ALRC Report (n 107) [323].
227 eg D Hensler and others, *Class Action Dilemmas: Pursuing Private Goals for Public Gain* (RAND, 2001).
228 This case is discussed in ch 9, s 3.

following: *Graham & Graham v Rechem*,[229] which was a case that was heard over a period of 198 days and involved 101 witnesses. Eventually the plaintiffs' case failed on causation. The defendant's costs were £4.5 million and the cost of Legal Aid was £1.5 million. Two additional English cases are the 2005 case of the *Buncefield Oil Disaster*, in which a GLO was refused and a number of successive settlements were made in a relatively fast timeframe of five years but there is no information as to the cost of this litigation,[230] and the *Corby Group Litigation*, which involved 18 claimants and where the trial lasted for 18 days in 2009 and resulted in a finding of liability followed by a confidential settlement.[231] The defence costs were £1.9 million. An interim payment of £1.6 million was made towards the claimants' costs, and reported total damages were over £4 million. Two Irish cases provide further illustrations of these difficulties: *Hanrahan v Merck Sharpe and Dohme*, where the plaintiffs eventually succeeded in the Supreme Court on causation only[232] and, finally, the *Irish Pyrite Litigation* in 2011, which involved 550 homeowners and continued for a period of two years, making it the longest-running case ever in the Irish Commercial Court. It eventually settled with the creation of a €25.5 million repair fund. These cases exemplify the difficulties of cost and delay but without detailed empirical information on additional cases it is not possible to include these as criteria in the analytical framework.

4. Management Role of MPAs

When each of the objectives in the MPA analytical framework is explored, a common theme emerges. This is the need for the most efficient use of judicial and other resources so as to maximise the delivery of justice. This is the essence of each of the MPA criteria. The overriding value informing each of these criteria is the use of MPAs as management devices to assist in achieving that end. All of the MPA objectives relate to this management role of MPAs and they are indicators of the effectiveness of MPA litigation. This becomes apparent throughout this study when examining the various modes of redress in several jurisdictions' legal systems. Even though these modes vary, their objective does not. Each of the methods is trying to achieve the same aim and is informed by the paramount needs for procedural efficiency and procedural justice. The different methods of collective redress adopted simply reflect the realities of the legal structures and systems in each national jurisdiction. In each of their respective contexts, each legal system is trying to achieve the same output. This means that, in reality, differences in enforcement approaches are incidental. For example, the divergent approaches of the US compared with the EU merely reflect a fundamental dichotomy in regulation. They are simply the routes through which different legal systems endeavour to maximise the efficient delivery of justice. The MPA objectives identified in this study support this management aim.

[229] *Graham & Graham v Rechem International Ltd* (1994) Env LR 158.

[230] The Competent Authority, *Buncefield: Why Did it Happen? The Underlying Causes of the Explosion and Fire at the Buncefield Oil Storage Depot, Hemel Hempstead, Hertfordshire on 11 December 2005* (2011) available at: http://www.hse.gov.uk/comah/buncefield/buncefield-report.pdf.

[231] *Group Litigation v Corby Borough Council* [2009] EWHC 1944 (TCC).

[232] [1988] ILRM 629.

Management is a utilitarian idea that, in the sphere of collective redress, assists with maximising outcomes for a maximum number of people. This connotes the utilitarian delivery of distributive justice in order to make redress accessible to the largest number of people. The need for effective management is the unifying theme that connects all MPA methods and the MPA objectives. MPA objectives such as procedural efficiency, fairness and predictability, while they are substantive, are necessary to achieve procedural efficiency. This will be highlighted in each of the jurisdictions examined. Collective redress systems need to be credible and to be seen to be offering a path to adequate compensation. The only way of achieving this is to ensure rigorous attention to substantive fairness and the efficient delivery of justice through collective redress mechanisms. It is important to recognise clearly that individual justice is subservient to the maximisation of the 'common good'. This however, begs the question of what the 'common good' might be, and also who decides this concept. Hence there is potential for abuse and a need for governance or oversight and transparency. It is unrealistic to expect that a judge can ever oversee what lawyers and funders are actually doing, for example in making tactical decisions and in negotiating settlements. Perhaps a better approach may be to use trustees to carry out this role.

This study argues that the efficient management of mass harm litigation so as to maximise just outcomes is the reason for the need for MPAs. There are notes of utilitarianism to this management theme. This jurisprudence philosophy propounds the doctrine that actions are right if they are useful for the benefit of a majority.[233] MPAs can have an important role in achieving this aim. This is based on procedural and substantive norms. While there are varying opinions as to the best MPA mechanisms,[234] MPAs undoubtedly serve valuable procedural purposes.[235] As for the substantive norms underlying MPAs, their aim is to deliver some redress to the largest possible category of potential claimants. This approach suggests that utilitarian and consequentialist theories of justice help to define the ultimate norms of MPAs. Utilitarian theories appeal to the interest of the majority. Utility it is the overriding norm. It measures what will make the majority of people most happy. The State's primary role is to secure group, majority or the wider social or public interests over minority interests.[236]

There are many illustrations of the management theme throughout this study. Each chapter gives many examples and these will be highlighted throughout. In the chapter examining mass harm and collective redress one of the key points to retain is the fundamental difference in the balance between public and private enforcement in various jurisdictions. This dictates the role that MPAs play in different jurisdictions and whether they are merely a managerial tool or more. In each of the common law jurisdictions examined, judges have adopted a managerial role and use MPA procedures to increase access for claims and efficiency. In the chapter dealing with MPA objectives, Lord Woolf's review highlights the need for 'balancing' and recognises that individual participation rights and procedural

[233] *Oxford English Dictionary* definition of utilitarianism. Major proponents of this theory are Jeremy Bentham and John Stuart Mill.

[234] eg some commentators argue that US class actions can result in a form of judicial blackmail and others counter that it is an effective means of policing behaviour and assuring victims fair compensation. See further M Redish and C Berlow 'The Class Action as Political Theory' (2007) 85 *Washington U L Rev* 753.

[235] M Redish, *Wholesale Justice: Constitutional Democracy and the Problem of the Class Action Lawsuit* (Stanford Law Books, 2009).

[236] Money-Kryle, 'The Origins and Roles of Class Action Laws across the World' (n 112).

autonomy must be compromised or curtailed to achieve efficient collective management, and a resolution of multiple, similar claims.[237] The Civil Procedure Rule Committee (CPRC) was also mindful of managerial need and recommended in 2003 that any further rules of court should enable the development of case management. This was echoed by the CJC when it cited Lord Woolf's commitment to procedural justice now being as important as substantive justice. This guided the CJC in making its recommendation for collective redress reform.[238] Mulheron also highlighted that the use of MPAs as managerial tools is an objective that is shared by varying MPA devices in several common law jurisdictions.[239] In the sphere of environmental mass harm there are growing calls for judges to take a more active role in some areas of the tort process. These concerns are to some extent procedural, for example the idea that in mass tort cases, the judge should take on a more managerial role.[240] The English and Welsh system is a good example of this both through its mechanism of the Group Litigation Order, which is a case management system not a collective or class action per se, and also in its use of case management. This will be discussed in further detail below, as well as in the chapter dealing with England and Wales, chapter eight.

The US system MPA system includes case management orders (CMOs), which are similar to consolidation. CMOs allow the pre-trial process to be managed so that discovery and settlement negotiations may be carried out in a synchronised way. Also the Multidistrict Litigation (MDL) statute allows related cases to be coordinated and consolidated for pre-trial discovery. The MDL also permits consolidation for the convenience of the parties and promotes just and efficient conduct of action. The MDL helps to manage complex and protracted lawsuits and enables parties to share all pre-trial costs, such as expensive discovery, and frequently results in settlement. Class actions are an obvious area where management is required. It is more economical for lawyers and courts to manage hundreds or thousands of similar cases as a group rather than on a case-by-case basis. Courts would be greatly overburdened if they had to deal with each case individually and the duplication of evidence and witnesses would generate needless expense. Class actions, through effective management, may resolve central issues and develop rational compensation schedules for the victims. Settlement also becomes a more attractive option for defendants where victims are members of a class. Overall, a class centralises all claims into one forum where a court can fairly resolve the issues by managing them collectively. It is interesting to note, however, that the trend in the US seems to have veered away from the rigid Rule 23 type class action towards the MDL (and class arbitration, for different reasons).

The use of MPAs in several other selected common law jurisdictions also gives plentiful illustration of MPAs assisting with management of mass harm cases. In Canada, it was stated in *Carom v Bre-X Minerals*[241] that:

> A class proceeding is the preferable procedure where it presents a fair, efficient, and manageable method of determining the common issues which arise from the claims of multiple plaintiffs and where such determination will advance the proceedings in accordance with the goals of judicial economy, access to justice, and the modification of the behaviour of wrongdoers.

[237] Gibbons (n 7) 227.
[238] CJC Report (n 30).
[239] Mulheron (n 10) 77.
[240] J Resnik, 'Managerial Judges' (1982) 96 *Harv L Rev* 374.
[241] (1999) 44 OR (3d) 173 (Gen Div).

This statement highlights most of the MPA objectives: access to justice; judicial and procedural economy; fairness; and deterrence. This evidences how MPA procedures, such as class actions, by providing management mechanisms, help to achieve these MPA objectives. Canadian courts are involved in case management of class actions in order to avoid this complicated type of litigation becoming unmanageable and to safeguard class members' interests.[242] For example, the Ontario Class Proceedings Act 1992 (CPA) requires case management of class actions and this is also normal practice in class actions outside of that province. Also, techniques may be used by which common issues may be bifurcated. Overall, Canadian MPA procedures appear to be efficient and innovative, greatly assisting the management of mass harm litigation.[243]

In Australia, owing to the shortcomings of traditional representative actions for managing collective redress, there was a clear need for additional effective MPA procedures and this was, therefore, a major rationale for the introduction of the grouped proceeding model known as representative proceedings. Under this procedure, the trial judges have wide-ranging 'managerial' powers and the ALRC has stated that 'without active court management, the interests of unidentified parties may not be taken properly into account'.[244] For example, the court has the power to order the discontinuation of proceedings.[245] Australian courts have further additional interventionist tools that they may invoke when necessary, the most important of which is section 33ZF (1). This allows the court to make 'any order … appropriate or necessary to ensure that justice is done in the proceedings'.[246] Again, this degree of court supervision and management safeguards group members' interests as well as those of unidentified parties, which indicates fairness, as well as judicial and procedural economy.

In relation to MPAs in England and Wales there have been considerable reforms that have introduced much greater judicial control through case management. For example in 1999, as a result of the Woolf reforms, the GLO was introduced as a means of case management. The GLO adopted general rules for managing individual litigation that were suitable for managing groups of similar claims. GLO rules establish a framework for the case management of claims that give rise to common or related issues of fact or law. They are intended to provide flexibility for the court to deal with the particular problems created by the cases. The court's case management powers enable it to deal with generic issues, for example by selecting particular claims as test cases. In a GLO, a managing judge is appointed with overall responsibility for the group litigation.[247] He has wide-ranging discretion to issue

[242] See eg opinion of Winkler J, 'Advocacy in Class Proceedings Litigation' (2000) 19 *Advocates' Soc J* 6, where he commented that case management judges have a 'weighty responsibility' and a 'broad discretion' in overseeing class actions.

[243] See generally W Bogart, J Kalajdzic and I Matthews, 'Class Actions in Canada: A National Procedure in a Multi-Jurisdictional Society?' (A report prepared for 'The Globalisation of Class Actions' Conference, Oxford University, December 2007).

[244] ALRC Report (n 107) [157].

[245] FCA, pt IVA, ss 33L, 33M, 33N and 33P; and pt 4A, ss 33L, 33M, 33N and 33P.

[246] A further example is that both the Federal Court and Victoria's Supreme Court have powers such as s 33X(5) which allows the court 'at any stage, [to] order that notice of any matter be given' to class members and by the court's direct involvement in 'administering and distributing monetary relief'.

[247] He may be assisted by a master or district court to deal with procedural issues and also by a costs judge.

case management directions[248] and may decide what issues and evidence are necessary or unnecessary. He may require parties to state their estimated costs and also order reductions or caps on costs. He may call case management conferences to manage and control the litigation effectively. Unviable cases may be struck out and also parties may be encouraged to mediate or settle cases. The judge's goal is always to resolve cases with minimal delay, at a low and proportionate cost, usually by agreement of the parties outside of the court. The GLO procedure gives the court maximum flexibility to use the appropriate management techniques tailored to each case and these can be innovative where necessary.[249] The *Corby* case is the benchmark for GLO litigation.[250] In addition to the GLO, there is effective use of case management. An example of this is shown in the *Buncefield* case, as it was a complex case that needed flexible management in order to resolve it. This case demonstrates that great efficiency, cost savings and flexibility can be achieved when such a managerial approach is invoked. In this case the judges imposed effective management and made speedy progress in litigation. Direct negotiations resulted in settlements. Mr Justice Steel considered that his main objective was to ensure that this litigation remained manageable. This again highlighted the court's inherent jurisdiction to manage cases. Under both the GLO and case management approaches parties may achieve what the MPA objectives define as 'access to justice'. Neither of these cases would have been adequately resolved without these management procedures, as the converse scenario would have entailed huge cost and other barriers for potential litigants if they had had to embark on individual litigation in order to obtain redress. Instead, by using MPA procedures and case management, the claimants benefited from cost-spreading advantages and other efficiencies to overcome these difficulties, as well as barriers to access to justice. It is notable, however, that the GLO, by using procedures designed for group litigation in cases that suit (where claimants have similar injuries), can deliver faster results than complicated case management which may be slow at dealing with non-common issues. Like the US trend towards MDL noted above, the GLO is located firmly within a matrix of judicial case management. *Buncefield* demonstrates that, in at least some circumstances, a flexible case management power is all that is required to deal with the litigation.

In Europe, there is evidence that most EU Member States did not introduce MPAs to improve access to justice but that, instead, often the reason for their introduction was to give a mechanism to judges to enable them to manage multiple similar claims. This is seen in the examples of Germany, which had to manage the massive *Deutsche Telekom* litigation and England and Wales, which was faced with numerous large-scale product liability cases, a phenomenon described as 'simply one of managerial need rather than enhancing access to justice or market health'.[251] This would appear to suggest that avoiding the courts and invoking alternative techniques through ADR, public enforcement and enhanced

[248] Law Reform Commission, *Consultation Paper on Multi-Party Litigation* (LRC CP 25-2003) states that this includes: varying the GLO issues; providing for one or more claims on the register to proceed as test claims; applying the results of the settlement of a test claim to other claims; appointing a solicitor as the lead solicitor for the parties on either side; setting a cut-off date for the entry of additional claims on the register; and removing a party from the register, 48 [2.40].

[249] A Higgins and A Zuckerman, 'Class Actions in England? Efficacy, Autonomy and Proportionality in Collective Redress' (2013) University of Oxford Legal Research Paper Series, 12.

[250] The *Corby* case will be discussed in detail in ch 8, together with the *Buncefield* case.

[251] Hodges (n 38) 82.14.

regulatory powers might achieve collective redress solutions. Where MPAs are needed, it seems that they are only effective if they are invoked for logistical reasons, in order to help manage mass harm litigation. Perhaps this may be a solution for EU policy—a collective management tool rather than a collective action. The Commission's Recommendation alluded to this managerial need when it stated that the judge in collective litigation should have the central role and should effectively manage the case and be vigilant against any possible abuses.[252]

In Ireland, the LRC recommended that any reform in the multi-party litigation area should be based on principles of procedural fairness, efficiency and access to justice. Again, this anchors any reform in this area to the MPA objectives, including those identified by the now Chief Justice of Ireland, Susan Denham, when she spoke at the launch of the Irish Law Reform Commission Consultation Paper on Multi-Party Litigation.[253] In particular, the LRC recommended that there should be active case management by the courts, which is in keeping with the general trend in the reform of civil procedure such as those in the Woolf Reform recommendations. As we have seen previously, the LRC, when examining MPA procedures, cited Hodges' opinion that '[i]n deciding on a managerial mechanisms… the paramount consideration is… that the selected approach will be dispositive of as many claims as possible'.[254] The LRC was also mindful of developments in case management of litigation and reforms recommended in England and Wales intended to reduce cost of litigation, such as the use of judicial management.[255] In terms of procedural efficiency, case management is an essential element of any State's legal system as it enhances the service provided to the public and minimises inefficiencies. Case management is only a recent phenomenon in the Irish legal system and has been emerging since the mid-1990s. As there has been a surge in the volume of litigation since that period there is a clear need to develop efficiency. This increase in volume of work has been matched by the increased complexity of cases. There has also been an increase in similar case litigation. The need for MPA-type procedures is an obvious corollary in order to ensure access to procedural justice. A rare example of case management was seen in some of the Irish asbestos litigation. It is important to note, however, that flexibility—and case management—detract from predictability, and this is not acceptable in some legal systems (notably civil law). It would appear that the Irish Law Reform Commission may have recommended the introduction of a multi-party action procedure partly because its recommended procedure would encourage Irish civil procedure towards case management. A key conclusion for Ireland, however, would appear to be that, as a common law country, it may be unwise to adopt a collective action procedure without having case management and one or more very experienced judges who could conduct and control such litigation effectively, and one whose decisions were not regularly appealed. How realistic such a possibility is remains to be seen.

It appears that mass harm raises managerial issues due to the volume and complexity of the harm that may result and that MPAs or case management solutions are required to deal with this challenge. Each of the MPA objectives identified in the analytical framework

[252] Recommendation (n 48) Point 4.

[253] See n 248.

[254] LRC, *Consultation Paper on Multi-Party Litigation* (n 248) 14 citing C Hodges *Multi-Party Actions* (n 17) 68, [5.11].

[255] LRC (n 248) 19.

in this study appears to be an indicator of the MPA methods' overarching aim, which is to ease the management of mass harm cases. It is suggested that this aim, in essence, is the function of MPAs.

5. Summary

Overall, the objectives of MPAs comprise the following: first, to increase the efficiency of the courts and the legal system and to reduce the costs of legal proceedings by enabling common issues to be dealt with in one action. Secondly, to enhance access by claimants to legally enforceable remedies where wrongful behaviour by the defendant is proven. This access to justice ought to be efficient and timely. On the other hand, MPAs ought to provide defendants with the opportunity to avoid unpredictable and conflicting decisions, possibly in different fora, over long periods of time. MPAs ought to provide outcomes and procedural rules that are predictable and that are proportionate in light of all the circumstances of the case.[256] It is important that MPA procedures provide safeguards against abuse in order to protect all the parties involved; therefore, the aim of non-abuse pervades all of the MPA objectives, particularly that of fairness. It is notable that the objective of deterrence is not shared unanimously among common law jurisdictions with MPA procedures. One of the biggest differences between US class actions and those in Australia is that Australia's objective is to compensate individuals, and not to punish defendants or to deter behaviour. Therefore it is not a valid objective of Australian class action jurisprudence to uphold a class action on the basis of its likely effect of modifying a defendant's behaviour. Identifying these MPA objectives helps to benchmark their aims and evaluate various mechanisms in several jurisdictions. An important underlying concomitant of the attainment of these MPA goals is the use of these devices as managerial tools to ease the logistical difficulties of administering cases of mass harm, and while Lord Woolf pointed out that they are not a panacea to achieving collective redress, they are 'the next step forward' in the debate that is trying to better achieve ways of 'managing the unmanageable'.

[256] Mulheron (n 10) 62.

4

Environmental Mass Harm and Collective Redress

1. Overview

Environmental mass harm is one area in which mass harm presents particular difficulties for claimants seeking collective redress. The phenomenon of environmental mass harm is explored as a case study of mass harm, as it illustrates some of the difficulties that may arise in mass harm litigation. The collective treatment of environmental mass harm cases may alleviate some of the difficulties in these cases. Environmental mass harm presents typical examples of circumstances in which the handling of multiple claims can give rise to common or related issues of fact or law and the clustering of such claims strengthens individual claims. This chapter will address the concept of environmental mass harm, the distinctive features and challenges it presents (such as difficulties relating to causation, evidential complexity and latency) then the solutions and difficulties that collective redress for environmental mass harm litigation through MPAs may entail. The experience of environmental mass harm litigation in various jurisdictions informs the examination in this chapter. This research will focus in particular on the possibilities for use of MPAs in common law jurisdictions and will not deal in detail with civil law jurisdictions, for reasons of space and the major procedural differences that exist between the two groups. The MPA procedures of some civil law jurisdictions and various common law jurisdictions will, however, be referred to occasionally for the purposes of illustration. Each of the forthcoming jurisdiction-specific chapters will contain a section on the treatment of environmental mass harm in that particular jurisdiction. The US has had the most experience of dealing with such litigation and, therefore, it inevitably greatly influences this discussion. Our understanding of this is vital to informing any examination of the use of MPAs.

As previously explained, there are obvious background differences to the approaches of the US and other common law jurisdictions to regulation, enforcement and litigation. While the varying approaches to tort law and public versus private law may be relevant, it is beyond the scope of this research to examine these in detail. Instead, this research will examine what, conceptually, is different and difficult about environmental mass harm and how MPAs may respond to these challenges or whether these problems are best addressed through other collective redress techniques. It will examine these issues from a global perspective, as many of the challenges are common in all jurisdictions. The solutions may stem from the solutions used in various common law jurisdictions. This study is looking for the broadest sample of comparative experience of environmental mass harm and MPAs as a general concept. It will draw on these to examine method, best practice, policy considerations and experience.

As the environment is a diffuse interest, it does not fit naturally within the framework that is traditionally recognised by the law for the protection of individual rights. In Ireland, for example, in both law and practice, private individuals and NGOs are inclined to have a secondary role in the regulation of environmental matters, as compared to public authorities. There is considerable acknowledgement by the Irish legislature that individuals or groups can have an interest in the environment, despite the more prominent role played by the regulatory authorities in this area and adjustments have been made to deal with problems such as legal standing. Examples of this can be seen in all aspects of planning law enforcement and in the civil liability provisions accompanying enforcement measures under some legislation, such as sections 57 and 58 of the Waste Management Act.[1] Existing tools for citizen enforcement are, however, still hampered by some practical impediments such as the prohibitive cost of litigation. In Ireland, a longstanding lacuna in the area of access to justice in Ireland is the lack of a procedural mechanism to enable MPAs for mass harm.[2] Such actions could be similar to collective action type lawsuits in a modified form so as to safeguard against abuse. The absence of a similar such mechanism potentially impedes citizens' access to justice and collective redress for mass harm in Ireland.[3]

There are key issues in environmental mass harm that differentiate it from other sectors of mass harm. Looking at these core characteristics of environmental mass harm, we must address why it should be examined separately to other mass harm areas. For example, there are practical difficulties associated with litigation involving environmental harm. This is because such cases can commonly involve conflicting and often novel expert testimony, as well as scientific uncertainty, and there is an obvious gap between legal and scientific culture. Evidence may require expert interpretation in order for it to be used in court. Tort problems can be exacerbated at mass level as judges, plaintiffs and defendants may struggle to deal with such technical evidence, perhaps where different types of injury are caused by one incident. Conversely, collective redress can be suited to resolving mass environmental harm where victims suffer similar injury, as plaintiffs in such cases may have issues such as causation dealt with collectively, obviating the need for them to prove this individually.[4] Also, environmental regulation can affect how tort law operates because it requires vast amounts of information to be supplied and made available to State agencies that collect and compile this information for purposes such as licensing and monitoring. The existence of this information is often key to providing information to would-be plaintiffs and defendants. It has resulted in the creation of an 'information explosion' as environmental legislation increasingly requires free access to information. For example, this has been the case for the past 25 years under EU law. This has changed the culture in relation to freedom

[1] Waste Management Act 1996 (as amended). These civil liability provisions provide for enforcement provisions in a tort-type way as proceedings may be initiated by anybody and so effectively resemble regulation in their effect.

[2] Ireland is an example of a common law jurisdiction that, at present, has no formal statutory or court rules for MPAs, so neither multi-party nor specifically collective action is yet permitted, save for very limited representative actions.

[3] Collective redress for environmental mass harm in Ireland will be discussed in detail in ch 10.

[4] This will be exemplified shortly in the discussion on the contrast between the *Corby Group Litigation* and the *Buncefield Litigation*. In the former, claimants suffered similar injury whereas in the latter the incident resulted in wide-ranging forms of injury.

of access to information and has put in place stringent and rigorous rules since 1990, as a result of the introduction of the original Directive on the freedom of access to information on the environment, Directive 1990/313.[5]

The functions of environmental mass harm litigation are similar to the aims of tort law generally, which principally involve compensation and deterrence. A key concern is access to justice for individuals and groups, to enable them to achieve collective redress. MPAs are an important mechanism to provide this for a number of reasons. MPAs and tort law generally, by increasing the possibility of errant polluters facing liability, force polluters to internalise pollution externalities. This can make tort liability systems more efficient by increasing the likelihood that liability will be imposed. The benchmarks outlined in chapter one will be used to examine collective redress mechanisms for environmental mass harm.

MPAs, by enabling victims of environmental mass harm to combine their legal actions, are a key tool in achieving their overall objectives of:

A. Access to Justice
B. Judicial and Procedural Economy
C. Fairness (also including proportionality, balancing individual rights and personal autonomy, non-abuse)
D. Predictability
E. Deterrence
F. Compensation

They can enable litigants to overcome many of the practical impediments facing citizens who take legal actions individually. These themes will be explored throughout this chapter. It is also noteworthy that the Aarhus Convention highlights the need to improve access to justice as a key facet of environmental governance in Europe.[6]

2. Regulatory Role—Environmental Law Enforcement Through Tort Law

Tort liability can play a regulatory role in relation to environmental harm in a way that it does not in other areas. This is seen particularly in the US. While this is not just a US phenomenon it is much more pronounced there. Such a role is evidenced in other common law jurisdictions in statutory systems that create tort-type liability. Ireland, for example, is also harnessing the regulatory potential of civil liability through statutory liability provisions that provide for civil liability for environmental harm,[7] and also through case law in

[5] Directive (EC) 90/313/EEC OJ 1990 L 158/56 provided for access to environmental information.

[6] UNECE Convention on Access to information, public participation in decision-making and access to justice in environmental matters, 38 ILM (1999) 517 (Aarhus, 25 June 1998); see further detail in S Kingston, 'Mind the Gap: Difficulties in Enforcement and the Continuing Promise of EU Environmental law' in S Kingston (ed), *European Perspectives on Environmental Law and Governance* (Routledge, 2013) 147.

[7] See eg Waste Management Act 1996 (as amended), ss 57 and 58; Local Government (Water Pollution) Act 1977, s. 12; Air Pollution Act 1987, s 4.

relation to the lifting of the corporate veil.[8] Enforcement through tort law and its role in environmental regulation are useful tools for achieving the objective of deterrence—it is deterrence taken to its logical conclusion. The EU and US have polar opposite approaches to public and private enforcement, while England and Wales seem to have a middle ground approach.

A. Tensions between Tort Law and Regulation

The roles of public law and private law in dealing with environmental problems need to be defined. They have completely different focuses. Private law, in particular tort law, has developed incrementally through the common law to meet the new challenges of modern-day living, for example mass marketing and industrialisation, and phenomena such as environmental and toxic torts.[9] Some commentators say that tort law is effective in this role.[10] Tort usually operates case-by-case looking retrospectively at a specific harm-causing event and the focus of litigation is usually the aim of compensation and deterrence.[11] This type of adjudication balances rights and responsibilities in modern society.[12] Kanner asserts that this balance is preferable to public law and bureaucracy.[13] Kanner, however, is perceived to be a lobbyist lawyer and it would appear that he is referring to the US private-enforcement-dominated context, not a European context. What is noteworthy is that what has driven the changes in tort law, especially when dealing with toxic torts, is different from what drives public law environmental regulation. Also, we can learn from this the importance of a continuing role for toxic tort litigation in a world where public law is becoming increasingly dominant. It may be possible that the private law processes, especially the tort litigation process, have advantages, in certain aspects, compared with public law environmental regulation.

Statutory liability regimes also play an important role in achieving environmental regulation as they use a kind of hybrid device of liability provisions, created under statute, to provide for civil liability for remediation. Such statutory liability is commonly used in England and Ireland, for example sections 57 and 58 of the Irish Waste Management Act, 1996, as amended. These remedies can even supplant tortious remedies in some circumstances. They are similar to what the US does in order to encourage private enforcement through tort law, except that in Ireland and England and Wales this can also be achieved by use of statutes.

Common law can also regulate and often does so, as we have seen in the previous chapter on mass harm. While tort law emphasises compensation and deterrence, in the US it can

[8] As seen in the cases of: *Wicklow County Council v Fenton* [2002] 4 IR 44; *Environmental Protection Agency v Nephin Trading Limited & Ors* [2011] IEHC 67 (High Court, Edwards J, 3 March 2011); *John Ronan and Sons v Clean Build Limited (in liquidation) and Others* [2011] IEHC 300.

[9] A toxic tort is tort caused by contact with a toxic substance, eg pesticides, chemicals and pharmaceutical drugs. Toxic torts include pollution torts, producer torts and mass disaster torts. Toxic torts will be discussed in detail in section 3A of this chapter.

[10] See eg M Shapo, 'Tort Law and Environmental Law Risk' (1991) 14 *Pace Envt'l L Rev* 531.

[11] Note that a different approach might be used for mass tort cases for medical monitoring, or for mature torts.

[12] D Farber, *Eco-Pragmatism: Making Sensible Environmental Decisions in an Uncertain World* (University of Chicago Press, 1999).

[13] A Kanner, 'Toxic Tort Litigation in a Regulatory World' (2002) 41 *Washburn LJ* 542.

provide certain remedies that can help that aim, but also, when applied to class actions, it can effectively resemble regulation.[14] More obviously, because tort law in the US provides for punitive damages, it also regulates. The American Supreme Court appears to be content with the role that tort law plays and this would suggest that tort law is not to be pre-empted, even in highly regulated areas. This position is reflected in English law, famously, in cases such as *Hunter v Canary Wharf*[15] and *Gillingham Borough Council v Medway*,[16] in both of which it was held that tort law is not to be supplanted by statutory or regulatory measures. One of the advantages of the common law is its incremental approach in delivering specific judgments on an individual case basis, which gives guidance to future cases. This approach, however, is undoubtedly challenged by mass torts, and this applies equally to mass environmental harm. Public regulatory law sometimes looks at relatively abstract issues and tries to use prospective approaches to problem solving, such as cost-benefit analysis. However, abstract public policy can ignore real rights, such as property rights.[17] Public regulatory law, however, does of course often enforce specific breaches. As for juries, they are best suited to dealing with the actual consequences of past actions, and therefore retrospective rather than prospective assessment. This is why they have a crucial role in US tort law. When dealing with environmental dispute resolution, it seems more appropriate to focus on real problems rather than expert speculation. As we have seen, we must differentiate the US approach, as the system there prioritises private enforcement over public enforcement. So, in this way the US is completely different. It positively incentivises private enforcement through MPAs. It encourages everyone to enforce, especially intermediaries.[18] As a result, the US substantive law has been aligned to allow this type of mass litigation, for example to help overcome problems of individual causation, and therefore there are lots of 'private attorneys general', as previously discussed. Hence in the US, in MPAs, claimants only have to successfully prove that there has been harm and it is very likely that they will then be awarded damages. This permission of public sanctioning achieves deterrence through juries and sanctions.

B. EU Perspective of Enforcement—a Different Approach

The EU has always had a sharp division between private and public enforcement. The EU is described as a regulatory state that has extensive public law rules that are primarily enforced by public authorities and their networks.[19] To date, private law rules have remained largely unharmonised, apart from the now large body of consumer protection law. Europe does not have a large tradition of private enforcement of public norms although there are some examples of this, such as Germany, that enforces all 'unfair competition' advertising and so

[14] Such as the remedy of medical monitoring, which will be discussed in detail in this chapter.
[15] [1997] UKHL 14.
[16] [1993] QB 343.
[17] Which would eg enable a landowner to seek tort damages against a polluter who has created a nuisance, despite the polluter having a licence, eg *Magnolia Coal Terminal v Philips Oil Co*, 576 So2d 475 (La 1991).
[18] They are given wide investigative powers; technical and economic barriers are removed; economic incentives are given.
[19] See eg G Majone, *Regulating Europe* (Routledge, 1996); F Cafaggi and H Muir Watt (eds), *The Regulatory Function of European Private Law* (Edward Elgar, 2009).

on through trade associations and NGO private actions instead of through public actors. Europe has a traditional model that keeps private enforcement of public norms separate from public enforcement of public norms, so it keeps regulation and compensation entirely separate. There are some exceptions to this, such as England and Ireland, which both have statutory liability measures that empower individuals to take action where there is a breach of statutory duty, as mentioned previously. Also, in both of these jurisdictions the common law tort remedy of breach of statutory duty exists as a ground for action, in theory at least, but it is rarely invoked. This specifically provides a private action remedy for a breach of a public norm. Also, many civil law Member States allow private claimants to piggyback on criminal investigations.[20] Overall, however, most European States do not have the US features that are designed to encourage litigation.

European lawmakers are concerned that collective procedures should not entail excessive costs. Also, if private actors are to be incentivised to take enforcement action, they need appropriate incentives. Ironically, what European commentators see as abuse in the US system are the intended consequences of a policy of private enforcement based on a *post facto* deterrence theory. US features such as the lack of cost shifting and the use of contingency fees are designed to increase financial incentives for private actors to bring actions. As evidenced above, the majority of the existing collective procedures in EU Member States are rarely used owing to the costs rules issues and problems of funding.[21] However, it is possible to surmise that if these were altered, then it may be likely that numerous claims would be attracted to these procedures. Another EU feature is the formal powers that private sector bodies, such as consumer associations, have in taking actions on behalf of groups for breaches of consumer law. Such associations can be highly successful watchdogs if they have the extensive funding necessary in order to be effective enforcement agents. In contrast, if private sector bodies were empowered to bring MPAs, and if these procedures did not contain adequate safeguards to guard against abuse, it is likely that these bodies would outsource this to lawyers, resulting in a similar system to the US. This would increase the number of claims but with inherent risks of abuse and conflicts of interest, as well as increasing litigation levels and court costs.

C. England and Wales—Perspective on Enforcement

First, a brief background on regulation, and in particular environmental regulation, in England and Wales. This involves many public regulation agencies. There is also a robust history of reliance on self- and co-regulation as well as increased trust in both private and public regulation. The public authorities have extensive formal enforcement powers under both criminal and civil law. The enforcement powers of most public authorities have been reformed in the past few years as the Government adopted all of the recommendations in the Hampton Report[22] and the Macrory Report[23] and enshrined the new regime on

[20] eg Case C-1/03 *Paul Van de Walle and Others v Texaco Belgium SA*, concerning the remediation of contaminated land.

[21] This will be discussed in further detail in ch 9.

[22] The Hampton Report, *Reducing Administrative Burdens: Effective Inspection and Enforcement* (HM Treasury, 2005) considered how to reduce unnecessary administration for businesses, without compromising the UK's excellent regulatory regime.

[23] The Macrory Report, *Regulatory Justice: Sanctioning in a post-Hampton World*; *Regulatory Justice: Making Sanctions Effective* (HM Treasury, 2006).

administrative sanctions in the Regulatory Enforcement and Sanctions Act 2008 (RESA). There is now a focus on achieving outcomes that deliver compliance and restoration of market balance and restitution to those harmed.[24] Increasingly, instead of requiring private parties to seek redress by initiating action in the courts for compensation or injunctions, public bodies can be highly effective in both facilitating and delivering redress. Such techniques can be more effective and economical than traditional civil action or other tools of redress. A regulatory approach can be particularly useful when large numbers of people or widespread business behaviour is involved. In this way, regulators can form effective agents for addressing mass or collective redress issues, without the cost, delay or abuse of private civil litigation. England and Wales has fundamentally reformed its approaches to regulation, enforcement and restitution in light of this. The result is an emerging new approach towards both enforcement generally and also towards incorporating restorative justice (namely redress, compensation and restoration of the status quo) as a key role for public enforcers. This has developed through changing ideas and policy on how regulators and others should control behaviour. The approach has changed from a traditional, authoritative 'command and control' approach to one based on responsive approaches towards behaviour, and how best to incentivise and regulate it within complex organisational structures. As a result, instead of requiring private parties to seek redress through themselves initiating action in the courts, public bodies can not only be involved in facilitating or delivering redress but they can be highly effective in this role.[25] Hodges notes that these techniques may be faster, more effective and more economical than traditional techniques. This approach to regulation is similar to the emphasis on ADR that is found in relation to the resolution of private law claims by avoiding the court system. ADR has essentially emerged within sophisticated, self-regulatory structures, notably through the development of many ombudsmen and specialist tribunals linked with business codes of conduct.[26] As a result of these changes, England and Wales has introduced a policy on public enforcement that is revolutionary, by basing its decisions firmly on academic theory and also economic priorities.[27] The overriding policy is of encouraging competitiveness and economic wellbeing. Specific policies are fostered, against this background, to adopt a risk-based and impact-assessment approach to regulation and enforcement, and also to reduce the administrative burden.[28] This policy's approach is that risk assessment should predicate regulatory and enforcement policy and also that the administrative burden of regulation on business should be reduced. This is based on the 'responsive regulation' theory propounded by Professors Ayres and Braithwaite based on their 'enforcement pyramid'.[29] Academic theory in restorative justice has also been adopted. This aims to influence behaviour

[24] This is as a result of the English 'Better Regulation' Policy, which aims at making both public expenditure and business costs more efficient and effective; the Hampton Report (n 22); and the Macrory Penalty Principles contained in the Macrory Report (n 23).

[25] C Hodges, *Law and Corporate Behaviour: Integrating Theories of Regulation, Enforcement, Compliance and Ethics* (Hart Publishing, forthcoming). This section is informed by an extract from a chapter on The Enforcement Powers of Individual Agencies.

[26] Ibid.

[27] www.epa.ie/pubs/reports/enforcement/OEE%20Policy.pdf.

[28] There is much written on Better Regulation Policy in the UK. The Hampton Report (n 22) proposed that the English regime should be simplified and enforcement made subject to a risk assessment.

[29] I Ayers and J Braithwaite, *Responsive Regulation* (Oxford University Press, 2002).

with the rectification of the harm caused by the wrongdoer's behaviour. Professor Macrory elaborated 'Six Penalties Principles' in order to achieve this:[30]

1. Aim to change the behaviour of the offender.
2. Aim to eliminate any financial gain from non-compliance.
3. Be responsive and consider what is appropriate for the particular offender and regulatory issue.
4. Be proportionate to the nature of the offence and the harm caused.
5. Where appropriate, aim to restore the harm caused by regulatory non-compliance.
6. Aim to deter future non-compliance.

While some of the above may resonate with private compensation law, Macrory focuses on a holistic process whereby those most directly affected by the wrongdoing come together to determine what needs to be done to repair the harm and prevent a recurrence. Although this approach focuses on sanctioning from the regulatory perspective, not from the perspective of compensation, this has led to innovative developments in compensation and restoration policy, especially for collective redress.[31] New enforcement policy has been adopted by the Environment Agency to reflect this. The Irish Environmental Protection Agency's (EPA) enforcement policy reflects elements of such an approach also.[32]

In examining the English Environment Agency (EA), its purpose is to 'protect or enhance the environment, taken as a whole', so as to promote 'the objective of achieving sustainable development'. It has extensive functions and impacts on a range of activities. It is logical to use public restorative remedies in relation to environmental damage, especially since private rights of action are restricted.[33] The EU Environmental Liability Directive[34] establishes a 'polluter pays' liability regime but it is enforced by public rather than private action. Therefore the EA and the statutory adviser on the natural environment in England, English Nature, were the first to be awarded the RESA Part 3 power to impose civil sanctions powers.[35] Civil sanctions were intended to provide new ways to protect the environment, supplementing the normal criminal-law based enforcement tools, and focusing on investment in environmental clean-up rather than paying fines. The two authorities were granted the full range of powers, including: the ability to impose financial penalties; the ability to issue a Compliance Notice, requiring steps within a stated period to ensure that an offence does not continue or happen again; the ability to issue a Restoration Notice requiring specified steps within a stated period to restore the position to what it would have been if no offence had been committed; the ability to issue a Stop Notice, which will prevent a person from carrying on an activity described in the notice until it has taken steps to come back into compliance; the ability to accept Enforcement Undertakings, which will enable a person, whom a regulator reasonably suspects of having committed an offence, to give an undertaking to a regulator to take one or more corrective actions set out in the undertaking; a person may give a Third Party Undertaking to compensate persons affected by an offence,

[30] Macrory Report (n 23).
[31] Hodges, *Law and Corporate Behaviour* (n 25).
[32] See www.epa.ie/pubs/reports/enforcement/oeeenforcementpolicy.html
[33] Hodges (n 25).
[34] Directive 2004/35/EC of the European Parliament and Council of 21 April 2004 on environmental liability with regard to the prevention and remedying of environmental damage. OJ L 143, 30.4.2004.
[35] As of 6 April 2010.

and the regulator, if it accepts the undertaking, must take it into account in determining the variable monetary penalty.[36] These powerful new tools in the armoury of the EA will further empower its role in regulation and enforcement.

D. Regulation and Adjudication

Public policy requires elite experts with technical ability and management skills to work together with independent agencies towards the goal of balancing economic growth and the environment. However, this view ignores that an agency can often act as both a regulator and promoter and, as such, have its own interests.[37] While democratic decisions may perhaps in some sense seem more legitimate than elite decisions, which, while ostensibly impartial, are generally abstract but can also be wrong sometimes.[38] Looking at the US example of the Food and Drug Administration (FDA), it is subject to criticism from both sides. It may be viewed as bureaucratic and slow on one hand and on the other as having 'allegiance to the medical profession and the drug industry…quick to approve new drugs without adequate evidence of safety…slow and inept in withdrawing drugs from the market'.[39] In Ireland and England and Wales, juries are no longer involved in these types of mass tort cases.[40] However, traditionally in US tort law, the jury decides all the facts required to resolve a dispute with the aim that their involvement in deliberations would result in a high degree of democracy in the award of damages. However, there have been growing calls in some areas for judges to take a more active role in the tort process. These concerns are to some extent procedural, for example the idea that in mass tort cases, the judge should take on a more managerial role.[41] This highlights the need for mechanisms to help with this management need and it would appear that MPAs could assist with this task by allowing mass cases to be collectively managed.

One outstanding issue, however, is whether environmental disputes should be resolved by common law decisions or be left to expert elites,[42] and whether they should be resolved on the case-by-case, fact-intensive basis of the common law. Kanner believes that political and bureaucratic public administration in the US suffers from the perception of the undue influence of narrow interest groups, while it appears that the civil justice system and tort law, once they are operating properly, seem to strike a balance between democratic control and expertise.[43] Public law is designed to resolve market failure and externalities,

[36] Hodges (n 25).

[37] B Commoner, 'The Hazards of Risk Assessment' (1989) 14 *Colum J Envt'l L* 365–66, explaining that 'new technology is chosen in advance of the risk assessment…which is not used to decide what technology to use, but rather how to best defend the choice already made'. See also D Elliot, 'The Future of Toxic Torts: Of Chemophobia, Risk as a Compensable Injury and Hybrid Compensation Systems' (1988) 25 *Hous L Rev* 781, 783–86.

[38] J Noonan, *Persons and Masks of the Law: Cordozo, Holmes and Wythe as Makers of the Mask* (Farrar, Strauss & Giroux, 1976) (criticising *Palsgraf* decision for ignoring detailed facts in favour of abstractions); D Richards, *The Moral Criticism of Law* (Dickinson-Wadsworth, 1977) ('Serious moral thought about social questions of any complexity obviously requires close attention to matters of empirical fact'.)

[39] R Crant, 'The Nature of Regulatory Choices' (1978) 33 *Food Drug Cosm LJ* 413.

[40] Apart from very few civil cases where juries may occasionally be used, such as defamation.

[41] eg J Resnik, 'Managerial Judges' (1982) 96 *Harv L Rev* 374.

[42] A Kanner, 'The Politics of Toxic Tort Law' (1997) 2 *Widener L Symp J* 163.

[43] Ibid 545.

with the pollution externality being a classic example as it is a social cost that common law and the free market arguably fail to force polluters to internalise. Regulation aims both to eliminate costs and promote certain goods where the market fails to do so. This is most suited to where harm is caused to public goods such as natural resources but least suited to individuals so it would seem that such unsuitability is amplified if dealing with groups of victims of environmental mass harm.

3. Distinctive Features of Environmental Mass Harm and Responses

A. Toxic Torts

As stated at the outset, there are features of environmental mass harm that present challenges for litigation. Environmental mass harm litigation is increasingly informed by, and centred on, toxic torts, so this area must be our primary focus when examining the phenomenon of environmental mass harm. For the purposes of this chapter, this study is concerned with such harm where it impacts on human health, property or the environment. While there is no single universally accepted definition of 'toxic torts', there is general agreement that toxic tort litigation deals with special types of injuries that are usually new to the law since World War Two—for example injuries resulting from exposure to asbestos, dioxin and toxic waste disposal.[44] In brief, toxic tort law deals with cases that have some, but not all, of the features of traditional tort cases and the remedies they provide, such as negligence, nuisance and product liability. However, toxic tort cases specifically involve hazardous substances and new harms that were either uncommon or non-existent in the past, which often cause newly emerging injuries. As a result, victims of toxic torts wishing to litigate their claims face challenges in bringing their cases, particularly in proving causation, often due to the scientific complexity of evidence. The law has had to evolve to deal with these emerging issues. As previously stated, these issues can be amplified at mass level but it would appear that MPA treatment of such harm can help to alleviate these difficulties, particularly, for example, where the courts must deal with technically complex and correspondingly expensive issues collectively, such as causation.

Looking at the US as an example, over the decades since toxic torts have become recognised there, tort law has evolved to meet the new challenges they have presented. These have entailed problems such as difficulties presented by case management,[45] causation,[46] statute

[44] Kanner, 'Toxic Tort Litigation in a Regulatory World' (n 13) 1.

[45] eg in *re Agent Orange Prod Liab Litig*, 597 F Supp 740 (DCNY 1984). Public law models have begun to impact on private law toxic tort cases, esp in civil procedure and evidence law. A greater variety of toxic tort claims are being handled as class actions and mass torts; eg *Petrovic v Amoco Oil Co*, 200 F 3d 1140 (8th Cir 1999) (affirming post-*Amchem* environmental and toxic tort class action settlement. Indeed, some remedies such as medical monitoring may be better suited to class action treatment. See *Ayers v Township of Jackson*, 525 A 2d 287 (NJ 1987) (class action by group of residents against township for nuisance arising from contamination of water by toxic pollutants leaching into aquifer from town's landfill—medical monitoring was granted).

[46] eg A Kanner, 'Ruminations on Trial by Jury: An Essay in Honor of Judge Robert S. Vance' (1990) 5 *Toxic L Rep* (BNA) No 12, pt I, 415.

of limitations,[47] expert evidence,[48] novel injuries[49] and multiple defendants.[50] All of these problems have been dealt with both collectively and individually. In this way, the courts have responded by developing jurisprudence to deal with the unique traits of toxic tort litigation.[51] There have, however, been some complaints by law reformers of the need for legislative or administrative solutions in the US.[52] A question that Europe ought to perhaps consider is whether the widening of US toxic tort law should be adopted in Europe, or perhaps this concept may be inconsistent with the ideas of balanced justice in Europe as between claimants and defendants.

It was from the late-1960s onwards that the US started to truly focus on the environmental problems associated with modern technology, such as those evidenced in toxic torts. As a result, the Environmental Protection Agency was created and also various environmental laws were enacted.[53] Both of these innovations dealt with new recording and monitoring requirements for industry and some of the laws also addressed operational conduct, such as clean-up. Crucially, at this time, public awareness and concern about pollution and its handling began to change, especially after some high-profile events such as the discovery of buried toxins at Love Canal[54] and the partial nuclear meltdown incident at Three Mile Island.[55] This resulted in strong public calls demanding clean-up and the development of political consensus to resolve such problems as a primary public concern.

In response to these events, the US has seen a number of key developments over several decades that have changed the face of toxic tort litigation there.[56] First, the courts have developed an approach to deal specifically with the distinctive characteristics of toxic tort litigation. For example, they have permitted recovery for a broader range of injuries, addressed statute of limitations problems that can affect multiple and time-delayed harms and removed problems of product identification associated with mass marketing.[57]

[47] A Kanner and E Trevor, 'Federal Expansion of State Statute of Limitations in Hazardous Materials Cases' (1988) 29 *The Barrister* 34.

[48] eg *Daubert v Merrell Dow Pharm, Inc*, 509 US 579 (1993).

[49] For more detail on new theories of compensable injuries, see J Weinstein, *Individual Justice in Mass Tort Litigation: The Effect of Class Action, Consolidations and Other Multi-Party Devices* (Northwestern University Press, 1995) 152.

[50] eg G LaMarca, 'Market Share Liability, Industry-Wide Liability, Alternative Liability and Concert of Action: Modern Legal Concepts Preserving Liability for Defective but Unidentifiable Products' (1981) 31 *Drake L Rev* 61 (various product identification theories); G Priest, 'The Invention of Enterprise Liability: A Critical History of the Intellectual Foundations of Modern Tort Law' (1985) 14 *J Legal Stud* 461, 462.

[51] eg R Baker and M. Markoff, 'By-Products Liability: Using Common Law Private Actions to Clean Up Hazardous Waste Sites' (1986) 10 *Harv Envt'l L Rev* 99, 100.

[52] See further W Ginsberg and L Weiss, 'Common Law Liability for Toxic Torts: A Phantom Remedy' 9 *Hofstra L Rev* 859 (1981); W Hurwitz, 'Environmental Health: An Analysis of Available and Proposed Remedies for Victims of Toxic Waste Contamination' (1981) 7 *Am J L & Med* 61; W Hurwitz, 'An Analysis of Common Law and Statutory Remedies for Hazardous Waste Injuries' (1980) 12 *Rutgers L Rev* 117; M Sokolow, 'Hazardous Waste Liability and Compensation: Old Solutions, New Solutions, No Solutions' (1982) 14 *Conn L Rev* 307.

[53] During the term of President Nixon.

[54] See A Gordon Levine, *Love Canal: Science, Politics and People* (Heath, 1982).

[55] This occurred in 1978 and was the worst incident in US commercial power plant history, resulting in the release of radioactive substances into the environment. See further *re Three Mile Island Litigation*, 605 F Supp 778 (MD Pa 1985). This was a class action for medical monitoring and economic loss.

[56] A Kanner, 'Future Trends in Toxic Tort Litigation' (1989) 20 *Rutgers LJ* 667.

[57] A Kanner, 'Emerging Conceptions of Latent Personal Injuries in Toxic Tort Litigation (1987) 18 *Rutgers LJ* 343.

Secondly, on a statutory level, Superfund legislation has changed the landscape in which toxic tort law exists.[58] This legislation aimed to address the clean-up of hazardous waste disposal sites and the imposition of liability for the cost of remediation on those responsible.[59] Among the aims of legislation such as Superfund were injury prevention and the detection and minimisation of severity of injury at an early stage.[60] The legislation encouraged a more cost-effective resolution of toxic tort cases. In this way, it was hoped that the cost of toxic injury to the individual victims, to the economy and to the civil justice system would be reduced. At least, the legislation has promoted suitable remedies, such as medical monitoring, and the involvement of the community has expedited and eased earlier difficulties.[61] A side-effect of the legislation was intended to be the reduction in harms and resulting tort claims, as more victims participate in the public law processes provided by the legislation and, as a result, that fewer private damage lawsuits would be brought by victims. The legislation does not provide compensation for those injured by hazardous chemicals, so it did not change the common law. Its main effect on private party toxic tort litigation has been the huge increase in information that must be made available. This 'information explosion' makes important data easily accessible to toxic tort plaintiffs. The legislation has resulted in increased reporting requirements and scientific information for victims on a database of toxicological and epidemiologic information and information such as notification of potentially dangerous contamination or 'substantial risk', which is required under the Acts.[62] This information is key to helping claimants gather evidence for litigation and this legislation has enhanced the availability of such data. An interesting aspect to Superfund is that academic commentators were quick to conclude almost unanimously that tort law was not equipped to address the problems of modern pollution and torts.[63] This would appear to undermine any role for MPAs in this sector. There are, of course, serious challenges posed by toxic tort litigation, but some consider that these are not insurmountable.[64]

[58] Comprehensive Environmental Response, Compensation, and Liability Act (CERCLA), 42 USC 9601-75, as amended by Superfund Amendments and Reauthorization Act of 1986 (SARA), Pub L No 99-400,100 Stat. CERCLA, commonly known as Superfund, was enacted by Congress on 11 December 1980. This law created a tax on the chemical and petroleum industries and provided broad federal authority to respond directly to releases or threatened releases of hazardous substances that may endanger public health or the environment. Over 5 years, $1.6bn was collected and the tax went to a trust fund for cleaning up abandoned or uncontrolled hazardous waste sites.

[59] Some commentators say that Superfund seems to have been an inefficient clean-up law. Opinion in the US has since turned full circle to support 'Brownfield Redevelopment' which is trying to release environmental clean-up from Superfund and redirect it to the private sector, which is economically incentivised to effective clean-up. See further A Kanner, 'Rebuilding America' (1995) 20 *Nat'l Ass'n Envt'l Prof'ls News* 17; A Kanner, 'Rethinking Superfund' (1995) 20 *Nat'l Ass'n Envtl Prof'ls News* 19.

[60] This can be achieved through medical monitoring, which will be discussed in detail in this chapter.

[61] Medical monitoring is the observation of a disease, condition or one or several medical parameters over time and will be discussed in more detail shortly. eg cases involving alleged long-term injury or diseases such as asbestos will require victims to be assessed periodically over an extended time.

[62] eg health effects are listed on the Center for Disease Control's (CDC) Toxic Disease Registry.

[63] See Ginsberg and Weiss, 'Common Law Liability for Toxic Torts (n 52); Hurwitz, 'Environmental Health (n 53); Hurwitz, 'An Analysis of Common Law and Statutory Remedies for Hazardous Waste Injuries' (n 52); Sokolow, 'Hazardous Waste Liability and Compensation' (n 52).

[64] On the problems facing potential plaintiffs seeking tort recovery for toxic harm, see Superfund no 301 (E) Study Group, *Injuries and Damages from Hazardous Waste—Analysis and Improvement of Legal Remedies—A Report to Congress in Compliance with no 301 (E) of the Comprehensive Environmental Response, Compensation and Liability Act of 1980*, pt 1, 55–56, 116–17, 196.

There were changes of attitude and law after *Love Canal* and there were concerns that private law was not equipped to remedy the new problems such as pollution and latent injuries, or the volume of problems arising from mass torts.[65] This would appear to suggest that mechanisms such as MPAs were needed to manage the logistics of resulting environmental mass harm litigation. A toxic tort lawsuit may be the final element in suits involving government bodies and victims. The information provided under legislation such as Superfund allows people to access data resources and even to participate in government action.[66] Owing to the improved public participation provisions in the legislation, the resulting or concurrent toxic tort lawsuit may have fewer claims because some injuries may have been mitigated or prevented entirely. Also, the suit will be more refined and better prepared because of government investigation and litigation, and less expensive, because expert proof and public information will be readily available. Difficulties with issues such as causation will hopefully be alleviated because the legislation provides that scientific evidence will be admissible in court and, therefore, can be taken into account in toxic tort cases.

As well as the jurisprudential and legislative responses to the toxic tort-type cases mentioned above, which highlight the potential difficulties these cases can entail, there are also many difficulties in relation to causation and evidential complexity, latency and foreseeability in these types of cases. These will now be examined in turn.

B. Causation and Evidential Complexity

One of the distinguishing features of toxic tort cases is the difficulty a plaintiff may experience in establishing causation. A plaintiff must prove that the harm was caused by that defendant's activities. It can be extremely problematic to prove causation under traditional causation rules, not just in mass harm cases. Generally, in toxic tort cases the complex nature of scientific and technical evidence can cause difficulty with issues such as causation and this may be greatly exacerbated in cases of mass harm.[67] It is important to note, as previously stated however, that collective treatment of environmental mass harm cases may alleviate some of the difficulties faced by individuals in these cases. An example of this is collectively dealing with issues of causation that can help resolve the difficulties that would otherwise be encountered by individuals trying to prove causation when dealing with technical scientific evidence.

In the US, Allan Kanner, one of the leading environmental and toxic tort class action trial lawyers, advises that the key to dealing with environmental mass harm cases is to understand that such harms turn on common questions of liability and general causation, which predominate in the life of certain types of cases.[68] This is especially true in property damage claims as well as claims for medical monitoring. Personal injury cases are more difficult to resolve unless one is dealing with an agent-specific harm that was suffered by an entire

[65] Kanner (n 13) 540.

[66] The Superfund Amendments and Reauthorization Act (SARA) amended CERCLA on 17 October 1986. SARA inserted a section in relation to public participation, although victims may bring their own actions.

[67] This difficulty has been alleviated in the US through judicial and legislative evolution of the law to deal specifically with toxic torts, as discussed.

[68] Kanner stated this in email correspondence in relation to this research in March 2013.

class. It is also extremely difficult to establish liability where the pollutant is dispersed into the wider environment; for example, in the US case of *Sterling v Velsicol Corporation*, the plaintiffs could not prove to the satisfaction of the Court that certain illnesses had been caused by drinking water contaminated by pollutants leaching from a waste burial site.[69]

Proving causation is difficult in the English and Welsh courts and Irish courts also. The Scottish case of *Graham & Graham v Rechem*[70] provides an extreme example of the practical problems that can arise in trying to establish causation in toxic tort cases.[71] This case involved an action in negligence and nuisance against the operator of a hazardous waste incinerator by local farmers for alleged damage to their cattle. The case involved a vast amount of cutting-edge scientific evidence. It lasted for 896 hours in court, spread over 198 days, and involved 80 lay witnesses and 21 expert witnesses on issues such as veterinary toxicology, agricultural accountancy, incinerator design, dioxin formation, pollution dispersion, analysis of trace organics and meteorology.[72] The Grahams submitted that the crucial issue on causation was whether the symptoms exhibited by their herd were indicative of contamination.[73] The lawyers had to have a detailed understanding of the scientific issues before legal arguments could be made. Furthermore, the importance of particular issues changed during the trial as the lawyers' understanding of the science increased. Ultimately, the case failed on the issue of causation, as it was found that there were other possible explanations of the cattle's injuries. Similarly, in Ireland, while there has not yet been extensive litigation of toxic torts, an early example of one such case is that of *Hanrahan v Merck, Sharpe and Dohme*, which shows similar difficulties in proving causation.[74] The facts were similar to those in the *Rechem* case above, with the plaintiffs failing to prove, at first instance, that the emissions from the neighbouring chemical plant had caused the illnesses being suffered by their livestock. They failed to rebut the vast array of technical and scientific evidence being propounded by the defence that raised questions over causation. Only on appeal to the Supreme Court did the plaintiffs finally succeed in their action, as they managed to convince the Court that there was no other possible cause for the illness other than the emissions from the pharmaceutical plant. Judge Henchy, in his Supreme Court decision, discussed at length the merits of reversing the burden of proof in toxic tort cases and placing it on the defendants instead, requiring them to prove that their activities did not cause the harm. He ultimately declined to reverse the burden in proof in this case but the appellants succeeded nonetheless. This case shows that, hopefully, judges may be willing to be more creative when addressing issues of causation in toxic tort-type cases in the future.

> What the plaintiffs have to prove in support of their claim in nuisance is that they suffered some or all of the mischief complained of and that it was caused by emissions from the defendants' factory.

[69] 855 F 2d 1188.

[70] *Graham & Graham v Rechem International Ltd* [1994] Env LR 158.

[71] There is however an important exception to this—the *Fairchild* exception to the general common law rule on causation (the 'but for' test) on indivisible diseases—so courts have created a policy exception where the risk of causing could be equated with causation in indivisible diseases (they do not permit this in any other area); *Fairchild v Glenhaven Funeral Services* [2002] 3 WLR 89 (HL).

[72] See further D Woolley and others, *Environmental Law* (Oxford University Press, 2000) 712.

[73] Polyhalogenated aromatic hydrocarbon (PHAH) toxicity. It was submitted that the standard of proof that would be required by the scientific community was far greater than that required to prove the proposition in a civil action and that the Grahams were only required to show on the balance of probabilities that PHAH toxicosis was a reasonable or probable cause of their problems.

[74] [1988] ILRM 629.

> To hold that it is for the defendants to disprove either or both of those matters would be contrary to authority and not be demanded by the requirements of justice. There are of course difficulties facing the plaintiffs in regard to proof of those matters, particularly as to the question of causation, but mere difficulty of proof does not call for a shifting of the onus of proof. Many claims in tort fail because the plaintiff has not access to full information as to the true nature of the defendant's conduct.[75]

There were indications of a change of attitude to the traditional causation stance in England and Wales in the case of *Fairchild v Glenhaven Funeral Services Ltd*, which has become a leading case on causation in English tort law.[76] It concerned malignant mesothelioma, a deadly disease caused by breathing asbestos fibres. Mr Fairchild had worked for a number of different employers, as a subcontractor for Leeds City Council; all of these employers had negligently exposed him to asbestos. He contracted pleural mesothelioma and died. His wife subsequently sued the employers on his behalf for negligence. A number of other claimants were in similar situations, and joined in the appeal. The problem was that a single asbestos fibre, inhaled at any time, could trigger the onset of mesothelioma. The risk of contracting asbestos-related disease increases depending on the amount of exposure to it. However, because of long latency periods it is impossible to know when the crucial moment of the harm occurring was, and consequently, which of the employers was responsible for his illness.[77] It was held that the appropriate test in this situation was whether the defendant had materially increased the risk of harm towards the plaintiff. The employers were held to be jointly and severally liable against the claimant.

While proving causation may be problematic now it may become less so because of legislative initiatives, such as the European REACH legislation and subsequent legislation in EU Member States, which could ease this difficulty.[78] This Regulation is crucial to toxic torts as it assesses the human and environmental impacts of chemicals and the information compiled by virtue of the accumulation of these assessments will form a vast database of scientific and technical data. This means that, with ease of access to such information, issues and difficulties of causation for future harms should be alleviated.

C. Legal Costs

There are a number of factors to be taken into account when accounting for costs in an MPA action, particularly for mass environmental harm. This reflects the MPA objective of fairness, according to which costs ought to be proportionately and reasonably incurred. They should also be proportionate and reasonable in amount to the value of the claim and to the importance of the matter to all parties, as we have seen in the discussion in chapter three. Depending on the system of determining legal costs, matters such as the skill, effort

[75] Henchy J. in *Hanrahan v Merck, Sharpe and Dohme* [1988] ILRM 629, [21].

[76] [2002] UKHL 22.

[77] It takes 25 to 50 years before symptoms of disease become evident.

[78] Regulation (EC) No 1907/2006 of the European Parliament and of the Council of 18 December 2006 concerning the Registration, Evaluation, Authorisation and Restriction of Chemicals (REACH), establishing a European Chemicals Agency, amending Directive 1999/45/EC and repealing Council Regulation (EEC) No 793/93 and Commission Regulation (EC) No 1488/94 as well as Council Directive 76/769/EEC and Commission Directives 91/155/EEC, 93/67/EEC, 93/105/EC and 2000/21/EC., OJ L 396, 30.12.2006.

and specialised knowledge of those involved may be taken into account. Another factor is obviously the amount of time spent working on the case by lawyers and other advisers. In England and Wales and Ireland, toxic tort litigation is generally extremely expensive as seen in *Graham & Graham v Rechem*. The defendant's costs were estimated at £4.5 million and the cost to the Legal Aid Board at £1.5 million.[79] Also, the potential costs to industry could be immense, as exemplified in the *Fairchild* ruling. In that case, Lord Justice Brooke in the Court of Appeal said that around 1,550 people a year are diagnosed with mesothelioma in the UK, of which about o1.500 cases are due to exposure to asbestos. Owing to the large number of potential claims, it has been estimated that this single ruling will lead to insurance claims of £6–8 billion over the next 20 years.[80] In England and Wales, fees may be on a 'no win, no fee basis'. However, previously, there was a success fee payable by the defendant that was not covered by the claimant's damages (this fee was effectively half of the amount of potential recovery in cases). Costs for the litigation of individual cases are often in line with damages but, for a GLO, these are usually much higher than normal and it may be possible to argue for the payment of significantly higher costs because of factors such as the complexity of the case. New legislation that came into effect in April 2013 means that the success fee is no longer payable by the defendant.[81] Also, the proportionality rule has been tightened up and will be applied strictly.[82] Insurance in England and Wales is 'after-the-event' and this means that the loser pays the winner's costs. Such costs can be very high. The loser pays the insurance premium and the cost of this can also be very high. In cases that involve injury, one-way cost shifting applies. This means that when the defendant loses, he pays the claimant's costs; when the claimant loses, each side bears its own costs. This is a factor in environmental cases, as costs will not apply if there is no proven injury. Therefore, if claimants are going to litigate environmental cases, they have to do so without insurance.

D. Latency

The cases discussed in relation to asbestos exposure highlight another common challenge of toxic tort cases, which is latency. There is often a delay between the exposure to the toxin and subsequent development of any disease, injury or symptoms. This is due to these being latent and therefore not obvious for a delayed period. This can cause difficulty for both plaintiffs and defendants, as it can be very difficult to assess harm in such situations. In the US, courts have recognised the possibility of two types of disease: one acute and the other chronic, and they have created a so-called 'two-disease' rule to deal with this, permitting a more orderly litigation process.[83] This is a very efficient managerial tool for toxic tort

[79] [1994] Env LR 158. This case is believed to have been the longest civil trial in English history.

[80] According to the BBC: http://news.bbc.co.uk/2/hi/health/1991023.stm. Furthermore, it is estimated that approximately 13 Britons die every day from asbestos-related diseases, and the rate of deaths is increasing.

[81] The Legal Aid, Sentencing and Punishment of Offenders (LASPO) Act 2012 introduces a wide range of reforms to the justice system as well as delivering structural reforms to the administration of legal aid. Pt 2 makes changes to the funding and costs of civil cases.

[82] This is as a result of the Rome II Regulation, (EC) No 864/2007. This is an EU Regulation regarding the conflict of laws on the law applicable to non-contractual obligations. From 11 January 2009, the Regulation created a harmonised set of rules within the EU to govern choice of law in civil and commercial matters (subject to certain exclusions) concerning non-contractual obligations, including specific rules for tort and specific categories of tort.

[83] *Mauro v Raymark Indus Inc*, 561 A.2d 257 (NJ 1989).

cases. For example, in cases of injury resulting from asbestos exposure, the right has been recognised to bring a second action for cancer after prior recovery for asbestosis caused by the same exposure to asbestos. This allows a victim to sue for later developing cancer even if she was previously aware of a separate injury caused by the exposure (such as asbestosis). This is instead of forcing one lawsuit for all the claims at an early stage, which would require suits for 'increased risk' of future harms under an inflexible statute of limitations. They have also begun to allow current actions for medical monitoring if these would mitigate possible future harm.[84]

The English asbestos cases also exemplify the challenges presented by latency. For example, the case of *Margertson and Handcock v JW Roberts Ltd*, in which the plaintiffs developed mesothelioma from exposure to asbestos while playing in the defendant's factory yard during childhood.[85] In that case, it was many years before the illness manifested itself in the victims as adults. JWR was found liable on the grounds that the risks associated with asbestos exposure had been known since 1925 and since the children were allowed to play in the immediate vicinity of the factory, it was foreseeable that they would be exposed to the risk of pulmonary illness. This case was also significant because it was the first time that the duty of care has been extended, beyond employees, so as to encompass those immediately outside the factory walls. In another asbestos-related case that came before the House of Lords, *Barker v Corus*, latency presented a different challenge in attributing liability.[86] The key question in that case was whether, if one of the employers responsible for materially increasing the risk of harm had become insolvent, should the later, solvent, employers pick up the proportion for which that insolvent employer was responsible.

Ireland has experienced similar asbestos litigation in the decision of the Supreme Court in the case of *Fletcher v The Commissioners of Public Works*.[87] This case has significant implications for the many asbestos-related claims being pursued in Ireland. It remains to be seen how strictly this decision will be interpreted in subsequent cases, as the Supreme Court has already distinguished its earlier decision.[88] This case arose out of what was admitted to be the failure of the defendants as employers to take proper precautions for the safety of the plaintiff, Mr Fletcher. He had been employed for many years as a General Operative in government buildings. The trial judge found as a fact that he had inhaled very large quantities of asbestos dust over a number of years and was satisfied that the defendants were guilty of gross negligence. The medical evidence was that, although the plaintiff was exposed to the risk of developing asbestosis and mesothelioma, he had not contracted either disease and it was unlikely that he ever would. He was diagnosed as suffering from 'reactive anxiety neurosis'. The trial judge was satisfied that the plaintiff's psychiatric illness was the result of his exposure to asbestos dust and not his exposure to the knowledge of it. The defendants appealed the matter on the basis that the trial judge's determination that the plaintiff

[84] *Ayers v Township of Jackson* (n 45).

[85] Joined cases: *Hancock v JW Roberts Ltd; Hancock v T & N Plc* [1996] Env LR 4 (304), [1996] PIQR 358 CA.

[86] [2006] UKHL 20.

[87] Supreme Court, unreported, 21 February 2003.

[88] In the case of *Swaine v The Commissioners of Public Works* [2003] IESC 30 (2003). The facts in this case were similar to those in *Fletcher*, where the plaintiff had been exposed to the risk of fatal injury from breathing asbestos in the workplace over an extended period. In the High Court, O'Neill J had held the defendant guilty of 'negligence of the grossest kind', awarding him €45,000 plus €15,000 aggravated damages. The defendant appealed quantum but did not contest liability. The Supreme Court overturned the award of €15,000.

was entitled to recover damages in respect of psychiatric illness, when unaccompanied by any physical injury, was wrong in law. In the Supreme Court, the Chief Justice, Mr Ronan Keane, felt that important policy issues needed to be considered in deciding whether the plaintiff was entitled to recover damages for the impairment of his mental condition that had resulted from his exposure to the risk of contracting mesothelioma. He stated that the courts had to adopt a more circumspect approach to cases of psychiatric illness because it is less susceptible to precise diagnosis. More importantly, the Chief Justice referred to:

> The undesirability of awarding damages to plaintiffs who have suffered no physical injury and whose psychiatric condition is solely due to an unfounded fear of contracting a particular disease … should not be awarded damages by the law of tort.

The Chief Justice was also mindful of the implications for the health care field of a more relaxed rule in respect of recovery for psychiatric illness. He was accordingly satisfied that the law in that jurisdiction should not be extended by the courts to allow the recovery by plaintiffs of damages for psychiatric injury resulting from an irrational fear of contracting a disease because of their negligent exposure to health risks by their employers, where the risk is characterised by their medical advisers as very remote. Mr Fletcher was found to be at risk of possibly contracting mesothelioma at some stage in the future, following exposure to asbestos, but it was impossible to know when and if this would occur. Despite the fact that he could not recover compensation from his grossly negligent employer, it would make sense that he (1) would be entitled to financial assistance in defraying the costs of medical check-ups; and also (2) that such cost would be payable by the employer, for the purposes of deterrence. Medical monitoring, by regularly observing the condition of the plaintiff's health, if it had been available as a remedy, would have achieved both.

On a strict interpretation of the *Fletcher* judgment it would appear that if the plaintiff had exhibited even the most minor of physical symptoms of asbestos-related injury, such as slight throat or eye irritation, then he would have recovered damages both for his physical symptoms and his much more significant psychiatric injury. In this case, however, the illness the plaintiff was suffering was psychiatric, a 'reactive anxiety neurosis', and the courts decreed:

> The law in this jurisdiction should not be extended by the courts so as to allow the recovery by plaintiffs of damages for psychiatric injury resulting from an irrational fear of contracting a disease because of their negligent exposure to health risks by their employers where the risk was characterised by their medical advisors as remote.[89]

Had the plaintiff exhibited any physical symptoms as a result of the asbestos exposure, however, the Court would certainly have allowed his claim.

> That specific policy considerations that disputed the imposition of liability in 'fear of disease' cases included the undesirability of awarding damages to plaintiffs who had suffered no physical injury and whose psychiatric condition was solely due to an unfounded fear of contracting a particular disease and the implications for the health care field of a more relaxed rule as to recovery for psychiatric illness (threats of numerous large monetary awards coupled with the added cost of insuring against such liability).[90]

[89] *Fletcher* (n 88) 465.
[90] Ibid.

E. Environmental Justice Issues

Some of the themes of the environmental justice movement and its aims are relevant to environmental mass harm. This is evident especially in some of the barriers that exist in areas such as access to justice for this kind of harm.[91] Schlossberg defines environmental justice as 'justice on environmental issues among the human population'.[92] He asserts that justice is about distribution, but it is also about individual and community recognition, participation and functioning.[93] Procedural justice is defined as fair and equitable institutional processes of a State.[94] It is important to explain that participation is procedural justice.[95] This is because it requires facilities such as access to information, procedure for review and other mechanisms facilitating participation by means of access to justice.[96] Shelton's research discerns this and points in particular to the procedural dimension of justice such as arrangements for dispute settlement. This aspect of environmental justice research may support the argument that MPAs have a role to play in providing access to justice. It would appear that MPAs, as mechanisms that help to provide procedural justice, enable access to justice.

Numerous studies, including those undertaken by the US Environmental Protection Agency (EPA) have affirmed that low-income, minority communities bear a disproportionate burden of pollution.[97] The EPA has acknowledged that polluting industries, incinerators and hazardous waste dumps are most often located in predominantly poor or minority communities.[98] The type of environmental imbalance does not just relate to the location of industrial facilities and the disposal of hazardous wastes, in or near minority or poor communities. It also impacts on the resulting disproportionate burden carried by those communities in terms of adverse health and environmental impacts.[99] Usually these facilities will remain where they are despite these concerns. This means that residents of these toxic communities will continue to bear a greater burden of the health, economic and other quality of life risks and burdens associated with pollution. The ideals of environmental justice require that these victims have the ability to vindicate their personal injury and property damage claims, especially those arising from the proximity of minority communities to

[91] A Kanner, 'Environmental Justice, Torts and Causation' (1995) 34 *Washburn LJ* 505.

[92] D Schlossberg, *Defining Environmental Justice: Theories, Movements and Nature* (Oxford University Press, 2007) 7.

[93] Kanner, 'Environmental Justice, Torts and Causation' (n 91).

[94] Schlossberg, *Defining Environmental Justice* (n 92) 25.

[95] A Hardberger, 'Life Liberty, and the Pursuit of Water: Evaluating Water as a Human Right and the Duties and Obligations it Creates' (2005) 4 *Northwestern J Int'l Hum Rights* 342.

[96] See eg D Shelton, 'Human Rights, and Environmental Rights, and the Right to the Environment' (1991) *Stan J Int'l L* 103; D Shelton, 'Environmental Rights' in P Alston (ed), *Peoples' Rights* (Oxford University Press, 2001) 214 and 258; D Shelton, 'Environmental Justice in the Postmodern World' in K Bosselmann and B Richardson (eds) *Environmental Justice and Market Mechanisms: Key Challenges for Environmental Law and Policy* (Kluwer Law International, 1999) 23.

[97] Environmental Protection Agency, 'Environmental Equity: Reducing Risk for All Communities' (June 1992). This report examined whether there was evidence that racial minorities and low-income communities bear a higher environmental risk than the general population, and considered action that the EPA might take on any identified disparities. It concluded that racial minority and low-income populations experience higher than average exposures to selected air pollutants, hazardous waste facilities, contaminated fish and agricultural pesticides in the workplace.

[98] Ibid.

[99] Ibid.

hazardous facilities.[100] It is probable that many of these victims may have valid claims for illness such as cancer or neurological problems and for environmental restoration and nuisance. Although private law actions combined with political action can be highly effective in these situations, serious obstacles still remain to the full vindication of rights on behalf of minority communities.[101] Clear examples of these private law hurdles that such communities may encounter are evidenced by the problems encountered by lower socio-economic groups. Difficulties with cost and proof of causation present obstacles for these groups, and so raise environmental justice concerns. This is usually the most difficult and controversial issue. Variables such as plaintiffs' lifestyle, residence, and socio-economic background may affect the extent to which an illness can be explained. These, together with issues of choice and fault all require complex formulae to evaluate.[102] What is often not taken into account, however, is that disadvantaged groups frequently do not have the same chance to escape unhealthy occupational or physical environments. In this way, such plaintiffs' chance of achieving justice is impeded.[103] In the context of a lawsuit, a defendant, in trying to justify the different exposure levels of different population groups, may try to blame the differentials on the fault of the victim. Also, these issues are rarely addressed by epidemiological studies.[104] The usual problems that most toxic tort litigation presents for plaintiffs exist, such as the cost of expert evidence and the 'battle of experts'. These hurdles may be insurmountable for disadvantaged communities and are exemplified in occupational litigation where existing occupational data may understate the health problems of certain socio-economic groups, for example.[105] The difficulty of dealing with technical and scientific evidence, discussed previously, can also be particularly problematic, as data in relation to environmental pollution causing health problems of minority communities located near toxic sites is not well studied.[106]

In terms of environmental justice generally, it is notable that Kramer has searched for possible environmental justice considerations in Europe. He contrasts the European jurisprudence and debate on environmental justice against that of the US and submits that

[100] J Ebesson and JP Okawa, *Environmental Law and Justice in Context* (Cambridge University Press, 2009) propound that comprehending environmental law includes justice considerations. This literature informs the relationship between environmental law—where it overlaps with tort law—and justice. It explains that environmental law concepts may reveal 'disproportionate burdening (for certain groups) when these concepts are applied'.

[101] See eg Louisiana Advisory comm. to the US comm'n on civil rights, 'The Battle for Environmental Justice in Louisiana' (September 1993) 48, where residents used legal action to challenge industry on environmental problems. They did so without substantial support from civil rights or environmental groups and attorneys played a primary role in the resolution process.

[102] M Faure, *Tort Law and Economics* (2nd edn, Edward Elgar, 2009) ch 10, 'Environmental Liability' 1 *Encyclopedia of Law and Economics* 247.

[103] A number of jurisdictions have recognised that 'economic coercion' may vitiate the assumption of the risk defence, eg *Borel v Fibreboard Paper Prods Corp* 493 F2nd 1076 (5th Cir 1973).

[104] See generally D Barnes and J Conley, *Statistical Evidence in Litigation* (Little, Brown and Company 1986, supp 1989).

[105] A clear example of where this data was available is a US Public Health study of chromate workers that demonstrated that, as a group, they were 29 times more likely to die of respiratory cancer than non-chromate workers. The different effect on African Americans and whites is astounding however: whites' actual-to-expected respiratory cancer death was 14.29 as against 80.00 for African Americans; N Ashford, 'Crisis in the Workplace: Occupational Disease and Injury' Report to the Ford Foundation (1976); M Davis, 'Occupational Hazards and Black Workers' (1977) 6 (5) *Urban Health* 16–18.

[106] Minority groups and the disparate impact of discrimination claims and whether the environmental harm disproportionately impacted a distinguishable group are, however discussed in case law (eg *Hatton v United Kingdom* (2003) 37 EHRR 28 [11]–[28]). See generally Barnes and Conley, *Statistical Evidence in Litigation* (n 104).

there is no perception in Europe of problems that link the social status of certain groups to the concerns of environmental justice. In other words, that the race and poverty arguments that have characterised the US environmental justice debate have no distinct parallels in Europe. His views support allegations that the European and US interpretation of environmental justice are currently at odds.[107]

Another difficulty is that often in toxic tort cases where personal injuries are alleged, defendant polluters try to place the blame for illness on the lifestyle or behaviour of the victim (for example rates of smoking and poor diet might be more prevalent in certain socio-economic groups). Poorer victims and those of lower socio-economic backgrounds may be less able to deal with this defence tactic, even if they have access to good counsel. They also suffer stereotypical allegations of bringing lawsuits to 'get something for nothing' and arguments about lack of risk avoidance. Finally, those less well-off are unlikely to be able to afford to document or take steps to mitigate harm to their health and, even if they seek a remedy such as medical monitoring, they may be accused of using a lawsuit to get a form of free health insurance.[108] In these ways, the toxic tort claimants are themselves put on trial. These difficulties experienced by more disadvantaged plaintiffs and those from some minority backgrounds are a key concern of the environmental justice movement. An exploration of this movement is useful to help understand the use of MPAs for environmental mass harm.[109]

On a constructive note, as there is huge reliance on reporting requirements and data recording in the area of public environmental law regulation and this information is usually, and increasingly, publicly available, this is likely to impact on the litigation of toxic torts in a positive way. For example, most companies will wish to avoid litigation and so will act to address problems. Furthermore, when litigation is required, it will be based on this accurate recorded data. These factors should assist in proving liability and causation. Overall, it is clear that issues of environmental justice are not just confined to racial concerns. As has been shown, scientific evidence is crucial in any toxic tort litigation. As a result of improved communications between victims and public information about pollution, there are changes to be expected in cases such as toxic torts. Kanner opines, however, that in some cases, political solutions may be more successful than trying to find a solution through litigation.[110] Despite this, he recommends that litigation should not be excluded as

[107] L Kramer, *Environmental Law and Justice in Context* (Cambridge University Press, 2009) ch 10.

[108] Medical monitoring, as explained, is the observation of a disease, condition or one or several medical parameters over time and will be discussed in more detail shortly. eg cases involving alleged long-term injury or diseases such as asbestos will require victims to be assessed periodically over an extended period.

[109] For further discussion on the litigation experience of environmental justice in practice, see H Osofsky, 'Learning from Environmental Justice: a New Model for International Environmental Rights' (2005) 24 *Stan Env'l LJ* 71. He discusses the complexity of legally characterising environmental harm to humans, focusing on human rights and he examines cases from the European Court of Human Rights, such as *Lopez Ostra v Spain* (1995) 20 EHRR 277. He draws on US environmental justice litigation approaches to create a model for deconstructing environmental harm to humans. In his view, since the advent of the environmental justice movement in the early-1980s, US lawyers and courts have struggled with how to address disproportionate environmental harm to humans.

[110] In Emelle, Alabama, site of the largest toxic waste dump in the US (black civil rights activists of the Minority Peoples Council and white environmentalists of Alabamians for a Clean Environment joined forces to work on the local hazardous waste problem—not a small point given the history of race relations on Alabama's black belt); R Bullard and B Wright, 'The Quest for Environmental Equity: Mobilizing the Black Community for Social Change' (1990) 3 *Race, Poverty and Env't* 5–16.

a remedy for toxic torts.[111] It is a challenge for the civil justice systems to respond to these developments, particularly in a way that meets the objectives for MPAs.[112] It would appear that it is therefore important to examine the ways in which mechanisms such as MPAs can help in providing procedural justice to those in need of such collective redress tools, as well as helping judges to manage the resultant, often unwieldy, litigation. The environmental justice movement's concerns raise challenges for legal systems of how best to achieve these goals.[113]

F. Other Issues that May Arise in Mass Environmental Harm Litigation

i. Jurisdiction

Jurisdictional issues were experienced in *Lubbe & Ors v Cape Plc* and can prove difficult to overcome.[114] This was a conflict of laws case, which is also highly significant for the question of lifting the corporate veil in relation to tort victims (which will be discussed below). In this case it was alleged and accepted by the House of Lords that, in principle, it is possible to show that a parent company owes a direct duty of care in tort to anybody injured by a subsidiary company in a group. Mr Lubbe was injured at work while manufacturing asbestos for a South African subsidiary company of the UK parent company, Cape Plc. The South African subsidiary was insolvent and Cape Plc had no assets in South Africa. His case was one of 3,000 claims. He alleged that the parent company, Cape Plc, owed a direct duty of care in tort to him as a worker in the company group. Cape Plc was applying to stay the actions on the basis of *forum non conveniens*, submitting that they were an abuse of process on grounds that intention to launch an MPA was not disclosed to the Court. Mr Lubbe argued that the claims should not be stayed since, in South Africa, the legal aid necessary to continue the claim had been withdrawn, no contingency fee arrangement was available and no other source of funding would be available. The Court of Appeal refused Mr Lubbe's arguments and continued the stay, and Mr Lubbe appealed to the House of Lords. The House of Lords held unanimously that although South Africa was the more appropriate

[111] Kanner (n 91).

[112] See further D Spence in *Enforcement of Environmental Law: The Case for Reform* (Law Reform Committee of the Law Society of Ireland, 2007) ch 1, where she discusses other patterns of punitive enforcement. Her conclusions relate both to MPAs and environmental mass harm, available at: www.lawsociety.ie/Documents/committees/lawreform/Envir%20Report.pdf. Spence discusses various methods by which environmental law may be better enforced by citizens and the State in Ireland and assesses weaknesses in current enforcement mechanisms, such as issues of accessibility and cost. She suggests the introduction of a number of recommendations, including mechanisms for citizen enforcement.

[113] J Steele's research in this area is concerned with justice as it relates to environmental decision-making, participation and remedies; J Steele, 'Participation and Deliberation in Environmental Law: Exploring a Problem-solving Approach' *Oxford Journal of Legal Studies* (Oxford University Press, 2001) 415–22. She assesses justice on a national, European and international level and propounds that issues of liability are principally concerned with attribution of the costs of pollution and that this should be on the basis of the polluter pays principle. Her view is that remediation costs alone do not provide adequate compensation. Steele has written widely that participation in environmental law is a key element in access to justice and remedies and she advocates a 'problem-solving approach'; J Steele,' Remedies and Remediation: Foundational Issues in Environmental Liability' (1995) 58 *MLR* 615–36; T Jewell and J Steele, *Law in Environmental Decision-Making: National, European, and International Perspectives* (Clarendon Press, 1998).

[114] [2000] UKHL 41.

forum for hearing the claim, it was highly likely that legal representation for the claimants would be unavailable. The expert evidence suggested a denial of justice would result, exacerbated by the lack of procedures in South Africa to accommodate MPAs. (This is further evidence that a lack of MPA procedure impedes access to procedural justice.) This meant that lifting the stay was appropriate and the action continued in the English courts. In this case, although the claims were against UK-domiciled companies, it was possible for the defendant to seek a stay based on *forum non conveniens* for five years. Similarly, in the case of *Connelly v RTZ Corporation Plc and Another UK*, the House of Lords ruled that a former employee of an African subsidiary of Rio Tinto Zinc (RTZ), the mining conglomerate, who claimed he was poisoned by uranium dust, had the right to sue for compensation in the English courts.[115] Fortunately, argument as to forum is no longer valid if advanced by an EU domiciled company.[116] Since this forum difficulty has been eased the incentives for law firms to take on such cases have therefore been increased.[117]

ii. Corporate Veil

This was another key factor in *Lubbe & Ors v Cape Plc*. There it was argued that a parent company was not liable because the corporate veil needed to be lifted in order to confer liability. The Court said that it was a question of whether the parent company was in control of the subsidiary. It was held that it was and that it had exercised this control negligently. The parent company was held liable because it owes a duty of care to a subsidiary company. The full rule was decreed to be:

> Whether a parent company which is proved to exercise de facto control over the operations of a (foreign) subsidiary and which knows, through the directors, that those operations involve risks to the health of workers employed by the subsidiary and/or persons in the vicinity of its factory or other business premises, owes a duty of care to those workers and/ or other persons in relation to the control which it exercises over and the advice which it gives to the subsidiary company.

A similar issue has arisen in Ireland in relation to tort-type statutory liability under the *Waste Management Act.*[118] *Wicklow County Council v Fenton* case[119] constituted a landmark judgment in which Court lifted the 'corporate veil' of a domestic company in order to give effect to the polluter pays principle. This principle of EU law is found in the Waste Framework Directive. The Waste Management Acts subsequently transposed this Directive. The Court interpreted sections 57 and 58 of the Waste Management Acts in a purposive way, to give full effect to the Directive and to the polluter pays principle. The Court held that it was necessary to lift the 'corporate veil' and impose personal liability on directors of a limited liability company for any shortfall in the remediation costs which the company

[115] [1997] UKHL 30; [1999] CLC 533.

[116] As a result of the Brussels II Regulation (EC) No 2201/2003 on conflict of law issues in family law between Member States, esp those related to divorce, child custody and international child abduction. It replaces Convention Council Regulation (EC) No 1347/2000 of 29 May 2000 on the jurisdiction, recognition and enforcement of judgments in matrimonial matters and in matters of parental responsibility for joint children.

[117] *Connelly v RTZ Corporation Plc and Another UK* [1997] UKHL 30. The Law Lords ruled that a former employee of an African subsidiary of Rio Tinto Zinc (RTZ), the mining conglomerate, who claimed he was poisoned by uranium dust, had the right to sue for compensation in the English courts.

[118] 1996 (as amended).

[119] [2002] 4 IR 44.

might not be able to meet by way of so-called 'fall-back orders'. The Court found that it was appropriate to do so, even where the directors were not directly involved in the relevant activities, to ensure that an innocent party, the community or State would not be required to step in to pay the remediation costs. In a subsequent case however, *Environmental Protection Agency v Nephin Trading Limited & Ors*,[120] the High Court refused to disregard the company's limited liability protection to impose clean-up costs on directors personally under section 57 of the Waste Management Act. In this case, regarding a landfill site polluting the surrounding area, the EPA sought 'fall-back' orders, that is to impose personal liability on directors for the costs of environmental clean-up, where the company did not have adequate funds to pay. The Court upheld the separate entity division between the company and its directors. In contrast to this, in the case of *John Ronan and Sons v Clean Build Limited (in liquidation) and Others*,[121] Judge Clarke held five former directors and shareholders of a liquidated company personally liable for the costs of remediating a site on which significant quantities of construction waste had been allowed to accumulate. This decision confirms that directors and shareholders of companies may be held personally and independently liable for environmental pollution. The Court avoided the need to decide whether it preferred the reasoning of Mr Justice O'Sullivan in the *Fenton* case, or Mr Justice Edwards in the *Nephin* case and so the conflict over whether the High Court has the inherent power to make a fall-back order against a director or shareholder remains unresolved. The Court did, however, confirm that a director or shareholder might be held personally liable where it is found to be *independently liable* under the Waste Management Acts for the environmental pollution in question, and that the polluter pays principle is a relevant consideration in the context of civil environmental enforcement. The case is also significant because it would appear to be the first occasion that a person other than a local authority or the EPA has taken direct civil enforcement action under sections 57 and 58 of the Waste Management Acts.

4. Novel Remedies for Environmental Mass Harm

The difficulties created by the features of environmental mass harm and that are encountered in the conduct of such litigation highlight the need for some novel remedies.

A. Interim Measures—such as Medical Monitoring (Emergence in the US)

Tort law is mainly concerned with remedying actual harm and is rarely successfully used to prevent harm or increased risk.[122] Of course, tortious remedies may include *quia timet* injunctions where, for example, a community may fear potential adverse effects from the construction of a new development. A court may give declaratory relief by way of a *quia timet* injunction to prevent such harm arising. Where there has been environmental harm

[120] [2011] IEHC 67 (High Court, Edwards J, 3 March 2011).
[121] [2011] IEHC 300.
[122] See Kanner, 'Emerging Conceptions of Latent Personal Injuries in Toxic Tort Litigation' (n 57).

and a victim has suffered actual injury, they have a greater likelihood of success in a private tort action than where they are merely at increased risk of harm.[123] There are, however, cases where interim measures, such as medical monitoring, have been granted to victims at higher risk of injury in the future.[124] Medical monitoring is the observation of a disease, condition or one or several medical parameters over time.[125] It is based on the idea that, as a victim of wrongful toxic exposure, a plaintiff is entitled to medical examinations and frequent testing to detect the development of any future illness that may be caused as a result, in order that such early detection may allow early medical treatment to minimise the severity of the injury. It is available as a remedy even if the risk being claimed may be speculative, whether or not the class members placed at risk were actually injured, and the cost is borne by the wrongdoer.[126] For example, cases involving alleged long-term injury or diseases, such as those resulting from exposure to asbestos, will require victims to be assessed periodically over an extended period. The general remedy of medical monitoring originated in US law, where it has been permitted for a long time[127] and it is expanding into the toxic tort domain.[128] It has been invoked there to deal with public health problems caused by issues including hazardous waste. Such pollution can result in a range of indeterminate health risks as well as other harms. It has become common practice that the cost of remedying and mitigating this type of harm should be borne by the wrongdoers responsible. The government alone cannot administer this resolution and, as a result, both Congress and the courts have endorsed the right of victims to pursue redress. This may be in order to achieve compensation for harm suffered or to deter wrongful behaviour. Medical monitoring may also be awarded even in circumstances where there has not yet been any evidence of physical injury. Most courts have dispensed with the rules requiring actual physical harm and physical impact to be shown when dealing with a claim for fear of future illness once there are sufficient grounds to believe that the victim's claim is genuine.[129] Victims may still bring a claim later even if they have been engaged in prior litigation based on the same tortious behaviour.[130] Three elements are required for medical monitoring, according to the case of *Merry v Westinghouse Elec Corp*:[131] (1) exposure to hazardous substances; (2) potential for injury; and (3) the need for early detection and treatment. The main legislation providing for medical monitoring is CERCLA, specifically section 107 of CERCLA, which recognises medical and environmental surveillance as compensable response costs in a lawsuit.[132] These 'response costs' are preventative. They are not the same as traditional damages, which are compensatory.

In recent decades, the UK has experienced an increase in toxic tort litigation and a growing body of case law shows how the law is evolving in response to this, for example in the field of asbestos.[133] This remedy of medical monitoring could be of use in such cases.

[123] Ibid.

[124] eg *Ayers v Township of Jackson* (n 45); Kanner, 'Medical Monitoring: State and Federal Perspectives' (n 125).

[125] For further reading on medical monitoring see A Kanner, 'Medical Monitoring: State and Federal Perspectives' (1989) 2 *Tul Envt'l LJ* 1.

[126] *Friends For All Children, Inc v Lockhead Aircraft Corp*, 746 F 2d 816 (DC Cir 1984).

[127] See eg Kanner (n 57) 366.

[128] eg *Ayers v Township of Jackson*, 106 NJ 557, 579–608, 525 A.2d 287, 298–313 (1987).

[129] eg *Hagerty v L & L Marine Servs, Inc*, 788 F 2d 315 (5th Cir 1986).

[130] *Mauro v Raymark Indus Inc*, 561 A.2d 257 (NJ 1989) [19].

[131] 684 F Supp 847, 850 (MD Pa 1988) (citing *Habitats Against Landfill Toxicants v City of York*).

[132] CERCLA legislation includes Superfund, established by 42 USC 9631 (1982).

[133] eg the English case of *Fairchild v Glenhaven Funeral Services* (n 71).

Medical monitoring could also have been useful in the Irish case of *Fletcher v Office of Public Works*.[134] If jurisdictions could adapt and adopt a remedy such as medical monitoring to prevent or mitigate further injury when dealing with mass harm toxic tort litigation, it could greatly assist both victims of toxic tort harm and also collective redress for such cases where mass harm occurs. The successful use of medical monitoring in the US as a remedy may be indicative of the effectiveness of MPAs for mass environmental harm actions. It may have arisen by virtue of these or perhaps mass harm actions are more suitable for granting these kinds of remedies. At present there is a lacuna for such remedies in Ireland, as the case of *Fletcher* indicates. Irish courts have not yet been innovative in granting these kinds of remedies and it is unlikely that they will be introduced any time soon. This is probably because the courts may fear the opening of the proverbial litigation floodgates, were such remedies to be afforded. However, as shown, a remedy such as medical monitoring would have addressed many of the policy concerns raised in *Fletcher*.

B. Acute versus Chronic Environmental Harm and Novel Remedies

It is important to distinguish the type of harm in question in environmental mass harm cases and to tailor the remedy sought to it. This is because the range of damage can vary greatly; for example, the type of harm emanating from an old waste disposal site versus an incident with a nuclear reactor. While the usual tort law remedies such as damages and or an injunction are likely to be pursued by the environmental mass harm victims, there are some remedies that are quite specific in relation to this harm, for example the remedy of medical monitoring, as seen in the US especially. Medical monitoring and injunctions may be more suitable remedies for harm resulting from creeping disasters, and remedies such as compensation may be more appropriate for single event disasters and other mass exposure cases. This is a key factor in the potential litigation of environmental mass harm. Together with traditional tort law remedies, more creative innovations may be required in granting alternative relief that may be more suited to toxic torts, particularly in an environmental mass harm context.

C. Equitable Relief and Problems with Legal Restitution

Obviously the primary aims of penalising those who pollute are deterrence and compensation. Often courts use a legal restitution approach in order to achieve these aims when awarding damages for harm to property. However, Kanner argues that this approach is inadequate on its own, for several reasons.[135] First, it does not provide deterrence. This is because, with environmental damage, often the cost to restore the land to its previous condition is greater than the diminution in its value, so instead, courts have commonly made polluters pay what was the fair market value for the land before the damage. This is often ineffective as a deterrent as it may be cheaper to pollute and to pay this than to properly

[134] Supreme Court, unreported, 21 February 2003.

[135] A Kanner, 'Equity in Toxic Tort Litigation: Unjust Enrichment and the Poor' (2004) 26 *Law and Policy* 209–30.

dispose of waste. By doing so, the polluter may be unjustly enriched by the cost saving of paying compensation to the victim rather than the cost of treating the pollution. This is exacerbated at mass level as greater harm can result, causing injury to more victims and further need for compensation. Secondly, this approach fails to account for market costs versus social value because it is impossible to put a true cost on environmental damage when the value of land is placed in the context of an entire ecosystem. Thirdly, this approach creates economic incentives for polluters to locate their polluting activities on low-value land, usually located near to the poorest members of society (resulting in a phenomenon known as 'environmental classism or racism'). The environmental justice movement argues strongly that these victims lack political power and financial strength to fight as victims of such pollution.[136] The legal restitution model creates incentives for industry both to pollute and to concentrate pollution in areas populated by such disenfranchised poor communities and in these ways, gives greater weight to the right of the wealthy to enjoy their property than to the poor.[137] This legal restitution model also clearly delivers an outcome that conflicts with the polluter pays principle. Such problems are exacerbated in cases of mass harm as a greater number of victims are affected.

Kanner advocates that an approach based on the equitable doctrine of unjust enrichment would be a preferable solution instead.[138] Under such a solution, a polluter should pay at least the amount saved by polluting if that amount is greater than the diminished value of the land. This would result in the enforcement of environmental policies and also reduces the risk of environmental classism. There are three remedies for unjust enrichment: the use of a constructive trust, the equitable lien and subrogation. It is at the discretion of a judge to use whichever remedy he or she feels is most appropriate in each case and, for environmental pollution, an equitable trust is usually the most appropriate solution. For example, a portion of the profits made by a polluting company could be held on trust for members of the community to compensate them for the diminution in value in the value of their land. Taking a case of where a polluter profited by US$10 million by not installing pollution abatement technology, they would be trustees to this amount for the pollution victims. The unjust enrichment model, in general, has the advantage of removing the incentive to target pollution at lower-valued lands (and the related environmental classism). Unfortunately, polluters often believe that they are less likely to be 'caught' polluting in areas where people have less income as such harm is likely to receive less publicity and court pressure to resolve the problem. Also, poorer communities are usually less informed about their legal rights, more pessimistic about the possibility of their problems being resolved by official bodies and they feel less empowered by the legal system than more affluent citizens. They are, therefore, less likely to take legal action.[139] Another factor is that deterrence should be the primary aim of environmental protection because, as previously stated, the value of land is inestimable and, if it is contaminated, the long-term damage is likely to be grave and unquantifiable, probably affecting more victims. There has been little research, however, on

[136] R Bullard, *Dumping in Dixie: Race, Class and Environmental Quality* (Westview Press, 2000); J Colopy, 'The Road Less Travelled: Pursuing Environmental Justice Through Title VI of the Civil Rights Act' (1994) 13 *Stan Env'l LJ* 125–89; M Knorr, 'Environmental Injustice: Inequities between Empirical Data and Federal, State Legislative and Judicial Responses' (1997) 6 *Univ Baltimore J Env'l L* 71–106.

[137] Osofsky, 'Learning from Environmental Justice (n 109).

[138] Kanner, 'Equity in Toxic Tort Litigation' (n 135) 222.

[139] Ibid.

how the enforcement of one particular group of private legal remedies may be more effective than another in terms of preventing harm or compensating victims in a way that allows them to restore their lives and environment. Restitution and equitable unjust enrichment may not be the panacea to all these problems, as they have inherent shortcomings, and so are not the perfect deterrent.[140] These theories of restitution and unjust enrichment are factors that ought to be taken into account when trying to provide remedies for mass harm. They influence the behaviour of potential polluters and wrongdoers and the punishment that they may face for such harm, as well as the ability of victims to pursue collective redress.

5. Solutions that MPAs May Offer for Environmental Mass Harm

This chapter has explored the phenomenon of environmental mass harm.[141] It has demonstrated that such harm comes in various forms, ranging from environmental disasters causing pollution, to environmental nuisances.[142] It is important to be aware that the routes to collective redress for such harm may take varying guises. The role of public law and regulation play a primary role in this, as do alternatives to litigation such as ADR and other techniques. Environmental enforcement through tort law also has a key role to play in overall environmental enforcement and in delivering collective redress. Environmental mass harm is an area that has a number of distinct features that can present difficult challenges for both its victims and for those endeavouring to manage the legal resolution of such harm. Examples of the issues that may arise include difficulties relating to causation, evidential complexity and latency. This research has analysed these distinctive features and some of the possible responses to them, including novel remedies that have emerged to deal with environmental mass harm. Unlike individual personal injuries, it is often the case that numerous victims are affected by exposure to such hazards and perhaps hundreds or thousands of people may be exposed. Large environmental and toxic tort cases entail challenges for litigants and judges alike due to the complexity and cost of technical evidence. The collective treatment of environmental mass harm cases may alleviate some

[140] First, a polluter may entirely evade justice for his behaviour. eg a polluter may still choose to pollute and take a chance that he will not be sued. There are many reasons why this can happen and there are fewer lawsuits than there are incidents of pollution: lack of experienced contingency fee attorneys with sufficient means to take cases; cover- ups and lack of information; lack of political organisation; lack of faith by landowners in government agencies to assist them etc. Secondly, even if a lawsuit is taken, plaintiffs may fail due to under-funding or inexperience of lawyers or their lawyers may prefer to settle the case before trial. Thirdly, some judges may be conservative and pro-industry and may use judicial rules to deny a plaintiff a jury. Fourthly, even a jury trial does not guarantee compensation, so this may further incentivise pollution. Also, some newer jurisprudence allows a judge to eliminate scientific evidence before it is even heard by jury. This effectively gives the decision-making power to the judge (see eg *Daubert v Merrell Dow Pharmaceuticals* (n 48). There have also been attempts by the US Chamber of Commerce to have all class actions tried in federal courts rather than by the more plaintiff-friendly state judges.

[141] This research will focus in particular on the possibilities for use of MPAs in common law jurisdictions and will not deal in detail with civil law jurisdictions, for reasons of space and the major procedural differences that exist between the two groups. Civil law jurisdictions and various common law jurisdictions will, however, be referred to for the purposes of illustration.

[142] eg noise from wind turbines or airports.

of the difficulties in these cases. Environmental mass harm presents typical examples of circumstances in which the handling of multiple claims can give rise to common or related issues of fact or law and the clustering of such claims strengthens individual claims. As both *Corby* and *Buncefield* showed, claimants in mass environmental harm cases can benefit from efficient case management. This may be through the use of GLO or creative case management, particularly for fact management.[143] *Corby*, for example, demonstrated how the obstacles of mass harm litigation that may confound individuals could sometimes be overcome as part of a group action.

As a case study, environmental mass harm illustrates how challenging mass harm litigation can be. Therefore, there is a need for management mechanisms to provide procedural justice and to enhance the overall management of such litigation. MPAs can have effective use in helping to ease some of the difficulties that those seeking environmental mass harm collective redress may encounter. For example, the class action law in Portugal expressly provides for its use to preserve environmental heritage and other matters. In Sweden, the class action procedure has been used to sue for environmental harm, such as noise pollution caused by airports that irritated inhabitants of surrounding neighborhoods. In Spain, there are some tools for collective action and an example is that of an environmental class action taken when the ship *Prestige* spilled oil off the coast of Galicia and the Spanish Government brought a criminal action and distributed compensation to fisherman. For environmental mass harm, instead of people suing individually, it would appear that it might be beneficial, in terms of access to justice and procedural justice, for them to join together in an environmental MPA. There are common liability issues (specifically environmental harm), common causation issues (also specific to environmental harm) and damage and so these issues are suited to collective treatment.

Also, for judges trying to manage complex environmental mass harm litigation, MPAs can be a helpful managerial device. However, in jurisdictions such as Canada, there has been limited class action activity in the area of environmental law.[144] Therefore, it seems that even though some environmental cases may be well suited to an MPA format, there is no guarantee that such cases will be certified as suitable for this in jurisdictions where such mechanisms exist.[145] The reality is that there is not a huge likelihood that environmental claims will be brought as collective actions, largely because, as identified at the outset of this chapter, first, the environment does not fit naturally within the framework that is traditionally recognised for the protection of private rights. Secondly, predominantly public authorities play a primary role. Thirdly, as we have seen, there are lots of difficulties with private enforcement (such as complex and conflicting expert evidence, scientific uncertainty, vast

[143] Fact management in group actions is one complexity, as is the assessment of quantum for loss of amenity. In cases such as these there can be hundreds of individual cases which all raise the same issues. Fact management is therefore complex but crucial. The challenge is to ensure that the claims are assessed efficiently, economically and proportionately; J Thornton, 'Group Actions for Private Nuisance: Fact Management and Assessing Quantum for Loss of Amenity' e-law November 2012, available at: www.lexology.com/library/detail.aspx?g=c022102a-ac8d-4b25-9f5c-32cafd1d2f1a.

[144] This is largely due to the difficulties encountered in the certification of such cases. This will be discussed further in ch 6 on collective redress in Canada.

[145] eg pollution claims usually require extensive and expensive expert evidence of cause and effect. Further, potentially large groups of persons might be adversely affected by a contaminating event, such as the release of a noxious gas cloud from an industrial facility or the pollution of a river with toxic effluents.

amounts of information, hence inherent uncertainty of outcomes, and huge costs and cost risks). Also, we have seen that, following Superfund, academic commentators concluded almost unanimously that tort law was not equipped to address the problems of modern pollution and torts. This seems to undermine any role for MPAs in the environmental mass harm sector. MPAs may have the potential to deter and affect behaviour but if they are not very suitable for mass environmental harm cases then they may not have huge impact in this regard. An important remedy for such cases to provide would be the obligation to repair the harm and to therefore restore the status quo to how it would have been were it not for the harm experienced. This could be achieved by mass litigation through the use of clean-up orders and similar provisions.

The use of MPA mechanisms and case management as a route to collective redress for environmental mass harm will be examined in particular in later chapters in light of the experience of a selection of common law jurisdictions. This examination will focus particularly on the US and England and Wales in separate chapters. We have seen the limited use of MPAs for environmental mass harm in Canada as they are unlikely to be certified there. It would appear that the findings for environmental mass harm seem to be very different from other mass harms. As this discussion has shown, environmental mass harm has various complexities and peculiarities that render it difficult for individuals to benefit from MPA treatment, as compared to other areas of mass harm (such as mass harm resulting in 'scattered damages', consumer mass harm, competition law infringements) that lend themselves to resolution through collective treatment. As for solutions that MPAs may offer for environmental mass harm, the evidence in this chapter would appear to suggest the conclusion that MPAs might be a largely illusory tool for remedying such harm.

Part II

Comparative Law Experience of Selected Common Law Jurisdictions and Europe

5

US Collective Redress

1. US Litigation Landscape

The US has been the forerunner in collective redress developments and an analysis of this experience is essential to any discussion of MPAs. There, the most well-known litigation procedure for aggregating large numbers of similar claims is undoubtedly that of the class action, such as may be brought under Rule 23 of the Federal Rules of Civil Procedure (FRCP). The majority of this US discussion will focus on such actions. It is important, however, to also outline the various other US aggregative mechanisms in order to fully describe US MPA litigation. Before examining US practice, a summary of the US legal system's federal and state court system may be useful.

A. US Federal and State Court System

The US is obviously a common law jurisdiction. There is a very important support role played by procedural and substantive law, which is found in the provisions of state and federal legislation. Major civil and criminal cases are heard in the trial-level courts of general jurisdiction in the individual states and in the federal system. There are also specialised courts of limited jurisdiction. The federal court system comprises trial courts (district courts), intermediate appellate courts and a supreme court. There are 94 district courts, 12 geographically defined circuit courts of appeal and a further thirteenth with specialist jurisdiction over administrative law and intellectual property.[1] These courts' decisions may be appealed to the US Supreme Court and heard at its discretion.[2] Federal courts principally deal with disputes of a federal nature. They may also hear state law claims in two situations: first, they may exercise 'supplemental jurisdiction' over a state law claim that is connected to a federal question.[3] Secondly, even where there is no federal question, the district court may hear any case where the litigants are from different states.[4] This is significant as it permits the federal courts to hear common law claims such as those based on tort.[5] The state

[1] Each circuit includes from 3 to 10 states.

[2] Note this jurisdiction is based on the discretionary writ of certiorari so the court only hears a small percentage of appeal cases.

[3] 28 USC § 1339.

[4] 28 USC § 1332.

[5] Federal law does contain a limited range of common law; it does not extend to claims such as contract and tort law.

court system is very similar to the federal system. Also, like the federal courts, state courts may hear 'mixed cases' involving both state and federal issues. In the civil courts of general jurisdiction, the role played by judges has traditionally been limited to ruling on pre-trial motions and overseeing how trials are conducted. Juries are usually used to decide questions of fact. Overall, trials are relatively rare and settlements are undoubtedly the most common way in which a case is concluded.

There has unquestionably been heated, ongoing debate about the scope and application of class actions in the US.[6] In some states there have been moves to restrain the use of mass consolidations and other large-scale aggregation procedures.[7] While it is unlikely that any new forms of collective litigation are going to be introduced in the near future, it is possible that the forms currently used may experience considerable modification.[8]

B. Important Features of US Litigation

From a comparative perspective, the lessons to be learnt from the US experience must be qualified by the significant differences in the way that litigation is financed and conducted there compared with other common law jurisdictions. First, in a civil case in the US, litigants have a constitutionally protected right to a jury trial. Plaintiffs tend to prefer this route because of the prospect of potentially high damages awards rather than opting for a bench trial. Jury trials, with their prospect of high punitive damages, may be perceived to incentivise class actions. Secondly, the costs regime of the US dictates that generally each side pays their own costs, so the defeated party is not liable for the costs of the winning party. Normally each side in a lawsuit is liable for its own legal costs, regardless of the result of the case.[9] Legal fees may be based on an hourly fee rate or they may be based on contingency fees (whereby the lawyer's payment is conditional on a successful outcome and calculated on a percentage of the amount awarded). This system allows plaintiffs to enter litigation without the threat of liability for costs and litigation expenses. Contingency fees are the principal method of securing representation for plaintiffs who have limited financial resources. They could also be based on a flat fee. Another option is a 'settlement-value only' action whereby a lawyer chooses a nominal plaintiff in the expectation that the defendant will settle in order to avoid litigation. However there have been allegations that these devices promote 'entrepreneurial' lawyer practice. Lawyers in the US have a very strong *pro bono* culture and this has enabled many class actions, especially in advancing civil rights. It is rare that there is public financing of litigation or third-party funding. Thirdly,

[6] eg A Miller, 'Of Frankenstein Monsters and Shining Knights: Myth, Reality, and the "Class Action Problem"' (1979) 92 *Harv L Rev* 664; D Hensler and others, *Class Action Dilemmas: Pursuing Public Goals for Private Gain* (RAND Institute, 2000); D Hensler and M Peterson, 'Understanding Mass Personal Injury Litigation: A Socio-Legal Analysis' (1993) 59 *Brooklyn L Rev* 961; M Galanter, 'Why the "Haves" Come Out Ahead: Speculations on the Limits of Legal Change' (1974) 9 *Law & Soc'y Rev* 95; D Hensler, 'Has the Fat Lady Sung? The Future of Mass Toxic Tort Litigation' (2007) 26 *Rev Litig* 883.

[7] See N Pace, 'Group and Aggregate Litigation in the United States' in D Hensler, C Hodges and M Tulibacka (eds), *The Globalization of Class Actions* (2009) 622 The Annals of the American Academy of Political and Social Science.

[8] Ibid.

[9] There are a few exceptions to this, most notably in class actions, but also under some circumstances that are defined by statute.

the damages system in both federal and state courts provides for exemplary or punitive damages. These are intended to deter misconduct and therefore are not related to genuine financial damages. Another factor in US tort law is the strict liability policies. Under strict liability, the manufacturer is liable if the product is defective, even if he was not negligent in making that product defective. Rather than the plaintiff having to prove that the defendant's behaviour was negligent, the focus is on the product itself. This has eased the burden of proof on plaintiffs. The US enforcement architecture has been explained in earlier chapters. It is important to highlight that the US system relies on mass tort litigation as a form of regulation. Finally, there is currently a deficiency in class action data as there is no national registry to compile statistical information and report on class action practices.[10]

2. US MPA Procedures

The US has a broad range of representative and group litigation procedures and it is useful to set these out in summary before discussing the class action mechanism in depth. From the list below, the two main forms of aggregative procedure are consolidation and class actions. These are governed by the FRCP. Generally these are replicated in the states' legal systems.[11] Several of these MPA procedures contain management features. This highlights the role of MPAs as 'managerial mechanisms' for mass harm litigation.

The formal and informal procedures for aggregating similar claims include:

A. Joinder
B. Consolidation
C. Multidistrict litigation (MDL) transfer of distinct but related claims into a single action
D. US bankruptcy proceedings for corporate reorganisation
E. Attorney 'inventories'
F. Representative litigation by associations—'private attorneys general litigation'
G. Representative litigation through government-initiated actions
H. Class actions

A. Joinder

There are rules in relation to 'permissive joinder' that gives a plaintiff the option of including other plaintiffs in the same action if they share common questions of fact or law and if their injuries arise from the same set of circumstances.[12] Similar rules have been adapted

[10] N Pace and W Rubenstein, 'How Transparent are Class Action Outcomes? Empirical Research on the Availability of Class Action Claims Data' (2008) RAND Working Paper Series WR–599–ICJ, available at: http://ssrn.com/abstract=1206315 (concluding that little data is available). Also Hensler and others, *Class Action Dilemmas* (n 6) ch 1.

[11] States determine their own rules, which apply in state courts, though most states have adopted rules that are based on the FRCP. Note also that the FRCP were most recently revised in 2006 with practical changes to discovery rules to make it easier for courts and litigating parties to manage electronic records.

[12] FRCP, r 20.

in most jurisdictions. When many plaintiffs are involved this may be called a 'mass action' or 'mass joinder'. The type of trial for this kind of action is similar to that used in mass consolidations, discussed below. In recent years there appears to be a reluctance on the part of courts to hold such mass trials of joined claims, especially for personal injury litigation.

B. Consolidation

Compared with joinder, consolidation is aggregation that is normally initiated by a judge. When separate actions that involve common questions of law or fact are pending before the court, the judge may order that they be consolidated.[13] Consolidation may also occur as a result of a motion from either a plaintiff or a defendant. Proceedings may be consolidated for various stages of the action, for only for the pre-trial stage of discovery, or for the trial stage.[14] At federal level, an important limitation on consolidations is the requirement that the cases must have been filed in the same federal district. Some states have a similar restriction that cases must be filed in the same courthouse. An approach that is similar to consolidation is that of using case management orders (CMOs) that apply to a whole body of litigation before all the judges in the same court or system. While this is not technically consolidation, as the actions proceed at the same time before all the judges, the CMOs allow the pre-trial process to be managed so that matters such as discovery and settlement negotiations can be carried out in a synchronised way. As will be discussed below, there is a clear judicial preference for consolidation as a means of resolving mass tort litigation in the US.

C. Multidistrict Litigation (MDL) Transfer of Distinct but Related Claims into a Single Action

Under the Multidistrict Litigation Statute, related cases may be consolidated for 'coordinated and consolidated pre-trial discovery' in advance of trial.[15] This can arise if cases involving related claims are filed in different federal district courts. The Judicial Panel on Multi-district Litigation (MDL Panel) has the authority to decide if these cases should be transferred to one federal judge in a single venue. The cases must share common questions of fact. Consolidation will be permitted provided that such transfer is for the convenience of the parties and witnesses and that it will promote the just and efficient conduct of such actions. This helps the management of complex and protracted civil lawsuits that are related to each other. It enables parties to share all pre-trial costs, such as expensive discovery, and frequently results in a comprehensive settlement, once the strength of the claims of the parties has been disclosed. Certain types of litigation are suitable for transfer and

[13] A procedure provided by federal statute—The Multidistrict Litigation Statute (28 USCA § 1407).

[14] FRCP, r 42 sets out the rules for consolidation and similar rules exist in most states although courts can tailor consolidated trials as they see appropriate; eg by dividing plaintiffs into smaller groups; holding 'bellweather' trials with small groups of related plaintiffs; or bifurcating the trial into 2 parts with a liability phase for common questions of law and fact and a subsequent causation/damages phase either for questions common to all plaintiffs or each individual plaintiff.

[15] 28 USC § 1407 in the United States Code. MDL Consolidation is also dealt with by r 42 of the FRCP.

consolidation to a single judge, such as actions involving a disaster or product liability.[16] Unlike joinder, common questions of law alone are not sufficient grounds for transfer. One of the most high profile MDL cases of recent years was the Deepwater Horizon BP Disaster in 2010. This is a high-profile example of environmental mass harm. In this case, more than 130 suits were filed against BP and other companies allegedly responsible for the disaster. Of those lawsuits, 77 were similar enough to be joined into one large case, known as MDL No 2179.[17] The outcome of this litigation was that BP agreed a deal with the Federal Government to establish a $20 billion fund to pay claims related to those lawsuits, which covers the majority of the injuries caused by the incident. As part of this settlement, thousands of people remain eligible to join the litigation and to receive settlement if they can demonstrate symptoms of medical conditions that resulted from this oil spill. Potential claimants include those living along the Gulf Coast or those who volunteered to assist with the clean-up. In order to determine their eligibility for compensation, claimants are subject to the US device of medical monitoring discussed in detail in the chapter four on environmental mass harm. This is the means by which victims with latent injuries can later be compensated for injury if illness that was not obvious at the time of litigation develops at a later stage. This is a very useful tool to overcome the difficulty that latency of injury can present in environmental mass harm cases in particular.

D. US Bankruptcy Proceedings for Corporate Reorganisation (Chapter 11)

This is one of the most widely used non-FRCP Rule 23 aggregation tools. It allows a company that is confronted with insurmountable debt to seek bankruptcy protection from current lawsuits, past judgments and expected future claims.

E. Attorney 'Inventories' of Clients Controlled by a Single Lawyer

Lawyers for plaintiffs can gather large numbers of clients with similar claims against one or several defendants. Even where such claims have not been filed as lawsuits or aggregated (through joinder, consolidation, MDL or FRCP class actions) an informal group resolution may still be negotiated with the defendants.

F. Representative Litigation by Associations

This term applies to lawsuits that may be taken by any individual or association to enforce certain statutes on behalf of groups of citizens, the public at large or the government.[18] It is

[16] Trade mark and patent infringement, securities violations and antitrust issues also typically use this aggregative process.

[17] Cited as *In re: Oil Spill by the Oil Rig 'Deepwater Horizon' in the Gulf of Mexico, on April 20, 2010*. On 14 November 2012, BP and the US Department of Justice reached a settlement. BP agreed to pay $4.5bn in fines and other payments. This case resulted in the largest settlement of its kind in US history.

[18] eg in relation to federal civil rights and state competition law.

so called litigation by 'private attorneys general'. Usually the relief granted is equitable and, if successful, the plaintiffs' legal fees and costs can be recovered. There is potential for fines to be imposed on defendants and for recovering large damages.[19]

G. Representative Litigation by Public Officials

These are government-initiated suits taken by state or federal Attorneys General can try to enforce statutes for consumer protection, competition law and other such laws, with the aim of getting injunctions, fines or compensation from defendants who have harmed the public. Such statutes usually expressly provide for government enforcement through civil rather than criminal litigation. In some cases, most notably in the recent tobacco litigation, the Attorneys General appoint private practice lawyers to bring the cases on a contingency fee basis.[20] Actions can also be brought to protect the welfare and health of citizens, for example by taking action to stop polluting behaviour in a neighbouring state. These are *parens patriae* actions, where government may seek injunctions or compensation in the public interest. In many jurisdictions, such action does not have to be based on any particular statutory authority.

H. Class Actions

These actions are brought under Rule 23 of the FRCP. This provides for representative litigation by individuals who voluntarily participate in a lawsuit. The US is the only jurisdiction with long-established experience of class actions. Many perceive the US to be the 'home of the class action'. In truth however, as previously explained, class actions originated in England circa the twelfth century, owing to the compulsory joinder rule whereby 'all parties materially interested in the subject of a suit had to be made parties so that there might be a complete decree to bind all'.[21] Nonetheless, the US federal class action regime gives invaluable insight into how class action litigation has evolved.

3. The US Federal Class Action Regime

The MPA discussion in this chapter will focus on class actions, as it would appear that this MPA procedure is most informative to this research's comparative examination. Rule 23 of the FRCP is the fundamental rule for federal class action litigation. State class action

[19] Sometimes treble damages.

[20] eg the *US Tobacco Litigation*; see www.justice.gov/civil/cases/tobacco2/index.htm.

[21] Irish Law Reform Commission *Report on Multi-party Litigation* (LRC 76-2005) 8, US literature recognises this link to the English representative rule: see *Newberg* (3rd) § 1.9, 3.1; T Rowe, 'A Distant Mirror: The Bill of Peace in Early American Mass Torts' (1997) 39 *Arizona L Rev* 711; W Weiner and D Szyndrowski, 'The Class Action, from the English Bill of Peace to Federal Rule of Civil Procedure 23: Is there a Common Thread?' (1987) 8 *Whittier L Rev* 935.

procedures and facilities vary from state to state but very often follow the federal approach. While similar rules are invoked in many individual states, state rules can vary considerably. It is estimated that about 3,300 new class actions are initiated in federal courts each year. The total number in the various state courts is unknown but it is generally supposed to be significantly larger than the federal numbers.[22] As previously outlined, the modern practice surrounding class action litigation in the US evolved through the civil rights era, the consumer movement and in recent times the movement towards mass tort litigation.[23] The more liberal rules on standing of the 1970s and 1980s have been eroded significantly in recent years by a series of seminal decisions. Initially, a class action could only be brought in equity cases. These involved disputes in which the parties did not necessarily seek monetary damages but instead might need some other type of relief. The adoption of Rule 23 of the FRCP in 1938 broadened the scope of the class action suit, providing that cases seeking monetary damages could be brought as class actions. Rule 23 is long and complex, with an explanation of the types of class action that is mainly historical. The 1966 revision of the Rule removed some of the more technical provisions of its operation. This revision also clarified the scope of the class action and Rule 23 was amended to provide that unnamed parties to a class action were bound by the final judgment in the action so long as their interests were adequately represented. A Rule 23 class action is essentially 'party neutral', and accordingly, defendant class actions are possible although they are quite rare in practice. This overview of the class action will concentrate solely on plaintiff classes.

Lawyers may initiate FRCP Rule 23-type class actions by filing a civil complaint in which a limited number of representative plaintiffs are individually named. The procedural language indicates that one or several named plaintiffs seek to recover losses or compel changes in the defendant's behaviour on behalf of both themselves and others similarly situated. Groups cannot file class action lawsuits unless a court recognises their legal standing to file a complaint and this is then certified. This requires an order certifying the proceedings as a class action and is called a *motion for class certification*, describing the proposed class and requesting the judge to review the class definition and the relief sought, with the aim of formally certifying a plaintiff class. The proposed class must consist of a group of individuals or business entities that have suffered a common injury, typically resulting from an action on the part of a business, or product defect or policy, that applied to all proposed class members in a uniform manner.

If a class is certified, one or more of the plaintiffs' attorneys will be named as class counsel. Any subsequent resolutions that bring about a settlement or verdict at trial will apply to the claims of all class members. If a class is not certified, then the matter can continue to be litigated, but the outcome will only have an effect on the individually named plaintiffs. In certain categories of certified class actions, for example those where principally monetary damages are sought, the class members are given notice (perhaps indirectly through published advertisements or directly through the post) of the fact that certification has occurred and they are notified of a timeframe within which they have the opportunity to opt out of the case if they do not wish to participate. If they decide to

[22] Pace, 'Group and Aggregate Litigation in the United States' (n 7).
[23] See Miller 'Of Frankenstein Monsters and Shining Knights' (n 6) 664.

opt out, they can still take their own individual action against the defendants. If they do not opt out, or neglect to do so either wittingly or unwittingly, then they will be bound by the outcome of the case and they cannot file their own individual lawsuits for similar claims against the same defendant. In other types of class actions, mainly those involving civil rights or those in pursuit of injunctive relief, there is no notice of certification nor is there an opportunity given to opt out. If the case goes to trial the verdict will apply to all class members.

More commonly, a settlement is negotiated and this agreement is delivered to the judge to decide whether the terms are fair, reasonable and adequate. This is one of the somewhat rare instances in the US legal system in which a privately negotiated settlement is subject to judicial review.[24] Before the judge issues his or her decision, the class is notified of the settlement and the members are given the opportunity to object to its terms or make comment on them. If the judge approves the settlement, he or she then decides the amount of the fee to be awarded to lawyers and the expenses to be paid by the defendant to class counsel. The fee can be determined as a percentage of the compensation obtained or based on the number of hours spent on the case by lawyers. If the judge does not approve the settlement, the parties are free to put forward a revised agreement or proceed to trial of the case. If the class members are to receive compensation, the sums can be shared out routinely, but in many cases, each of the class members will have to submit a claim for their individual share. It is not unusual that large numbers of the estimated class fail to submit claims. Pace emphasises that it is important to remember 'just about any civil lawsuit in the United States has the ability to morph from one with a limited number of individual parties to one where entire classes of plaintiffs or defendants are involved'.[25] There are a few, very narrowly defined exceptions to this, as some jurisdictions prohibit class actions for certain proceedings.[26] On the whole, once there are questions of fact or law that are common to a large group of individuals or bodies in a civil case, then FRCP Rule 23 can be used to bring a class action.

In terms of the comparative element of this research, it is notable that the US class action categorisation approach, which will be explained shortly, was expressly rejected by the law reform agencies in Australia and Ontario. For this reason, it is the category of Rule 23(b)(3) (which encompasses damages claims) that comprises the main focus of this research. Commentators such as Phair stress that the aim of Rule 23(b)(3) was to provide greater access to the courts, particularly for those who 'individually would be without effective strength to bring their opponents to court at all' but it does not exclude cases in which individual damages run high.[27] It is also remarkable that the Canadian and Australian class action regimes stand apart from the US rule in that they *expressly* contemplate claims for damages for mass tort cases, whereas US rules do not refer to damages.[28]

[24] Pace (n 7) 37.

[25] Ibid 37.

[26] eg class actions may be prohibited in some administrative proceedings, in certain taxpayer challenges, in certain instances where enhanced types of damages are available, in small claims courts, in domestic relations or probate matters, or in cases brought under statutes with specific restrictions usually very narrowly defined.

[27] R Phair, 'Resolving the "Choice-of-Law Problem" in Rule 23(b)(3) Nationwide Class Actions' (2000) *U of Chicago L Rev* 839.

[28] J Fleming, 'Mass Torts' (1994) 42 *Am J Comp L* 521.

4. Rule 23 of the Federal Rules of Civil Procedure (with 2003 Amendments)

Rule 23 governs the procedure and conduct of class action suits brought in federal courts. It is a complex rule with numerous subcategories.[29] In assessing the US class action requirements, Rule 23 provides that class actions can only be maintained if all its prerequisites in Rule 23(a) are met and the proposed class falls into one of four subcategories listed under Rule 23(b).

A. Rule 23(a) Prerequisites to a Class Action

One or more members of a class may sue or be sued as representative parties on behalf of all only if:

(1) The class is so numerous that joinder of all members is impracticable,
(2) There are questions of law or fact common to the class,
(3) The claims or defenses of the representative parties are typical of the claims or defenses of the class, and
(4) The representative parties will fairly and adequately protect the interests of the class.

These requirements of numerosity, commonality, typicality and adequacy of representation are designed to ensure that class treatment is both necessary and desirable in the circumstances, having regard also to the interests of the absent class members of the potential class. They relate to the MPA objectives of judicial and procedural economy and also to the objective of fairness. Their aim is ensure that class action treatment is truly necessary. The onus is on the promoter of the class to show that these prerequisites are fulfilled. These are the four prerequisites of any class action. Numerosity requires that a judge must first find that the class is 'so numerous that joinder of all members is impracticable'.[30] This means that it is logistically inconvenient or problematic to name each individual class member as a separate party to the lawsuit. Numerosity is met when there are 40 or more plaintiffs. Commonality requires there must be 'questions of law or fact common to the class'. This is most likely the most difficult of Rule 23's requirements. The plaintiffs must highlight one or more issues of law or fact that affect every class member.[31] Typicality requires that the claims or defences

[29] For information purposes, r 23 is set out as an appendix to this research. For a brief history of the rule, see F James and others, *Civil Procedure* (5th edn, Foundation Press, 2001) 10.21–10.22.

[30] See R Roth, 'Mass Tort Malignancy: In the Search for a Cure, Courts Should Continue to Certify Mandatory, Settlement-Only Class Actions' (1999) 79 *BUL Rev* 577.

[31] The US Supreme Court has made this requirement even more restrictive since *Wal-Mart Stores v Dukes* (20 June 2011, No 10-277) in 2011. This was a decision in one of the largest class action lawsuits ever made. Betsy Dukes and approximately 1.5 million current and former female Wal-Mart employees brought a suit for discrimination against women in Wal-Mart's promotion and pay policies. The US Supreme Court ruled against class certification in a decision that has significantly changed the legal landscape for large-scale federal class action lawsuits. It held that, for a potential class action lawsuit to be certified by federal courts, the lead plaintiffs must produce 'significant proof' that their claims share such strong commonality with those of the general class members that the determination of the validity of each claim can be resolved in one class-wide stroke. The Court also made it clear that claims for individualised monetary relief such as back-pay cannot be certified under the r 23(b)(2) 'injunctive-type' lawsuits; instead, suits involving *any* type of individualised monetary claims can now only be brought as a r 23(b)(3) 'damages-type' lawsuit irrespective of whether the injunctive or monetary relief predominates.

of the representative parties are typical of the claims and defences of the class. This requires that class members' and the representative plaintiffs' common claims need to be based on the same issues of liability and arise from the same events or practices.[32] Adequacy of representation requires that the class representatives will 'fairly and adequately protect the interests of the class'. The court will look at several factors to ensure that that the representative plaintiffs' interests would not be in conflict of interest with those of the class members.[33]

B. Rule 23(b) Class Actions Maintainable

Once these four pre-requisites above are satisfied, Rule 23(b) must be also satisfied. This imposes further requirements related to judicial economy. A class action may be certified if the court is shown that the action falls into one of the categories listed. It defines three kinds of class actions. These are set out in Rule 23(b)(1) or (b)(2) or (b)(3). These categories are 'functional in that they sort class actions according to the class's particular objectives'.[34] For the sake of simplicity, these can be grouped into those with 'mandatory classes' and those with 'opt-out classes'. Mandatory class cases are certified under Rule 23(b)(1)(A), Rule 23(b)(1)(B) or Rule 23(b)(2). These are often cases involving civil rights or seeking social change. In these cases judges are not required to give absent class members notice of certification or of the option to exclude themselves from the litigation. These cases mainly seek injunctions or declaratory judgments rather than monetary damages. Because this kind of equitable relief is indivisible and is for the benefit of all who fall within the class definition, arguably it does not make any difference whether they know they are class members or exclude themselves from the class. Other good reasons for mandatory classes include the potential that the defendants might be faced with conflicting judgments of the issue if opt-outs were permitted and circumstances where a very limited amount of funds is available to pay all claimants. The first type of mandatory class action outlined in 23(b)(1)(A) and (B):

> (1) The prosecution of separate actions by or against individual members of the class would create a risk of
>
> (A) Inconsistent or varying adjudications with respect to individual members of the class which would establish incompatible standards of conduct for the party opposing the class, or
>
> (B) Adjudications with respect to individual members of the class which would as a practical matter be dispositive of the interests of the other members not parties to the adjudications or substantially impair or impede their ability to protect their interests;

This has formed the basis for a glut of class actions in the area of civil rights. It may be brought where separate lawsuits might adversely affect other members of the class or the defendant in either of two ways. First, if the piecemeal litigation resulting from separate suits might impose inconsistent standards of conduct on the defendant, or, secondly, if multiple suits might 'impair or impede' the class members from protecting their various interests. In the next type of mandatory class action, Rule 23(b)(2), a class seeks an

[32] If the matter goes to trial, the class representative's individual claims would be decided by the judge or jury and the outcome would be effectively applied to the whole class.

[33] eg that their lawyers are sufficiently qualified, experienced, unconflicted and have adequate financial means to robustly prosecute the litigation.

[34] Roth, 'Mass Tort Malignancy' (n 30) 583.

injunction or some type of relief compelling the defendant either to cease a certain activity or to perform some other type of action:

> (2) The party opposing the class has acted or refused to act on grounds generally applicable to the class, thereby making appropriate final injunctive relief or corresponding declaratory relief with respect to the class as a whole

The final category of opt-out classes is those under Rule 23(b)(3). Often the principal aim of these 23(b)(3) cases is to seek restitution or monetary damages that can include claims involving mass torts, employment, competition law, securities and shareholders, or various consumer issues.[35] These are known as 'money damage' cases and they have two extra requirements: the *predominance* test and the *superiority* test, outlined below, which impose further requirements: that the common questions of law or fact common to the members predominate over any individual questions affecting only individual members; and that a class action is superior to other methods of adjudication.[36]

> (3) The court finds that the questions of law or fact common to the members of the class predominate over any questions affecting only individual members, and that a class action is superior to other available methods for the fair and efficient adjudication of the controversy. The matters pertinent to the findings include:
>
> (A) The interest of members of the class in individually controlling the prosecution or defense of separate actions;
>
> (B) The extent and nature of any litigation concerning the controversy already commenced by or against members of the class;
>
> (C) The desirability or undesirability of concentrating the litigation of the claims in the particular forum;
>
> (D) The difficulties likely to be encountered in the management of a class action.

These requirements indicate a requirement that a class action suit is a more efficient means to resolve a dispute and that the court is mindful of judicial and other economy, particularly procedural economy. They reflect the MPA objective of judicial and procedural economy. There is a requirement that notice be given to all potential class members that a class has been certified and that they have the choice of excluding themselves from any proceedings. Courts have held that due process requires that absent class members under Rule 23(b)(3) class actions be given adequate notice, adequate representation and adequate opportunity to opt out, before they can be bound by a final judgment in the suit.[37] If there is a settlement proposal, notice of this must be sent to all members of the certified class. If class members do not opt-out within the specified time period they will be bound by any judgment or court-approved settlement. This notification requirement can be difficult and expensive to satisfy but is a necessary concomitant of the MPA objective of fairness. This burdensome requirement is not necessary for class actions brought under Rules (b)(1) and (b)(2). Litigants frequently decide to sidestep the Rule 23(b)(3) notice requirements by instead

[35] Note, while FRCP, r 23 provides the foundation for securities-related class action litigation, such cases operate under a very different set of rules from other opt-out money damage class actions. The Federal Private Securities Litigation Reform Act 1995 and the Federal Securities Litigation Uniform Standards Act 1998 are instrumental in how these cases are litigated.

[36] These 2 further requirements for r (b)(3) class actions were added in 1966 by the Rules Advisory Committee; see Rules Advisory Committee, 'Notes to 1966 Amendments to Rule 23' (1966) 39 FRD 69, 102–03.

[37] *Phillips Petroleum Co v Shutts*, 472 US 797, 105 S Ct 2965, 86 L Ed 2d 628 [1985].

proceeding under Rule 23(b)(2). If this is done, claims for damages can be added on to claims for injunctive relief under this rule. This prompted the Advisory Committee in 1966 to discourage the use of class actions in tort cases and they have also been cited as reasons for declining certification.

Overall, Rule 23 gives the trial court extensive powers in relation to the certification and management of class actions.[38] The certification order may be altered at any time prior to a verdict on the merits.[39] The court may also divide the class into subclasses where members have claims that raise common issues particular to that subclass that are not shared by all the class members. Each of these subclasses is treated as a class in its own right.[40] A crucial role is played by the court in the supervision of any settlement of a class action. Rule 23(e) demands court approval of any 'dismissal or compromise' of the action and also for the provision of notice to all members of the class 'in such a manner as the court directs'. As class action settlements can be very complex and this can impede rigorous judicial scrutiny, occasionally courts will organise special hearings on the fairness of a settlement and may perhaps also assign a guardian to inform of its adequacy.[41]

If a class action is successful, a period of time is given for those who can prove they fit the class to file claims to participate in the judgment amount. Class actions are obviously difficult and expensive to file and follow through. The results can benefit claimants who could not afford to carry a suit alone. Also, they can have a strong deterrent effect and can force businesses that have caused widespread damage or who disregard public welfare to change their practices and/or pay compensation. They could also possibly result in high fees for the winning lawyers. As mentioned already, often lawyers operate on the basis of contingency fee, such as one-third of the final judgment, which could be millions of dollars. In summary of US class actions, they impose increased responsibility on judges. First, judges must decide whether to certify a class for the purpose of efficiency and then, subsequently, they must defend the interests of the class against the potential conflicts of interest between the class and its lawyers.[42] Such anxieties appear to be a fundamental reason for the apparent unwillingness of courts to certify classes in mass tort cases.

5. Evaluation of US Class Actions against MPA Objectives

In the US as in other jurisdictions, there is debate about whether class action litigation is the best route for resolving mass tort cases.[43] The merits and demerits of class action suits have been the subject of political and social controversy in the US over the years.[44] The analytical framework of the MPA objectives established in this research will be invoked to assist in an

[38] The court may order that a class be ordered for certain purposes but not for others or that certification be conditional.

[39] FRCP, r 23(c)(1).

[40] Ibid r 23(c)(4).

[41] James and others, *Civil Procedure* (n 29) 10.23.

[42] See further E Sherman, 'The Class Action Fairness Act 2005' (2006) 80 *Tul L Rev* 1593 (Class Action Fairness Act of 2005, Pub L No 109-2, 119 Stat 4 (codified in scattered sections of 28 USC)).

[43] R Mulheron, *The Class Action in Common Law Legal Systems: A Comparative Perspective* (Hart, 2004) 3.

[44] See eg the works cited at n 6.

evaluation of class actions in their role as MPA procedures. These objectives have previously been used as benchmarks in the general discussion of MPAs, so this section will endeavour to avoid repetition.

A. Access to Justice

We recall Judge Iacobucci's definition of access to justice as including the ability to institute legal proceedings and to have it reach a resolution.[45] In assessing access to justice, we have observed how, essentially, the focus is on procedural aspects, such as issues of costs and timeliness, as these are key determinants of access to justice. There is an argument that class action litigation has a tendency to be more complicated and slower than conventional litigation and a greater burden on resources.[46] However, a counter-argument is that, although cumbersome, a single class action is more cost-effective than numerous individual proceedings, particularly as evidenced in 'scattered damages' scenarios. It is helpful to recall Phair's opinion that the aim of the US class action, and in particular Rule 23(b)(3), was to provide greater access to the courts, especially for those who 'individually would be without effective strength to bring their opponents to court at all'.[47] Case law regularly illustrates the 'overriding principle that providing sufficient incentive to get at small claims is an important goal of class litigation'.[48] The US Supreme Court emphasised this in stating that one of the justifications that led to the development of the modern class action was to facilitate spreading litigation costs among numerous litigants with similar claims.[49] Once again, these are reminders of the 'economies of scale' identified by the LRC and Lord Woolf. We have seen how, in the US, the class action's ability to level the balance of power may be regarded as 'the new equity'.[50] This is because class actions can give strength to victims of mass harm.[51] However, it is also clear that regulation may be an additional means of achieving this, as well as through other tools such as ADR.[52]

This idea of timeliness has been endorsed in some modern procedural regimes[53] and has been recognised in class action jurisprudence.[54] It is important to note, however, that as

[45] This definition includes two components: (1) to provide claimants with an opportunity to pursue their claims in court; and (2) to obtain an appropriate restorative result, where warranted; see F Iacobucci, 'What is Access to Justice in the Context of Class Actions' in J Kalajdzic (ed), *Accessing Justice, Appraising Class Actions: Ten Years after Dutton Hollick and Rumley* (LexisNexis, 2011) 20.

[46] R Seltzer, 'Punitive Damages in Mass Tort Litigation: Addressing the Problems of Fairness, Efficiency and Control' (1983) LII *Ford L Rev* 37, 69; The Federal Judicial Center, *An Empirical Study of Class Actions in Four Federal District Courts: Final Report to the Advisory Committee on Civil Rules* (17 January 1996) 9; The Federal Judicial Center, *Preliminary Report on Time Study Class Action Cases* (9 February 1995) 19.

[47] Phair, 'Resolving the "Choice-of-Law Problem" in Rule 23(b)(3) Nationwide Class Actions' (n 27) 839.

[48] Mulheron, *The Class Action in Common Law Legal Systems* (n 43) 54.

[49] *US Parole Comm v Geraghty*, 445 US 388, 402, 100 S Ct 1202 (1980), cited in *re General Motors Corp Pick-up Truck Fuel Tank Prods Liab Litig*, 55F 3d 768, 784 (3d Cir 1995).

[50] S Finn, 'In a Class All its Own: The Advent of the Modern Class Action and Its Changing Legal and Social Mission' (2005) 2 *Can Class Action Rev* 333, 371.

[51] Such as the consumer who has been injured by a widespread corporate malpractice.

[52] Iacobucci, 'What is Access to Justice in the Context of Class Actions' (n 45).

[53] eg the English Civil Procedure Rules, introduced in 1998, explicitly state this as an overriding objective of civil procedure there: CPR, r 1.1(2)(d): 'ensuring that [the case] is dealt with expeditiously and fairly'.

[54] M Davis, 'Towards the Proper Role for Mass Tort Class Actions' (1998) 77 *Oregon L Rev* 157, 232 ('timely and meaningful vindication of rights and enforcement of responsibilities').

Mulheron has said, some class actions can proceed at a 'glacial pace'[55] and that this hinders the aim of judicial economy that class action legislation aims to achieve but certain class action features reflect the principle that timeliness of the decision for class members is as important as the right decision.[56] The use of devices such as 'tolling' of class actions may help to ameliorate the harsh elements of the Statute of Limitations in some circumstances.[57] In assessing the other components of access to justice we can gain a better insight into features of the US class action system that can enhance and inhibit the achievement of these objectives.

B. Judicial and Procedural Economy

First, the aggregation of a large number of individualised claims into one representative lawsuit has been recognised as conferring some advantages. It can increase efficiency of the legal process and lower the costs of litigation. Where common questions of law and fact arise they may avoid the necessity of repeating 'days of the same witnesses, exhibits and issues from trial to trial'.[58] There has also been judicial recognition that class actions may help to overcome the 'scattered damages' phenomenon surrounding 'the problem that small recoveries do not provide the incentive for any individual to bring a solo action prosecuting his or her rights'.[59] This ensures that a defendant who engages in widespread harm, but does so minimally against each individual plaintiff, must compensate those individuals for their injuries. Those in favour of class actions claim that the class action format has most often been used to aggregate small claims that were not worth litigating separately. For this reason a class action is an effective means for holding defendants accountable for widespread harm that would otherwise go unchecked. There is public value in allowing this type of class action, even if the amount payable to each member of the class is small. Furthermore, in 'limited fund' cases (where defendants have limited financial means), these actions may ensure that all plaintiffs receive relief, not just those who file cases early and have first access to the fund. Supporters of class actions contend that trivial cases are rare and that neither high settlement rates nor small individual recoveries demonstrate frivolous litigation. Moreover, criticism of large attorney fees ignores the 'entrepreneurial' risk that class action attorneys arguably take in starting such lawsuits. Not every class action

[55] J Kleefeld, 'Class Actions as Alternative Dispute Resolution' (2001) 39 *Osgoode Hall LJ* 817.

[56] eg features such as the requirement to consider all dispute resolution methods or to use judicial devices to manage non-common issues; Mulheron (n 43) 55.

[57] 'Tolling' in the US refers to a situation or circumstances in which the Statute of Limitations will be extended beyond the limit named in the state statute.

[58] *Jenkins v Raymark Indus Inc* 782 F2d 468, 473 (5th Cir 1986) (granting certification of an asbestos class action).

[59] *Amchem Prods Inc v Windsor* 521 US 591, 617 (1997) (quoting *Mace v Van Ru Credit Corp*, 109 F3d 388, 344 (7th Cir 1997)). 'A class action solves this problem by aggregating the relatively paltry potential recoveries into something worth someone's (usually an attorney's) labour'; *Amchem Prods Inc* at 617 (quoting *Mace* at 344). In other words, a class action ensures that a defendant who engages in widespread harm—but does so minimally against each individual plaintiff—must compensate those individuals for their injuries. eg thousands of shareholders of a public company may have losses too small to justify separate lawsuits, but a class action can be brought efficiently on behalf of all shareholders. Perhaps even more important than compensation is that class treatment of claims may be the only way to impose the costs of wrongdoing on the wrongdoer, thus deterring future wrongdoing.

will be successful and the costs of litigation can be substantial. Without a financial incentive, attorneys will not take these on and plaintiffs will not find redress for certain types of injury. Those who defend the use of class actions also point out that personal injury lawyers receive large portions of the awarded damages through contingency fees. They claim that class action attorneys should not be treated differently.

The US Supreme Court has stated that class certification in class actions can promote 'the efficiency and economy of litigation which is the principle purpose of the procedure'.[60] Despite this, it seems that there is no denying that there can be negative aspects to mass tort litigation and this is seen in the US opposition to class actions for mass torts and the demands for procedural safety measures for individual case management in group proceedings. The US class action rules explicitly support the achievement of efficiency. This is seen in the FRCP that govern civil procedure for civil lawsuits in United States district federal courts, particularly in the use of FRCP Rule 23(b)(3) actions where the court is to have regard to the 'fair and efficient adjudication of the controversy'. There has been criticism that judicial economy was not given the consideration that it ought to have been given in the US asbestos litigation and that this was one of the reasons for repetitive trials:

> Why should a defendant or group of defendants be entitled to thousands of chances to convince thousands of jurors that one identical set of facts does not give rise to liability? This is what happened in the asbestos litigation that consensus says has been a dismal failure of judicial efficiency and fairness to litigants.[61]

The Alberta Law Reform Institute, in reviewing the US class action regime, has stated that the opportunity for early closure is a benefit of class action regimes to defendants:

> Rather than waiting for individual claims to pile up, corporate defendants can clean up their liabilities in one proceeding without risking inconsistent decisions or facing multiple lawsuits in numerous jurisdictions.[62]

Compared with some other common law jurisdictions, Rule 23 of the FRCP will not allow a class action unless it is established that there are clearly common issues of law or fact. The English representative action requires a high degree of overlap between class members' claims. In practice there even small differences can preclude group litigation status. In contrast, Australia's class action procedure is more liberal than the US and England as Australia does not have certification requirement and those seeking class treatment must only show one issue common to the class.[63] The Australian predominance issue can, in theory, be avoided by using an 'issue class', which is a class action limited to proof of certain issues. Australian class actions are effectively all issue classes. US law has not yet gone this far, as issue classes are rare, although they are regarded as possible in theory under the rules.[64] The efficiency of class actions must also be measured in terms of settlements. It commonly occurs that class actions are settled in the US but statistics are difficult to

[60] *General Telephone Co of Southwest v Falcon* 457 US 147, 159, 102 S Ct 2364 (1982).

[61] Davis, 'Towards the Proper Role for Mass Tort Class Actions' (n 54) 232.

[62] Alberta Law Reform Institute Report 'Report on Class Actions, Final Report No 85, Dec 2000' (AltaLRI Report) [122].

[63] See G Miller, 'Group Litigation in the Enforcement of Tort Law' in J Arden (ed), *Research Handbook on the Economics of Torts* (Edward Elgar, 2013) 264.

[64] Ibid 265.

obtain. It is, however, clear that many class actions are resolved by methods other than settlements, such as voluntary dismissals.[65]

It seems that the greatest discontent with US class actions has been evidenced in 'mass tort class actions involving, for example, product liability, which can involve thousands of would-be class members with different, distinct claims'.[66] These became a notorious feature of the US legal scene in the 1970s and 1980 and were led by numerous class actions against asbestos manufacturers. With large caseloads involving multiple litigants, courts started to certify class actions just to relieve this pressure, and parties then settled what had become unmanageable lawsuits. As the media hype regarding this phenomenon grew so did the numbers of new filings.[67] Lessons learnt from the experience of such litigation demonstrate that the very scale and complication of such cases means that they are inappropriate for class action treatment.[68] Whether a class action is superior to individual litigation depends on the case, and is determined by the judge's ruling on a motion for class certification, as previously noted. The Advisory Committee Note to Rule 23, for example, states that mass torts are ordinarily 'not appropriate' for class treatment. Class treatment may not improve the efficiency of litigation of a mass tort because the claims frequently involve individualised issues of law and fact that will have to be re-tried on an individual basis.[69] Mass torts also involve high individual damage awards, thus, the absence of class treatment will not impede the ability of individual claimants to seek justice. Other cases, however, may be more conducive to class treatment. More recently, the US courts have moved back to the original foundations of Rule 23 and have refused to certify mass class actions that may be unmanageable and eventually settled.[70] Consumer class litigation entailing multiple claims for small monetary losses (scattered damages) has also been controversial. Supporters argue that such actions help an important public interest as they uphold the rights of less advantaged plaintiffs and they also have a deterrent effect on defendants. Opponents assert that undeserving consumer claims are boosted by this 'strength in numbers' and that the only true winners are the class action lawyers. There are similar allegations against securities fraud class actions.[71] Some commentators argue that 'to exploit litigation

[65] See N Pace, S Carroll, I Vogelsang and L Zakaras, *Insurance Class Actions in the United States* (RAND Corporation, 2007), which found that negotiated class-wide settlements occurred in only 12% of closed insurance cases filed as class actions.

[66] J Coffee, 'Class Wars: The Dilemma of the Mass Tort Class Action' (1995) 95 *Colum L Rev* 1343.

[67] James and others, *Civil Procedure* (n 29) 10.22; L Harbour, 'Class Actions: An American Perspective' in C Hodges, *Multi-Party Actions* (Oxford University Press, 2001) 13.19–13.22.

[68] Irish Law Reform Commission, *Consultation Paper on Multi-Party Litigation* (LRC CP 25-2003) 2.14.

[69] See *Castano v Am Tobacco Co*, 84 F 3d 734 (5th Cir 1996) (rejecting nationwide class action against tobacco companies).

[70] See *Barnes v The American Tobacco Co* 161 F 3d 127 (3rd Cir 1998). This decision affirmed a district court's refusal to certify a nationwide class of nicotine addicts; see also: *Castano v Am Tobacco Co* (n 69) (reversing partial certification of class claims in a similar suit against tobacco manufacturers); *In re American Med Sys Inc*, 75 F 3d 1069, 1089 (6th Cir 1996) (reversing certification of a nationwide class consisting of between 15,000 and 120,000 men who had been implanted with penile prostheses manufactured by the defendant); *Valentino v Carter-Wallace Inc* 97 F 3d 1227 (9th Cir 1996) (reversing certification of a class of persons who had taken an epilepsy drug). The US Supreme Court has supported this more cautious approach: *Amchem Prods Inc v Windsor* (n 59).

[71] Irish Law Reform Commission, *Consultation Paper on Multi-Party Litigation* (n 68) 2.15 at 37 mentions that the worst cases allegedly entailed efforts to coerce settlements through spurious fraud class actions based on falls in the price of company shares. Congress responded with the enactment of the Private Securities Litigation Reform Act 1995 15 USC §§ 77z-1(c), 78u-4(c) and the Securities Litigation Uniform Standards Act 1998 15 USC §§ 77p, 78bb(f). See James and others, *Civil Procedure* (n 29) 10.22 (which notes that these statutory developments have not reduced the number of securities fraud class action filings).

scale economies fully, courts should automatically and immediately aggregate all potential claims arising from mass tort events into a single mandatory-litigation class action, allowing no class member to exit'.[72] This argument is based on the normative premise that the law should promote individuals' wellbeing and that, as a consequence, the law should seek to minimise the sum of accident costs.[73] In Rosenberg's opinion, this presupposes that the 'social objective' of common law mass tort liability is the prevention and compensation of tortious harm and that the function of class actions is to develop and promote 'equity' among plaintiffs.[74] He argues that fairness is more likely to be at risk where mechanisms of aggregative procedures such as class actions are not available. The evaluation of MPAs in this study indicates that class actions facilitate the objectives of mass tort liability by allowing plaintiffs to combine their cases in a group action against the defendant, avoiding the procedural and cost risks of individual actions, particularly in metaphorical 'David and Goliath' situations. Instead, MPAs allow plaintiffs to gain litigation-al 'strength in numbers'. This research has already established that the objectives of MPAs exceeds the aims stated by Rosenberg's aim of compensation and include many other goals such as proportionality and predictability. What Rosenberg propounds complies with these objectives at least in relation to fairness and the possibility of judicial economy.

The aims of judicial and procedural economy can be enhanced by settlements. It has been shown already that when a class action is settled in a way that provides prescribed amounts of damages for plaintiffs then this obviates the need for separate trials to assess individual damages, which can arguably be one of the most expensive aspects of class action litigation. However, such settlements do raise concerns about compromising due process and fairness to all litigants to ensure judicial economy. The MPA objective of fairness will be discussed in further detail below. The Rule 23(c)(4) provision, whereby a court may also divide the class into subclasses where members have claims that raise common issues particular to that subclass that are not shared by all the class members and each of these subclasses is treated as a class in its own right, gives rise to further judicial and procedural economy. Furthermore, liability and causation may be determined on a class basis and damages by way of individual 'mini-trials'[75] or 'bifurcated proceedings.[76]

This reflects the need to make mass harm litigation more manageable. The US class action MPA mechanism, by providing for this subclass division, enhances the manageability of such litigation, hence reflecting MPA use as management mechanisms.

C. Fairness

(In this section, fairness includes proportionality, balancing individual rights and personal autonomy, and non-abuse.)

[72] D Rosenberg, 'Mandatory-Litigation Class Action: The Only Option for Mass Tort Cases' (2002) 115 *Harv L Rev* 831, 1.

[73] Ibid.

[74] Ibid 2.

[75] Harbour and others, 'Class Actions: An American Perspective' (n 67) 913.15 and 13.40.

[76] FRCP, r 42(b) provides: 'The Court, in furtherance of convenience or to avoid prejudice, or when separate trials will be conducive to expedition and economy, may order a separate trial of any claim ... or of any separate issue or of any number of claims'.

The preamble to the Class Action Fairness Act of 2005 asserted that:[77]

> Class-action lawsuits are an important and valuable part of the legal system when they permit the fair and efficient resolution of legitimate claims of numerous parties by allowing the claims to be aggregated into a single action against a defendant that has allegedly caused harm.

Class actions have been availed of with great success to advance civil rights against public and private actors, for example in employment discrimination. They have also achieved moderate success in single-issue tort cases.[78] On the other hand, the preamble to the Class Action Fairness Act states that some abusive class actions, by allowing settlements that gave most of the financial benefits to lawyers, have harmed class members with legitimate claims.[79] It also states that by assessing unjustified awards some abusive cases have harmed defendants who have acted responsibly. It further states that they have raised the cost of doing business and therefore have adversely affected inter-state commerce and undermined public respect for the country's legal system. This is because, in terms of the damages awarded by US juries, these can be perceived as a considerable financial threat to industry. A further criticism is that often class members receive little benefit after large fees. It may also be argued that unjustified awards are made to certain plaintiffs at the expense of other class members. For example, sometimes a decision can bind all class members with a low settlement as a way to forestall major liability by precluding a large number of people from litigating their claims separately, to recover reasonable compensation.[80] However, the law requires judicial approval of all class action settlements, and in most cases, class members are given a chance to opt out of class settlement. Critics of class actions remain unconvinced about the social and legal value of group lawsuits. They argue that the lawyer has the largest economic stake in the outcome, leading to settlements that guarantee high attorney fees and minimal payouts to the class members. Further criticisms also dispute the value of the private attorney general role. Most class action lawyers, they contend, are seeking lucrative financial awards rather than social justice. Moreover, class actions may interfere with the regulatory and oversight functions of the appropriate government agency; for example, the agency may conclude that the injuries attributed to the defendant are insignificant and do not warrant prosecution. Furthermore, defendants in mass tort class actions have an incentive to search for and negotiate with the plaintiffs' attorney for the lowest settlement amount.

In looking at Rule 23 of the FRCP itself and its requirements, the four prerequisites in Rule 23(a) are designed to ensure that class treatment is both necessary and desirable in the circumstances, having regard also to the interests of absent class members of a potential class. This is a strong indicator of fairness. This is particularly evident in Rule 23(a)(4) which requires adequacy of representation so that the class representatives will fairly and adequately protect the interests of the class. For opt-out classes under Rule 23(b)(3), the requirement that adequate notice be given to class members that a class has been certified and giving them a choice to exclude themselves from any proceedings is a further indicator of fairness. This gives them the freedom to pursue their own claims if they so wish.

[77] Class Action Fairness Act 2005 (n 42) (codified in scattered sections of 28 USC).

[78] In cases where common issues prevail over individual issues.

[79] S Harmon Wilson, 'Public Law Litigation and Public International Law in the US', *The US Justice System: An Encyclopedia* (ABC-CLIO LLC, 2012) 278.

[80] Such as 'coupon settlements' which offer benefits for a nominal amount or voucher.

Furthermore, if there is a settlement proposal, notice of this must be sent to all members of a certified class. Obviously, the corollary of class members not receiving notice, either of the class or the settlement, does have potentially unjust implications as they will be bound by the outcome of the case and will be precluded from taking their own individual action for their claim in the future if they do not opt out of the class, either wittingly or unwittingly. As mentioned previously, in situations where settlements obviate the need for separate trials and in 'limited fund' cases there is no need to provide notice to all class members, or to permit them to opt out. Doing this, however, does raise concerns about compromising due process and fairness to all litigants in order to ensure judicial economy. As class actions and their settlements can be very complex, the degree of judicial control over the conduct of the proceedings gives reassurance of fairness to class members. This is particularly so with the court supervision of settlements.[81] Furthermore, the requirement of Rule 23(e) for court approval of any dismissal of the action and also the requirement that notice must be provided to all class members further protect participants.

There are some further points in relation to the need to balance individual rights and autonomy with the interests of the class that need to be recalled. For example, outcomes and settlements may benefit plaintiffs with weak claims to the detriment of those with stronger claims.[82] Also, there are obvious conflicts of interests between the various actors and elements of the class such as the representatives, the lawyers and absentee class members (the protection of whose rights requires especially rigorous judicial supervision) that have to be considered. In class action litigation, because control of the case is transferred from the individual's lawyer to the class counsel, it is arguable that an individual's interests may not receive the same level of priority care that they would otherwise hope to benefit from. For such reason there is frequently opposition to class action proceedings from the individual's lawyer but this is likely to be also for reasons that are in the lawyer's own financial interests because his fees will be fixed by the trial judge, not by the usual means of contingency fee. It is hoped by claimants engaging in class actions that, overall, the benefits of class participation will outweigh these potential negative aspects. As for large claim class actions, a concern is that the victims may not always be fairly served. Large claim cases raise doubts about the capacity of the class action format to provide justice for individuals. Another question is the ability of class attorneys to represent effectively the various needs of class members. Furthermore, it is important to be mindful of the impact on future class members who do not, at the time of litigation, have a ripe claim because their injury is not yet apparent due to latency. In these large claim cases, it could be argued that defendants have sought class action status as a way of limiting liability. In some cases, the parties propose a settlement before a complaint has ever been filed, suggesting the possibility of collusion between lawyers for both sides.

A way of alleviating these concerns is to modify legislation and court rules to give more power to the courts to examine class action applications. If this were so, courts could carefully review the applications and deny class status to small claims cases with little social value. Another alternative may be to reduce lawyers' fees, which would reduce the incentive for frivolous actions. Judges have an important role in defending the interests of the class

[81] Also, the fact that courts may occasionally organise special hearings on the fairness of a settlement and perhaps assign a guardian to ensure its adequacy; see James and others, *Civil Procedure* (n 29) 10.23.

[82] *In re Agent Orange* 818 F 2d 145 (2nd Cir 1987).

against the potential conflicts of interest between the class and its lawyers; the anxiety that this too can cause judges may also contribute to the apparent unwillingness of courts to certify classes in mass tort cases.

As for proportionality, it has been previously noted that multi-party litigation inevitably entails a common tension between the individual rights, in terms of fairness, and judicial economy, because of concerns such as time, cost and court resources. Lord Woolf stated in 1996 that 'the effective and economic handling of group actions necessarily requires a diminution, compromise or adjustment of the rights of individual litigants for the greater good of the action as a whole'.[83] He subsequently noted the need to provide 'proportionate methods of resolving [multi-party] cases'.[84] As Zuckerman observed whereas once rectitude of decision was an overriding value of civil procedure, consideration of timely justice and reasonable costs are now relevant and important factors in the allocation of finite judicial resources.[85] This attitude has been recognised in relation to class actions and, as one US commentator has stated, '[t]he fact that the class action procedure requires compromises is an insufficient reason to fear and thus reject it'.[86] For example, the principle of proportionality is applied to a cost-benefit analysis of whether a MPA action warrants its commencement at all.[87] Furthermore, there may be a point at which the costs to class members outweigh the benefit to class members individually, 'a point at which the consumer or person suffering injury must reasonably accept the risk of injury because the cost of providing compensation is too high relative to the benefit'.[88] It has even been noted in US case law that it is possible that individual plaintiffs could recover higher damages if they were to pursue their own claims.[89] Therefore, as Mulheron has stated, 'certifying a class action may well entail the proportionality of lower compensatory awards'.[90]

D. Predictability

In the US, it has been stated that the class action 'protects defendants from inconsistent obligations that may be created by varying results in different courts, and similarly, it promotes the equitable principle that similarly situated plaintiffs should receive similar treatment'.[91] This might be extended to similar treatment whereby cases are heard similarly. Lawyers are the first to advise on the appropriateness of such litigation in the circumstances and their evaluation is a key factor in the eventual allocation of courts' resources and judicial efficiency.[92] It is important, however, to remember the argument that class actions may raise the threat of arbitrary conclusions. For example, where multiple claims are combined in

[83] Lord Woolf *Access to Justice Inquiry: Issues Paper (Multi-Party Actions)* (1996) [2], [2(a)].
[84] Lord Woolf, *Access to Justice Final Report*, ch 17, [2].
[85] A Zuckerman, *Justice in Crisis: Comparative Dimensions of Civil Procedure* (Oxford University Press, 1999) 17–18.
[86] Davis (n 54) 232.
[87] Mulheron (n 43) 50.
[88] Australian Law Reform Commission (ALRC), *Managing Justice* (Rep No 89, 1999) [342].
[89] *Marcarz v Transworld Systms Inc*, 193 FRD 46, 55 (D Conn 2000).
[90] Mulheron (n 43) 51.
[91] *US Parole Comm v Geraghty*, 445 US 388, 402–03, 100 S Ct 1202 (1980); see further Phair (n 27) 837.
[92] Acknowledged by the ALRC, *Managing Justice* (n 88) 7.90.

a class action there may be a greater pressure on defendants to settle despite the merits of individual claims. In terms of procedural certainty, the detailed case certification requirements and case management by the class action judge certainly lend an air of predictability to the legal proceedings, which can be reassuring for both claimants and defendants.

E. Deterrence

There has been widespread academic acknowledgement in the US of the deterrence function of class litigation, such as its role in 'transforming non-threatening individual claims into mass tort litigation',[93] 'filling the gaps left by regulators'[94] and 'counter-balancing corporate weight'.[95] There is also judicial acknowledgement of this deterrence function[96] and a large literature examines the effectiveness of tort law including the use of class actions and the role of damages in achieving deterrence.[97] According to some commentators, this would appear to suggest that the US class action system may have a powerful influence on the behaviour of actual or potential defendants.[98] It is notable that US public institutions are not exempt from tort claims.[99] The potential for behaviour modification is considered to be a worthy goal of class action certification in the US but this view is not unanimously shared in all common law jurisdictions.[100] For example, in Australia, the ALRC stated that the objectives of increased access to justice and judicial efficiency did not enhance deterrence as a goal of its representative proceedings.[101]

Critics maintain that state and federal law enforcement organisations may investigate and punish widespread small-scale fraud and offer an alternative means of addressing wrongful conduct. Private enforcement through a class action reduces this and delegates control over enforcement priorities to the plaintiffs' lawyer. Those who defend class actions argue that the class action type of lawsuit has a legitimate social purpose. A lawyer who prosecutes a class action can be viewed as a 'private attorney general' who aggressively enforces various regulatory laws or who alerts the public to problems. At a time when the US Government is seeking to reduce government regulation, class action lawsuits may provide an opportunity for the private sector to take up this surveillance function. The effect that a class action can have on the behaviour of an entity that had previously been acting in reckless disregard of the public, for example, can be powerful in forcing such entities to change their behaviour, as well as to possibly compensate their victims, thereby achieving a powerful deterrent and sometimes, as a by-product, a regulatory result.

93 J Kellam, 'Toxic Torts' (1998) 8 *Aust Product Liability Reporter* 161, 67.

94 D Lennox, 'Building a Class' (2001) 24 *Advocates' Q* 377.

95 C Harlow and R Rawlings, *Pressure Through Tort Law* (Routledge, 1992) 113.

96 Examples are *Blackie v Barrack*, 524 F 2d 891, 903 (9th Cir 1975); *In re Gap Stores Securities Litigat*, 79 FRD 283, 295 (ND Cal 1978).

97 eg T Galligan, 'Deterrence: The Legitimate Function of the Public Tort (2001) 58 *Wash & Lee L Rev* 1019.

98 These are often governmental agencies or large corporations.

99 The Federal Tort Claims Act (25 June 1946, ch 646, Title IV, 60 Stat 812, '28 USC Pt.VI Ch.171' and 28 USC § 1346(b)) ('FTCA') is a 1946 federal statute that permits private parties to sue the United States in a federal court for most torts committed by persons acting on behalf of the United States. Historically, citizens have not been able to sue their state—a doctrine referred to as sovereign immunity. The FTCA constitutes a limited waiver of sovereign immunity, permitting citizens to pursue some tort claims against the government.

100 *Scott v TD Waterhouse Investor Services (Can) Inc* (2001), 94, BCLR (3d) 320 (SC) [142].

101 See ALRC, *Managing Justice* (n 88) [2.23].

A class action may, however, be the only way to impose the costs of the wrongdoing on the wrongdoer, thus deterring future wrongdoing. In areas where there is limited confidence in public regulation, MPAs can provide an important means of potential regulation. Rosenberg opines that

> Mass exposure cases are frequently products of the deliberate policies of businesses that tailor their safety investments to profit margins. Such risk-taking policies should be especially amenable to control through threats of liability.[102]

F. Compensation

We have seen how those who defend class actions claim that mass harm cases benefit from using a class action structure. When victims of mass harm seek substantial compensation for injuries caused by a defective product, such as asbestos, it makes sense to aggregate the claims. This is particularly true to enable the management of such claims and MPAs play a crucial role in achieving this. As we have seen in the example of environmental mass harm, it is more economical for lawyers and the courts to manage hundreds or even thousands of similar claims as a group rather than on a case-by-case basis. The courts would be greatly overburdened if each case had to be handled individually, and the duplication of evidence and expert witnesses would generate needless expense. A class action can resolve the central issues and develop rational compensation schedules for the victims. Settlement also becomes a more attractive option for defendants when the victims are members of a class. Overall, class actions centralise all claims into one venue where a court can fairly resolve the issues. It is useful to recall that conceptually, compensation is the fundamental point of tort law and, according to Hodges, 'it is axiomatic that a primary purpose of tort law and of collective mechanisms in both the US and in Europe is to deliver compensation'.[103]

6. Concluding Observations on US Mass Harm Litigation

US class action lawsuits became a controversial topic in the 1990s. Once seen as a way of empowering individuals with small claims to access court, class actions are viewed by some as a way for plaintiffs' lawyers to benefit from their clients', sometimes, unmeritorious cases. Furthermore, there is a criticism of the use of class actions by defendants in mass tort cases, such as the asbestos litigation, allegedly in order to frustrate the large and legitimate claims of individual victims. In summation of the US experience of class actions, it is very important to stress that, despite the common misperception, especially held abroad, class actions have rarely been certified for mass tort claims.[104] This is perhaps due to confusion with the practice of consolidation or because a few exceptional high-profile cases may have led

[102] D Rosenberg, 'The Causal Connection in Mass Exposure Cases: A "Public Law" Vision of the Tort System' (1984) *Harv L Rev* 849, 929.

[103] See C Hodges, 'Objectives, Mechanisms and Policy Choices in Collective Enforcement and Redress' in J Steele and W van Boom (eds), *Mass Justice* (Edward Elgar, 2011) 102.

[104] eg class or multidistrict actions have been repeatedly rejected for asbestos claims.

to this impression. The fact that it can be increasingly difficult to get certification and that there has been a major shift to arbitration and class arbitration have reduced the number of class actions being brought in the US. Surprisingly, defendants can be more in favour of the use of class actions in tort cases than plaintiffs, as are trial judges who are overburdened with claims. Most plaintiffs' lawyers oppose class actions because the judge decides the lawyers' fees, as opposed to by pre-arranged contingency fees, and it is the lawyers who cover the litigation costs prior to judgment. Perhaps class actions are best suited to consumer protection where the matters at stake for individuals are too small to merit litigation but the collective stakes would justify it, as seen in the 'scattered damages' cases, previously discussed. This seems to be the approach taken by a number of civil law jurisdictions that have introduced class actions for such consumer protection.[105] It is also noteworthy to recall that mass harm litigation requires judges to assume a very proactive role in judicial case management whereby they try to assist parties to resolve their disputes. Under the MDL statute this has had a high success rate and after common discovery there has been a large reduction in the need for individual trials.[106] This again highlights the key function of MPAs as management mechanisms for mass harm litigation.

The changing judicial opinion on certification is reflected by the observation by Davis, that:

> Early attempts to certify class actions in mass tort cases after the 1966 amendments were few and routinely met with defeat ... In the late 1970s and early 1980s, at about the same time that products liability actions generally were on the increase, three 'defective' products gave rise to thousands of injury claims, creating 'mass torts' that have since grabbed the attention of society and federal judiciary. The presence of these mass torts—asbestos, Agent Orange, and the Dalkon Shield intrauterine device—in the judicial system seem to have affected a change in the attitude of the trial, and to a lesser extent, appellate, judiciary which was evidenced by a greater willingness to certify class actions.[107]

Mulheron opines that, notwithstanding the uncertainties that surround its most appropriate application, the US class action has become increasingly utilised, with one study noting that, 'from 1990 to 2001, the number of class actions filed annually in federal courts increased steadily, from 922 to over 3000'.[108] As explained, the practice of class actions has largely originated in the US and is still predominantly a US phenomenon but it is notable that several European civil law countries have made changes in recent years to allow consumer organisations to bring claims on behalf of large groups of consumers. Some may question why mass litigation has not been evidenced to the same extent elsewhere. A primary cause is that the US has been under greater pressure to adapt to the demands of mass litigation. There is a widely known reliance on litigation in America, as a result of its social context and enforcement architecture. Briefly recapping, there are numerous reasons for this. First, as previously mentioned, victims of harm are forced to seek redress through the judicial process due to the lack of a comprehensive social security or national health system.

[105] eg Spanish law allows nominated consumer associations to take action to protect the interests of consumers. A number of groups already have the power to bring collective or class actions: certain consumer associations, bodies legally constituted to defend the 'collective interest' and groups of injured parties.

[106] eg again the *Agent Orange case* (n 82) where Weinstein J succeeded in getting the parties to agree a settlement.

[107] Davis (n 54) 407.

[108] Pace (n 7) 15.

Secondly, personal injury lawyers are paid through contingency fees, giving them with a financial interest in their clients' case. This has resulted in wide-ranging accusations that, in pursuit of larger fees, lawyers encourage litigation. Thirdly, the American public are very aware of their rights and the legal process as a result of media coverage of litigation and for them the legal route is perceived as a common fact of life.[109] What might be regarded as a litigious culture seems particularly to centre on mass litigation. All of these factors contribute to the greater pressure on the US to adopt particular legal mechanisms to deal with mass harm litigation, compared with other legal systems. Furthermore, in the US the contingency fee system removes the fear of the prohibitive expense of litigation, including the risk if the claim fails of having to bear the costs of the other side, including lawyers' fees. This risk is a reason for lower levels of litigation in other legal systems. This is another factor for higher levels of litigation of all types in the US. Finally, as mass harm litigation has developed in the US, so has the skill of lawyers there to handle such cases. Perhaps these skills are spreading to the other side of the Atlantic with the recent advent of a number of English law firms now specialising in mass harm litigation.[110] As highlighted already, despite an erroneous widely held misperception, in the US there has been little eagerness to endorse the use of class actions for mass harm litigation. It is helpful to recall the words of the Irish Law Reform Commission that: 'the reality is that class actions have proved effective in some but not all of the extraordinarily wide range of legal contexts to which they have been applied'.[111] It is also important to recognise a fundamental limitation to be drawn from this MPA analysis, namely the lack of reliable statistics. This makes it difficult to assess the extent to which the MPA objectives have been achieved. This limitation applies to all the jurisdictions examined in this work.

7. Future Developments in the US

It may be reasonably assumed that Rule 23 of the FRCP and its equivalents in individual states will remain relatively unchanged in the future, although the court decisions, statutes and legal doctrines that mould how these rules are applied may change significantly. For example, the federal Class Action Fairness Act (CAFA) 2005[112] relaxed the rules for transferring state court class actions with inter-state repercussions into the federal courts. Some allege that having these cases heard by federal judges rather than state judges will result in far fewer certified classes, even though the originating states use class action rules that replicate FRCP Rule 23.[113]

According to Pace, another significant change may involve how appellate courts finally decide on the application and validity of mandatory arbitration clauses in consumer

[109] Fleming opines that this contributes to the spirit of litigiousness noted by foreign observers; Fleming, 'Mass Torts' (n 28).

[110] See firms such as Davies Arnold Cooper, in London, Pannone LLP in Manchester, and Leigh Day & Co with a reputation for specialty in this area—in areas ranging from Thalidomide, to asbestos and drug litigation.

[111] Irish Law Reform Commission, *Consultation Paper on Multi-Party Litigation* (n 68) 36.

[112] Class Action Fairness Act 2005 (n 42) (codified in scattered sections of 28 USC).

[113] Pace (n 7) 39.

contracts.[114] If these clauses are commonly held to prevent contracting consumers from participating in a FRCP Rule 23-type class, this may strictly curtail class action litigation arising from consumer transactions.[115]

Klonoff describes how, in recent years, the US courts have dramatically restrained the ability to bring class action lawsuits.[116] The result, in his opinion, has undermined the compensation, deterrence and efficiency functions of the class action device. Since the mid-1990s the US courts have been concerned about the pressure on defendants to settle once the decision to certify a class had been made. There were also concerns from the business community that many multi-state class actions were being brought in pro-plaintiff, state court venues. In 1998, the FRCP Rule 23(f) was adopted which enabled defendants to obtain interlocutory review of federal district court decisions certifying class actions. Also, CAFA has resulted in most key class actions being brought in federal court.[117] This has created a large body of federal appellate court case law, the results of which show the emergence of several trends.[118] First, the requirement by many courts that plaintiffs now prove large parts of their cases on the merits at the class certification stage. Secondly, it has become more difficult to establish several of the class certification requirements, including class definition, numerosity, commonality, adequacy of representation, Rule 23(b)(2) and Rule 23(b)(3), following several US Supreme Court decisions restricting certification.[119] Thirdly, class settlements have been rejected by a number of courts that have inflexibly applied the requirements for class certification even though the need for a trial had been obviated by the settlement. Fourthly, several courts have practically nullified so-called class issues under Rule 23(c)(4) by obliging the courts to scrutinise whether the case as a whole meets the predominance requirement of Rule 23(b)(3). Finally, as previously mentioned, unconscionability challenges to binding arbitration clauses that forbid resolution of disputes on a worldwide basis have been upheld by the Supreme Court.[120]

Overall, the impact of these trends has been to restrict significantly the capacity of plaintiffs to obtain class treatment. Some class actions do, however, remain feasible, such as antitrust class actions. The use of the class action as a mechanism, which was once deemed to be a 'revolutionary' means for achieving mass justice, seems to have lost this status, as courts have become sceptical about its certification and have heightened the hurdles to be surmounted before they are granted.[121] One argument is that some courts have gone too far in restricting class actions.[122] Cases such as *Dukes* and *Concepcion* have had effects beyond adopting new rules and seem to echo sentiments of suspicion about class actions generally. This is based on the hypothesis that the class action is an unwieldy instrument to force

[114] Ibid.

[115] eg as seen in Supreme Court decisions of *Wal-Mart Stores v Dukes* (20 June 2011, No 10-277). Also, the Supreme Court decision in *AT&T Mobility v Concepcion*, 563 US Reports, 27 April 2011, in which the Court held that corporations can use arbitration provisions in consumer and employment contracts to ban class actions, and that state contract law is preempted to the extent that it deems class-action bans unconscionable. This will make it much harder for consumers to file class action lawsuits.

[116] R Klonoff, 'The Decline of Class Actions' (2013) 90 *Wash UL Rev* 729.

[117] Class Action Fairness Act 2005 (n 42).

[118] Klonoff, 'The Decline of Class Actions' (n 116) 729.

[119] *Wal-Mart Stores v Dukes* (n 115).

[120] *AT&T Mobility v Concepcion* (n 115).

[121] O Fiss, 'The Political Theory of the Class Action' (1996) 53 *Wash & Lee L Rev* 21, 25.

[122] Klonoff (n 116) 828.

settlement and achieve large fee awards for lawyers. Klonoff concludes that the class action tool, when responsibly invoked by competent lawyers under court supervision, provides a private remedy for the achievement of collective redress.[123] This is because, apart from using a public enforcement action, class actions are the only means of redress for small-claim cases in the US. The deterrence function of the threat of class action remains an important weapon against potential misconduct. As we have seen, class actions also avoid the need for the same common issues to be resolved repeatedly for each victim. Courts should not overlook the fact that class actions can be useful and efficient managerial mechanisms for mass harm litigation. Again, we are reminded of the objectives of MPAs such as judicial and procedural economy, and deterrence.

With ongoing debates about MPAs worldwide, particularly surrounding the use of class actions, jurisdictions are experimenting with the approaches of different models. This is likely to produce much needed control against abuse and to increase efficiency. Funding of litigation is undergoing changes that may ease access for consumer cases in particular and will increase the need for regulation. These changes may vary the litigation landscape. So once again, it would appear that the field of collective redress is undergoing fundamental changes at present, with litigation being discredited as the best solution for mass harm collective redress. Instead, areas such as settlement, mediation ADR and compensation schemes are appearing to be more efficient, and therefore preferable, routes to collective redress.

8. US Class Actions and Environmental Mass Harm

In reflecting on the chapter four, which examines environmental mass harm in detail, it may be useful to highlight how some of the US MPA features, such as the requirements of Rule 23, might impact on the litigation of environmental mass harm. This is in order to compare jurisdictions in a focused way and also to highlight what is relevant to mass environmental harm considerations. We have seen how, for example, the predominance requirement can usually only be satisfied in cases of single event disasters where there is a common cause issue, unlike drug and toxic tort cases. This presents difficulties for environmental mass harm cases that do not fall into this single event category. As a way of avoiding this problem, claimants may try for settlements that provide benefits without proof of causation linking the injury to the alleged cause. This has occurred in a couple of major US class actions, where funds were established without the requirement that claimants prove that their ailments were caused by the defendants' products.[124] In Fleming's opinion, while the amount of damages weighs against the 'superiority' of class action treatment, a settlement that provides prescribed amounts of compensation obviates the need for separate trials to assess individual damages.[125] By amending these requirements of -tort liability, settlements effectively retroactively validate the class certification in conformity with its

[123] Ibid.

[124] eg *in re 'Agent Orange'* (1987) product liability litigation 597 F Supp 740 (EDNY)—(toxic defoliant) and *Dow Corning* (1994)—(breast implants) as reported in the American press in March 1994.

[125] Fleming (n 28) 507.

prescribed conditions.[126] In doing so, settlement circumvents the need for certification. In limited fund cases the advantage of this is that it is neither necessary to provide notice to all class members nor permit anyone to opt out.[127] However these cases raise concerns about compromising due process and fairness to all litigants in order to ensure judicial economy. Furthermore, there is a concern that in large class actions the victims may not always receive fair treatment, as class actions may not provide individualised justice. Another difficulty is the ability of class lawyers to represent effectively the various needs of all class members.

In relation to trends involving class actions in the US, environmental mass harm appears to be a complex area. Sherman notes that:

> The most contentious arena for class actions in modern times concerns mass disasters (such as plane crashes or building collapse), environmental disasters (like the escape of toxic chemicals into the air or water) and defective products (like asbestos, prescription drugs etc).[128]

In response to questioning on the future use of class actions for environmental mass harm in the US, Kanner highlighted the practical difficulties in such litigation. In his opinion:

> Class action practice is constantly evolving. For example, predictability in certification has become a very difficult issue. Many experienced lawyers will say the selection of the judge is outcome determinative. More courts are requiring extensive expert proof prior to certification and a merits analysis. Because of the costs, delay and risks of this path, many attorneys are using mass tort actions (MDL) as an alternative. There are a great many other issues pushing this trend, and many reasons to oppose it. The recent *Roeder* case, however, surprised many lawyers who thought that environmental class actions were dying off. This was a recent class action settlement for the contamination of groundwater and drinking water as a result of alleged wrongful storage and disposal of hazardous substances associated with an abandoned copper mine. The settlement is believed to be worth up to $19.5 million and comprised two settlement classes that were certified: a property settlement class; and a medical monitoring settlement class. *Philip Roeder et al v Atlantic Richfield Co and BP America Inc.* Case No.11-105 (D.Nev.). Control is another evolving issue. In the past lawyers were selected by individual clients. Class actions changed that but they contain built in procedural safeguards regarding the appointment of class counsel. Now many of these cases are ending up in MDLs where the court simply picks an MDL lead or liaison counsel who has extraordinary control over the fate of litigants without any of the procedural safeguards associated with class action practice.[129]

This indicates the crucial need for safeguards in MPA mechanisms, a fact of which EU policy seems to be very aware. Traditionally, the MPA mechanism most often used for environmental mass harm was the opt-out class action. It has been used in many mass environmental harm cases, for example, the case of *Ren-Dan Farms, Inc v Monsanto Co.*[130] Another example is the action by numerous Ecuador citizens who sued Texaco for damage caused

[126] Ibid.

[127] At the cost of the representative plaintiffs.

[128] E Sherman, 'Group Litigation under Foreign Legal Systems: Variations and Alternatives to American Class Actions' (2002) 52 *DePaul L Rev* 401, 407.

[129] By email on 5 March 2014.

[130] 952 F Supp 370 (WD La 1997). This case concerned a national class of farmers who succeeded in suing Monsanto for damages arising from genetically altered cotton. The potentially unknown risks of releasing such altered organisms can have long-term and wide-ranging implications. In this case, agriculturalists cross-pollinated some strains of corn to create a hybrid seed that did produce a greater yield but which was less resistant to a harmful fungus, which decimated 15% of the US corn crop in 1970, causing an estimated $1bn in losses.

by a toxic spill and the destruction of rain forest.[131] A further, infamous, example is that of the US class action in Bhopal, where Indian residents were killed or injured together with destruction to the environment by release of methyl isocyanate by Union Carbide Corporation.[132] As Kanner highlights above, however, this class action trend may be changing, due to reasons such as the costs, delays and risks involved in class actions. It appears that mass tort actions through MDL are being invoked more often in their place. Even so, it seems clear that MPA mechanisms are necessary in the US as a route to a remedy for environmental mass harm. This is because they may be helpful management mechanisms for the litigation of such cases. There is a fear of US class actions in Europe but it is important to remember that US MPA mechanisms are necessary because of the enforcement function that they play.

The environmental mass harm chapter shows how the US has progressively dealt with the challenges presented by environmental mass harm litigation such as scientific evidence, environmental justice issues and concerns such as latency. In an effort to overcome these difficulties, it has introduced legislative innovations and encouraged judicial creativity, for example by creating procedures such as the device of medical monitoring. The example of the Deepwater Horizon Disaster involving BP illustrates these innovations, even though it was MDL, rather than a class action. It is also notable that BP, as part of the settlement, agreed to spend $105 million over five years to set up a Gulf Coast health outreach programme and pay for medical examinations. The US experience appears to indicate that, in appropriate cases, where there is no alternative to litigation, there can be advantages to both claimants and defendants in collectively resolving cases of environmental mass harm. This would suggest that other common law jurisdictions could learn valuable lessons from the US experience of using MPAs for environmental mass harm, particularly in relation to its innovative legislative remedies and creative approach to toxic tort cases.

[131] In February 2011, an $18bn judgment was rendered against Chevron by a court in Lago Agrio, Ecuador, for alleged contamination resulting from crude oil production in the region. This is the largest environmental damages award in history.

[132] The Bhopal disaster was an industrial disaster that took place at a Union Carbide India Limited pesticide plant in the Indian city of Bhopal, Madhya Pradesh. On 3 December 1984, methyl isocyanate (MIC) gas was accidentally released from the plant, exposing more than 500,000 people to MIC and other chemicals. The Government of Madhya Pradesh confirmed a total of 3,787 deaths related to the gas release. It left an estimated 40,000 individuals permanently disabled, maimed, or suffering from serious illness, making it one of the world's worst industrial disasters in history. Union Carbide was sued by the Government of India and agreed to an out-of-court settlement of US$470m in 1989. The plant site clean-up and India's demand for the extradition of then-Union Carbide CEO Warren Anderson are yet to be resolved.

6

Canadian MPA Experience

This chapter is the beginning of the examination of the experience of selected other common law jurisdictions, apart from the US, and their varying collective redress MPA mechanisms. As stated in the overview of MPA procedures in chapter two, outside of the US, not many common law countries have adopted legislative changes to facilitate mass harm through collective redress procedures. Australia and Canada provide exceptions to this as both have introduced class actions for cases of mass torts.[1] Both of these jurisdictions eschew the US categorisation approach to class actions as this was expressly rejected by the law reform agencies in Australia and Ontario. It is also remarkable that the Canadian and Australian class action regimes stand apart from the US rule in that they *expressly* contemplate claims for damages for mass tort cases, whereas US rules do not refer to damages.[2]

1. Canadian Litigation Landscape

A. Overview

Canada is a bi-juridical, bilingual nation but the legal system in most of its provinces and territories is dominated by the common law adversarial system. This is based on common law as inherited from Great Britain through its colonisation and English is the main language spoken. In Quebec, however, French is the predominant language and there is a large civil law influence on the legal system, inherited from France. Nonetheless, Quebec has taken on aspects of the adversarial system for its civil litigation procedures in general, and

[1] In Canada, class actions were first introduced in Quebec in 1978 by Lois Que 1978 c 8; Code of Civil Procedure (CCP), Arts 999–1051, followed in 1992 by Ontario with its Class Proceeding Act 1992 (c 6). In Australia, both the federal system and the 2 states of Victoria and New South Wales have introduced representative or group proceedings regimes which are similar to US style class actions. These Australian procedures have been available in the Federal Court since 4 March 1992, in Victoria since January 2000 and in New South Wales since 4 March 2011. In each instance, those regimes have been established by the passage of legislation. The federal procedures were introduced under the Federal Court of Australia Amendment Act 1991 in the form of pt IVA, an amendment to the Federal Court of Australia Act 1976 (Cth). The state procedures were introduced through pt 4A of the Supreme Court Act 1986 (Vic) and pt 10 of the Civil Procedure Act 2005 (NSW). However, owing to the limited scope of federal jurisdiction, this is more or less limited to product liability.

[2] J Fleming, 'Mass Torts' (1994) 42 *Am J Comp L* 521.

particularly for class actions.[3] The constitutional structure of Canada gives its provincial superior courts jurisdiction over civil rights and property within their territory. There is also a Federal Court of Canada that has jurisdiction throughout the country. However, this Federal Court's role in civil litigation is restricted for several reasons, chiefly owing to its limited subject matter jurisdiction as stipulated by statute.

B. Evolution of MPA Landscape

Canadian law generally allows class actions in all of its provinces.[4] Ontario, Quebec and British Columbia currently operate active class action regimes.[5] There were hesitant efforts by some courts to expand class actions during the 1960s and 1970s in response to pressure from environmentalists, consumer groups and competition campaigners. However, there was a long spell of opposition to class action and resistance to its introduction by those who felt threatened by the changes that class actions would bring, namely the fear of their potential to injure the business community. Quebec, even though it is a civil law system, was the first province to introduce US style class actions proceedings legislation in 1978. In the rest of Canada, the Ontario Law Reform Commission led attempts at class action reform during the late-1970s and early-1980s, culminating in its enormous three-volume report in 1982 that recommended legislative change.[6] The impasse was broken in the early-1990s by a liberal Attorney General who negotiated with the main parties who felt unsure about such reform.[7] Ontario passed its class action legislation in 1993, followed by the British Columbia legislation in 1995. Since 2008, class action procedures have been introduced in all Canadian provinces and territories, apart from Prince Edward Island, as well as in the Federal Court of Canada.[8] It is beyond the scope of this research to look at the class action regime in all of Canada in detail, so it will examine procedures at federal level and also in two provinces in particular, Ontario and British Columbia, because these are legally important common law jurisdictions for reasons of population and volume of litigation.[9] It will also examine one that is heavily influenced by the civil code tradition, Quebec.

[3] J Kalajdzic, W Bogart and I Matthews in D Hensler, C Hodges and M Tulibacka (eds), *The Globalization of Class Actions* (2009) 622 The Annals of the American Academy of Political and Social Science 41.

[4] Both plaintiff and defendant classes are possible. It is important to note that all Canadian provinces are common law except for Quebec.

[5] Elsewhere in Canada, multi-party litigation is dealt with under the historic representative procedure similar to the Irish ord 15, r 9 and other miscellaneous procedures.

[6] Ontario Law Reform Commission, *Report on Class Actions*, vols 1, 2 and 3 (Toronto, Canada, Ministry of the Attorney General, 1982).

[7] Kalajdzic and others (n 3) 42.

[8] This was achieved through amendments to the federal rules of practice as outlined in the Class Proceedings in the Federal Court of Canada, Federal Court of Canada Circular No 2/2000.

[9] For more detail on Canadian class actions, see generally J Prestage and G McKee, 'Class Actions in the Common Law Provinces of Canada' in C Hodges, *Multi-Party Actions* (Oxford University Press, 2001); G Watson 'Class Actions: The Canadian Experience' (2001) 11 *Duke J Comp & Int'l L* 269; P Cashman, *Class Action Law and Practice* (Federation Press, 2007) 657; G Coonan, 'Public Interest Law and the Irish Legal System: All Crass and No Class' (2002) 5 *Trinity CL Rev* 44.

2. MPA Litigation

Canada's civil procedure rules allow joinder or consolidation of multiple claims in all provinces, as well as class actions.[10] The current class action procedures are broadly based on the Uniform Class Proceedings Act[11] and Rule 23 of the US Federal Rules of Procedure. Unlike the US style approach, the Canadian approach specifically addresses damages claims. The requirements arising under Canadian legislation for class action proceedings and certification are not quite as arduous as those of the US in Rule 23. However, all the class action legislation requires that leave to proceed with the litigation as a class is obtained from the court by way of a motion to certify the proceedings as a class action. In general, for the action to be certified, the promoter of the class proceedings is required to satisfy five criteria. These require that:

1. the pleadings disclose a cause of action;
2. there exists an identifiable class;
3. there are common issues among the claims of the class members ('common issues');
4. a class action would be the preferable procedure for resolving these common issues ('preferability'); and
5. the class representative will fairly and adequately represent the interests of the class on the basis of a workable trial plan.[12]

The tests for certification vary slightly in each state's legislation. For example, as for the 'preferability' criterion, generally the class action needs to be the preferable procedure in relation to the common issues.[13] While Ontario and other provinces stipulate preferability, what is required is left to the court's judgment.[14] As stated in *Carom v Bre-X Minerals*:[15]

> A class proceeding is the preferable procedure where it presents a fair, efficient, and manageable method of determining the common issues which arise from the claims of multiple plaintiffs and where such determination will advance the proceedings in accordance with the goals of judicial economy, access to justice, and the modification of the behaviour of wrongdoers.

These aims echo the objectives identified in this study for MPAs generally. They also highlight the role of class actions as MPA managerial mechanisms. Quebec, however, does not specify preferability; it has an express requirement that the action raises similar or related questions of law and fact and that the composition of the group makes joinder difficult or impracticable.[16] The Supreme Court of Canada has held that judicial economy should be considered and evaluated when determining whether the requirement of preferability is met in the relevant class action statutes.[17]

[10] See eg Ontario Rules of Civil Procedure, RRO 1990, reg 994, rr 5 and 6.
[11] Adopted by the Uniform Law Conference of Canada in 1996.
[12] The representative must be appropriate. See Irish Law Reform Commission, *Consultation Paper on Multi-Party Litigation* (LRC CP 25-2003) 38.
[13] See generally Prestage and McKee, 'Class Actions in the Common Law Provinces of Canada' (n 9) 1421.
[14] See eg Class Proceedings Act 1992, SO 1992, c 6 (Ontario CPA), s 5(1)(d).
[15] (1999) 44 OR (3d) 173 (Gen Div).
[16] Quebec CCP, Art 1003(a).
[17] *Hollick v Metropolitan Toronto (Municipality)* 2001 SCC 68, 205 DLR (4th) 19 (SCC) [15], [27].

The requirement that a class be 'identifiable' merely means that it be possible to determine that a person is a class member but the identity and quantity of individual class members need not be definite. While the 'common issues' requirement is a critical element of the certification, neither the Ontario nor the British Columbia legislation dictates that the common issues must 'predominate'. Also, a representative plaintiff does not need to be typical of the putative class once he does not have a conflict of interest and can show that he will progress the class claims fairly and effectively. Even though it may seem that the threshold set by these requirements is quite easy to establish, certification can still be as difficult to attain as in the US. However, in Ontario, class action certification is considered easier to obtain than in the US, especially after the passage of the US Class Action Fairness Act 2005.[18] Watson notes that:

> Certification has been a major battleground. Defendants have fought hard to achieve certification, with mixed success. Courts, however, have sometimes refused certification for reasons having little to do with statutory criteria- judges identify an action as a 'bad class action' (which is never really defined) and the reasons for refusing certification may be disingenuous and lack transparency.[19]

While there is generally no limit on the type of relief that may be sought or by whom, once the proposed representative plaintiff satisfies the prescribed requirements, some jurisdictions do impose limitations on corporations and other non-natural persons acting as representative plaintiffs.[20] The majority of representative plaintiffs are, however, individuals seeking monetary relief. There are differing views on whether it is necessary that a representative plaintiff should have a personal cause of action against each defendant. In British Columbia, it has been held that once a representative plaintiff would fairly or adequately represent the class for the purposes of the certified common issues then he or she can act.[21] This allows for so-called industry class actions to be filed by one individual.[22] A defining trait of all the relevant legislation is that it aims to protect the interests of class members. This protection generally requires the court to use the mechanisms available to it in the legislation to make sure that class members are treated justly all the time. This appears to suggest a prevailing objective of fairness in the Canadian class action regime. The Canadian approach is largely opt-out,[23] although there are exceptions to this. British Columbia, for example, while it operates an opt-out regime, obliges class members who are not resident in the province to opt in.[24] Apart from this, a judgment on common issues will bind all class members. Ontario is well known as an opt-out jurisdiction.[25]

Class members must be notified of certification. The content of the notice is prescribed by the legislation and it must be court-approved. The legislation states that notice may be given to members of the class at each of the critical stages in the proceedings and the court must approve both the notice content and the way in which it is published.[26] In some cases

[18] Pub L No 109-2, 119 Stat 4 (codified in scattered sections of 28 USC).

[19] Watson, 'Class Actions' (n 9); see generally Cashman, *Class Action Law and Practice* (n 9).

[20] eg Quebec CCP, Arts 999 and 1048.

[21] British Columbia Class Proceedings Act, RSBC 1996, s 14(3).

[22] Ibid.

[23] Ontario CPA (n 14), s 9.

[24] BC CPA (n 21) s 16(1).

[25] Once the proceeding is certified the members of the class are presumptively included and are bound by any settlement or judgment unless they actively 'opt out' within a certain specified timeframe.

[26] eg Ontario CPA (n 14) ss 17 and 29(4).

there is close court scrutiny of the form and effectiveness of notice.[27] It is at the court's discretion how the notice is to be conveyed and who bears this cost. Notification to class members is not formally necessary before a class action is begun but, generally, informal notice of potential class members' claims is often given. The court may decide to abolish notice entirely.[28] Usually, although this is not required by legislation outside of Quebec, the court will insist that all class members are also given notice of the hearing at which a proposed settlement will be considered. Class members have the right to appear at such a hearing and object to the adequacy or fairness of the settlement proposal. Many class action law firms use websites and press releases to publicise class proceedings and their updates as well as using direct mail and media advertisements.[29] If a class is certified, then any decision of court or settlement will bind members of the class unless they opt out within a specified time after certification.

Canadian law explicitly provides the possibility of bifurcating common issues and individual issues within a single procedural agenda. This means that once an action has been certified and notice has been given, a court will usually deal with the issues common to the class, followed by those common to any subclass, then any issues relating to individual members of a class.[30] The Ontario and British Columbia systems provide for the certification of sub-classes in this way. The trial judge has wide discretion to impose whatever conditions or to make whatever orders he deems fitting in the interests of convenience or fairness. As for discovery, in both of the common law provinces, which are Ontario and British Columbia, and in the Federal Court, the civil procedure rules allow documentary and oral discovery of opposing parties.

One of the most remarkable traits of the Canadian class action regime is the way in which class actions are funded. Most class actions are funded through the use of contingency fee agreements with class counsel. In such agreements counsel undertake to fund the litigation and recoup fees. The representative plaintiff will only have to pay these fees if the litigation outcome is successful, either because of settlement or at trial. Such agreements are normally for 20 to 40 per cent of the award. Class counsel sometimes arrange for a consortium of third-party investors to finance the litigation by giving a loan to the representative plaintiffs that is repayable only in the event of a successful outcome to the litigation.[31] The use of contingency fees or funding arrangement is common because, in the jurisdictions where cost awards can be obtained, court-ordered costs will, by themselves, be insufficient financial incentive to entice counsel to act in the proceedings.[32] Court approval is required

[27] In some cases, counsel have retained 'class-notification experts' to design notice programmes and provide the court with evidence as to the expected effectiveness of the notice programme. eg notice of the proposed $1bn settlement of the Indian Residential Schools case was given in 27 languages in every province, in print, radio and television advertisements. See, for example, The Hilsee Group LLC, the class action notification experts., www.hilseegroup.org

[28] Ontario CPA (n 14) s 17(2).

[29] See eg Sutts, Stosberg LLP 'Vioxx National Class Action Canada', available at: www.vioxxnationalclassaction.com.

[30] eg in a class action for damages in tort, liability might be established through the resolution of common issues. The court would then proceed to make an aggregate award of damages in favour of the class or to conduct further proceedings leading to individualised assessments.

[31] See *Toronto Star*, 'Investors Betting Lawsuits Will Bring Big Payoffs' (22 February 1998).

[32] This refers to what is known as 'party and party costs', which will include the successful party's reasonable disbursements.

for any fee agreement between a lawyer and representative plaintiff, whether contingent or not, and the fee has to be justified by the class counsel. The courts take a range of factors into consideration when deciding what fee is fair in the circumstances.[33] These include the amount of time and work involved, the novelty of the legal issues in question, the outcome of the proceedings and the risk taken by class counsel.[34] Ontario and Quebec have government funds to which representative plaintiffs may apply for litigation funding. The Ontario Law Society also operates a Class Proceedings Fund, which is a highly original mechanism.[35] This provides funding for disbursements only. The Class Proceedings Fund was created in order to alleviate potential hardship of the losing class representative and it provides two things. First, the representative may apply for funding towards expenses of the proceedings.[36] Secondly, where the representative sought funding and this was awarded but the class action then failed, the Fund will absolve the representative plaintiff of liability for the defendant's costs. As a *quid pro quo* for this facility, a levy is imposed by the Fund on beneficiaries who consequently win their cases.[37] While this innovative approach hypothetically shows potential, the reality is that, in practice, the Fund has only achieved moderate success owing to its failure to attract representative plaintiffs, especially in the large, successful class actions.[38] The small numbers who have sought funding and the smaller still numbers of those who have been given it has meant that the levy is effectively a redundant way of financing the Fund.[39] It seems to have failed to reach its intended aim of facilitating access to justice by alleviating the financial barriers faced by representative plaintiffs. Some class action lawyers say that the main reasons that plaintiffs do not seek funding more often are the low approval rate of the Class Proceedings Committee, which decides whether to give the financial support by assessing the merits of an action, and the low level of funding given and the relatively very large share of the settlement or judgment that is collected by the Fund.[40] In Quebec, funding may be available for both disbursements and fees.

As for litigation costs, the extent and nature of the plaintiff's liability differs in each of the provinces. Like Ireland, in Canadian litigation generally the rule for costs is that the losing party must pay the costs of the winning party as 'costs follow the event'. This applies equally to class actions, but astoundingly it is only the representative plaintiff who is liable for the costs of the other side in the event the class action is defeated. Some of the provinces have adopted a no costs rule, by which litigants usually bear their own costs and some provinces

[33] Ontario CPA (n 14) ss 32(3) and 33.

[34] A list of factors discussed can be seen eg in *White v Canada* (Attorney General), [2006] BCJ No 760, [27] (SC) (QL).

[35] It is administered by their Class Proceedings Committee.

[36] They apply to the committee and funding is awarded based on several factors, eg the merits of the class action, the representative's ability to raise funds elsewhere and the existence of financial controls to make certain that the monies are spent suitably.

[37] Where a plaintiff who had received funding succeeds in the class action, 10% of the damages award must be given to the Fund.

[38] eg *Nantais v Telectronics Proprietary (Canada) Ltd* [1995] 129 DLR (4th) 110 (Ont Gen Div) (Can), *prob juris noted* 127 DLR (4th) 552 (Can$23.1m settlement in heart pacemakers); *Serwaczek v Medical Engineering Corp* [1996] 3 CPC (4th) 386 (Gen Div) (Can$29.1m settlement in breast implants case); *Dabbs v Sun Life Assurance Co of Canada* [1998] 40 OR (3d) 776 (Gen Div) (Can) (multi-million dollar settlement in a fraudulent life assurance case).

[39] In 2007, only 3 applications for funding were made and 2 of these were approved. The total amount awarded to applicants in 2007 was Can$257,209.

[40] See W Branch, *Class Actions in Canada* (Canada Law Book, 2007) 4.

retain a two-way costs rule whereby the loser pays. In Ontario, a representative plaintiff will only escape liability for costs if the court feels that the action was a test case, or raised a novel point of law or involved a matter of public interest. To offset this disincentive to litigate, Ontario law expressly exempts class actions from the province's general prohibition on contingent fees in civil proceedings. Apart from funding difficulties that putative plaintiffs face there is also the additional obstacle of the risk of an adverse costs award if the defendants succeed (in provinces with the two-way costs rule). The Canadian courts have been generally very aware of the risks that large costs pose to class action viability. They have recognised the role played by class actions in increasing access to justice in the legal system and have stated that 'large cost awards against unsuccessful plaintiffs will have a chilling effect and likely discourage meritorious class actions'.[41] Despite this statement, there have been some sizeable costs awards made against unsuccessful plaintiffs and some commentators believe that the courts are becoming less protective towards plaintiffs as a result of the 2007 Supreme Court decision in *Kerr v Danier Leather*.[42] In that case, the appellate court overturned the trial judgment in favour of investors in a securities class action. Anecdotally, practitioners argue that the case will be confined to its particular facts. The case concerned a wealthy representative plaintiff who suffered hundreds of thousands of Canadian dollars in share losses but who commenced a class action instead of taking an individual action. In awarding costs against him, Justice Binnie stated:

> It should not be assumed that class proceedings invariably engage access to justice concerns to an extent sufficient to justify withholding costs from the successful party.[43]

Such a decision might appear, either intentionally or by accident, to create an incentive for the use of the 'man of straw' as a plaintiff, as has been seen in both Ireland and Australia, in order to avoid potentially crippling costs awards. This also raises concerns of fairness when one asks how fair it is on the defendant if there is only a small chance of being awarded its costs.

Courts are involved in case management of class actions in order to avoid this complicated type of litigation becoming unmanageable and to safeguard class members' interests.[44] Once again, we see the role of MPAs as managerial mechanisms assisting with mass harm litigation. For example, the Ontario Class Proceedings Act 1992 (CPA) requires case management of class actions and this is also normal practice in class actions outside of that province. In the common law provinces examined it is generally the same judge that hears all pre-trial motions in a class action, as well as the motion for certification. The provinces differ in relation to whether the case management judges should preside over the trial of the common issues. In Ontario, the case management judge does not officiate at the trial of the common issues unless the parties agree to this.[45] Other provinces, like British Columbia,

[41] *Pauli v Ace INA Insurance Co*, [2004] AJ No 883 at [31] (CA) (QL).

[42] 2007 SCC 44.

[43] Ibid para 69. For comments on the impact of this decision on future class action litigation, see generally K Baert and A Guindon, 'Class Proceedings in Ontario: the Growing Risk of Adverse Costs Awards Against Representative Plaintiffs' ('5th Annual Symposium on Class Actions', Toronto, April 2008).

[44] See eg opinion of Winkler J, 'Advocacy in Class Proceedings Litigation' (2000) 19 *Advocates' Soc J* 6, where he commented that case management judges have a 'weighty responsibility' and a 'broad discretion' in overseeing class actions.

[45] Ontario CPA (n 14) s 34.

do not place any restrictions on this.[46] As there are no legislative provisions for national class actions, courts have used their case management authority innovatively to control class actions that involve the same subject matter in different provinces and have been doing so on a consent basis among the judges and parties concerned. However, courts are aware that they are not able to impose binding coordinating orders on an extra-provincial court without such consent.

As for the determination of class actions, there may be settlement or trial. If there is a settlement, this must be approved by the court.[47] Some commentators have noted that Canadian judges, when scrutinising settlements, are more demanding than their US equivalents.[48] Settlements are negotiated by counsel for the parties, sometimes helped by a judge acting as mediator but this must not be the case management judge. The representative plaintiffs are seldom involved in negotiations and there is no need for them to sanction the settlement before it will be approved on behalf of the class by the court. The role of the judge at the settlement hearing is to ensure that the proposed settlement is 'fair, reasonable and in the best interests of those affected by it'.[49] The settlement does not have to be perfect; rather, the court must be satisfied that the settlement falls 'within a zone or range of reasonableness' for the class as a whole.[50] The vast majority of class actions are settled and it appears that less than 5 per cent of all class actions go to trial.[51] Class counsel must keep the interests of the class as their primary concern when they are negotiating the settlement, as they owe them a fiduciary duty.

Class actions offer a wide range of remedies to class members. As regards monetary relief, there are detailed provisions including the participation of individual class members for the determination of their own particular issues.[52] Other possibilities include the assessment of aggregate awards[53] and the distribution of judgments, including a form of *cy près*.[54] In the context of class actions, this refers to the application of an aggregate award or settlement in a way which may reasonably be expected 'to compensate or benefit class members, where actual division and distribution of the award among the class members is impossible or impracticable'.[55] Precise Canadian class action statistics are not available but research has shown that there has been a significant increase in class action proceedings in recent years.[56]

Following this brief look at the Canadian experience of class actions, it seems that they have been widely used there. There has, however, been much debate surrounding how multiple, overlapping and/or national class actions are to be conducted and managed as

46 BC CPA (n 21) s 14(3).

47 As being fair and reasonable and in the best interests of the class.

48 eg in *Parsons v Canadian Red Cross Society* [1999] 40 CPC (4th) 151 (Ont S C), 101 ACWS (3d) 694 (Can), the trial judge refused to approve an initial settlement proposal for a Can$1.5 bn settlement of a class claim in relation to Hepatitis C-contaminated blood.

49 *Sutherland v Boots Pharmaceutical PLC*, [2002] OJ No 1361, [10] (SCJ) (QL).

50 *Ontario New Home Warranty Programme v Chevron Chemical Co*, [1999] OJ No 2245, [89] (SCJ) (QL).

51 Precise Canadian class action statistics are not available. For 2012 statistics, see http://harrisonpensa.com/wp-content/uploads/2012/07/Summary-of-Common-Issues-Trial-Activity-Across-Canada-Jul-11-12-FINAL-Read-Only.pdf Settlements can happen either before or after certification or the common issues trial.

52 Ontario CPA (n 14) s.25.

53 Ibid ss 23 and 24.

54 Ibid s 25.

55 See generally R Mulheron, *The Class Action in Common Law Legal Systems—A Comparative Perspective* (Hart Publishing, 2004) 426.

56 Baert and Guindon, 'Class Proceedings in Ontario' (n 43).

national classes, with members all over the country.[57] If there is no generally applicable agreement for national classes then, at least in some situations, an opt-out provision will enable class actions in those provinces to include members from all over Canada. This helps to assuage fears that most class members are passive and would otherwise not proactively include themselves in the class proceedings.[58] For a number of reasons, the Federal Court has limited subject matter jurisdiction prescribed by statute; for example, this is confined to: actions against the Federal Government; actions involving admiralty issues; and certain matters of intellectual property. Thus, the Federal Court's role in civil litigation, in general, and class actions, in particular, is circumscribed.[59] The Federal Court, therefore, offers limited opportunities for national class actions. In contrast, the provincial courts have general subject matter jurisdiction but limited territorial jurisdiction. As regards the provincial courts, the legislation of Ontario and of Quebec does not explicitly deal with issues of national class actions. Commentators believe that there are compelling arguments for certifying an otherwise valid class action as a national class action where members of the class are spread throughout the country. These arguments include the objective of enhancing access to justice for class members, avoidance of duplication of litigation and overall savings to the administration of justice.[60] As a result of this, there have been a number of decisions in Ontario and Quebec certifying classes to include members not resident in the province.[61] Some court decisions in those provinces have not followed this approach.[62] There has been an effort to better manage and synchronise class action litigation involving plaintiffs from all over the country and proposals to facilitate this were put forward by the Uniform Law Commission of Canada.[63]

There are criticisms, for example, about the ability and appropriateness of courts of individual provinces for certifying national class actions. However, none of the criticisms attacks the existence of class actions or their authenticity. More importantly, the public has not been critical of the benefit of class actions to class members. The consequences of class action litigation have had effect throughout Canada,[64] because the Ontario and British Columbia regimes have enabled quite a few nationwide class actions. There has been a broad range of areas that have been the subject of class actions and this includes

[57] See generally C Poltak, 'Ontario and Her Sisters: Should Full Faith and Credit Apply to the National Class' (2006) 3 *Canadian Class Action Rev* 437; C Jones, 'Disorderly and Unfair: The Weird Present and Uncertain Future of 'Full Faith and Credit' in Inter-jurisdictional Class Actions, Paper presented to the '4th Annual Symposium on Class Actions', Toronto, 26–27 April 2007, [unpublished].

[58] Kalajdzic and others (n 3) 44.

[59] P Hogg, *Constitutional Law of Canada*, vol 1 (15th edn, Thomson Canada Limited, 2007) 7-26–7-27.

[60] W Bogart, J Kalajdzic and I Matthews, 'Class Actions in Canada: A National Procedure in a Multi-Jurisdictional Society?' (A report prepared for 'The Globalisation of Class Actions' Conference, Oxford University, December 2007) 11.

[61] The leading Ontario case is *Nantais v Telectronics Proprietary (Canada) Ltd* [1995] 129 DLR (4th) 110 (Ont Gen Div) (Can), *prob juris noted* 127 DLR (4th) 552 (Can$23.1m settlement in heart pacemakers); the leading Quebec cases are *Société canadienne des postes c Lépine*, 2007 QCCA 1092 (CA)(QL) and *Masson v Thompson* (29 January 1992), Montréal 500-06-000005-914 (Que SC) [unreported] (certification decision), aff'd [1993] RJQ 69 (CA); [1994] RJQ 1032 (SC) (jurisdiction over non-resident class members), aff'd [1995] RJQ 329 (CA) (application to sever third-party proceedings).

[62] See eg *McNaughton Automotive Ltd v Co-operators General Insurance Co* (2003) 66 OR (3d) 112 (SCJ).

[63] For detail in the report, see the Uniform Law Conference of Canada (9 March 2005).

[64] Even in the province where no class action legislation has been enacted, Prince Edward Island.

consumer claims;[65] employment claims;[66] mass torts;[67] product liability claims;[68] and economic claims.[69] It is difficult to measure the success of class actions in Canada because of the lack of statistics and precise empirical studies. It is useful to look in summary at class action developments in Canada in the past decade since the Canadian Supreme Court released a trilogy of class actions decisions, *Centres v Dutton*, *Hollick v Toronto a* nd *Rumley v British Columbia*.[70] These cases elaborated on the commonality and preferability criteria to be used in all certification motions and they also established other important procedural tests. According to Kalajdzic, they effectively codified the objectives of class actions and signalled the entrenchment of class actions in the Canadian civil justice system.[71] In *Dutton*, in particular, the Supreme Court affirmed the importance of class actions in modern litigation.[72]

3. Evaluation of Canadian Class Action Experience Against MPA Objectives

Looking now at the MPA objectives to evaluate the Canadian regime against these, it is worth reiterating a statement from *Carom v Bre-X Minerals*[73] that echoes several of the MPA objectives:

> A class proceeding is the preferable procedure where it presents a fair, efficient, and manageable method of determining the common issues which arise from the claims of multiple plaintiffs and where such determination will advance the proceedings in accordance with the goals of judicial economy, access to justice, and the modification of the behaviour of wrongdoers.

A. Access to Justice

Class actions improve access to justice by dividing the costs of litigation between class members and without them 'the doors of justice remain closed to some plaintiffs, however strong their legal claims'.[74] Class actions have been consistently lauded and justified on the basis that they improve access to justice and for many commentators it is self-evident that such litigation helps surmount economic, social and psychological barriers to claiming

[65] eg illegal credit card charges.
[66] eg wrongful dismissal.
[67] eg institutional child abuse, eg *Lumley v British Columbia* [1999] BCJ No 2633.
[68] eg defective medical devices.
[69] eg breach of copyright, franchising.
[70] *Western Canadian Shopping Centres v Dutton*, [2000] SCJ No 63, [2001] 2 SCR 534 (SCC) (*Dutton*); *Hollick v Toronto (City)*, [2001] SCJ No67, [2001] 3 SCR 158 (SCC) (*Hollick*); and *Rumley v British Columbia*, [2001] SCJ No39, [2001] 3 SCR 184 (SCC) (*Rumley*).
[71] J Kalajdzic (ed), *Accessing Justice, Appraising Class Actions, Ten Years After Dutton, Hollick & Rumley* (Lexis Nexis, 2011) 3.
[72] *Dutton* (n 70) [46].
[73] (1999) 44 OR (3d) 173 (Gen Div).
[74] *Dutton* (n 70) [28].

redress.[75] Kalajdzic highlights that despite this, the Supreme Court itself has expressed doubt that class actions inevitably engage access to justice considerations.[76] One of the judges in the Supreme Court trilogy, *Dutton*, *Hollick* and *Rumley*, The Honourable Frank Iacobucci, stated that these cases approached access to justice in quite a narrow way: access to justice was equated with access to the courts; class actions improve access to justice by making viable claims that individually are uneconomical to prosecute.[77] It has been suggested, however, that while undoubtedly class actions increase the numbers and types of claims being litigated, the extent to which they are successful in providing a remedy that is fair for the injuries that the class has suffered is not self-evident.[78]

On a positive note, an examination of the three Supreme Court decisions endorses the beneficial attributes of class actions. Chief Justice McLachlin in *Dutton* opined that the reform of class actions in Canada had been 'motivated in large part by the recognition of the benefits that class actions can offer the parties, the court system and society'. In *Rumley*, the Court lauded the inherent flexibility of the class action mechanism. It stressed that courts are ultimately trying to balance efficiency with fairness, and that for vulnerable class members, such as survivors of institutional abuse like those in *Rumley*, allowing the case to proceed as a class action helped to somewhat mitigate the emotional and psychological barriers facing some plaintiffs. Finally, in *Hollick*, the Court opined that the Class Proceedings Act in Ontario 'reflects an increasing recognition of the important advantages that the class action offers as a procedural tool'.

In examining the specific features of the Canadian regime, the fact that the Canadian requirements for certification are not as demanding as those in the US may initially suggest easier access to justice. However, it has been shown above that although the threshold to meet these requirements may be easy to establish, court certification itself can still be as difficult to attain as in the US. There are clearly inherent funding difficulties in the system and large costs pose a strong threat to the viability of class action. The courts are aware of how these risks may impede access to justice. The innovative solution of the Class Proceedings Fund aimed to increase access to justice but it has not been very effective in alleviating this threat. All of the following objectives are included in the aim of access to justice, so are briefly elaborated on below and then summarised in the conclusion.

B. Judicial and Procedural Economy

Overall, Canadian procedure appears to be efficient and innovative.[79] For example, there is case management of class actions to avoid them becoming unmanageable and techniques may be used by which common issues may be bifurcated. In Canadian class action statutes, the concept of judicial economy is only implicitly included. However, the Supreme Court of Canada has held that judicial economy should be considered and evaluated when determining whether the requirement of preferability is met in the relevant class action

[75] Kalajdzic, *Accessing Justice, Appraising Class Actions, Ten Years After Dutton, Hollick & Rumley* (n 71) 4.
[76] *Kerr v Daniel Leather Inc*, [2007] SCJ No 44, [2007] 3 SCR 331, [69] (SCC).
[77] F Iacobucci, 'What is Access to Justice in the Context of Class Actions?' in Kalajdzic (n 71) 21.
[78] Kalajdzic (n 71) 4.
[79] See generally Bogart, Kalajdzic and Matthews, 'Class Actions in Canada (n 60).

statutes.[80] This shows a conscious effort of the judiciary to evaluate proactively whether the use a class action is the preferable means to resolve a dispute in order to achieve efficiencies and judicial economy.

C. Fairness

Notwithstanding the reservation above that the extent to which class actions are successful in providing a remedy that is fair for the injuries that the class has suffered is not self-evident,[81] it is clear the Canadian class action legislation and procedure aim to protect the interests of class members and to ensure that they are treated fairly at all times. The court scrutiny of the notification process is an example of this as it aims to ensure that the class action is accessible to all who are eligible to opt in. The courts have wide discretion over issues such as which party bears the cost of notification and also to impose whatever conditions or orders that are considered to be fitting in the interests of fairness. The need for court approval of settlement is a further safeguard and it may be argued that some Canadian judges may be more demanding than those in the US in this regard.[82] Furthermore, the ability of class members to appear and object in a settlement proposal hearing further ensures fairness. Case management by judges also aims to safeguard members' interests. Judges may act as mediator in achieving settlement and overall will aim to achieve a fair settlement for the parties. As shown above, a remarkable feature of the Canadian class action system is that it is only the representative plaintiff who is liable for the costs of the other side if the class action is defeated. The use of contingency fees and the requirement that they be court-approved helps to mitigate any unfairness that this may cause. Ostensibly, the difficulty of financing funding is further eased by the existence of the Class Proceedings Fund but this has only been moderately successful. In *Rumley*, as we have seen, the court praised the inherent flexibility of the class action mechanism and recognised that the courts are ultimately trying to balance efficiency with fairness. This does not appear to be an easy balance to achieve.

In relation to the objective of balancing individual rights and personal autonomy, the class action procedure endeavours to provide this balance. For example, some of the compensation provisions allow the participation of individual class members for the determination of their own particular issues.[83] Also, class members are given notice of the hearing at which the proposed settlement will be considered and they have a right to appear at this and to object to the adequacy or fairness of such settlement.

As for the objective of proportionality, although the Canadian courts do not expressly employ this concept,[84] they certainly try to achieve balance. The detail discussed in

[80] *Hollick v Metropolitan Toronto (Municipality)* (n 17) [15], [27].

[81] Kalajdzic (n 71) 4.

[82] eg in *Parsons v Canadian Red Cross Society* (n 48), the trial judge refused to approve an initial settlement proposal for a Can$1.5bn settlement of a class claim in relation to Hepatitis C-contaminated blood.

[83] Ontario CPA (n 14) s 25.

[84] eg the English CPR requires proportionality, which relates to 'saving expense' and 'allotting an appropriate share of the court's resources [to the case], while taking into account the need to allot resources to other cases'.

Canadian procedures overall indicates that the courts will aim to achieve reasonableness for the class as a whole. It may be that this is implicit in the objective of fairness and balancing individual rights and personal autonomy.

D. Predictability

The requirements of Canadian procedure are clear and predictable, for example the notice requirements. As discussed in the chapter three on the objectives of MPAs, where class actions have been introduced, calls for further guidance have followed and, in many cases, law reform commissions have responded by recommending the introduction of a developed class action regime.[85] Such reform has had considerable benefit and was endorsed by the Supreme Court of Canada.[86]

E. Deterrence

In Canada, class action regimes aim to change the behaviour of others 'by making it feasible for victims to recover damages from wrongdoers who were previously insulated from having to account for their wrongs because of economic and other barriers to individual proceedings'.[87] Kalajdzic has recognised above that Canadian class action is justified by its tripartite aim, one of which is to ensure behaviour modification.[88]

F. Compensation

As shown above, the Canadian approach specifically addresses damages claims, unlike the US. Also, as there is generally no limit on the type of relief that may be sought or by whom, the availability of a wide range of remedies offered to class members enables effective compensation. Some class action scholars view class actions as 'an evolutionary response to the existence of injuries unremedied by the regulatory action of the government'.[89]

[85] Examples include Ontario Law Reform Commission (OLRC), *Report on Class Actions*, vols 1, 2 and 3 (Toronto, Canada, Ministry of the Attorney General, 1982); Australian Law Reform Commission (ALRC), *Managing Justice* (Rep No 89, 1994); Manitoba Civil Justice Litigation Committee, *Civil Justice Review Task Force Report* (1996) and Alberta Law Reform Institute Report (AltaLRI Report) 'Report on Class Actions, Final Report No 85, Dec 2000'.

[86] *Hollick v Metropolitan Toronto (Municipality)* (n 17), in which the Court stated that 'while it would have been possible for courts to accommodate moderately complicated class actions by reliance on their own inherent power over procedure, this would have required courts to devise *ad hoc* solutions to procedural complexities on a case-by-case basis ... The Class Proceedings Act, 1992, was adopted to ensure that the courts had a procedural rule sufficiently refined to allow them to deal efficiently, and on a principles, rather than an ad hoc basis, with the increasingly complicated cases of the modern era'.

[87] *Hollick v Metropolitan Toronto (Municipality)* (1998), 18 CPC (4th) 394 (Ont Gen Div) [19].

[88] Kalajdzic (n 71) 6.

[89] B Garth, I Nagel and Plager, 'The Institution of the Private Attorney General: Perspectives from an Empirical Study of Class Action Litigation' (1988) 61 *S Cal L Rev* 353, 361, citing *Deposit Guaranty Nat'l Bank v Roper*, 445 US 326, 339 (1980).

4. Environmental Mass Harm Litigation

It appears that in Canada there had been limited class action activity in the area of environmental law. This is due to strict restricted certification requirements. Therefore, it seems that even though environmental cases may be well suited to an MPA format, there is no guarantee that such cases will be certified in jurisdictions where such mechanisms exist.[90] The case of *Hollick v Metropolitan Toronto (Municipality)*[91] provides a good example of these stringent certification requirements. This concerned an action taken by 30,000 residents who were living in close proximity to a landfill site. They alleged that toxic fumes and noise pollution from this site interfered with the use and enjoyment of their properties. After the action was initially certified this was overturned on appeal. Certification was deemed to have been inappropriate owing to the failure to satisfy the preferability prerequisite and also because the individual issues overwhelmed any common issues. The Supreme Court of Canada did not rule out the possibility of environmental class actions, however, as it emphasised that all cases have to be determined on their own facts.

The subsequent case of *Pearson v Inco Ltd* was considered to be a watershed decision.[92] In 2001, the plaintiff claimed $750 million against Inco, a nickel refinery, for widespread contamination that it was alleged to have caused since 1918. The motion judge and the Divisional Court denied certification. The Court of Appeal, however, certified the action on the basis that the plaintiff had narrowed the scope of the claim and also had withdrawn all claims for health-related damages. The only remaining claim was for the diminution in property value caused by the pollution. This case makes it clear that class actions may be used to prosecute harms occurring over a long period where they are caused by a single event or source. Since this decision it appears that there is increasing scope for environmental class action certification. This is because courts are certifying more cases in relation to long term harm from a single source. However, there is still careful scrutinisation of putative class actions. It also appears that there are an increasing number of cases going to common issues trial. This is because fewer defendants are settling and more are seeking to have their cases go to trial, despite the possible risk of costs being awarded against them. There seems to be a lack of success in certifying health claims, however, as courts remain reluctant to certify health-related environmental issues because of the importance of individual issues. The lessons to be learnt from this Canadian experience are that environmental class actions pose significant potential risks for those guilty of environmental mass harm. Such litigation is financially lucrative for plaintiff lawyers and they, therefore, offer representative plaintiffs attractive fee arrangements for pursuing claims. The *Pearson* decision confirms that once environmental class actions are properly framed, they can be the basis for a successful action, particularly for contamination arising from long-term operations. The crucial determinant, however, remains that of certification. Where certification is defeated, individual claims may not be advanced against the defendant or their value may

[90] eg pollution claims usually require extensive and expensive expert evidence of cause and effect. Further, potentially large groups of persons might be adversely affected by a contaminating event, such as the release of a noxious gas cloud from an industrial facility or the pollution of a river with toxic effluents.

[91] *Hollick v Metropolitan Toronto (Municipality)* (n 17).

[92] (2005), 261 DLR (4th) 629 (Ont CA).

be significantly decreased. Therefore, it seems that even though environmental cases may be well suited to an MPA format, there is no guarantee that such cases will be certified as suitable for this.

5. Summary

In conclusion, since the Supreme Court trilogy of cases, all of Canada, apart from Prince Edward Island, has enacted class proceedings legislation. The class action is justified in all of these jurisdictions by its tripartite aim to promote judicial economy, to ensure behaviour modification and to increase access to justice.[93] In assessing the role of class actions in Canada, it has been shown that although it is a procedural device, it is one with enormous potential to effect political, financial and social consequences.[94] In summary, three of the commonly approved aims of class actions are clearly evidenced: improved access to justice; enhanced judicial economy; and increased deterrence of wrongful behaviour. However, without reliable statistics it is difficult to assess the extent to which these benchmarks have been achieved. Additionally, there is a lack of statistics showing the total costs of class actions. The Canadian Supreme Court has stated succinctly that class actions reflect 'the rise of mass production, the diversification of corporate ownership, the advent of the mega-corporation, and the recognition of environmental wrongs'.[95] The Canadian scheme is clearly amenable to environmental claims as all of the above are particularly applicable to environmental mass harm. In conclusion, Canadian class action reform has brought considerable benefit, as explained by the Supreme Court of Canada:

> While it would have been possible for courts to accommodate moderately complicated class actions by reliance on their own inherent power over procedure, this would have required courts to devise *ad hoc* solutions to procedural complexities on a case-by-case basis … The Class Proceedings Act, 1992, was adopted to ensure that the courts had a procedural rule sufficiently refined to allow them to deal efficiently, and on a principles, rather than an ad hoc basis, with the increasingly complicated cases of the modern era.[96]

[93] Kalajdzic (n 71) 6.
[94] Ibid 6.
[95] *Western Canadian Shopping Centres Inc v Dutton* [2001] SCC 46 (SCC) 26.
[96] *Hollick v Metropolitan Toronto (Municipality)* (n 17).

7

Australian MPA Experience

1. Australian Litigation Landscape

Australia's legal system and laws are based on the common law of England and Wales. Like the US and Canadian legal systems, it has both a federal court system and an independent court structure in each of the six states[1] and two self-governing territories.[2] Consequently, as well as the hierarchy of courts in each state and territory, presided over by the Supreme Court in each, there is the Federal Court of Australia, which takes care of matters over which the Commonwealth has constitutional power. The ultimate appellate court is the High Court of Australia, the highest court in Australia. The legal system is based on the English model. Practice and procedure are based on the adversarial model, which means that civil proceedings are usually heard by a judge sitting without a jury. Juries are not used in any Australian representative actions or representative proceedings. As for costs, like in England and Wales, these generally follow the event. Australia, like Canada, eschews the US categorisation approach to class actions as this was expressly rejected by the law reform agencies in Australia and Ontario. It is also remarkable that the Canadian and Australian class action regimes stand apart from the US rule in that they *expressly* contemplate claims for damages for mass tort cases, whereas the US Rules do not refer to damages. Owing to the scope and scale of this research, discussion will focus on the federal system and that of the states of Victoria and New South Wales. This is because these have the most highly developed legislative and judicial systems for MPAs, so they will be taken as the best examples for discussion.

2. Evolution of MPA Landscape

Until 1992, class action type procedures did not form part of the Australian legal landscape. There was much debate in this area including a report published in 1988 by the Australian Law Reform Commission (ALRC).[3] The rules of the various Australian courts did, however,

[1] These are: Victoria, New South Wales, Queensland, South Australia, Western Australia and Tasmania.

[2] These are the Australian Capital Territory and the Northern Territory.

[3] Australian Law Reform Commission (ALRC), *Grouped Proceedings in the Federal Court* Report no 46 (Sydney, Australia, 1988) para 1. 11 years were spent preparing this report. The ALRC subsequently recommended numerous enhancements to the FCA in 2000 and advised the Federal Government to order a review of the operation of pt IV; see further ALRC, *Managing Justice—A Review of the Federal Civil Justice System* Report no 89 (Sydney, Australia, 1994) para 7.128.

provide for what were known as 'representative actions'. These were based on common law and the old English rules. These were of comparatively limited application and they were generally considered to have no useful application in modern society. They still exist and have similar weaknesses to their Irish equivalent, especially the prerequisite that the parties have the 'same interest' in the proceedings. This requirement restricts the availability of the representative action procedure and has been narrowly interpreted by Australian judges.[4] Therefore, until relatively recently, multi-party litigation was limited to this common law representative action. This changed in 1992, when the Federal Parliament amended the Federal Court of Australia Act 1976 (the FCA) to introduce to the federal court system what are referred to in that legislation as 'representative proceedings'.[5] These are, in essence, analogous to US class actions. Most 'class actions' in Australia are commenced under this mechanism.[6] However, owing to the limited scope of federal jurisdiction, this is more or less limited to product liability. In 1994, an advisory committee made a recommendation that 'fair and efficient [class] action procedures should be available in all Australian jurisdictions. The Commonwealth provision for [class] actions in the Federal Court is ... a suitable model'.[7] As a result, in November 2000, the State of Victoria also introduced a class action regime that is almost the same as the federal regime, followed by New South Wales in March 2011.[8] In June 2013, there were proposals by the Western Australian Law Reform Commission (WALRC), supported by the Law Council, that Western Australia (WA) adopt legislation to create a scheme allowing representative proceedings on substantially similar terms to Part IVA of the FCA.[9]

The 1992 amendments to the FCA formed part of a package of reforms that included amendments to the Trade Practices Act[10] that established a new product liability regime

[4] This requirement is set out in the Federal Rules of Court, ord 6, r 13. See, for an example of judicial interpretation, *Markt and Co Ltd v Knight Steamship Co Ltd* [1910] 2 KB 1021 (CA), where the English Court of Appeal held that the 'same interest' requirement, under the traditional representative action procedure, meant that the procedure was unavailable in actions where separate and individual contracts were involved or in cases where damages were claimed.

[5] The Representative Group Proceedings Act 1991 provided for this and it was introduced, through the addition of a new pt IVA to the Federal Court of Australia Act 1976, as inserted by the Federal Court of Australia Amendment Act 1991 (No 181 of 1991) s 3. Pt IVA provided for representative proceedings. Under this regime, proceedings can be commenced if 3 threshold requirements are met: (1) 7 or more persons have claims against the same respondent; (2) the claims of all those persons are in respect of, or arise out of, the same, similar, or related circumstances; and (3) the claims of all those persons give rise to a substantial common issue of law or fact.

[6] These Australian 'representative proceedings' procedures have been available in the Federal Court since 4 March 1992, in Victoria since January 2000 and in New South Wales since 4 March 2011. In each instance those regimes have been established by the passage of legislation.

[7] Advice of a committee established by the Federal Parliament: Access to Justice Advisory Committee, *Access to Justice—An Action Plan* (Canberra, Australia, 1994) para 2.105.

[8] The state procedures were introduced through pt 4A of the Supreme Court Act 1986 (Vic) and pt 10 of the Civil Procedure Act 2005 (NSW). A regime similar to the federal regime's pt IVA took effect from 1 January 2000 through the inclusion of pt 4A of the Supreme Court Act 1986 in Victoria. This followed a Supreme Court challenge to the court rules for their introduction. See report by V Morabito, 'Class Actions, Group Litigation and Other Forms of Collective Litigation: National Report Australia', 622 Annals of the American Academy of Political and Social Science (March 2009) 320–32.

[9] This resulted from the WA Law Reform Commission Discussion Paper 2009—Project No 103. Details of this may be found in *The Annals of the American Academy of Political and Social Science* Vol. 622, The Globalization of Class Actions (Mar., 2009), pp. 320–327

[10] Trade Practices Act 1974.

based on strict liability. At the same time as these changes were made by the Federal Parliament the various state and territory legislatures amended the rules governing the practice of law in Australia so as to remove the longstanding restrictions on lawyers advertising for clients.[11] Contingency fees are prohibited in Australia so lawyers are not permitted to take a proportion of clients' awards but they can use 'no win no fee' agreements to charge a success fee for successful outcomes. This can amount to twice their normal fees. Taken as a whole, these changes significantly increased the level of litigation in Australia. Lawyers began to advertise in the media, offering to act for plaintiffs on a 'no win no fee' basis. This led to the emergence of a number of prominent law firms specialising in large-scale litigation on behalf of plaintiffs. In many instances this litigation is attempted to advance claims in Australia that were identical with proceedings being run by their associates in the US. It is now generally accepted that the reforms of the early-1990s contributed to the public liability crisis that came to prominence in 2002. This led to the Federal Government establishing a review of key areas of the law of negligence and resulted in the subsequent passage by all state and territory governments of civil liability reform legislation.[12] In some jurisdictions, notably New South Wales, this has included attempts to re-impose restrictions on advertising by lawyers. All of the representative proceedings regimes in existence in Australia surpass the limitations on traditional representative actions, especially as they allow proceedings for the recovery of damages. To date, most of the class actions that have been initiated have included product liability claims,[13] shareholder litigation[14] and claims against government agencies[15] and public utilities.[16] In the last few years, there has been a transformation in the Australian legal system and it is now a commonly held perception that, apart from the US, Australia is the most likely place for a plaintiff to bring class action type proceedings.[17]

There have been several other long-term influences on the growth of class actions in Australia. For example, following the contraction of personal injury law practices as a result of reform of Australian tort law in 2002, the traditional plaintiff law firms have concentrated on class actions as having significant business growth potential. Also, there is a growing focus on corporate governance and the role of private litigation in enforcement and some of the heads of Australia's regulators have endorsed the role that class actions play in enforcement and deterrence. Furthermore, court procedures have been introduced and amended to facilitate bringing such proceedings. All of the above factors, together with the availability of third-party funding, have created and developed plaintiff-focused class action practices and relationships with third-party funders. Anecdotally, some call these

[11] eg in 1993 the New South Wales Parliament inserted s 38J into the Legal Profession Act 1987 which entitled a barrister or solicitor to advertise in any way that he or she thought fit.

[12] Ipp Committee Report (October 2002).

[13] eg *Philip Morris (Austl) Ltd v Nixon* (2002) 170 ALR 487 (action against tobacco manufacturers).

[14] See eg *King v GIO Australia Holdings Ltd* (2000) FCA 1649.

[15] See eg *Zhang v Minister for Immigration, Local Government and Ethnic Affairs* (1993) 45 FCR 284 (action against a State minister).

[16] See eg *Johnson Tiles Pty Ltd v Esso Australia Ltd & Anor* [1999] 94 FCA 167 (action against suppliers of Melbourne's gas).

[17] See generally J Kellam and S Stuart Clark, 'Multi-Party Actions in Australia' in C Hodges, *Multi-Party Actions* (Oxford University Press, 2001) ch 15; and also S Stuart Clark and C Harris, 'Multi-Plaintiff Litigation in Australia: A Comparative Perspective' (2001) 11 *Duke J Comp & Int'l L* 289.

the 'perfect storm' conditions for class action growth. Despite this, there has not been a significant increase in the number of such actions filed in recent years. Class actions have, however, evolved to become part of the Australian legal landscape and there has been an increase in the number of high-value high-profile class actions being taken. The contexts in which class actions are being taken have expanded also. Traditionally, class actions in Australia related mainly to product liability but this has expanded to many other areas, ranging from securities class actions to shareholder actions, which have overtaken product liability claims as the most common type of class action. In recent years, there have been a number of mass consumer claims and also resurgence in product liability claims and a number of claims alleging anti-competitive behaviour and environmental harm. In terms of resolution of class actions, most class actions are settled. This is a reflection of the fact that the risks associated with class action litigation are too high for both defendants and the class. It is also not unusual for class actions to be settled even before they are filed.

3. MPA Overview

A. The Quasi-Class Action Regime in the State of South Australia

This is a unique regime that endeavours to address some of the major shortcomings of the traditional rules governing representative actions but in a less detailed manner than the federal and state class action regimes.[18] Its origins can be traced back to a report on class action reform that was released by the Law Reform Committee of South Australia in 1977, which recommended a reasonably detailed legislative class action regime.[19] This recommendation was never implemented by the South Australian legislature. Instead, in 1987, several new sections of the Supreme Court Rules 1987 (SA) came into operation.[20] In September 2006, new Supreme Court Civil Rules 2006 (SA) came into operation and these rules were replaced by Rules 80 and 81, which provide that where a group of persons

> has a common interest in the subject matter of an action or proposed action and a member of the group is authorized in writing by the other members of the group to bring or defend the action as representative of the group, the person may bring or defend the action as representative of the group.

Rule 81 implements, with respect to representative actions brought under Rule 80, Australia's only certification regime. This quasi-class action regime has hardly ever been used, which would appear to suggest that the intended goal of removing in South Australia the barriers that are faced by multiple claimants who wish to commence a representative action in South Australia has not been achieved.[21]

[18] This is available through the provisions of r 80(1) of the Supreme Court Civil Rules 2006 (SA); Supreme Court Rules, r 34.

[19] Law Reform Committee of South Australia, *Report Relating to Class Actions* (Rep no 36, 1977).

[20] rr 34.01–34.06.

[21] For further detail on this, see generally report by V Morabito, 'Group Litigation in Australia—"Desperately Seeking" Effective Class Action Regimes' (National Report for Australia prepared for the 'Globalisation of Class Actions' Conference, Oxford University, December 2007).

B. Traditional Representative Actions

Order 6, Rule 13 of the Federal Court Rules provides that:

> Where numerous persons have the same interest in any proceeding the proceedings may be commenced, and, unless the Court otherwise orders, continued, by or against any one or more of them as representing all except one or more of them.

Each Australian state and territory has procedural rules that allow representative actions under provisions similar to the above.[22] Proceedings brought pursuant to these rules are commonly referred to as representative actions. The rules governing these procedures have essentially remained unchanged over the past 100 years.[23] Victims of mass harm have encountered multifarious problems that prevented them from using these procedures to get access to the courts and there is strong agreement that representative proceedings are grossly inadequate vehicles for managing legal disputes involving multiple claimants.[24] In particular, the availability of this procedure had been significantly restricted as a result of the narrow judicial interpretation of the 'same interest' prerequisite[25] and the failure of the rules governing this procedure to provide guidance to the courts and litigants with respect to the numerous and complex issues raised by multi-party proceedings. Owing to the shortcomings of these actions as mechanisms for managing collective redress there was clear need for additional effective multi-party litigation procedures and this was, therefore, a major rationale for the introduction of the grouped proceeding model known as representative proceedings. This highlights the contribution that effective MPAs can make as managerial mechanisms.

C. Representative Proceedings

These are effectively class actions and are provided for under Part IV of the FCA.[26] One of the main features of Australian representative proceedings is that there is *no* requirement that the proceedings are judicially certified under either regime, unlike the US and Canadian systems. A representative plaintiff may commence class action proceedings under Part IVA of the FCA once three threshold requirements are met:

1. the class comprises at least seven persons;
2. the claims of the class members arise out of the same, similar or related circumstances; and
3. the claims give rise to at least one substantial common issue of law or fact.[27]

[22] D Grave and K Adams, *Class Actions in Australia* (Lawbook Co, 2005) 578–84.

[23] See *Mobil Oil Australia Pty Ltd v Victoria* (2002) 189 ALR 161, 205 (per Callinan J). However, an exception to this statement is that in November 2007 significant provisions were added to the rule governing representative actions in New South Wales.

[24] Morabito, 'Class Actions, Group Litigation and Other Forms of Collective Litigation: National Report Australia' (n 8) 32–37.

[25] See eg *Markt and Co Ltd v Knight Steamship Co Ltd* (n 4), where the English Court of Appeal held that the 'same interest' requirement, under the traditional representative action procedure, meant that the procedure was unavailable in actions where separate and individual contracts were involved or in cases where damages were claimed.

[26] See R Mulheron, *The Class Action in Common Law Legal Systems: A Comparative Perspective* (Hart Publishing, 2004) 481–90.

[27] FCA, pt IVA, s 33C(1).

A full discussion of this procedure will follow below. It is important to note that while both the federal and state legislation use the terms 'representative proceedings' and 'group proceedings', respectively, to describe these mechanisms, commentators and Australians commonly refer to such proceedings as class actions. Similarly, those represented in a representative proceeding are referred to in the FCA as 'group members' rather than class members. As a result of this, the terminology can be confusing. For the purposes of this discussion, however, the legislative terminology of representative proceedings and group proceedings will be used.

D. Joinder, Test Cases and Consolidation

Where neither representative proceedings nor representative action procedures are available or are not used, there are three other options for dealing with disputes that involve multiple claimants.[28] One option is to join all of the plaintiffs with a common claim in one action through use of a joinder procedure. In this way, for example, two or more persons may be joined as plaintiffs in any proceeding.[29] Another option is to commence separate actions for each claimant, and then try 'test cases' to resolve the common issues. The ALRC has described test cases as proceedings 'brought by a single applicant in circumstances where many other people may have the same or similar claims. This may be done by the unilateral action of the claimant'.[30] The third option is to consolidate existing non-group proceedings that relate to the same dispute with respect to the same defendants.[31] However, there are a number of problems that exist with the use of these procedures as devices for dealing with legal disputes involving numerous claimants. For example, in Lord Woolf's opinion 'joinder is not satisfactory where the interests of claimants differ'.[32] A further problem is that it is not clear how damages are to be determined. If the judge were responsible for calculating damages for individual plaintiffs in complex matters, this would waste rather than save judicial time.[33] In the opinion of the Ontario Law Reform Commission, the joinder procedure:

> Will be of minimal assistance to individuals with small claims. While some small claims may be transformed by joinder ... into claims that are individually recoverable—because the cost of proving certain issues can be shared—most such claims will continue to be individually nonrecoverable. The reasons for this are quite straightforward. The individual litigant will be liable to pay his own lawyer's fees, whether the action succeeds or fails. Moreover, if the action fails, he likely will

[28] V Morabito, 'Australasia' in D Hensler, C Hodges and M Tulibacka (eds), *The Globalization of Class Actions* (2009) 622 The Annals of the American Academy of Political and Social Science 320.

[29] This is an example of how the joinder of parties procedure operates in Australia under r 9.02 of Victoria's Supreme Court (General Civil Procedure) Rules 1986.

[30] ALRC 1988 Report (n 3) para 52.

[31] The rules in the State of Victoria are a good example of how this procedure may be used. r 9.12 provides that where several proceedings are pending, the court may order those proceedings to be consolidated, or tried at the same time, or tried one immediately after another, or may order them to be stayed until the determination of any of them. This power may only be exercised where it appears to the court: that some common questions of law or fact arise in both or all of them; that the rights to relief claimed therein are in respect of, or arise out of, the same transaction or series of transactions; or that for some other reason it is desirable to make an order under the rule.

[32] Lord Woolf, *Access to Justice—Final Report to the Lord Chancellor on the Civil Justice System in England and Wales* (1996) 225.

[33] Morabito, 'Group Litigation in Australia (n 21) 9.

> be ordered to pay a portion of the defendant's costs. Consequently, most small claims, even though they be aggregated, will remain individually nonrecoverable.[34]

The use of test cases can also be problematic. Some of these problems are because, unlike a class action, the test case litigation is not binding on the plaintiffs who are not named plaintiffs.[35] The Irish Law Reform Commission considered that the test case device 'is essentially an individualised means of resolving collective grievances'.[36] While it is possible that the outcome of the test case may influence the outcome of any future proceedings initiated by the other claimants, they stated that:

> The extent to which the test case serves as a benchmark for subsequent proceedings varies depending upon the nature of the action and the prevalence of common claims among the putative plaintiffs. The matter is straightforward where the original ruling declares a legislative or administrative act to be unconstitutional and, at the other end of the scale, considerably more complicated where there is a need for individualized assessments of damages.[37]

As for the use of consolidation, Grave and Adams consider that this procedure represents:

> A means of dealing with proceedings which have already been commenced and which raise common questions. It does not assist in achieving the policy objective [of enhancing access to justice] where the cost of litigation or other factors are a barrier to the bringing of proceedings.[38]

These are a few examples of the shortcomings of these MPA devices for use as a means of resolving disputes involving mass harm and they indicate that these mechanisms fall short of the MPA objectives identified in this research. For these reasons, as well as many more, Morabito considers these three mechanisms to be 'extremely unsatisfactory'.[39]

4. The Representative Proceedings Regime

A. Background

In February 1977, the ALRC was asked by the Federal Attorney General to report on the adequacy of the existing law relating to collective redress in the Federal Court and other courts whilst exercising federal jurisdiction or in courts exercising jurisdiction under any law of any territory.[40] It was not until 1988 that the ALRC's report was released to Parliament. This delay must have been as result of considerable debate within the ALRC, as noted by Senator Durack: 'I am unaware of any other report that took such a long time as the one on the subject of class actions. It is quite clear that the [ALRC] was considerably divided on the subject'.[41] This report contained a proposal to introduce in the Federal Court a new

[34] Ontario Law Reform Commission, *Report on Class Actions* (Rep no 48, 1982) 85.
[35] D Hensler, 'Revisiting the Monster: New Myths and Realities of Class Action and Other Large Scale Litigation' (2001) 11 *Duke J of Comp & Int'l L* 179, 191.
[36] Irish Law Reform Commission, *Consultation Paper on Multi-Party Litigation* (LRC CP 25-2003) para 1.32.
[37] Ibid para 1.34.
[38] Grave and Adams, *Class Actions in Australia* (n 22) 19.
[39] See generally Morabito (n 21) 7–11.
[40] ALRC 1988 Report (n 3) para 1.
[41] Commonwealth, *Parliamentary Debates*, Senate, 13 November 1991, 3019 (Senator Durack).

grouped proceeding model. A key reason for the introduction of this was the need to avoid the problems inherent in the representative action procedure that had prevented victims of mass harm from getting access to the courts. In the ALRC's opinion, its recommendation would advance 'the objectives of access to the courts and judicial economy, while providing safeguards against possible abuse',[42] because:

> Such a procedure could enable people who suffer loss or damage in common with others as a result of a wrongful act or omission by the same respondent to enforce their legal rights in the courts in a cost effective manner. It could overcome the costs and other barriers that impede people from pursuing a legal remedy. People who may be ignorant of their rights or fearful of embarking on proceedings could be assisted to a remedy if one member of a group, all similarly affected, could commence proceedings on behalf of all members. The grouping of claims could also promote efficiency in the use of resources by enabling common issues to be dealt with together. Appropriate grouping procedures are an essential part of the legal system's response to multiple wrongdoings in an increasingly complex world.[43]

In this way, the ALRC identified ways in which the new mechanism would enhance access to justice and improve judicial and procedural economy, while at the same time removing the barriers that can inhibit those wishing to pursue a claim for mass harm. The ALRC addressed the problems inherent in the representative action procedure, by: (1) providing more liberal and precise requirements for the commencement of a grouped proceeding; (2) making it clear that a number of judicial principles, which significantly restricted the circumstances in which the 'same interest' requirement could be adhered to, could not be applied to restrict access to the new regime; and (3) providing courts with extensive powers to deal with the various phases of group litigation.[44] The Federal Government acted on the ALRC's proposals in September 1991 when the Federal Court of Australia Amendment Bill 1991, containing Part IVA, was introduced to the Senate. It was passed without any amendments and Part IVA came into operation in March 1992. The then Federal Attorney General discussed the objectives of Part IVA as follows:

> The Bill gives the Federal Court an efficient and effective procedure to deal with multiple claims. Such a procedure is needed for two purposes. The first is to provide a real remedy where, although many people are affected and the total amount at issue is significant, each person's loss is small and not economically viable to recover in individual actions. It will thus give access to the courts to those in the community who have been effectively denied justice because of the high cost of taking action [the access to justice goal of the class action device].
>
> The second purpose of the Bill is to deal efficiently with the situation where the damages sought by each claimant are large enough to justify individual actions and a large number of persons wish to sue the respondent. The new procedure will mean that groups of persons, whether they be shareholders or investors, or people pursuing consumer claims, will be able to obtain redress and do so more cheaply and efficiently than would be the case with individual actions [the judicial economy goal of the class action device].[45]

[42] ALRC 1988 Report (n 3) para 2.

[43] Ibid para 69.

[44] Morabito (n 21) 4.

[45] Commonwealth, *Parliamentary Debates*, House of Representatives, 14 November 1991, 3174 (Mr Duffy—Federal Attorney General). Similar reasoning was embraced by the Victorian Attorney General, Mr Hulls, when he introduced pt 4A in the Legislative Assembly of the Victorian Parliament: Victoria, *Parliamentary Debates*, Legislative Assembly, 31 October 2000, 1252, as cited by Morabito (n 21) 4.

In identifying these objectives, the Attorney General highlighted the difficulty in 'scattered damages' scenarios and the need to achieve judicial economy through collective redress overall. These aims are helpful in demonstrating how the Australian representative procedure wished to overcome previous MPA difficulties.

B. The Regime

The Scottish Law Commission has described the Australian 'class action' procedure as a 'sophisticated and improved version' of the representative action procedure.[46] This endorsement indicates that it has overcome the shortcomings of the representative action, which was the motivation for the introduction of the representative procedure in the first place. The drafters of both the federal and Victorian class action regimes favoured an opt-out system. For this regime to function, it is provided that an application to begin proceedings need not 'name, or specify the number of, the group members'[47] unless they opt out of the proceedings.[48] In the federal and state regimes, the consent of a person to be a group member in representative proceedings is not required unless he or she is the Commonwealth; a territory or state; a minister, officer or certain agencies of any of these.[49] Instead, the Australian rules empower the court with a broad discretion to direct the way in which the group members are to be notified of the proceedings[50] and they also allow any member to opt-out by giving written notice within a specified period.[51] However, the court has the power to not require group member notice where the relief the class is seeking does not include damages.[52] Otherwise, the court must approve the content and form of the notice and it may also decide who is to bear the cost of the notice distribution.[53] The high degree of judicial supervision in these steps appears to safeguard the interests of group members. The action must only describe the class in general terms. The group can be defined by a list of names or a set of criteria. It may, however, be defined in a way that effectively requires members to opt in to the class, including for example by entering into a retainer with a particular law firm or an arrangement with a particular litigation funder. The claim is brought on behalf of all group members by one, or a small number of, representative plaintiffs. The representatives are the only group members to be parties to the proceedings. There is no requirement that the claims of the representative parties should be typical of those of the class nor that the common issues predominate over the individual issue. This is in stark contrast to the US Rule 23. The system in Australia provides for the consideration of individual issues as well as common issues and provides for the use of subclasses if necessary. FCA, section 33C(2)(a) provides that a class may be commenced whether or not the relief sought is, or includes, equitable relief or damages; or includes

[46] Scottish Law Commission, *Multi-Party Actions* (Rep no 154, 1996) para 6.1. See generally R Mulheron, 'From Representative Rule to Class Action: Steps Rather than Leaps' (2005) 24 *Civil Justice Q* 424.

[47] FCA, pt IVA, s 33H(2); and pt 4A, s 33H(2).

[48] Ibid s 33H.

[49] Both regimes have a s 33E that states this.

[50] FCA, s 22X and s 33Y.

[51] Ibid s 33J. Notice must be given to class members of commencement of the proceeding and of their right to opt out of the group prior to the date the court has fixed.

[52] Ibid pt IVA, s 33X(2); and pt 4A, s 33X(2).

[53] Ibid, pt IVA, s 33Y(2); and pt 4A, s 33Y(2).

claims that may require individual assessment or is the same for each person represented. FCA, section 33C(2)(b) provides that proceedings may be brought regardless of whether they concern separate transactions, acts or omissions between the defendant and individual group members. Once the proceedings have been commenced all members of the group are bound by the outcome of the proceedings unless they opt out. In order to take that step the group member must give written notice to the court of their intention to opt out. Once the class action has been initiated, the court may terminate proceedings as a class proceeding, if, upon application by the defendant, it is satisfied that the litigation does not satisfy the threshold requirements. The onus is on the defendant to persuade the trial court that the proceedings should be concluded.[54] Even where the judge holds that the requirements have been met, the court can discontinue the class proceedings in certain circumstances. The most important of these is FCA, section 33 N(1), which allows the court to order that the action no longer constitutes a class proceeding because it is in the interests of justice to do so as:

1. the costs that would be incurred if the proceedings continued as a class action are likely to exceed the costs that would be incurred if each group member conducted a separate action;
2. the relief sought can be obtained by action other than a class proceeding;
3. the class proceeding will not provide an efficient and effective means of dealing with class members' claims; or
4. it is otherwise inappropriate that the claims are pursued by means of class action.

Under the opt-out system in both regimes all class members are bound by any judgment of the court.[55] Crucially, a class action may not be ceased or settled without court approval.[56] The court requires evidence that the members of a class have been adequately notified of the terms of a settlement before it will be approved. Each of the regimes has adopted the ALRC's recommendations of empowering trial judges to take an active role in protecting the interests of those parties not present in court. The trial judges have wide-ranging 'managerial' powers and the ALRC has stated that 'without active court management, the interests of unidentified parties may not be taken properly into account'.[57] This again highlights the important role that MPAs can play as managerial mechanisms. For example, the court has the power to order the discontinuation of proceedings;[58] the substitution of a representative plaintiff who is not adequately representing the class members' interests;[59] and the creation of subgroups for issues common to only some of the class members together with their own subgroup representative.[60] Settlement requires the court to be satisfied that the settlement is fair and reasonable and in the interests of class members. Courts have further

[54] eg according to FCA, s 33C and s 33N, on the ground that the action is frivolous or oppressive or that the procedure is not the most efficient and effective means of disposing of the claims in question.

[55] Ibid s 33Z provides that a judgment delivered in a class proceeding 'binds all such persons [described or otherwise identified in the judgment] other than any person who has opted out of the proceeding' ie those who fall within the class description who have not opted-out in writing.

[56] Ibid pt IVA, s 33V(1).

[57] ALRC 1988 Report (n 3) para 157.

[58] FCA, pt IVA, ss 33L, 33M, 33N and 33P; and FCA, pt IVA, ss 33L, 33M, 33N and 33P.

[59] Ibid pt IVA, s 33T; and pt 4A, s 33T.

[60] Ibid pt IVA, ss 33Q; and pt 4A, s 33Q.

additional interventionist tools that they may invoke when necessary, the most important of which is s 33ZF(1). This allows the court to make 'any order … [it] thinks appropriate or necessary to ensure that justice is done in the proceedings'.[61] Again, this degree of court supervision and intervention safeguards group members' interests as well as those of unidentified parties, as well as striving to achieve judicial and procedural economy. As regards damages, the court has a wide discretion and if the class action is successful it may award damages to the class as a whole, to any subclass or to individual members.[62] It is useful to recall another important distinction in the Australian system compared with the US is that it expressly contemplates claims for damages for mass torts (as does the Canadian system), whereas the US rules do not refer to damages.[63]

As regards costs, Australia has a similar system to Canada in that it uses the traditional rule that costs follow the event, but it has a narrow interpretation in terms of who is liable if the plaintiff is unsuccessful. If a class action is defeated, only the representative plaintiffs and not the individual group members will be liable for costs. This is because, as previously mentioned, group members are bound by the outcome of representative proceedings without being formal parties to the litigation.[64] Effectively, this confers them with immunity from adverse costs awards. Without fee and retainer agreements between individual group members and the lawyers that the class representatives have employed, group members are not liable for the costs and fees involved in organising the proceeding for the plaintiffs.[65] As a result, those group members who are not formally parties to the litigation are often described as 'free riders'.[66] Often it is not financially realistic for putative class representatives to bring representative proceedings unless they can do something about their potential exposure to cost liability including lawyers' fees and adverse cost awards. In Canada, and in Ireland in particular because of the lack of civil legal aid, in an effort to sidestep this problem, plaintiffs' lawyers have used the tool of nominating a 'man of straw' (a person with no assets) as the plaintiff.[67] In response, defendants have sought orders for security for costs requiring the plaintiff to pay into court an amount equal to the estimated cost of proceedings. The Australian courts seem more willing to grant these orders and it is likely that this has discouraged some putative class plaintiffs.[68] Increasingly, solicitors acting for class representatives have begun effectively to fund many Australian representative proceedings by entering into no win no fee agreements with representatives. Also, litigation funders often finance these proceedings and their fee can comprise up to 40 per cent of an award. In these cases, an essential part of their involvement is that the representative group is restricted to

[61] A further example is that both the Federal Court and Victoria's Supreme Court have powers such as s 33X(5) which allows the court 'at any stage, [to] order that notice of any matter be given' to class members and by the court's direct involvement in 'administering and distributing monetary relief'.

[62] Damages may consist of specified amounts, amounts calculated in a particular manner or an average amount to be divided among class members.

[63] See J Fleming, 'Mass Torts' (1994) 42 *Am J Comp L* 521.

[64] *Johnson Tiles Pty Ltd v Esso Australia Ltd* [1999] 94 FCA 167, 738 (per Merkel J).

[65] This is expressly stated by s 43(1)(A) of pt IVA and s 33ZD of pt 4A.

[66] Morabito (n 28).

[67] Two examples of this are the Irish cases of *Hanrahan v Merck Sharpe and Dohme* [1988] ILRM 629 and *Molumby v Kearns* Unreported High Court 19 January 1999; in both of these cases the courts did not insist on the usual requirement of a proprietary interest in order to bring a nuisance action.

[68] Stuart Clark and Harris, 'Multi-Plaintiff Litigation in Australia: A Comparative Perspective' (n 17) 302.

those claimants that are prepared to enter into funder agreements with litigation funders and also to enter fee agreements with the lawyers for the class representatives.[69] The full Federal Court of Australia has held that such arrangements were not inconsistent with the terms and policy of Part IVA.[70] A feature that has perhaps forestalled any over-exuberance from entrepreneurial lawyers is the Australian prohibition on contingency fees for lawyers, mentioned at the outset, but this prohibition does not apply to litigation funders.

While the Australian representative proceedings device is often portrayed as similar to that of the US, there are a number of significant differences between the two countries' procedural requirements, all of which tend to make the Australian procedure more 'plaintiff-friendly' than that in the US. The significant differences between class actions in Australia and the US can be identified summarily. As regards class certification, it has been shown that the Australian class action procedure has no certification procedure or requirement. Therefore, there is no threshold requirement that the proceedings be reviewed and certified by the court as appropriate to be determined as a class action. This is in sharp contrast with the US where the lead plaintiff in a class action must come before the court at an early stage in the proceedings and demonstrate that the formal requirements to commence a class action have been satisfied and that it is appropriate that the proceedings continue as a class action. Whereas, in contrast, in Australia, the onus is on the defendant to establish that the threshold requirements have not been met. As for the common issues, in Australia there is no requirement that the common issues between class members predominate over the individual issues. Rather, there is merely a requirement that there be at least one 'substantial' common issue of law or fact. Once again, this is in contrast with the US where the plaintiffs must demonstrate to the court that the common issues between class members predominate. As for costs, in the US these are borne by each party irrespective of the outcome. In Australia, the unsuccessful party will generally be ordered to pay the successful party's costs as well as their own costs. Contingency fees are permitted in the US, whereby lawyers may charge based on a percentage of any amount received. In Australia, contingency fee structures are generally prohibited for lawyers and instead they are permitted to charge on a 'no win no fee' basis. As mentioned previously, another important difference from the US is the fact that the Australian regime, like Canada, expressly provides for damages for mass torts. Finally, the Australian procedure also expressly provides for the determination of 'subgroup', or even individual issues as part of the proceedings. Thus, even though a claim may commence as representative proceedings, it can quickly degenerate into a mass of what are, in effect, individual claims that must be considered by the court on an individual basis.

[69] The Victoria Law Reform Commission (VLRC), *Civil Justice Review Draft Proposals* (Melbourne, Australia, 2007) 49–50 stated that: 'Some commercial funders are prepared to finance the litigation, meet any obligations to provide security for costs and provide an indemnity in respect of any adverse costs order. This is usually in consideration of an agreement by the assisted parties to pay to the litigation funder a specified percentage of the amount recovered if the litigation is successful. However, such agreement cannot be entered into by the representative party on behalf of the class. Thus, in order to secure a legal entitlement to share in the amount recovered by class members litigation funders usually endeavour to get individual class members to enter into contractual litigation finance arrangements. Moreover, litigation funders are usually only agreeable to fund litigation on behalf of those individual class members who have agreed to enter into litigation finance agreements. These commercial considerations have led to a proliferation of class actions where the defined classes are limited to persons who have agreed to enter into litigation funding arrangements with commercial litigation entities'.

[70] See eg its December 2007 decision of *Multiplex Funds Management Limited v P Dawson Nominees Pty Limited* (2007) FCAFC 200.

These differences are more than just theoretical distinctions. As a result of these differences Australian plaintiffs have been able to pursue representative proceedings that would not be allowed as class actions in the United States. For example, claims against pharmaceutical companies or the manufacturers of medical devices will generally not be heard in the United States as class actions. This is because the determination of each class member's claim will, ultimately, turn on individual issues. No such restriction exists in Australia. As a consequence, the Australian courts are now obliged to hear and determine complex product liability claims that would not even be commenced in the US.

5. Litigation Funding

Commercial third-party litigation funders have been operating in Australia since the 1990s.[71] Australia's largest litigation funder has been listed on the Australian Stock Exchange since 2001 and expanded its business to representative proceedings. This was controversial and led to many challenges mostly based on public policy and abuse of process arguments related to third-party entrepreneurialism in the litigation process.[72] In 2006, however, the High Court of Australia approved third-party funding for representative proceedings when it held that it was not contrary to public process or an abuse of process.[73] This ruling ended questions about the validity of litigation funding and has encouraged new funders to enter the market.[74] It has been the most important factor in the development of the Australian MPA landscape in recent times, with more than three times the number of representative proceedings being commenced in the three years following this decision than in the three years preceding it.[75] Now it is highly unusual for such proceedings to be pursued without third-party funding. A crucial detail in relation to third-party funding in Australia is the requirement that third-party funders need to have contracts with all group members so as to recover their fee and to exclude 'free riders', and to therefore maximise the group membership. This requirement has led to a *reversal* of the initial opt-out model into a de facto opt-in model. This obviously has had huge implications for the Australian regime. Various appeal court decisions in recent years have imposed regulatory requirements on third-party funders. For example, the requirement that representative proceedings funders comply with the regulatory scheme for managed investment schemes and requiring all funders to hold an Australian financial services licence. The Federal Government soon after introduced temporary class order relief from the implications of these decisions and has recently implemented legislation, effective from July 2013, to reverse the effect of the decisions. The legislation effectively ensures that the third-party funding party market is largely unregulated and therefore anyone can provide funding, except for the lawyers involved in the case.

[71] In insolvency cases.

[72] Following the abolition of the torts of maintenance and champerty in most Australian states.

[73] *Campbells Cash and Carry Pty Ltd* [2006] HCA 41.

[74] See Allens, *Focus*: 'High Court Gives Green Light to Litigation Funding' (August 2006) and also Allens, *Focus*: Yet Another Tick for Litigation Funding' (October 2009).

[75] V Morabito, 'An Empirical Study of Australia's Class Action Regimes: Class Actions Facts and Figures' (Department of Business Law and Taxation, Monash University, December 2009).

Initially this action was taken on policy grounds based on the desirability of third-party funding in providing access to justice through class actions. This could be the final step in ensuring the establishment of third-party funding in Australia but it is likely that this will develop further.

6. Evaluation of Australian Representative Proceedings against MPA Objectives

A. Access to Justice

Access to justice has been cited to justify representative proceedings; for example, one of the goals behind the amendment of legislation was to 'provide a real remedy' to those in the community who individually had uneconomically viable claims, but where, overall, the total amount at issue was significant (the 'scattered damages' scenarios discussed previously).[76] The absence of a class certification process and the low common issues threshold make it easier to commence and maintain representative proceedings in Australia than in the US. As a result, the Australian regime has been described as 'one of the most liberal class action rules in the entire world'.[77] The Australian position in respect of costs is, however, generally acknowledged as being a significant deterrent to speculative litigation and a key reason why Australia has not seen a proliferation of class action activity despite the establishment of litigation funding.

B. Judicial and Procedural Economy

These aspects of Australian representative proceedings are only implicitly included in legislation. They have, however, been highlighted by the ALRC[78] and the Federal Attorney General as objectives of representative proceedings legislation.[79] As shown in chapter three, the Australian Federal Court noted in *Murphy v Overton Investments Pty Ltd* that the question of judicial economy is a direct determinant of whether or not class action proceedings are considered 'inappropriate' under the Federal Court Act, section 33N(1), in which case the proceedings must be discontinued.[80] There are multiple examples of the important managerial role that MPAs play in Australian mass harm litigation and these have been

[76] Extracted from the speech of the then Attorney General at the second reading of the Federal Court of Australia Amendment Bill 1991, referring to the new pt IVA of the Act; *Parliamentary Debates*, Senate, 14 November 1991, 3174 (Mr Duffy).

[77] G Miller, 'Some Thoughts on Australian Class Actions in Light of the American Experience' in the Hon Justice KE Lindgren (ed), *Investor Class Actions*, Ross Parsons Centre of Commercial, Corporate and Taxation Law (2009) 4.

[78] ALRC 1988 Report (n 3) para 69.

[79] Commonwealth, *Parliamentary Debates*, House of Representatives, 14 November 1991, 3174 (Mr Duffy—Federal Attorney General).

[80] [1999] FCA 1123, [69], [87].

highlighted throughout the preceding discussion. Most notably, the need for representative proceedings as an effective MPA mechanism arose as a result of the shortcomings of traditional representative actions as mechanisms for managing mass harm litigation. Furthermore, it is clear that Australian judges have wide-ranging managerial powers and the need for these was recognised by the ALRC when it stated that 'without active court management, the interests of unidentified parties may not be taken properly into account'.[81] Case management plays important roles also, therefore, in achieving the MPA objective of fairness.

C. Fairness

It is questionable whether the opt-out system is inherently fair because all group members will be bound by a judgment unless they opt out of the proceedings, but this is a negative feature of opt-out regimes in general. One of the guarantors of fairness is that proceedings may not be ceased or settled without court approval. It must be proved that class members have been adequately notified of the terms of a settlement before the court will approve it. Another indicator of fairness in class action proceedings is the ability of the court to terminate proceedings either upon application of the defendant or where the court wishes to do so in the interests of justice. Also, this is illustrated by the fact that in exercising their case management powers, Australian judges take an active role in protecting the interests of those parties not present in court. The fairness of the Australian costs system is questionable in the way that only the group plaintiffs and not the individual group members will be liable for costs. The immunity from adverse costs awards conferred on other group members encourages the risk of 'free riders' and has resulted in the tool of 'men of straw' being invoked as plaintiffs and the corresponding demands from plaintiffs for protective costs orders. The increase in the use of third-party funding arrangements has eased funding difficulties but the restrictions on contingency fees for lawyers has somewhat tempered the risk of entrepreneurial practices.

It has been shown above, under the heading of procedural and judicial economy how case management can also play an important role in achieving the MPA objective of fairness. It also therefore assists with the objective of balancing individual rights and personal autonomy. The opt-out system obviously has implications for autonomy of putative plaintiffs. Furthermore, the consent of group members is not a precondition of the initiation of class actions as it is not necessary to name the class members unless they opt out of the proceedings. It has been shown, however, that classes may be defined in such a way as to require members to opt in by complying with certain requirements, for example entering a funding arrangement. This helps to safeguard individual rights of those who do not wish to participate in the litigation. The court has powers over notice requirements and may not require group member notice where the relief sought does not include damages but this will not negatively impact on potential plaintiffs. Finally, as the Australian system provides for the consideration of individual issues and for the use of subclasses if necessary, this further

[81] ALRC 1988 Report (n 3) para 157.

protects individual autonomy. Also, as regards awarding damages, these can be tailored to individual needs because the court has a wide discretion to award damages to the class as a whole, to any subclass or to individual members. This is a key lever that the court can use in terms of balancing the rights of individuals and individual autonomy.

D. Predictability

There do not appear to be any obvious differences in Australian aims of achieving the objectives of proportionality and predictability compared with other common law jurisdictions.

E. Deterrence

As previously discussed, one of the biggest differences between US class actions and their Australian equivalent is that Australia's objective is to compensate individuals and not to punish defendants or to punish behaviour. The ALRC stated that the objectives of increased access to justice and judicial efficiency did not enhance behaviour modification or deterrence as a goal of its potential class action proceedings.[82] It remarked that whilst 'the expansion of access to legal remedies might lead to greater enforcement of legal liabilities, and, as a result, increase the amount of monetary relief paid' by defendants, that was merely 'incidental' to the primary aim of providing access to the remedy the law prescribed.[83] Traditionally the defendant in representative proceedings has been the company most connected with the alleged harm but there have been increasing claims against others arguably responsible for the loss, which has implications for both deterrence and behaviour modification. The high rate of settlement of class actions may, however, impede their potential for achieving both of these objectives.

F. Compensation

As discussed in the deterrence section above, the ALRC has stated that whilst 'the expansion of access to legal remedies might lead to greater enforcement of legal liabilities, and as a result, increase the amount of monetary relief paid' by defendants, it did remark, that this was but 'incidental' to the primary goal of providing access to the remedy the law prescribed.[84] Representative proceedings in Australia, however, by providing access to justice through MPA procedures, do improve the availability of compensation. As seen above, the ability of the court to exercise discretion in how damages are awarded means that it has flexibility in delivering compensation. It is also clear that the use of representative proceedings has expanded to many areas ranging from mass consumer claims to those for environmental harm thus improving access to compensation.

[82] Ibid para 2.23.
[83] Ibid para 67 and 323.
[84] Ibid.

7. Environmental Mass Harm in Australia and Summary

Recent jurisprudence in Australia shows an increasing trend for the use of representative proceedings by those similarly situated suffering losses from the same cause.[85] Examples of this include environmental problems such as contaminated water, as well as claims against governments and agencies and for product liability.[86] One of the most high-profile environmental mass harm cases taken in Australia is still ongoing and it is the litigation related to the *Kilmore East Kinglake Bushfire*. This fire caused the deaths of 119 people on a day known as Black Saturday. It is the biggest civil case in Victorian history. The thousand plaintiffs allege negligence on the part of SP AusNet and Utility Services Corporation that caused the fire. They maintain that SP AusNet, the electricity provider, had inadequate systems in place and that those that were in place were poorly maintained. Furthermore they allege that the inspections, training and monitoring carried out by the defendants were inadequate. This negligence on several levels resulted in the electrical current coming into contact with the vegetation and causing the fire. The blaze razed 125,000 hectares and destroyed more than 1,000 homes. The plaintiffs maintain that the cause of the fire is not in dispute and allege that the defendants were aware that older and faulty electricity infrastructure could cause a devastating bushfire in extreme weather conditions but failed to take steps to make it safe. The Department of Sustainability and Environment, the Country Fire Authority and the State of Victoria are also being sued.

In summary of representative proceedings in Australia, they are now an established and important part of the Australian legal landscape. Factors that have contributed to this growth include the legal developments that have, in part, resulted from Federal Government support for such proceedings, as well as third-party funding, increasingly plaintiff-friendly representative proceedings laws and the growth of plaintiff representative proceedings law practices. The inbuilt checks and balances in the Australian system however, have helped to avoid what some feared in the mid-2000s to be an 'explosion' of class action suits. Notwithstanding this, as stated earlier, Australia has become the most likely jurisdiction in which a corporation will face significant class action-type litigation, outside of the US. The relative ease with which such proceedings can be commenced in Australia has led to actions being commenced in a wide variety of circumstances. While there were surprisingly few commenced in the years immediately following the introduction of the new procedure, however, that has radically changed over the past two or three years and there appears to be a new impetus to mass harm litigation in Australia.[87]

[85] eg *Godi v Toronto Transport Comm* (Gen Div, 20 Sep 1996) (subway disaster); *Johnson Tiles Pty Ltd v Esso Australia Ltd* [1999] 94 FCA 167 (gas supply).

[86] eg *Philip Morris (Austl) Ltd v Nixon* (n 13).

[87] For further empirical studies of Australian mass harm litigation, see generally V Morabito, 'An Empirical Study of Appeals by Class Members in Australia's Federal Class Actions' (2013) 42 *Common Law World Review* 240–68; V Morabito and J Caruana, 'Can Class Action Regimes Operate Satisfactorily without a Certification Device? Empirical Insights from the Federal Court of Australia' (2013) 61(3) *American Journal of Comparative Law* 579–615; V Morabito, 'Clashing Classes Down Under—Evaluating Australia's Competing Class Actions through Empirical and Comparative Perspectives' (2012) 27 *Connecticut J Int'l L* 245–318; J Caruana and V Morabito, 'Turning the Spotlight on Class Representatives—Empirical Insights from Down Under' (2012) 30 *Windsor Ybk of Access to Justice* 1–38; V Waye and V Morabito, 'Collective Forms of Consumer Redress: Financial Ombudsman Service Case Study'(2012) 12 *Journal of Corporate Law Studies* 1–32; J Caruana and V Morabito, 'Australian Unions—The Unknown Class Action Protagonists' (2011) 30 *Civil Justice Q* 382–410.

8

Collective Redress in England and Wales

1. Litigation Landscape

MPAs can trace their origins to England, as discussed previously.[1] However, such actions were very rare in the following centuries and the group action was a phenomenon that only began properly in the 1980s due to the availability of legal aid and a core group of lawyers who had explored the techniques in managing US class actions. Significantly, this movement was launched by a series of disasters, such as the Piper Alpha fire. Subsequently, there were a number of cases resulting from 'creeping disasters'. Examples of these include the following: those resulting from allegations of defective medical products such as the Dalkon Shield; defective pharmaceutical products; defective blood products supplied by the NHS which caused hepatitis or HIV infection. Many English lawyers learned MPA skills in these cases and developed ways of working together and with the courts that could be applied in new areas to facilitate mass harm litigation. A recent growth area is that of financial actions. There are several categories of examples of these: first, anti-competitive conduct (often US lawyers involved in US litigation seek European clients injured by such behaviour); secondly, securities actions, where there are allegations by shareholders that they have been injured by negligence or fraud by directors[2] and; thirdly, financial services. A final category is that of consumer mass harm, where, for example, many claimants suffer from relatively small but still significant harm. Such claims often cannot be effectively pursued as small claims and may not be overseen by an effective regulator and are therefore still in need of effective remedy.

This discussion relates to the treatment of collective redress through MPAs in England and Wales. Northern Ireland and Scotland are separate jurisdictions and they have similar public law. England and Wales obviously have a common law system where civil procedure is traditionally adversarial and decisions on liability and quantum are made by judges. Juries are only used in a small number of specific types of civil cases, for example defamation. There have been considerable reforms since 1999 that have introduced much greater judicial control through case management and that have eased funding difficulties. Courts have the power to limit the number of expert witnesses, the amount of documentary

[1] As discussed in ch 2, 'Collective Redress and Mass Harm', s 4 of that chapter ('The History and Background of Mass Torts') explains that the earliest trace of group litigation was an action brought on behalf of an entire parish against their rector who was alleged to have failed to provide their church with appropriate financial support in the case of *Master Martin Rector of Barkway v Parishioners of Nuthampstead*. See further S Yeazell, *From Medieval Group Litigation to the Modern Class Action* (Yale University Press, 1987) 54.

[2] These may involve cases against the companies or against individual directors; eg cases such as Enron and Worldcom.

evidence and oral argument admitted in litigation, and settlement through mediation is encouraged. It is very rare that punitive damages are awarded.[3] England and Wales, like Ireland, have a small claims procedure for claims under a certain financial threshold.[4] Similarly, England and Wales have been more cautious than the US in relation to fully embracing formal collective action mechanisms, with both England and Wales and Ireland being notable exceptions to the selected common law regimes in this research that have fully adopted such procedures. This situation is currently changing in England and Wales following significant developments whereby, in 2013, the Government published plans for reforming the regime for private competition law actions. This includes the creation of a new opt-out collective action for competition law on behalf of both consumers and businesses in the Competition Appeal Tribunal (CAT). This chapter will examine the existing mechanisms of collective redress for mass harm in England and Wales. In particular, there will be a detailed discussion of the representative action and the Group Litigation Order (GLO), both of which procedures facilitate multi-party litigation under the English Civil Procedure Rules (CPR). It will trace the evolution of the MPA landscape including the reasons for the previous rejection of the collective action mechanism.

England and Wales have several kinds of MPA mechanisms. The first is for those based on statutes that have a mainly regulatory nature, particularly for consumer protection, and these are commonly based on EU provisions.[5] These are limited to injunctive relief, although some claims for damages are now possible. The second form of collective relief is based on procedural rules of court that can be used for any sort of individual claim. There has been significant concern over the introduction of collective damages cases because of the perils of promoting litigation, especially in the scattered damages scenario where claims are of limited financial value but may result in large costs, as this could endanger economic competitiveness. The Government's policy has been to promote public authorities' supervision of restitutional payments as part of their regulatory enforcement activities. It is also encouraging fast and economical settlement and good behaviour through alternative collective redress avenues, such as ombudsmen,[6] mediation, sectoral schemes[7] and compensation schemes.[8]

2. Existing MPA Procedures

A. Public Representative Procedures

These are commonly used for consumer protection and competition law enforcement, often based on EU legislation that provides for representative claims in this area. These

[3] *Kuddus v Chief Constable* [2002] 2 AC 122 (HL).

[4] In England and Wales this is £5,000 for general claims or £1,000 for personal injuries cases.

[5] Public representative procedures are commonly used for consumer protection and competition law enforcement, often based on EU legislation that provides for representative claims in this area. These include powers for consumer organisations to bring claims that are usually limited to injunctive relief.

[6] eg the Financial Services Ombudsman and the Local Government Ombudsman.

[7] eg the medical injury scheme proposed under the NHS Redress Act 2005.

[8] There are various disparate compensation schemes in the UK: see forthcoming book by Macleod and Hodges on compensation schemes.

include powers for consumer organisations to bring claims that are usually limited to injunctive relief.[9] However, these tools are intentionally restrictive and rarely used. This is because the main model of enforcement requires such action to be in the hands of public authorities. Such enforcement was often undertaken by the now disbanded Office of Fair Trading (OFT). It used to be the OFT that took court proceedings, often based on referrals by consumer associations who did not bring actions themselves. The OFT's functions have been distributed to a number of various organisations, such as the Competition and Markets Authority (CMA). If there is an EU law element to the infringement then a cross-border injunction may be used. Section 47B of the Competition Act 1998 permits a representative action to be brought by a specified body for 'consumer claims made or continued on behalf of at least two individuals'. These are a type of collective action procedure under English law that may be used in competition cases. They are follow-on actions for damages in cases of previously proved breaches of competition law. It is only once an anti-competitive breach has been established by the CMA, the CAT, or the European Commission (EC) that a representative claim under section 47B may be made.[10] However, claims can only be brought by a 'specified body' as an 'ideological claimant' acting as a representative claimant, not by a directly affected consumer as a representative claimant. Consumer bodies need government approval to bring such actions and the only 'specified body' that has been licensed to take such action so far is the national consumers' association 'Which?'.[11] This would indicate that there may be underlying policy reasons for allowing a consumer body to take such action rather than individuals. Only consumers may be included in the class, not businesses that may have suffered harm as a result of the anti-competitive behaviour. These Competition Act representative actions are 'opt-in', so the consent of each consumer is required in order for his participation in the class. This prerequisite helps to ensure that only genuine claims are included and avoids frivolous or vexatious claims. If those consumers lose in the follow-on class action they have immunity from any adverse costs order. The Enterprise Act 2002 introduced additional powers that empower a designated consumer organisation to make a 'super-complaint' to the regulator (the CMA) where consumer interests seem to have been harmed in the English market.[12] It is the CMA that then takes action.

Some commentators suggest that both section 47B of the Competition Act and the other existing collective redress mechanisms in England and Wales fail to provide effective redress for victims of anti-competitive behaviour.[13] An example of this failure is seen in the only case that has been brought to date by Which? under section 47. The case was taken against JJB sports for anti-competitive behaviour in its pricing of England and Manchester United Replica T-shirts.[14] It followed the OFT's decision to fine JJB £6.7 million for fixing prices for replica shirts in 2000 and 2001. Which? settled the case with JJB out of court. Under

[9] Known as an 'enforcement orders' in the Enterprise Act 2002, s 21.

[10] Competition Act 1998, s 47A(5) and s 47A(6).

[11] Specified Body (Consumer Claims) Order 2005, SI 2005/2365.

[12] Under the Enterprise Act 2002, s 11(1) a super-complaint is defined as a complaint submitted by a designated consumer body that 'any feature, or combination of features, of a market in the UK for goods or services is or appears to be significantly harming the interests of consumers'.

[13] A Higgins and A Zuckerman, 'Class Actions in England? Efficacy, Autonomy and Proportionality in Collective Redress' (2013) University of Oxford Legal Research Paper Series, 14.

[14] The claim was settled. See 'Which? 'JJB to make payments to consumers for replica football shirts' (Press Release, 9 January 2008).

the settlement, each claimant received £20, which was the amount of the estimated illegal mark-up. A notable feature of the litigation is that, although there was widespread publicity, only 130 consumers opted into the proceeding, fewer than 0.1 per cent of those affected.[15] Following this case, Which? decided that it would no longer be taking any cases under section 47B because the opt-in nature of the system meant that it was not a proportionate use of resources for a charitable consumer organisation.[16] As a result, Which? called for the introduction of opt-out class actions.[17] The *Emerald Supplies Ltd and Others v British Airways plc*[18] case, discussed below, will show how Which? would have been unable to act in that case under section 47B because the case involved claims by both consumers and businesses, so it would have not have been permitted under the consumer only procedure of section 47B. Both of these cases demonstrate the reasons that both the Government and the senior judges responsible for administering competition law in England believed that there was a distinct need for reform of collective redress procedures.[19] Higgins and Zuckerman argue that

> It is only though a well-designed class action procedure that individuals, consumers and small businesses can obtain the level of protection available in the US. While there are disadvantages to opt out class actions, and the US model in particular, these can be clearly outweighed by the advantages. By providing easier access to court for individuals and businesses with legitimate grievances, it is reasonable to suppose that resulting higher levels of enforcement has also included higher standards of compliance amongst the provider of services and the suppliers of goods than would otherwise have been possible. Moreover, the capacity of individual litigants to prejudice the rights of others who are similarly situated, or cause unnecessary expense to publicly funded courts and vexation to opposing litigants, a strong case can be made for making class actions mandatory for those wishing to enforce or defend claims involving a generic question of fact or law.[20]

Sir Gerald Barling, President of the English CAT, expressed the view that 'there are a number of benefits that may flow from introducing an opt-out regime'.[21] In recalling the MPA objectives in this research, it is clear that just because an MPA procedure does not achieve results under one objective, this does not preclude it from succeeding in other areas. MPAs, as we have seen, can achieve a whole range of purposes ranging from compensation to deterrence. For example, the JJB case failed to recognise and compensate all those injured by the anti-competitive practice, and therefore it failed to achieve its compensation aims. It may, however, be viewed as having been successful in terms of the deterrence objective because the decision was likely to discourage similar anti-competitive practices in the future.

[15] Although some others have settled on similar terms since this settlement: Department for Business, Innovation and Skills (BIS), 'Private Action in Competition Law: A Consultation on Options for Reform' (Consultation Document, April 2012) [5.4].

[16] British Institute of International and Comparative Law (8th Annual Trans-Atlantic Dialogue, London, 15 May 2008).

[17] According to D Prince, then Head of Legal Affairs at Which?, as quoted in R Mulheron, 'Reform of Collective Redress in England: A Perspective of Need' (2008) Research Paper for Submission to the Civil Justice Council 41.

[18] *Emerald Supplies Ltd and Others v British Airways plc* [2009] EWHC 741 (Ch).

[19] Higgins and Zuckerman, 'Class Actions in England?' (n 13) 15.

[20] Ibid 46.

[21] G Barling, 'Collective Redress for Breach of Competition Law: A Case for Reform?' (2011) 10 *Competition LJ* 5–20. See also R Mulheron, 'A Missed Gem of an Opportunity for the Representative Rule' [2012] *Eur Bus L Rev* 49–60, both cited by Higgins and Zuckerman (n 13) 15.

B. Representative Actions, Consolidation, Joinder and Group Litigation Orders (GLOs)

While the English legal system, until very recently, did not contain any private collective action mechanism like those seen in the US, Canada or Australia, the occurrence of multi-party litigation is well established there. This has traditionally been carried out by the combination of some of the methods also used in Ireland such as the representative procedure, joint proceedings, consolidated proceedings, test cases and the allocation of several similar cases to a specific judge. As for joinder and consolidation of individual claims, the court has general powers to combine a number of individual proceedings into one action and can order that two or more claims be tried together. Both of these can result in efficiencies of cost and other economies but they do not result in a decision that binds all parties.

In 1999, a new system for conducting MPAs was introduced as part of a comprehensive reform of England and Wales's Civil Procedure Rules 1998 (CPR). These rules include various procedures for multi-party litigation. There are four additional procedures, including a procedure for representative actions, particularly where a single representative party may represent all the parties that have the same interest.[22] These new rules came about as a result of the Woolf Report in 1996 that made recommendations for litigation reform.[23] They aimed to encourage swifter and more cost-effective dispute resolution. The Woolf Report suggested that MPAs ought to be facilitated in England and Wales. There were fears that this could lead to US style class actions because, at the time, there were no specific rules in England and Wales for MPAs. Instead, procedures developed to a large extent as cases proceeded, often increasing costs. Lord Woolf's recommendation was to devise a new scheme for proceedings that require collective treatment. In 1999, as a result of these reforms, the Group Litigation Order (GLO) was introduced as a means of case management.[24] Under the rules, a court can make a GLO when numerous claims 'give rise to common or related issues of fact or law'.[25] It provides that a number of similar claims can be officially organised and coordinated, then managed and adjudicated by the same judge.[26] It arose out of a practice that had developed spontaneously to enable a series of large pharmaceutical multi-party cases to be managed by the courts in the 1980s and 1990s.[27] A new 'codified' approach reflecting this practice was included in the new 1999 CPR. These adopted general rules for managing individual litigation that were suitable for managing groups of similar claims. This highlights the need for managerial mechanisms to manage mass harm litigation and

[22] In addition to the normal tools of joinder or consolidation of individual actions, CPR, pt 19.II, specifies 4 different mechanisms:

1. representative parties with the same interest (r 19.6);
2. representation of persons who cannot be ascertained in relation to the estate of a deceased person (r 19.7);
3. representation of a person who has died (r 19.8); or
4. a claim by one or more members of a company, body or trade union … to be given a remedy to open it (a 'derivative claim': r 19.9).

[23] As discussed in ch 3; Lord Woolf, *Access to Justice: Final Report* (1996).

[24] Court Rules on Co-ordinated Management of Multiple Claims through Litigation.

[25] CPR, r 19.10 and r 19.11.

[26] See generally C Hodges, *Multi-Party Actions* (Oxford University Press, 2001) chs 2–8; N Andrews, 'Multi-Party Proceedings in England: Representative and Group Actions' (2001) 11 *Duke J Int'l & Comp L* 249.

[27] Further details of this history can be found in Hodges, *Multi-Party Actions* (n 26).

it would appear that MPA mechanisms play an important role in responding to this need. Before addressing the GLO, representative actions will be examined.

i. Representative Actions

In their English and Welsh form these are the closest equivalent to collective actions. They comprise a legal action in which one or a few members of a class sue on behalf of themselves and other members of the same class. They are the oldest procedure for obtaining collective redress in English law.[28] By using a representative action, claims can be pursued where one representative claimant or defendant acts on behalf of a class of individuals. Pursuant to Rule 19.6 of the CPR, representative actions may be brought 'by or against one or more persons who have the same interest' in a claim 'as representatives of any other persons who have that interest'. Any judgment or order given is then binding on all persons represented, but can only be enforced by or against a person who is not a party to the claim with the permission of the court. This 'same interest' requirement is designed to ensure that the interests of all bound by the action are adequately represented. It aims to avoid risks that may arise where a representative party may not pursue aspects of the case in which he has no direct interest. It also aims to avoid conflicts of interest between class members where the representative party may advance a case that undermines the interests of the other class members.

Court permission is not required for representative action proceedings, nor is consent needed from the represented person. Therefore a party may appoint himself as representative of others in legal proceedings—and thus make them potentially liable—regardless of whether he has been authorised to do so, and without any review by the court.[29] For these reasons, the court has interpreted the representative action requirements very narrowly, in particular the requirement that all persons in the representative class have the 'same interest'.[30] Historically, this procedure was not available if the action was for damages, because group members would be likely to be entitled to different damages.[31] Although these restrictions have been partly relaxed, the *Emerald Supplies* case, which will be discussed below, demonstrates that courts are reluctant to allow the procedure where there are different defences available against class members.[32] The reason for such reluctance is the concern that allowing such action would mean either that the interests of some class members were not adequately represented, or, that it could prevent a defendant from raising a defence that he has against some of the persons represented but not others.[33] As a result of these concerns, the procedure has been very rarely used. It is most commonly invoked where the claims arise out of one accident or tort or the breach of one contract. The restrictive approach to bringing a representative action has been confirmed in *Emerald Supplies Ltd*.[34] This is a renowned representative action that involved admitted price fixing

[28] See J Sorabji. 'The Hidden Class Action in English Civil Procedure' (2009) 28 *Civil Justice Q* 498.
[29] *Independent Ltd v Music Trading On-Line (HK) Ltd* [2003] EWHC 470 (Ch); *Howells v Dominion Insurance Co Ltd* [2005] EWHC 552 (QB).
[30] J Seymour, 'Representative Procedures and the Future of Multi-Party Actions' (1999) 62 *MLR* 564.
[31] *Markt v Knight* [1910] 2 KB 1021 (CA).
[32] *Emerald Supplies Ltd and Others v British Airways plc* (n 18).
[33] *London Association for Protection of Trade v Greenlands* Ltd [1916] 2 AC 15 (HL).
[34] *Emerald Supplies Ltd and Others v British Airways plc* (n 18).

by British Airways and other international airlines in respect of airfreight cargo. Price fixing obviously can have serious deleterious effects on markets and cause substantial losses to both direct and indirect consumers. The case concerned a claim by importers of cut flowers who alleged that BA had entered into concerted practices with other airlines to inflate airfreight prices. The claimant company, S, which used the services of BA to import flowers, brought a representative action on its own behalf and as representative on behalf of all other direct and indirect purchasers of airfreight services affected by the alleged concerted practices of price fixing between December 1999 and March 2006.[35] Emerald was seeking a declaration as to the outcome of seven points in dispute in this representative action:

1. that BA was a party to agreements or concerned practices with other air carriers who supplied airfreight services, directly or indirectly, to fix the prices of those airfreight services;
2. that the object or effect of those agreements or practices was to prevent, restrict or distort competition;
3. that those agreements or practices spanned the seven-year period noted above;
4. that the agreements or practices involved one or more of the air carriers identified in the litigation;
5. that the object or effect of the agreements or practices was to inflate the prices at which airfreight services were supplied to purchasers above those that would have prevailed had there been no such agreements or practices;
6. that the agreements or concerted practices constituted infringements of European and domestic competition law;
7. that the three particular types of damages were recoverable in principle from the defendants.

While it sought a declaration about each of those points, Emerald Supplies argued that proof of the individual losses that both it and the class of price-fixed victims had suffered would be individually determined outside the context of the representative action. Without proof of damage, it would not be possible to state that BA or its co-defendants were liable to the class members, given that proof of damage was a necessary element of the cause of action of each of those purchasers.[36] Hence, total liability could not be determined within the representative action itself. Emerald submitted that the declaration incorporated those issues that were pertinent to all class members' claims.[37] BA applied for an order striking out the representative element of the claim on the grounds, inter alia, that the other claimants that S sought to represent did not have the 'same interest' in the claim so as to meet the preconditions of a representative action under CPR, r 19.6.[38] The representative element of the claim was struck out by Vice Chancellor Morritt. His judgment illustrates a reluctance to support US style class actions, and shows that that reluctance also exists in relation to follow-on damages actions in competition law.

This decision was affirmed on appeal. The Court acknowledged the seriousness of the complaints and the gravity of the losses suffered by victims of price fixing. However, the

[35] Noted in [2010] EWCA Civ 1284 [34].
[36] Ibid [34].
[37] Ibid [58].
[38] This section of the CPR governs representative action.

Court upheld the Vice Chancellor's decision that the claim was not maintainable as a representative action because the represented group did not have the 'same interest' under CPR, r 19.6. The representative element of the claim was struck out because the class did not have a common interest in the claim and a common grievance when the claim was issued. It was not possible to say of any given person that he was a member of the class because membership depended upon the success of the action. Even if this flaw could be corrected by way of amendment to the statement of the case, the relief sought in the action was not equally beneficial to all members of the class because it included some who had absorbed the alleged inflated price as well as those who had passed it on. This resulted in disparate and possibly conflicting interests between class members.[39] The Court rejected the claimants' attempts to widen the representative action procedure to encompass elements of a 'class action'. It held that the GLO procedure provided a mechanism for managing multiple actions and that it was not in the interests of justice for actions to be pursued on behalf of persons 'who cannot be identified before the judgment in the action'.[40] While the courts' approach to CPR, r 19.6 has the benefit of providing certainty and simplicity, it has, however, rendered the procedure excessively narrow so as to be inapplicable in most cases.[41] Even in cases with genuine collective interests, the procedure may be frustrated by defendants who can demonstrate that they have defences against some class members but not all. For example, in a pollution case, a defendant may argue that only some class members, but not others, were affected by the way that the pollution was dispersed. Commentators believe that the representative rule, even following the CPR reform, has not been successful in aiding multi-party litigation, due to its limited scope and technical requirements.[42] The *Emerald* decision reinforces that conclusion.[43]

In 2001, the Lord Chancellor's Department proposed new procedures for representative claims. This idea was based on the Government's pledge to give various bodies the right to bring representative actions, such as consumer groups, environmental organisations and public enforcement agencies.[44] These proposals provided general amendments to representative proceedings. They included first, that there should be a pre-action protocol to the commencement of representative claims setting out the steps that should be taken by parties or their legal advisers before proceedings are issued. Secondly, it was proposed that a person or entity wishing to sue in a representative capacity would require the permission of the court to issue proceedings. Thirdly, that the application should be in writing and served on the defendant. Fourthly, that the membership of the represented group should extend to unnamed persons as well as named persons who would have a direct cause of action. Furthermore, it was proposed that individuals should be given an opportunity to opt out of the proceedings. Also, that applicants should be required to satisfy the court that they could adequately represent the group and that the representative claim is an appropriate way to proceed. Finally, it was proposed that organisations should be able to apply to the court for a determination that proceedings in the public interest should be conducted on a no costs

[39] *Emerald* (n 18) [64], [69].
[40] Ibid [35].
[41] Higgins and Zuckerman (n 13) 9.
[42] R Jackson, *Review of Civil Litigation Costs: Final Report* (December 2010) 330.
[43] Higgins and Zuckerman (n 13) 11.
[44] Some of these measures were required by EU instruments, such as the EC Directive on Unfair Terms in Consumer Contracts, as previously discussed.

basis or on the basis that if the action fails, the body will not be liable for costs.[45] Subsequent MPA developments will be detailed after an examination of the GLO mechanism.

ii. Group Litigation Orders (GLOs)

Apart from the representative action, the other principal mechanism for collective redress litigation in England and Wales is the Group Litigation Order, which can be made under CPR, r 19.11 for claims which 'give rise to common or related issues of fact or law'. GLOs are regulated by their own specific regime.[46] The fundamental difference between a GLO and a collective action is that a GLO comprises multiple distinct suits that are administered together, rather than a single suit. A GLO may be applied for by either a claimant or by a defendant, or the court on its own initiative may order a GLO.[47] This may occur at any time before or after any claims have been issued. The Law Society Practice Advice Service operates the Multi-Party Action Information Service (MPAIS) that assists in organising putative GLO applicants. Before applying for a GLO the solicitor acting for the proposed applicant should consult the MPAIS in order to obtain information about other cases giving rise to the proposed GLO issues. The parties must have regard to the practice direction governing group litigation.[48] This states that it will often be convenient for the claimants' solicitors to form a Solicitors' Group and to choose one of their group to take the lead in applying for the GLO and in litigating the GLO issues. The lead solicitor's role and relationship with the other members of the Solicitors' Group should be carefully defined in writing and will be subject to any directions given by the court under CPR, r 19.13(c). Certain information must be included in the application, such as: a summary of the nature of the litigation; the number and nature of the claims already issued; the number of parties likely to be involved; the common issues of fact or law that are likely to arise; any matters distinguishing small groups of claims within the wider group. The GLO regime can only be initiated with court approval.[49] The GLO indicates the issues that are shared by the cases coming within its scope. It may also dictate the way in which the order is to be publicised. When the GLO has been made, a group register is then set up containing details of the cases subject to the order. If someone wishes to join the group they are required to opt in. They may apply to have their case entered on the register before a deadline set by the court. Thus claimants can avoid some of the formalities of taking individual claims. A litigant's claim may also be consolidated to a group action by the court. In this way, group litigation presumes a definite decision to litigate.[50] This is in clear contrast to class actions, which usually contain

[45] Irish Law Reform Commission, *Consultation Paper on Multi-Party Litigation* (LRC CP 25-2003) 40, [2.44].

[46] Rules, practice directions and subordinate legislation, ie s III of the Civil Procedure Rules, rr 19.10–19.15; Practice Direction 19B—Group Litigation.

[47] *sua sponte.*

[48] Practice Direction 19B—Group Litigation states that 'It will often be convenient for the claimants' solicitors to form a Solicitors' Group and to choose one from their number to take the lead in applying for the GLO and in litigating the GLO issues. The lead solicitor's role and relationship with the other members of the Solicitors' Group should be carefully defined in writing and will be subject to any directions given by the court'. Available at: www.justice.gov.uk/courts/procedure-rules/civil/rules/part19/pd_part19b.

[49] Whether the parties have requested the GLO or it has been court-ordered, the order requires the consent of the Lord Chief Justice (for Chancery Division proceedings) or of the Vice Chancellor (for county court proceedings).

[50] Andrews, 'Multi-Party Proceedings in England: Representative and Group Actions' (n 26) 260.

opt-out mechanisms and also in contrast to representative actions, which do not require any decision by those being represented.

As stated, for a GLO to be established, the claims must give rise to common or related issues of fact or law. An example of how courts have treated this requirement is seen in *Hobson & Others v Ashton Morton Slack Solicitors and Others*.[51] There, the Court refused to grant a GLO in respect of claims brought by a group of miners and ex-miners regarding the enforceability of agreements made between the claimants and their trade unions. Under these agreements, the claimants agreed to pay to the trade union a proportion of the compensation awarded to them in separate litigation, as no group litigation issue had been sufficiently or precisely identified. The only unifying feature in the litigation was that all of the claimants were miners or ex-miners. The individual agreements between the claimants and the trade union were different and the assessment of liability depended on the facts of each case. The Court also found that a GLO was not an appropriate means of resolving the dispute, as the cost of pursuing this grossly exceeded the amount of damages claimed. Consolidation of the actions or the trial of selected cases were deemed to be a more appropriate and cost-effective means of resolving the claims.

In a GLO, a managing judge is appointed with overall responsibility for the group litigation.[52] He has wide-ranging discretion to give case management directions[53] and may decide what issues and evidence are necessary or unnecessary. He may require parties to state their estimated costs and also order reductions or caps on costs. He may call case management conferences to manage and control the litigation effectively. Unviable cases may be struck out and also parties may be encouraged to mediate or settle cases. The judge's goal is always to resolve cases with minimal delay, at a low and proportionate cost, usually by agreement of the parties outside of the court. The judge will normally select one or more individual cases to try as test or lead cases and the resolution of these should shed light on how many others may be resolved or settled. The managing judge has a general power to direct trial of common issues and/or individual issues.[54] Lord Woolf said that:

> the effectiveness and economic handling of group actions necessarily requires a diminution, compromise or adjustment of the rights of individual litigants for the greater good of the action as a whole.[55]

With this in mind, the GLO approach recognises that both the court and the parties have to make compromises in their usual rights to enable the group to make the required 'orderly progress'.[56] A judgment or order on a GLO is binding on all parties on the register at the time the judgment or order is made.[57] A party who is negatively affected by a judgment or

[51] [2006] EWHC 1134 (QB).

[52] He may be assisted by a master or district court to deal with procedural issues and also by a costs judge.

[53] Irish Law Reform Commission, *Consultation Paper on Multi-Party Litigation* (n 45) 40 [2.40] states that this includes: varying the GLO issues; providing for one or more claims on the register to proceed as test claims; applying the results of the settlement of a test claim to other claims; appointing a solicitor as the lead solicitor for the parties on either side; setting a cut-off date for the entry of additional claims on the register; and removing a party from the register.

[54] Practice Direction 19B—Group Litigation (n 48) cl. 5.

[55] Lord Woolf, *Access to Justice Inquiry: Issues Paper (Multi-Party Actions)* (1996).

[56] *AB and Others v John Wyeth & Brother Ltd* [1996] EWCA Civ J1213-8.

[57] This is unless the court orders otherwise. The court may also extend any judgment or order to any late claimants.

order may seek leave to appeal. The outcome of a test claim will be binding on all similar claims on the register.[58]

As mentioned above, one of the advantages of the GLO is that it equips the court with broad case management powers in order to provide that the class is adequately represented and that the case is handled justly. This includes steps such as appointing lead solicitors for the group and ensuring that one or more of the claims can be heard as test cases. The overall effect of a GLO is that all those subject to it will be bound by a judgment on the common (GLO) issues. The court also has power to vary these issues. The GLO procedure is broader in its scope than the representative action as it provides for situations where a number of claims 'give rise to common or related issues or fact of law'.[59] The GLO procedure gives the court maximum flexibility to use the appropriate management techniques tailored to each case and these can be innovative where necessary.[60] The GLO is an example of the managerial mechanism role that MPAs may play in order to assist the administration of mass harm litigation.

As regards costs in a group litigation situation, the general rule is that costs will follow the event, so the normal rules on civil litigation costs apply. Therefore, group litigants will be liable for the other side's costs if the group loses the action as 'loser pays winner's costs'. Group litigants will usually be given an order for common costs which will entail each group litigant being severally liable for an equal share of the common costs. Individual group litigants will be liable for costs relating to their own individual claims. Complex arrangements may be required for funding GLOs and a cost/risk analysis of individual group members may be undertaken in order to determine common costs. Some argue that the complexity and size of costs create a barrier to group cases. This will be discussed in the section that follows dealing with funding.

Surprisingly, the GLO has not been invoked as often as might have been expected and it has been eschewed in cases in which it may have appeared an obvious solution, for example in the *Buncefield* disaster, which is discussed in detail in a case study in this chapter. The court may refuse a GLO where insufficient consideration has been given to following a more cost-effective way of resolving the dispute, by using test cases or consolidating individual actions, as well as failure to identify a 'group litigation issue'. There is ongoing debate about potential reform, in which the Government is endeavouring to balance the challenges of improving access to justice while preventing the growth of a 'compensation culture'.[61] It is trying to achieve this by pursuing a new approach that involves public authorities supervising restitution as part of regulatory enforcement.[62]

The outcome for claimants' success in MPA litigation has been mixed. The legal costs far outweigh the damages and the difficulty in getting legal aid for such cases exacerbates this. This mixed success is despite the introduction of the GLO, which appears to not be being used frequently in practice. The general perception seems to be that MPAs are becoming outmoded as a route to achieving collective redress. This is apparent in the restrictive approach to bringing a representative action taken by the courts, as seen in *Emerald*

[58] It will also be binding on any subsequent claims if the court so directs.

[59] CPR, rr 19.10–19.15.

[60] Higgins and Zuckerman (n 13) 12.

[61] See Department of Constitutional Affairs, *Tackling the 'Compensation Culture': Government Response to Better Regulation Task Force Report 'Better Routes to Redress'* (2005).

[62] Hodges (n 26).

Supplies for example.[63] There the representative element of the claim was struck out as it was not possible to say at the time the action was begun who was a member of the class and the relief sought was not equally beneficial to all members of the class. The Court rejected the claimants' attempts to widen the representative action procedure to encompass elements of a collective action. As previously mentioned, it found that the GLO procedure provided a mechanism for avoiding multiple actions and that it was not in the interests of justice for actions to be pursued on behalf of persons 'who cannot be identified before the judgment in the action'. This point may indicate that the GLO may have had a role in preventing collective actions and that the GLO may be used as a mechanism for avoiding representative actions. Perhaps one of the rationales behind the introduction of the GLO in England and Wales was as a compromise to provide some form of group litigation but to avoid the introduction of collective actions. If so, then perhaps if GLOs are effectively used as MPA managerial mechanisms, they could play a role in preventing collective actions.

There is no up-to-date information on the number of GLOs that are currently being managed by the English courts. However, data from 2010 indicated that about 75 GLOs had been managed by the courts, but less than 10 GLOs were commenced in each of the previous five years.[64] The GLO has been invoked in a broad range of cases, particularly for product liability for medicinal products, the majority of which cases have failed. Examples of well-known successful product liability GLOs include those relating to PIP breast implants, the 'Toxic Sofa Cases', which resulted in a £20 million pay-out and the GLO taken for product liability against McLaren Buggies. As for MPAs generally, according to the Law Society, such cases cover a range of different areas of law:

> MPAs occur when a significant number of claimants have closely related or similar claims arising from the same event. They fall into three broad categories. Firstly, sudden disasters, such as personal injury or fatal accident claim, including damage to property. The Paddington rail crash is one such example. Secondly, rolling claims, which are claims arising from a single cause such as an allegedly defective drug or product. Thirdly, consumer claims where the claims are related to defective goods or services, personal injury or financial loss, such as mis-sold endowment policies.[65]

3. Evolution of MPA Landscape

It appears that the MPA landscape in England and Wales was changing as a result of the introduction of the GLO in 1999 and with the subsequent Lord Chancellor's Department's proposed new procedures for representative claims in 2001.[66] These proposals stemmed from the Government's pledge to give various bodies the right to bring representative actions, such as consumer groups, environmental organisations and public enforcement authorities.[67] They provided general amendments to representative proceedings.[68] While

[63] *Emerald* (n 18).

[64] www.arnoldporter.com/resources/documents/EnglandWales.pdf.

[65] www.lawsociety.org.uk/advice/practice-advice-service/multi-party-action-information-service/.

[66] Lord Chancellor's Department, *Representative Claims: Proposed New Procedures* (Consultation Paper) (February 2001).

[67] Some of these measures were required by EU instruments, such as the EC Directive on Unfair Terms in Consumer Contracts, as previously discussed.

[68] For further detail, see s 2B for discussion on Representative Actions.

the proposals were mostly welcomed, there were reservations expressed about the need for such a procedure in England and Wales, especially given the relative success of group litigation and the risk of opening the metaphorical floodgates to US style class actions.[69] While there is no fully-fledged class action system in England and Wales yet, English and Welsh courts repeatedly commented with regret on the absence of such mechanism in their own unaided efforts to structure alternative procedural techniques for mass tort claims.[70] Representative actions and group litigation have helped in some way to fill this void. Some commentators opine that such collective action 'is mainly for the benefit of claimants who perceive that they have a greater chance of success if they are united rather than appearing separately and at less cost' which is a philosophy similar to that of class actions.[71]

As mentioned at the outset, there have been significant developments in England and Wales recently as the Government has been considering the introduction of collective actions for competition law breaches. This followed the advice given by the Civil Justice Council (the CJC) to the Lord Chancellor in a December 2008 report.[72] In a move similar to the recent EU collective redress proposals for the introduction of horizontal collective actions, the CJC's report recommended that in order to improve access to justice, it should be possible for collective actions to be brought by representative bodies in respect of any type of civil law claim. The Government, however, did not support the introduction of a generic right of collective action and resolutely rejected the CJC's recommendation that a generic class action rule should be introduced.[73] It stated that there was no prospect, at least in the foreseeable future, of a generic collective action for England and Wales. It believed that instead, such rights should be considered, and where appropriate introduced, in respect of specific 'sectors'. The Government's opinion was that this was the only practical solution given the potential structural differences between the sectors that will necessitate different consideration. Furthermore, before implementing any reform it stated that it would be necessary to undertake full assessment of the likely economic and other impacts of such action. This response highlights the wider economic risk of defendants in certain economic sectors being particularly vulnerable to the bringing of disproportionate 'blackmail suits', which have been seen in the US as forcing defendants to settle on an objectively unreasonable basis. The Government stated that other techniques for achieving collective redress should be considered before introducing court-based options, as litigation was not the best route to achieving such redress. It recommended the use of regulatory options as an alternative in particular. It acknowledged certain regulators' concerns that delivering compensation could distract them from their core role, but where regulatory bodies exist and are in a position to act on behalf of consumers or other groups, they could,

[69] Lord Chancellor's Department, *Representative Claims: Proposed New Procedures* (Consultation Response) (April 2002).

[70] J Fleming, 'Mass Torts' (1994) *Am J Comp L* 522. eg 'There may well be a strong case for legislative action to provide a jurisdictional structure for the collation and resolution of mass product liability claims, particularly in the pharmaceutical field'; *Nash v Ell Lilly* [1993] 4 All ER 383, 409 (CA).

[71] Puxon, 'Comment' (1996) 7 *Med L Rev* 229.

[72] CJC Report, *Improving Access to Justice through Collective Actions: Developing a More Efficient and Effective Procedure for Collective Actions*. As discussed in ch 3, the CJC is an Advisory Public Body which was established under the Civil Procedure Act 1997 with responsibility for overseeing and coordinating the modernisation of the civil justice system…

[73] It did so, per the Ministry of Justice (MoJ), through *The Government's Response to the Civil Justice Council's Report* (July 2009).

for example, be given power to order compensation to be paid to consumers in addition to or instead of financial penalties. The decision on whether to adopt this type of model will be for the government department responsible for the relevant sector, as the regulatory environment will inevitably vary between sectors. In the Government's view this may be a more economical and efficient way of dealing with cases involving a large number of small claims.

One of the main CJC recommendations was that the courts should control whether collective actions may be brought and whether they should be on an opt-in or opt-out basis. They advised that this should be done by way of a certification process. Again, the Government's view was that the appropriate model or models for representative actions would need to be considered on a sector-by-sector basis rather than adopting a full opt-out model. The EU proposals, by way of contrast, advocate a horizontal approach rather than one based on sectoral needs. The Government response highlighted the difficulties with an opt-out model such as identifying sufficient members of a class at an early stage in order to demonstrate the cost benefit of the action and to secure funding. It further noted the concerns surrounding the calculation of damages in the opt-out approach, whereby damages have to be calculated on the basis of estimates of the class as a whole, rather than by quantifying the losses of known individuals. In light of these concerns, it considered that the same objectives from a full opt-out model would be better met in most cases by one of the hybrid models. The Government agreed with the CJC recommendation that the courts should control any collective actions that may be brought through the certification process. This process would consider factors such as the availability and suitability of alternative options, legal merit and whether the likely benefits justify the costs. The Government was also keen in its response to underline the importance of effective Alternative Dispute Resolution (ADR) mechanisms in any collective action. Its response also addressed the issues of costs and cost shifting in the context of collective actions. Cost shifting (or the 'loser pays' principle), as has been shown, is regarded as significantly deterring blackmail settlements. The Government believed it is for the court to decide on the issue of costs, the court retaining full discretion to shift costs on to the loser. The responsibility for the necessary primary legislation to introduce collective actions on a sector-by-sector basis would fall to the government departments concerned, following consultation with stakeholders and an assessment of economic and other impacts. It will be for each department to decide whether to consider introducing collective actions in any given sector and the timetable for doing so. To ensure that all the relevant issues are considered and, where appropriate, consistent conclusions are reached, the Government stated that it intended to develop a policy framework document to assist policymakers and others to address all the relevant issues. In addition to this, the Government pledged to work with the CJC to develop proposals for procedural rules to be put to the Civil Procedure Rule Committee (CPRC). The aim of such collaboration was to develop flexible generic procedural rules within which any collective action scheme can operate.

Anecdotally, it appears that the CJC's approach was intended to attract collective cases to be resolved in the English courts. This was based on its idea that this would benefit London's legal services market and the English judicial system. In reality, neither business nor government would welcome this potentially huge increase in large-scale litigation. A White Paper has shown the development of regulatory techniques in the consumer area, with last resort assistance through the use of a judicial compensation method controlled by a new quasi-ombudsman known as the Consumer Advocate.[74] This proposal by the Labour Government, however, was subsequently dropped when the Coalition came to power. For financial services claims the main emphasis is on self-regulation and ADR by financial institutions with support from the Financial Ombudsman Service (FOS), and also with support from the Financial Services Compensation Scheme. There is also now an increased regulatory oversight power for the Financial Conduct Authority and judicial representative claims are a last resort.[75] In endorsing a sectoral approach, it appears that the Government is laying emphasis on the differences between the nature of claims arising under different sectors and the different needs of treatment that arise as a result, for example the differences between a claim arising under competition law and a claim arising under consumer law.

In 2009, the CJC established a subcommittee, a CJC working group, to develop proposals and to draft rules of court for collective actions. They aimed to produce a set of generic court rules of sufficient flexibility that they might be used for any different model of collective proceedings that primary legislation might permit. The MoJ committed itself to work with the CJC to develop proposals for draft rules of court for collective actions, which would then be submitted to the CPRC. The CJC created its 'Draft Court Rules for Collective Proceedings'[76] and these were submitted to the Lord Chancellor and the CPRC in February 2010.[77] The need for these draft rules was probably encouraged by the notorious English bank charges litigation—in which over 53,000 claims were filed between March 2006 and August 2007. The unpredictability and uncertainty surrounding this litigation appeared to be one of the political motivations for the proposed reform of collective actions via the means of the introduction of a new collective action in the Financial Services Bill.[78] This regime, intended to apply to financial services claims, contained an opt-in or opt-out class action, depending on the judicial choice. That proposed regime was ultimately abandoned prior to the General Election in May 2010, and the supporting rules that were drafted for the CPR were not promulgated.[79]

In January 2013, following the consultative process between the CJC and the MoJ, the Government announced its plans for reforming the English regime for competition law private actions, including radical proposals for the creation of a new 'opt-out' collective action for competition law claims on behalf of both consumers and businesses in the

[74] Department for Business, Innovation and Skills, *A Better Deal for Consumers. Delivering Real Help Now and Change for the Future* (Cm 2669, 2009).

[75] Financial Services Bill, cl 18–25, proposed that an individual may bring representative proceedings on behalf of others who are entitled to bring proceedings of the same, similar or related issues of fact or law, subject to the court approval of a collective proceedings order. The court would decide whether an opt-in or opt-out model would apply; see Draft Court Rules for Collective Proceedings by the Civil Justice Council.

[76] The Financial Services Bill was published just as the working group commenced its work, available at: www.publications.parliament.uk/pa/cm200910/cmbills/049/10049.1-7.html. This Bill contained provisions for collective proceedings in relation to specified financial services claims. The Bill differs from the Draft Rules in its use of terminology in two respects:

(1) The court rules generally refer to a 'class'- a term that has been avoided in the Bill.
However, the Bill was introduced into Parliament on the basis that it provides for 'class' actions. The working group considered this a useful description to use in the court rules.
(2) The rules refer to a 'class representative' (the Bill uses only 'representative').

[77] The CJC understood that in the light of these draft rules the CPRC would produce proposals for amendments to the Civil Procedure Rules and that it will carry out a full consultation before reaching any final decision.

[78] Financial Services Bill, cl 18–25.

[79] As proposed CPR, pt 19.IV.

CAT.[80] In April 2013, the Government published its consultation on competition law private actions, which proposed that under an opt-out regime claims could be brought on behalf of a defined group, without the need to identify individual group members. All those who fall within the group will be bound by the result unless they actively opt out of the case. This is a significant departure from existing procedures for multi-party litigation in England and Wales, which generally require potential claimants to opt in to proceedings.[81] The consultation recognised concerns that an opt-out class action may encourage vexatious or unmeritorious claims. The proposals were highly controversial owing to concerns that such procedures may lead to some of the 'excesses' of US style competition litigation that are often alleged to encourage defendants to make blackmail settlements. The consultation paper acknowledged this and propounded that these concerns can be addressed by various safeguards, including a thorough certification process, retention of the 'loser pays' rule and the continued prohibition on contingency fees in collective action cases. Under the proposals, claims will only be allowed by claimants or by genuine representatives of the claimants, such as trade associations or consumer associations, not by law firms, third-party funders or special purpose vehicles. One aspect of the Government's plans that is likely to be particularly unpopular with defendants is that any damages remaining unclaimed will be paid to the Access to Justice Foundation rather than reverting to the defendant. Accordingly, the damages that defendants will have to pay will be based on losses suffered by the entire class, not only those who come forward to claim their damages. Parties will however be free to agree a settlement on a different basis, subject to approval from the CAT.

Under the proposed opt-out regime, claims can be brought on behalf of a defined group and damages awarded to that group, without the need to identify individual group members. All those who fall within the group will be bound by the result, including a settlement, unless they actively opt out of the case. Under the proposals, the CAT will be required to certify whether an action should proceed on an opt-in or opt-out basis. The opt-out aspect will apply only to England and Wales-domiciled claimants. Those domiciled outside the jurisdiction will need to opt in if they wish to participate in the litigation. The Government is also proposing a new opt-out collective settlement regime for competition cases, whereby parties could ask the CAT to approve an agreed settlement on an opt-out basis (for England and Wales-domiciled claimants) without the need for a claim to be brought. This is similar to the Dutch mass settlements regime, save that the Dutch system purports to cover claimants domiciled outside the Netherlands (including potentially England and Wales-based claimants).[82] There will also be new powers for the CMA, to certify voluntary redress schemes. The Government made it clear that it does not support a generic collective redress mechanism, which would apply to all sectors. These proposals for competition law claims may make it more likely that similar initiatives will be brought forward for other sectors.

[80] Department for Business, Innovation and Skills, *Private Actions in Competition Law: A Consultation on Options for Reform—Government Response* (January 2013) available at: www.gov.uk/government/uploads/system/uploads/attachment_data/file/70185/13-501-private-actions-in-competition-law-a-consultation-on-options-for-reform-government-response1.pdf.

[81] The one exception, for representative actions under CPR, r 19.6, is not widely used owing to the strict test that applies, as confirmed by the Court of Appeal in the *Emerald Supplies* case.

[82] Similar to the Dutch Collective Settlement Act 2005, to allow businesses to settle cases quickly and easily on a voluntary basis.

It is still early days in terms of seeing how these proposals will be adopted. There has been one prediction that England could be Europe's class action capital in times to come.[83] However, it is slightly extreme to draw analogies with the US system at this stage. We have seen how factors such as widespread use of contingency fees for class actions and large damages awards encourage more speculative class actions in the US. There is a continued prohibition on contingency fees in collective action cases in England and Wales. The occurrence of speculative actions is likely to be linked closely to legal aid reforms. Such reform will have the reduction of costs as their main aim and this will therefore help potential claimants.

4. Funding Regime and Recent Changes

In terms of funding cases in England and Wales, since 1995 public funding through legal aid has been heavily restricted.[84] Contingency fees were not permitted for contentious work in England and Wales until recently.[85] In 2009, Lord Justice Jackson, a Court of Appeal judge, carried out a year-long review of civil litigation costs. He published his final report, *Review of Civil Litigation Costs*, in January 2010.[86] In his report he found that the costs of civil litigation were too high and were fuelled by the way in which conditional fee arrangements (CFAs) operated. Under such arrangements, lawyers could conduct litigation and would get a success fee of up to 100 per cent of the normal fee if the case succeeded and nothing, or sometimes a discounted fee, if the case were lost. The use of such arrangements has been possible for some time.[87] Under these agreements, the claimant was effectively at no financial risk, the risk being borne by the claimant's lawyer and the defendant. On the other hand, a losing defendant had to pay not only the claimant's base legal costs, but also the CFA success fee and the claimant's after-the-event (ATE) insurance premium, both of which were recoverable from the losing side and which could add substantially to costs. Lord Justice Jackson made recommendations for the introduction of contingency fees in part because he considered it desirable that as many funding methods as possible should

[83] eg www.legalweek.com (30 October 2007) stated that the UK is regarded as the most 'fertile' ground in Europe for class actions, according to the results of a new survey of company executives and corporate counsel. 59% of respondents to the poll, carried out by the Economist Intelligence Unit and sponsored by US law firm Bryan Cave, said they expected to see collective litigation take root in the UK over the next 3 years. Over half (59%) of the 240 participants in the poll said they expected consumer goods companies to be targeted in particular, with two-thirds (67%) highlighting product liability as a key area.

[84] For many years the UK spending on legal aid for civil litigation has been the highest of any EU Member State: see Council of Europe (European Commission for Efficacy of Justice), *European Judicial Systems 2002* (Strasbourg, France, 2004) 30. See Access to Justice Act 1999; Legal Services Commission, *The Funding Code*, available at: www.legalservices.gov.uk/civil/guidance/funding_code.asp.

[85] Contingency fees were permitted, however, for employment and other tribunal work (which is technically considered non-contentious business).

[86] www.judiciary.gov.uk/Resources/JCO/Documents/Reports/jackson-final-report-140110.pdf.

[87] Under the Conditional Fee Agreements Regulations 2000, SI 2000/692, reg 3(1)(a), and The Conditional Fee Agreements Order 2000, SI 2000/823. A CFA has 2 parts: a 'no win no fee' provision and an increased fee if the claimants win their case. The 'no foal no fee' amount will comprise the normal basic fee which is based on an hourly rate, plus the uplifted fee for success, which is a proportion of the basic fee. Statute, contract, the court and the regulator of professional conduct regulate the percentage uplift in an individual case. The agreement must set out the reasons for the agreed uplift and it is capped at 100% of the normal fee and should not exceed 25% of the damages recovered.

be available to litigants, particularly once CFA success fees and ATE insurance premiums would no longer be recoverable from the losing party. He also saw particular merit in the freedom of contract argument that if the client wishes to enter into a contingency fee agreement with its lawyer, it should be free to do so. The Government has confirmed that the use of contingency fees, or damages-based agreements (DBAs) as they are also known, will be prohibited for the new form of collective action that is to be introduced for competition law claims. This is intended to act as a safeguard against the risk of frivolous or unmeritorious cases arising from the introduction of an opt-out regime. The Legal Aid, Sentencing and Punishment of Offenders (LASPO) Act 2012 no longer permits claimants to recover the success fee (or after-the-event insurance if it is taken out) from the defendant. It means that the claimant has to pay the success fee, after-the-event insurance premium or, for example, costs for experts. The cost risk will reduce the attractiveness of opt-out collective actions. Presumably, DBAs will be available for other forms of collective action, whether brought as representative actions or under GLOs or on any other basis.

The Government carried out a full consultation between November 2010 and February 2011 on implementing Lord Justice Jackson's main recommendations for the reform of funding arrangements. It published its response to the recommendations in March 2011.[88] In this, the Government confirmed that the CFA reforms and other related measures would be implemented. The Government's proposals were enacted in Part 2 of the LASPO Act and came into effect in April 2013. Most notably, under this new legislation, contingency fees are now permitted for contentious work in England and Wales. This means that they will be permitted for litigation or arbitration proceedings.[89] As a result, for the first time, lawyers can conduct litigation and arbitration in this jurisdiction in return for a share of any damages. There is, however, a continued prohibition on contingency fees in collective action cases. Until these changes, only third parties could fund litigation in return for a share of the proceeds. This is known as third-party funding, or litigation funding. Litigation funders are regulated by a voluntary code of conduct, which was introduced in 2011. Cases need to show very good chances of succeeding before they will attract funding from lawyers under CFAs[90] or from third-party investors and from insurance companies who will cover the risk of the adverse costs.[91] The appearance of third-party investors is predicted to have wide-ranging effects. Now expensive cases are financed by consortia that involve lawyers on CFAs, insurers, investors, as well as by the parties themselves. It is also common that lawyers and case managers can advertise. Ironically, these traits seem to resemble features of the US class action system, that England and Wales had been determined to avoid. The costs of MPA litigation are high and, in an effort to combat this, a number of changes have been introduced whereby the court can make an order to cap costs at an early stage in the

[88] MOJ, *Reforming Civil Litigation Funding and Costs in England and Wales—Implementation of Lord Justice Jackson's Recommendations: The Government Response*, available at www.gov.uk/government/uploads/system/uploads/attachment_data/file/228974/8041.pdf.

[89] The Legal Aid, Sentencing and Punishment of Offenders Act 2012 (LASPO Act), s 45 amends s 58AA of the Courts and Legal Services Act 1990 to permit DBAs. Certain requirements that DBAs must meet in order to be enforceable are set out in the Damages-Based Agreements Regulations 2013 S.I. No. 609.

[90] These were introduced under the Courts and Legal Services Act 1990, s 58.

[91] The cost of after-the-event premiums are recoverable from losing defendant: Access to Justice Act 1999, s 29.

case or that claimants be protected.[92] England and Wales have also introduced the concept of Protective Costs Orders, but only for judicial review in public law cases. These orders allow a judge, at an early stage in proceedings, to limit the costs payable by a party if they lose. This means that the court can specify what costs and to what limit each party will be liable. The advantage of such orders is that they eliminate the uncertainty regarding potential future costs liability that may otherwise deter a potential litigant. These orders are used primarily in relation to public environmental law. All of these developments will help in the funding of cases and ease access to justice for claimants.

5. GLOs and MPA Objectives

The case study of environmental mass harm at the end of this chapter will evaluate the use of the GLO and case management as methods of collective redress for such harm and will be discussed in detail there. Hodges, in a historical review of MPAs, has produced a schedule of 'a succession of major cases since the early 1980s' in England and Wales that give additional analysis of the English MPA experience.[93]

Chapter three on MPA objectives has also examined the aims of collective redress and its evolution in England and Wales through the various mechanisms and also the input of contributions by Lord Woolf and the CJC. Therefore, this section will make only brief reference to the MPA objectives.

A. Access to Justice

The main restriction of the GLO regime, in terms of barriers to entry and the ability to obtain collective redress, is that all members of the group must commence their own individual proceedings. In this way, the GLO is more of an effective case management instrument where there are a large number of related claims, each of which merits individual proceedings. It is not a collective action procedure. Another crucial constraint to its use is the costs liability for all those who are subject to a GLO. CPR, r 48.6A provides that a costs order against group litigants imposes several liability for an equal portion of the common

[92] A Protective Costs Order is an order made at the outset of the proceedings in question which provides that the party applying for the order shall, regardless of the outcome of the proceedings, either not be liable at all for the other party's costs or be liable only for a fixed proportion thereof but if successful may be entitled to recover all or part of his costs from the other party. The first recorded case of this in England was *R v Lord Chancellor, ex p Child Poverty Action Group* [1999] 1 WLR 347; [1998] 2 All ER 755, QBD. The implementation of the Aarhus and related EU rules in England and Wales was codified in April 2013 following a MoJ consultation. In effect, this enables claimants in judicial review claims within the scope of the Aarhus Convention to have a PCO with a maximum liability of £5,000 if they are individuals and £10,000 if they are other legal persons such as NGOs or companies. There is a reciprocal limit on recovery of £35,000. Using a PCO in public law cases, where the issues raised are of general public importance and the applicant does not have a private interest in the case, will limit or extinguish that claimant's exposure to costs: *R (on the application of Corner House Research) v Secretary of State for Trade and Industry* [2005] EWCA Civ 192 (CA).

[93] See further Hodges (n 26).

costs, rather than joint liability, unless the court orders otherwise. In addition to this, a group litigant is also liable for the costs in relation to his individual claim. Both of these factors are considerable impediments to access to justice in terms of the MPA benchmarks. Taking the *Emerald* case as an example, the fact that a GLO requires every group member to commence their own proceedings and holds them liable for a share of the costs of the proceeding is likely to be the main reason why a GLO was not sought in that case. The GLO regime evidences many of the existing economic and social barriers to access to justice previously identified in mass harm cases, especially in scattered damages scenarios.[94] Furthermore, there are high transaction costs for the lawyers and litigation funders who support the litigation because they have to obtain instructions to issue a claim from all those wishing to partake in the action. Also, those pursuing a GLO may be observed by 'free riders'. This term refers to those who have identical claims but prefer to stay out of the litigation, hoping that if the GLO succeeds they would be able to get redress from the defendant without having to prove the common issues or incur the risk of considerable costs. By way of contrast, in a representative action and a US class action there is no need for each represented party to issue their own proceedings before they can benefit from the result of such an action.

B. Judicial and Procedural Economy

This also is discussed in detail in the environmental mass harm section. It is clear that the use of the GLO provides for efficiencies in both procedural and judicial economy. We have seen how Lord Woolf identified judicial economy as being important when he dictated that any new procedure should 'provide expeditious, effective and proportionate methods of resolving cases'.[95] It has also been noted already that part of the objective of the CPR is the need for efficient and economical use of court resources. The importance of this aim was judicially endorsed in the *Emerald case*, where it was it was found that whether there was the requisite 'same interest' in that representative litigation 'is determined with a view to promoting the litigation objectives of justice, economy, efficiency and expedition'.[96] It was eventually held there that the representative action was procedurally ineffectual.

It has been shown that the English reforms of collective redress view economy and efficiency in a broad context and that the CJC intended some wider aims in its 'key findings' in its report *Improving Access to Justice Through Collective Actions*:

> Effective collective actions promote competition and market efficiency, consistent with the Government's economic principles and objectives, benefiting individual citizens, businesses and society as a whole. Equally they are effective mechanisms through which individual rights can be upheld. Collective claims can benefit defendants in resolving disputes more economically and efficiently, with greater conclusive certainty than can arise through unitary claims.[97]

These wider objectives were taken into account by the CJC when, in 2008, it proposed a new generic collective action for England and Wales. This recommendation was adopted for the sectoral reform proposed in the Financial Services Bill 2010. Experience has shown

[94] Higgins and Zuckerman (n 13) 13.
[95] Lord Woolf, *Access to Justice: Final Report* (n 23) ch 17[2].
[96] [2010] EWCA Civ 1284 [4].
[97] December 2008 Report, in particular key findings number highlighted above.

that where MPAs can help to resolve cases speedily and efficiently for parties, then they may make a valid contribution to ensuring access to justice.

C. Fairness

Lord Woolf emphasised that fairness and balance between litigants was crucial, to the extent that collective redress should 'achieve a balance between the normal rights of claimants and defendants, to pursue and defend cases individually, and the interests of a group of parties to litigate the action as a whole in an effective manner'.[98] In 1998, the CPR[99] included this as part of its overriding objective. It expressly requires that, in order to deal with cases justly, this should include, 'as far as is practicable', both 'ensuring that the parties are on an equal footing'[100] and 'ensuring that [the case] is dealt with expeditiously and fairly'.[101] The CJC December 2008 report emphasised that fairness 'remains a valid benchmark' when considering any collective actions reform and design.[102] Lord Woolf's review highlighted that the need for 'balancing' recognises that individual participation rights and procedural autonomy inevitably must be compromised or curtailed to achieve efficient collective management, and a resolution of multiple similar claims.[103] It has been shown how this may potentially involve significant interferences; for example, under a GLO, individual group members may find that they cannot freely choose or instruct lawyers,[104] or they may be excluded from influencing the pleadings, selection of experts and presentation of evidence. In Ireland, or other jurisdictions, such a situation might produce constitutional difficulties. For example, there was a recent Irish Supreme Court decision in relation to the right to legal representation. The case of *Declan O'Brien v PIAB Ireland*[105] concerned an application by a victim of an accident in the course of his employment, demanding the Personal Injuries Assessment Board (PIAB), the statutory body whose role it is to assess compensation paid to persons who have endured a personal injury, to deal with his solicitor in relation to his claim for personal injury. O'Brien alleged that his constitutional right to be represented by a solicitor was being breached by the actions of the PIAB, in that it sought a right to deal directly with him, rather than through his solicitors. He successfully sought a declaration from the High Court that the Board's actions breached the relevant legislation. In his High Court judgment Mr Justice MacMenamin held that the claimant's lawyer could not be excluded from dealing with the Board on the claimant's behalf, as there was no such provision contained in the Act establishing the Board to that effect. He recognised the necessity of obtaining legal advice as:

> Such steps and such decisions may have serious consequences for a claimant. The right to legal representation and the lawyer/client relationship exist in a common good. Most significantly they

[98] *Access to Justice: Final Report* (n 23).

[99] As stated previously, these are the Civil Procedure Rules (CPR) that apply to all litigation, including collective redress litigation, conducted in England and Wales.

[100] CPR, r 1.1(2)(a).

[101] Ibid r 1.1(2)(d).

[102] CJC, *Improving Access to Justice through Collective Actions* (n 72) 51.

[103] S Gibbons, 'Group Litigation, Class Actions and Lord Woolf's Three Objectives—A Critical Analysis' (2008) 27 *Civil Justice Q* 208, 227.

[104] eg where lead solicitors are appointed and a claimants' steering committee is formed to liaise with them.

[105] [2007] 1 IR 328.

help to guarantee equality of arms in litigation and various types of adversarial process and the maintenance of fairness between the strong and the weak.

This decision has implications for the right to legal representation in these situations and could likely, by implication, extend to representation in MPAs. In relation to the GLO and settlement terms, these may be negotiated and agreed without the involvement of individual group members or they may find their cases 'stayed' while other test claims trials proceed. They may be bound by these decisions and also be forced to pay a share of these costs. Furthermore, most significantly, in the opinion of Gibbons, not only group members but also group litigants who take entirely separate, parallel proceedings may find that their 'normal' rights are circumscribed in order to give priority to the GLO parties' interests.[106] This, she opines, falls within Lord Woolf's broad wording which therefore permits 'balancing' 'not only where conflicts of interest arise between group members, between individual group members and the group as a whole, and also between the group as a whole and individual litigants engaged in other, entirely separate proceedings'.[107]

As for the objective of proportionality, as seen earlier, all provisions within the CPR, including those concerning collective actions, are subject to the 'overriding objective of dealing with cases justly'[108] and relate proportionately to 'saving expense' and 'allotting an appropriate share of the court's resources [to the case], while taking into account the need to allot resources to other cases'.[109] The importance of considering the effect of the CPR's overriding objective has also been stated in relation to the GLO[110] and has been referred to by judges in case law, for example in *Emerald*.[111]

In his *Final Report on Access to Justice*, Lord Woolf identified as his third objective that the multi-party litigation regime in England ought to have, that the rules for such procedures should 'achieve a balance between the normal rights of claimants and defendants, to pursue and defend cases individually, and the interests of a group of parties to litigate the action as a whole in an effective manner'.[112]

D. Predictability

As previously shown, the unpredictability and uncertainty surrounding the English bank charges litigation, as well as the inconsistencies in the various litigation strategies that were developed to cope with the volume of claims,[113] appeared to be one of the political motivations behind the proposed reform of collective actions and the introduction

[106] *Gibbons*, 'Group Litigation, Class Actions and Lord Woolf's Three Objectives' (n 103) 208, 227. She cites the case of *T (formerly H) v Nugent Care Society (formerly Catholic School Services)* [2004] EWCA Civ 51; [2004] 1 WLR 1129 (CA).

[107] Ibid.

[108] CPR, r 1.1[1].

[109] CPR, r 1.1(2)(b); CPR, r 1.1(2)(e).

[110] eg *Taylor v Nugent Care Society* [2004] EWCA Civ 51 [22].

[111] Where Chancellor Morritt held that the CPR's overriding objective of dealing with the fixed price victim's litigation against airlines fairly would be best achieved by having their recourse to the GLO mechanism rather than the representative action being sought in that case.

[112] Following this report in 2000, the CPR were amended by the introduction of CPR, r 19.4. CPR, pt 19 sets out the rules governing multi-party disputes, including representative party actions and GLOs.

[113] In which over 53,000 claims were filed in the English county courts between March 2006 and August 2007.

of a new collective action in the Financial Services Bill 2010.[114] Furthermore, it has been shown in the use of the GLO shows how two approaches may be used depending on the circumstances- the test case and generic issues.[115] This makes the use of the GLO mechanism more uncertain.

E. Deterrence

MPAs, as we have seen, can achieve a whole range of purposes ranging from compensation to deterrence. For example, the *JJB* case failed to recognise and compensate all those injured by the anti-competitive practice, and therefore it failed to achieve its compensation aims. It may, however, be viewed as successful in terms of the deterrence objective because the decision was likely to discourage similar anti-competitive practices. This case may indicate that deterrence may be a key function rather than compensation. While not suggesting that any MPA system ought to go as far as the US because of the enforcement environment there, it is still important that MPAs may have a deterrent effect. The CJC noted that deterrence is an important ancillary consequence of effective private enforcement:

> Effective enforcement would involve compensatory damage awards that were appropriate according to established substantive law principles of disgorgement of profits. It is a consequence of its primarily compensatory function that effective private enforcement arises, through which it provides a real deterrent effect that such actions are said to have on unlawful conduct. In this context both the OFT and the European Commission have publicly stated that they see private actions by victims in competition law as a necessary complement to their own public enforcement efforts.[116]

F. Compensation

The objective of compensation has not been specifically addressed by the English studies examined as an MPA objective, perhaps either because it is implicit in the notion of access to justice or because it is a by-product of effective multi-party mechanisms.

6. Combined Case Study of Environmental Mass Harm

The system in England and Wales is a perfect example of where mass harm may be remedied through the use of MPAs as management mechanisms, or through the use of case management techniques, in order to enhance access to justice.[117] Both the GLO and case

[114] This was intended to apply to financial services claims and provided for an opt-in or opt-out class action (depending on the judge's choice). This proposal never survived the General Election in May 2010 and was not introduced.

[115] eg the test case approach was used in *Pirelli Cable Holding NV v Revenue and Customs Commrs* [2007] EWHC 583 (Ch) and the generic issues approach was used in *Esso Petroleum Co Ltd v Addison* [2003] EWHC 1860 (QB).

[116] CJC, *Improving Access to Justice through Collective Actions* (n 72) 78–79.

[117] In general, however, these tools alone are insufficient.

management techniques have been adopted there to enable mass harm litigation and they can be used for any claim including environmental mass harm.[118] GLOs aim to ensure effective management of multi-party litigation and this is preferable to trying to manage large numbers of individual cases relating to the same facts. The use of 'test cases' increases access to justice by making claims more manageable for claimant lawyers and judges.

England and Wales does not have a highly developed culture of public interest law firms compared with the US, probably because of lack of resources from legal aid and so the claimant firms often have to act for the group, which can be a burden on the law firm's cash flow as it has to pay for outlays such as the cost of experts and gathering evidence. It can be difficult to know the length of time that a case may take and this uncertainty may further increase risk and cost. There is only one law firm in England with the experience and expertise to pursue environmental mass harm actions, Leigh Day and Co. They have been involved in most MPAs in England. Since 1990, they have acted in the tobacco litigation and also in one of the first environmental actions in England and Wales against Sellafield on behalf of childhood leukaemia victims. They specialise in overseas claimants suing British multinational companies and have acted in cases such as *Lubbe & Ors v Cape Plc*;[119] *Motto v Trafigura*;[120] and *Bodo Community v Shell Petroleum Development Company.*[121] In the opinion of Richard Meeran, of Leigh Day, private lawyers need an incentive to take on such cases and that this should entail certain benefits and attractions.[122] This, he believes, is crucial in terms of ensuring access to justice for claimants. Recent developments in England and Wales have benefited claimant lawyers and have made these cases easier to bring, hence increasing access to justice.[123] The fact that the English system does not allow potential

[118] eg a GLO was made in respect of the *Corby Litigation* which has recently been settled after a first instance judge found in favour of the claimants on the subject of the breach: *Corby Group Litigation* [2009] EWHC 1944 (TCC). This was an action against a local authority that the claimants argued was responsible for birth defects, given the manner in which it cleaned up contaminated land in the area. This, however, is a rare success for claimants in an environmental 'toxic torts' case in the UK. A much less successful claim was *Hunter v Canary Wharf* [1997] AC 655 (HL), brought by various residents of the London Docklands, which was eventually heard by the House of Lords.

[119] *Lubbe v Cape Plc* [2000] UKHL 41.

[120] *Motto and Others v Trafigura* [2011] EWCA Civ 1150 (CA) was a group action involving approximately 30,000 claimants injured by the dumping of toxic waste in the Ivory Coast by a ship chartered by the defendant, a Dutch-based oil and commodity shipping company. The action had been commenced in November 2006. Liability was initially denied, but later accepted. Despite allegations of severe injury and death, it transpired that the victims suffered only flu-like symptoms. The claims were all settled in September 2009 on the basis that Trafigura would pay £30m damages (ie approximately £1,000 per claimant) and they would pay claimants' costs on the standard basis, to be assessed if not agreed. The claimants' bills totalled nearly £105m including 100% success fees for solicitors and counsel and a £9.7m ATE insurance premium. For reference, the defendant's costs were £14m in total. There was no agreement as to the costs.

[121] Leigh Day sued Shell after negotiations with Shell over the payment of compensation for 2 massive oil spills broke down. The legal action, on behalf of 11,000 members of the Bodo community, represents the first time Shell or any oil company has faced claims in the UK from a community from the developing world for environmental damage caused by its oil extraction operations. In August 2011, Shell admitted liability following 2 massive oil spills in the Niger Delta, which experts have advised amounted to about 500,000 barrels from a Shell pipeline in 2008. The oil devastated the environment surrounding the community of Bodo, in Gokana Local Government Area, Rivers State, Nigeria. Leigh Day & Co represents the Bodo Community and brought the multi-million pound claim, coupled with a demand for clean-up of the oil spills, against Shell Petroleum Development Company (Nigeria) Ltd in the High Court, in London in 2012. The Bodo community is a rural coastal settlement that now consists of 49,000 people who live in 35 villages. The majority of its inhabitants are subsistence fishermen and farmers.

[122] In addressing the 'Conference on Collective Redress', *Increasing Access to Justice through Class Actions: A Conference for Litigators and Policy-Makers* (Brussels, November 2012).

[123] eg LASPO Act.

claimants to opt out of litigation, however, may present problems. For example, victims who are unaware that they are suffering from harm such as a latent disease may be precluded from taking an action at a later stage under this system.

For the purposes of this study, it is useful at this point to look at a practical example of environmental mass harm litigation in England and Wales, as the closest comparator to the Irish legal system. This is done through a combined case study of two contrasting landmark English mass environmental harm cases. The first case is the *Corby Group Litigation*,[124] which was resolved using a GLO. The second case is the *Buncefield Oil Disaster*, where the option of granting a GLO was not exercised. Instead, creative case management was successfully invoked to resolve the case. The experience and outcome of both cases can be compared in order to learn lessons about how these two different techniques aided collective redress for environmental mass harm. What the resolution of both cases appears to suggest is the need for managerial mechanisms in order to overcome the challenges presented by needs of such redress.

Before looking at the GLO case study in Corby, it is useful to recap on the GLO procedure. Part 19 of the CPR governs group litigation.[125] Rule 19.10 provides that a GLO is an order made under Rule 19.11 to provide for the case management of claims which give rise to common or related issues of fact or law. Under these rules, the court has power to make a GLO enabling the court to manage the claims covered by the order in a coordinated way. Rules 19.10 to 19.15 of Part 19 are designed to achieve the objectives of providing access to justice where large numbers of people have been affected by another's conduct, but individual loss may make an individual action economically unviable. A practice direction supplements these CPR rules for GLOs.[126] The rules and practice direction cannot, however, be treated as a complete guide to the appropriate court procedures for conducting every group action. They simply establish a framework for the case management of claims that give rise to common or related issues of fact or law. They are intended to provide flexibility for the court to deal with the particular problems created by these cases. The GLO will contain directions about the establishment of a 'group register' on which the claims to be managed under the GLO will be entered and will specify the management court which will manage the claims on the register. Judgments, orders and directions of the management court will be binding on all claims within the GLO. The court's case management powers enable it to

[124] *Group Litigation v Corby Borough Council* [2009] EWHC 1944 (TCC).

[125] CPR, r 19.11 provides as follows:

(1) The court may make a GLO where there are or are likely to be a number of claims giving rise to the GLO issues. (The practice direction provides the procedure for applying for a GLO.) A GLO must—
  (a) Contain directions about the establishment of a register (the 'group register') on which the claims managed under the GLO will be entered;
  (b) Specify the GLO issues which will identify the claims to be managed as a group under the GLO;
  (c) And specify the court (the 'management court') which will manage the claims on the group register.

(2) A GLO may—
  (a) In relation to claims which raise one or more of the GLO issues (i) direct their transfer to the management court (ii) order their stay until further order; and (iii) direct their entry on the group register;
  (b) direct that from a specified date claims which raise one or more of the GLO issues should be started in the management court and entered on the group register; and
  (c) Give directions for publicizing the GLO.

[126] Practice Direction 19B—Group Litigation (n 48).

deal with generic issues, for example, by selecting particular claims as test claims. These case management powers are contained in Rule 19.13.[127] In addition to Rule 19.3(b) providing for tests claims, Rule 19.15 specifically provides:

> (1) Where a direction has been given for a claim on the group register to proceed as a test claim and that claim is settled, the management court may order that another claim on the group register be substituted as the test claim.
> (2) Where an order is made under paragraph (1), any order made in the test claim before the date of substitution is binding on the substituted claim unless the court orders otherwise.

Neither the rule nor the practice direction provides any guidance on when and how test cases might be selected. In fact, group litigation can be case managed in a number of different ways, including division of the group into subgroups, identification of generic or common issues, use of a master pleading, trial of particular issues, and some investigation of a sample of all individual claims, as well as the test case approach. By only referring to test cases, the rule implies that this is the preferred option.

A. Group Litigation Using a GLO in *The Corby Group Litigation Case*

i. Facts

In the 1980s, Corby Borough Council acquired a large tract of contaminated land from the British Steel Corporation. It wished to regenerate the land following the closure of the steel works. Years of steel manufacture meant that the soil on the site contained toxic substances. The Council constructed a tip for the contaminated soils and transported hundreds of lorry loads of soil along the roads in Corby linking the former steelwork sites to the tip. A number of children were born in the Corby area between 1986 and 1999 with deformities of their upper limbs. Their mothers lived close to or had contact with this area at the time of the works, which coincided with their pregnancies. They formed the Corby Litigation Group representing 18 children born during this period. The group alleged that the reclamation works created toxic dust, mud and sludges along the public roads between the sites. The group sued Corby Borough Council for damages for personal injury allegedly caused by the Council's negligent handling of the contaminated soils. In the High Court, the judge found that the negligence of the Council could have caused the injuries complained of. The trial of the case, during which specific issues that were generic and common to all of the claimants were examined, lasted for 38 days. 18 claimants and/or their parents gave evidence along with 20 other factual witnesses, together with a host of scientific experts. Vast amounts of time were spent examining key issues in detail, including: what sorts of substances were present on the site; what the Council's

[127] This provides that: 'Directions given by the management court may include directions: (a) varying the GLO issues; (b) providing for one or more claims on the group register to proceed as test claims; (c) appointing the solicitor of one or more parties to be the lead solicitor for the claimants or defendants; (d) specifying the details to be included in a statement of case in order to show that the criteria for entry of the claim on the group register have been met; (e) specifying a date after which no claim may be added to the group register unless the court gives permission; and (f) for the entry of any particular claim which meets one or more of the GLO issues on the group register'.

activities consisted of; whether a duty was owed by the Council to the claimants; whether the activities had been conducted to the proper standard; whether failure to adhere to the proper standard could have caused the types of birth defect complained of; and whether the harm in question was foreseeable.

ii. Outcome

The case did not determine which children could recover and how much they would receive. This was to be decided at a later hearing. Such a hearing, however, never took place because, shortly after the case, Corby Borough Council agreed a settlement with the families, although the amount of compensation remained confidential under the settlement agreement. There are a number of features that are particularly relevant to mass toxic tort litigation in this case. First, expert scientific evidence was presented. This was based on claims submitted by the mothers of children. They claimed that during their pregnancies they were exposed to contamination from the waste removal operation. They sought to bring a legal action to try to prove a link between the mismanagement of the toxic waste and the birth defects suffered by their children. The evidence presented included reports detailing the higher rate of birth defects, and alleged that exposure to the toxic waste was the likely cause of the children's deformities. They also presented a report written by Roger Braithwaite, an environmental expert instructed by the families, which concluded that the negligent handling of the waste by Corby Borough Council demonstrated:

> Naivety, arrogance, ignorance, incompetence and a possible serious conflict of interest ... At this early stage it would seem to me that these ... badly polluted lands have never been effectively or comprehensively assessed, properly permitted, regulated, monitored or adequate records maintained ... This is environmental negligence on a grand scale.

Secondly, the GLO certification: After having reviewed the evidence presented by all parties to the case, the then Lord Chief Justice, Lord Phillips of Worth Matravers, approved an order that set out the terms of the litigation in relation to the Council's management and execution of the 'land reclamation contracts' between 1985 and 1999 and any duty they had to the families. Permission was given for the parents to pursue the claim against Corby Borough Council as an MPA involving children born between 1985 and 1999. In his High Court ruling, Mr Justice Akenhead said it was clear that the Council had permitted toxic waste to disperse into the atmosphere. He also said that there was a 'statistically significant' cluster of birth defects between 1989 and 1999, and that:

> Toxicologically, there were present on and from the Corby Borough Council sites, over the whole period from 1985 (and possibly before) until 1997, the types of contaminants which could cause the birth defects complained of. There was an extended period between 1983 and August 1997 in which Corby Borough Council was extensively negligent in its control and management of the sites, which they acquired from British Steel and otherwise used. That negligence and, as from April 1, 1992, breach of statutory duty on the part of CBC permitted and led to the extensive dispersal of contaminated mud and dust over public areas of Corby and into and over private homes, with the result that the contaminants could realistically have caused the types of birth defects of which complaint has been made by the claimants (save in limited respects)... Corby Borough Council is liable in public nuisance, negligence and breach of statutory duty, obviously subject to it being established in later proceedings by individual claimants that their particular conditions were actually caused by the defaults identified in this judgment.

Mr Justice Akenhead said that while the parents had been 'wholly honest', the Council's motive was to develop and sell the land quickly without thought for the consequences of those nearby, and without appreciating 'the enormity, ramifications and difficulty' of its task in moving the material. In a lengthy judgment, the judge held the Council liable in public nuisance, negligence and breach of statutory duty.[128]

Thirdly, causation: following the judgment, the claimants were not yet entitled to an award of damages. Each of the claimants then needed to show that their particular condition was actually caused by the Council's identified shortcomings. They were supported by the judgment on generic group issues. To get to the trial stage the Council was anecdotally reported to have incurred defence costs of £1.9 million. In addition, it then had to make an interim payment of £1.6 million in respect of the claimants' costs, which was rather less than the claimants had requested but was nevertheless very significant (the claimants are reported to have asked for an interim payment of over £3 million against their total costs of over £4 million).

In 2009, Corby Borough Council voted to appeal against the ruling but said that it would follow a 'twin track' approach, preferring to attend independent mediation sessions to come to an out-of-court settlement with the families. The chief executive gave a statement that if a causal link between the toxins and the limb deformities was ever proven he would 'offer an unreserved apology'. In April 2010, the Council released a joint statement with the families' solicitors announcing it was dropping its appeal and that it had agreed a settlement with 19 families. The terms of the settlement remained confidential, and the agreement forbids disclosure of the financial arrangements.

iii. Commentary

The group action decision in the Corby Group Litigation seems to be the benchmark for mass harm litigation involving GLOs at present.[129] The case bears many of the hallmarks of 'classic' environmental toxic tort litigation and the challenges that these can present all those involved in achieving collective redress. Some toxic tort actions allege exposure of groups of individuals to a substance that has been introduced into the general environment by the defendant's actions. In England, it is extremely rare for environmental toxic tort actions to make it to trial, and rarer still for the claimants to actually win. Evidentially, claimants face tough challenges in proving their case, and the cost of putting a case together is usually prohibitive. When claimants can put together a credible case, however, defendants can find themselves in a very difficult position. It is often difficult to shift media attention away from

[128] The judge made the following findings: (1) there was a statistically significant cluster of birth defects to the children of mothers living in Corby during much of the relevant period. A cluster like this could not be explained by chance alone; (2) toxicologically, there were present on and migrating from the site over the whole period from 1985 (and possibly before) until 1997 the types of contaminant that could cause the birth defects complained of by the claimants; (3) there was an extended period between 1983 and 1997 in which the Council's activities at the sites were conducted in such a way that they fell below the proper standard; (4) the activities led to the extensive dispersal of contaminated mud and dust over public areas of Corby and into and over private homes with the result that the contaminants could realistically have caused the types of birth defect of which complaint has been made by the claimants (save in limited respects); and (5) in respect of children conceived after August 1997, it could not be demonstrated that their birth defects could be caused by any breaches of duty or public nuisance occurring before that time; and there were no significant emissions of the relevant contaminants after that time which could have caused the birth defects.

[129] *Group Litigation v Corby Borough Council* (n 124).

the emotional or perceived moral aspects of the case onto the more legally relevant ones. Settling can be difficult owing to the likelihood of adverse public relations and the possibility of further copycat actions by additional claimants. Fighting the case often turns out to be the most attractive option for defendants, even though gathering the evidence to counter the claimants' case is costly and the chance of recovering in respect of all costs—even if the defence is successful—is not great. In this case it was held that Corby Borough Council had been negligent in cleaning up former steelworks and, as a result, that birth defects in children in the area could have been caused by the mismanagement of toxic waste. This case provides an example that illustrates how obstacles, particularly those of mass environmental harm litigation, which may confound individuals where they are attempted solely, can be overcome when they are addressed as part of a group action. This is a significant advance in the field of such litigation whereby individuals still maintain their own claims, but actions can now be grouped together for technical requirements, such as establishing causation in negligence. This clustering of claims strengthens individual claims. A similar approach might be taken to conditional fee arrangements (which include a premium allowing a law firm to get insurance against the loss of the action). Such advances show how the innovative use of MPAs may assist in the attainment of justice.

There are lessons to be learned from *Corby*. The judge stressed that the Corby project was a 'one off' in many ways. Large environmental toxic tort cases rarely get to trial owing to the complexity and cost of the technical evidence required. As a general rule, if the organisation has behaved in line with the prevailing standards at the time, or has selected and supervised independent contractors with reasonable care and skill, it will be difficult to make a claim against them. However, organisations ought to be vigilant, particularly in relation to falling short of appropriate standards. The judge in *Corby* said that the Council had sowed the seeds of liability by simply 'biting off more than it could chew' on an unfamiliar project rather than having a systemic breakdown. Also, as this case shows, liability in environmental toxic tort cases can lie dormant or undetected for decades and catch an organisation off guard when it surfaces. If there is an increase in the number of environmental toxic tort cases in England and Wales (due to the emergence of more sophisticated claimants' lawyers and a friendlier costs environment), and because the financial cost, management challenges and reputational risks to the company are so high (even if the claim fails), potentially vulnerable defendants are best advised to take steps to ensure that they have suitable insurance cover in place should a claim arise, and that any future activities that might have an environmental impact are managed in accordance with the law.

B. Case Management—*The Buncefield Oil Disaster*

i. Facts

This disaster concerned a major oil storage facility at Buncefield, north of London, which was the site of a major explosion and fire in December 2005.[130] There were multiple causes,

[130] The Competent Authority, *Buncefield: Why Did it Happen? The Underlying Causes of the Explosion and Fire at the Buncefield Oil Storage Depot, Hemel Hempstead, Hertfordshire on 11 December 2005* (2011) available at: www.hse.gov.uk/comah/buncefield/buncefield-report.pdf. The term 'Competent Authority' is used in EU law to designate a Member State's public authority that is responsible for regulating a sector or activity under specific EU legislation.

including negligence, and it resulted in large-scale damage to the surrounding areas as well as serious personal injuries. There were clear design, maintenance, operational and behavioural failings that caused this event. As well as the fire and explosion damage, there was contamination of groundwater from fuel and fire-fighting liquids. The event was the largest peacetime explosion ever to have occurred in Europe, measuring 2.4 on the Richter scale and it could be heard 200 kilometres away. The disaster was investigated by the Competent Authority (comprising the Health and Safety Executive and the Environment Agency), which published a report on its findings.[131] The extensive damage resulted in a considerable environmental, social and economic toll. Local business and residential properties suffered from the after-effects, with some properties destroyed and others badly damaged.[132] The principal defendants were Hertfordshire Oil Storage Limited (HOSL), which owned and operated the tanks.[133] The estimate of total quantifiable cost from the incident came close to £1 billion.

Following the event, there were calls for action to stop pollution and some calls for a public inquiry. Experience of public inquiries in England had shown that they could be very slow and costly. An independent investigation board, the Buncefield Major Incident Investigation Board (MIIB), was established to undertake the public supervisory role. The entire process meant that there were several parallel procedures taking place.[134] Five companies were prosecuted for various offences and the ruling included record fines for a single incident in the UK.[135] Extraordinarily, the civil compensation litigation made swift progress and was resolved before the regulatory process. No GLO was used in this case, despite it seeming suited to such treatment. The claimant group involved over 100 groups. They filed approximately 3,000 claims, comprising claims by individuals and companies for sums amounting to up to £1 billion. These included about 250 individuals.[136] Most of the claimant householders were represented by one law firm, that of Des Collins. This firm had a high local profile in personal injuries cases after handling cases such as the Corby children's limb deformities cases. Leigh Day & Co also had some involvement. This was unusual because in many other cases of multi-party litigation the claimants had diverse legal representation.

ii. Outcome

At the outset, the oil companies made a strategic policy decision that they would respond appropriately to the damage and proactively invite claims to come forward.[137] Collins applied for a GLO. In March 2006, at a Case Management Conference (CMC),[138] the GLO

[131] Ibid.

[132] Following a 5-day fire.

[133] This was a joint venture between Total UK Limited (60% ownership) and Chevron Limited (40%).

[134] This included the MIIB scrutiny, the COMAH investigation and prosecutions, environmental protection activities and civil claims. Under COMAH, the EA was looking at whether 'Operators' had taken 'all measures necessary'.

[135] Total UK Ltd, eg, pleaded guilty to 3 offences and was fined £3.6m and ordered to pay costs of £2.6m. HOSL and two other defendants pleaded not guilty but were found guilty.

[136] With a total claim value of £20m, of which many claims were for less than £10,000.

[137] This policy had been successfully adopted in the Lloyd's litigation: Hodges (n 26) 14.

[138] This was convened by the Senior Master of the High Court, Master Turner, in the Queen's Bench Division of the High Court.

application was adjourned and a general structure was established for civil claims. It was ordered that all claims were to be issued in or transferred to the High Court, marked '*In Re The Buncefield Incident*' and the Law Society was to be informed, in relation to its semi-official Multi-Party Action Information Service role in coordinating solicitors. At the next CMC in October 2006, Master Turner decided that there would not be a GLO but instead continuance of a 'structured settlement' process that had already begun. He ordered HSOL to mediate with the householders and in March 2007 there was a mediation that was unsuccessful. It was agreed to transfer the cases to the Commercial Court, where Mr Justice David Steel took over their management. At a further CMC in April 2008, the judge was concerned at the cost of all the representation and he strongly encouraged parties to collaborate to save costs.[139] The Commercial Court has vast experience of handling big cases and has a reputation for flexibility that is greater than that of some other courts. However, concern over costs and delays led to a series of recommendations for the adoption of further innovations in procedure, and the *Buncefield* case became the first paradigm case to test new techniques.[140] The judge was persuaded that a GLO would be unnecessary and that the case could be progressed as managed litigation.[141] Instead of the parties sequentially exchanging pleadings, the legal teams each filled out a large matrix document identifying what the issues were and this enabled the judge to identify how the various claims should be managed. This was in order to support both court determination of key issues and settlements as efficiently as possible.[142] Following trial, the claims that had not been settled were sent on for assessment of quantum. 140 individual claims for quantum were transferred to the Technology and Construction Court. These claims were eventually settled, with support from the judge, despite a four-year delay. The final issue was liability for costs. Collins was of the view that the cost arrangements would have been organised from the outset if a GLO were in place. All of their clients entered into privately funded arrangements, mostly conditional fee arrangements. Under a CFA, Collins bore financial responsibility for cash flow but it would recover a success fee if the case resulted in a successful outcome. The clients also entered into complicated cost-sharing arrangements, which involved some disagreement.

iii. Commentary

This case study shows the need for flexible management when processing complex cases. As stated at the outset, a pre-existing procedure, such as the GLO, was not used. Settlement was achieved thanks to the power to adopt flexible case management.[143] A crucial impetus for

[139] Estimated to involve 60 solicitors and 60 barristers as well as multiple householders and insurers.

[140] Judiciary of England and Wales, *Report and Recommendations of the Commercial Court Long Trials Working Party* (2007).

[141] By Jeremy Stuart-Smith QC.

[142] A great deal of work was done in the run-up to the trial. The disclosure process was phenomenal as 1.7 million documents were processed in 6 months. A large part of the trial was dominated by the argument between Total and its joint venture partner Chevron over liability and the extent to which Total was responsible for HSOL.

[143] Requirements on settlement and case management were introduced into the CPR upon their fundamental reform in 1999.

this was the formal procedural requirement in the CPR to achieve settlement. The regulatory system also exerted pressure by proactively seeking claims and settlement. The judge and leading lawyers exercised great control in the matrix management. It was challenging for them to deal with such a diverse range of claims and parties. Great efficiency and cost savings were demonstrated by all parties either at their own initiative or encouraged by the Court. The judges and lawyers showed great flexibility and resolved the cases very speedily.

The solicitors were under pressure to attract clients and there was media involvement in this case, which was a burden. Possibly as a result of this, some steps in the litigation process, such as making an application for a GLO, were taken at too early a stage to enable the lawyers and the courts to have sufficient information to decide what the correct action ought to be. In this case, the early application for a GLO could not be supported by a clearly defined legal case, and the various judges simply disregarded it. The essential feature in the successful resolution of this case was that all of the four judges involved were experienced in handling multi-party cases. The degree of judicial control they provided resulted in continuity and consistency. Another essential feature was the ability of the judges to impose effective management and to make speedy progress in the litigation. Their encouragement of direct negotiations resulted in settlements. Mr Justice Steel considered that his main objective was to ensure that the litigation remained manageable. In the opinion of all the judges, the claims were successfully resolved thanks to senior, experienced lawyers with significant experience in managing large cases. The process worked so well that there was no need for a procedural structure in the form of a pre-existing format. Both judges and lawyers were focused on the CPR's formal aim to achieve settlement. In addition to this, there was a great deal of cooperation and agreement between the parties and their lawyers, which facilitated efficient resolution.

From this case study it is clear that mass harm litigation such as this requires considerable resources and experience in terms of management of personnel and logistics. Overall, the entire litigation was effectively resolved within six years, with many of the claims having been settled earlier. The judges and lawyers engaging in flexible, creative management achieved this successful outcome. They refused to be constrained by procedural rules and instead they exercised significant discretion over case management as they went along. The regulatory and compensation aspects of *Buncefield* were dealt with separately through different systems and courts. It is normal practice in England and Wales that the incidents involving companies such as in this case are subject to public scrutiny. This results in administrative action and enforcement. Such incidents are dealt with by public agencies such as the Health and Safety Executive and Environment Agency, and they are also responsible for handling criminal prosecutions and public investigation reports. The civil courts dealt solely with the compensation aspect of the case.

In summary, this example clearly illustrates the need for management in mass harm cases. In this case, the mechanism by which the judges managed this litigation was based on the courts' inherent jurisdiction to manage cases—no new rules were required and neither the GLO nor any pre-existing procedure was used. All of the actions remained separate and were not formally joined within any formal coordinated structure. A GLO may be technically appropriate where there is a homogenous group of individual claimants and a single defendant. However, in a case such as *Buncefield*, where there are different groupings of both claimants and defendants, there is a need for creativity and efficiency in order to managing such litigation justly.

7. GLOs Compared with Case Management

As *Corby* shows, environmental or personal injury claims are typical examples of circumstances in which the handling of claims involving multiple parties gives rise to common or related issues of fact or law. Other examples are cases involving sudden disasters, industrial disease or accident, product liability claims involving the taking of medicines, or the use of defective products. In the *Corby* litigation, a GLO was made at an early stage. Such an order was appropriate in light of the common issues of fact and law that were likely to arise in the litigation. Despite 18 individual claims being issued under CPR Part 7 on behalf of individual children born with limb defects, no directions were made by the management court for any individual claim on the group register to proceed as a test claim. While the five specific issues which were expressly the subject of the GLO were largely, by agreement, amplified by the addition of a further 25 sub-issues, the central GLO on the issue of causation was: 'Whether any such breach (of duty) had the ability to cause upper and/or lower limb defects to the claimants of the type complained of'.

In contrast, no GLO was made in respect of the *Buncefield* proceedings. Although the claimants involved several parties with closely related claims, many claimants were content to await the outcome of the trial between Total and Chevron. Two claimants' groups emerged to represent claimants outside the fence made up of: one group appearing for companies situated in the local industrial estate, and a second group representing individual claimants from the Hemel Hempstead area. A Case Management Conference took place in the Commercial Court and this made provision for a trial of preliminary issues. The order called for an exchange of lists of proposed issues for approval by the court. It was further ordered that all findings of fact or rulings of law were to be binding on all parties in the *Buncefield* action. In the *Buncefield* litigation there were three areas of expertise on which oral evidence was called: (1) data analysis;[144] (2) operational negligence;[145] and (3) accountancy.[146] In the *Corby* litigation the claimants and Corby Borough Council each relied on expert scientific, medical and epidemiological evidence. More than a year before the trial, directions were made by the court for experts in the fields of management of waste disposal programmes, toxicology, foetal development, epidemiology, and air pollution science and safety risk management, to hold discussions and produce joint statements in accordance with CPR, r 25.12 on issues arising in their common fields, and to exchange reports in their like fields.

In terms of the role of experts in such litigation, at the trial the epidemiological evidence concentrated upon a consideration of whether or not there was a 'cluster' of limb reduction defects in Corby. In his judgment Mr Justice Akenhead said:

> It is an unfortunate fact of life that children are born with birth defects for some known reasons but generally for unknown reasons. Science and statistics have not been able at this stage of history

[144] The focus here was on the information and database tables stored on computer drives. Chevron called a specialist in mechanical engineering with particular expertise in the investigation of fires and explosions. Total called a senior project engineer with particular experience in electronic control analysis.

[145] Chevron relied on a logistics support operation manager at its Aldermaston Petroleum Storage depot. Total relied on a consultant safety engineer with Vectra Group Limited.

[146] Total called a chartered accountant who had examined Total's accounting records so as to determine whether any premiums incurred in effecting the Total group insurance programme had been charged to the joint venture company, Hertfordshire Oil Storage Limited.

> to identify the causes of the defects in each case or indeed in many cases. In some cases, there is a genetic throwback for a particular defect in the child's family. Sometimes, abusive substances, such as cocaine, cause defects. Thalidomide, to which various experts have referred, was a prime example of a prescribed drug causing birth defects. It therefore becomes of interest and use to determine whether something out of the ordinary has happened in any given case or whether what has happened is an unfortunate chance event or series of events. It is in that context that the epidemiological experts address the available statistics … It is however clear that the epidemiological evidence, whatever I find, is not directly or fully probative. As both experts accepted, the outcome of the epidemiological debate in this case is at best simply a pointer, albeit it may be a strong one. It does not prove conclusively that the cause of all or some of the claimants' problems were a cause that was specific to Corby (such as the reclamation works). However, it does become increasingly important to the extent that other areas of the evidence show the existence of circumstances which point to something specifically present or happening in Corby at the relevant times.

After a review of the epidemiological evidence Mr Justice Akenhead concluded:

> Congenital limb reduction defects are relatively rare events which, current statistics indicate, affect about 5 in 10,000 babies. The aetiology is often difficult to determine but it is established that teratogenic substances can cause such defects; there can often be a genetic component as well. Given that there have been a number of reports and investigations, for instance in the area of landfill sites in the UK and Europe, it is scientifically plausible that there is or at least may be a connection between contaminants of one sort or another and the creation of birth defects.

After examining the tables of the number of births in Corby and elsewhere in the Kettering Health Authority, Mr Justice Akenhead found at 'that the rate of upper limb-reduction defects in Corby was significantly higher than elsewhere in KHA for 1989–1998 whilst it was even higher for the later five-year period, 1994–1998'. As to the toxicological evidence, the judge held that embryos and foetuses are much more sensitive to toxic chemicals than adults. The dosage of a teratogen required to induce birth defects can be much lower than that which would be required to cause toxic effects in adults and, although its teratogenic effects may be the result of induction by high doses, they may also be induced by low-level exposures. Most known teratogens have been identified through experimental animal studies. It is not ethical for any teratogenic tests to be done on pregnant mothers let alone on embryos and foetuses. A problem with this is that there is no exact or mathematical correlation between what will affect a mouse foetus and a human foetus. Notwithstanding these difficulties, the judge concluded:

> That it is more probable than not that the human birth defects complained of in this case were capable of being caused by the mother's exposure to some or a mixture of PAHs, dioxins and heavy metals (in particular Cadmium, Chromium and Nickel) and there is no reason why they could not be capable of causing limb defects of the type complained of in this case. It is unnecessary for me to decide if any individual Claimant's birth defects were caused by the teratogens present on the CBC site being disturbed or moved during the period 1984 to 1999. What I can do and do conclude is that the PAHs, dioxins, Cadmium, Nickel and Chromium were capable of causing the birth defects complained of by the Claimants.

After reviewing the engineering and waste management evidence and the air pollution and safety risk management evidence, the judge considered the foetal medicine and neonatal evidence. In relation to the latter, the judge recorded:

> It is accepted by the experts that the period of greatest risk to the foetus or embryo of suffering significant abnormalities to organs and limbs is in the third to the eleventh week of pregnancy

> during the period of organogenesis, which is while the foetal organs and limbs are forming. It is also, rightfully, accepted that the impact of terotagens on a given foetus or embryo may well vary widely. A given mother may have built up a certain amount of terotagenic substances in her body. A given mother, foetus or embryo may for a wide variety of reasons have more or less resistance to a given substance or combination of substances.

The judge concluded that it was very much a combination of facts that led him to his overall findings. There was a statistically significant cluster of birth defects. Toxicologically, the contaminants that were present on and from the Corby Borough Council sites were of a type that could cause the birth defects complained of by the claimants. There was negligence and breach of statutory duty on the part of Corby Borough Council which permitted and led to the extensive dispersal of contaminated mud and dust over public areas of Corby and into and over private homes with the result that contaminants could realistically have caused the types of birth defects of which the complaint had been made by the claimants. The foetal medical evidence showed that it was feasible for the identified contaminants to cause most of the birth defects in question. Accordingly, Corby Borough Council was liable in public nuisance, negligence and breach of statutory duty, obviously subject to it being established in later proceedings by individual claimants that their particular conditions were actually caused by the defendants identified by the judge.

Both of these cases demonstrate the underlying need for management of mass harm cases. Both cases illustrate that the claimants in mass environmental harm cases can benefit from either the use of the GLO as MPA managerial mechanisms or from the use of effective, creative case management. The GLO seems best suited to a multi-party toxic tort action where similar injuries have occurred. In *Corby*, the action based on remediation activities in Corby overcame an important hurdle in the fight for compensation. Claimants there were able to overcome the difficulties inherent in dealing with technical scientific evidence and trying to establish causation individually. Instead, the GLO, by dealing with such issues collectively, produced an efficient result. Case management as seen in the *Buncefield* case seems to prove case management as a preferable solution where varying injuries occur and issues such as causation cannot be resolved as easily collectively. In that case, settlement was a priority and a key objective of the judges. They demonstrated great creativity, flexibility, experience and determination in achieving this outcome.

8. Environmental Mass Harm Litigation in England and Wales Summary

Overall, when dealing with environmental pollution, the aim of tort law is both justice (usually by way of awarding compensation) and deterrence. It appears that best solution to achieve these aims is to have the greatest possible range of legal remedies in order to deter pollution, to compensate harm and to protect the environment. MPAs and case management can offer clear advantages in terms of access to justice, reduced costs and cost-sharing as well as procedural efficiency, to highlight the most obvious benefits. According to Mulheron, the second highest category of GLO actions initiated since the introduction of the GLO procedure is that of environmental claims.[147] More recently however, few group actions, let alone toxic tort claims, have been successfully initiated in the English courts given the complexity of evidence and the consequent costs of funding the action.[148]

A. Access to Justice

In addressing the first of the benchmarks, access to justice, the primary concern in MPA litigation should be how the individual fares in mass litigation and how each victim can be treated as an individual and have his or her needs addressed. In applying this to environmental mass harm litigation, in *Corby* the claimants had the opportunity to pursue their claims in court, through the use of the GLO, and to obtain an appropriate restorative result. This was possible particularly because the injuries suffered were similar and therefore were suited to group treatment. By grouping their claims together, the claimants were able to overcome obstacles such as the difficulties of having to prove causation individually. In *Buncefield*, the injuries suffered were so varied that they did not lend themselves easily to collective treatment and the priority in that case seems to have been to achieve a speedy resolution. While *Buncefield* was settled and the victims did not technically have a victory in court, this was the optimum result for claimants, rather than having to wait for lengthy and complicated determinations of the numerous varying issues. Under both the GLO and case management approaches, parties achieved what has earlier been analysed as access to justice. Neither of the cases discussed would have been adequately resolved without these MPA managerial mechanisms. Without these mechanisms there would have been huge costs and other such barriers for potential litigants if they had had to embark on individual litigation in order to seek redress. There would have also been many managerial and logistical challenges for the judges. Both cases exemplified the scenario where the defendants have greater financial resources than the victims and this would have been a strong advantage in defending individual litigation. Instead, by using the MPA procedures, claimants were able to benefit from cost-spreading advantages and other efficiencies to overcome these difficulties, as well as other barriers to access to justice. The procedural and substantive features of both the GLO and case management approaches provided effective mechanisms for enabling their claims.

In referring to Mulheron's four aspects to the objective of access to justice, the first is that MPAs 'provide the substantive law with teeth'. In equipping claimants with an effective and efficient route to redress both approaches delivered this, although *Buncefield* did take four years to eventually reach a settlement, and *Corby* took six years, arguably a lengthy time but understandable in the challenging circumstances. The second aspect is to 'overcome cost-related barriers' and, again, by delivering an affordable route to compensation through MPA procedures for victims both mechanisms assisted with this and delivered economies of scale. In *Buncefield*, the judge was mindful of the costs difficulties for claimants and strongly encouraged the parties to collaborate to avoid excessive costs arising. *Buncefield*

[147] Environmental claims comprised 15% of GLO actions in the period since the procedure's introduction in 2000 to 2010. See Mulheron, 'Reform of Collective Redress in England and Wales (n 17).

[148] Ibid. Since the introduction of the GLOs in 2000 there are just 69 such actions listed on Her Majesty's Court Service website for 2010—about 7 each year- across all types of claim.

did, however, present issues in relation to liability for costs and all of the parties had to enter into complicated, privately funded cost-sharing arrangements with their solicitors to cover their costs, which involved some disagreement. In the opinion of the claimants' solicitors, this would have been organised at the outset if a GLO had been in place. These solicitors recovered a success fee as a result of their clients' outcome, and this arguably resulted in increased costs overall. The third aspect of Mulheron's analysis is to 'ensure that the parties are on an equal footing' and both mechanisms have provided this by balancing the position of claimants and defendants and allowing their claims to be managed in a fair and efficient manner and particularly by enabling victims to overcome the barriers that can exist in such litigation if such collective mechanisms are not available or invoked. Mulheron's final facet of access to justice is 'timeliness of commencement, conduct, trial or settlement'. While the concept of timeliness is relative, perhaps *Buncefield* may seem to fall short of achieving this objective, due to the four-year timeframe it took to finally achieve settlement. In comparison, *Corby* delivered settlement shortly after the hearing of the case concluded although some cases took up to six years to resolve. Both cases, overall, in the challenging circumstances, achieved a relatively swift delivery of justice to victims. From this analysis, it appears that the use of a GLO, by using procedures designed for such group litigation in cases suited to such treatment (ie where injuries are similar), can deliver more expeditious results than complicated case management, which can understandably struggle to deal with non-common issues in a timely manner. It is a credit to the expertise, creativity and pragmatism of those involved in *Buncefield*, that such complex litigation was resolved relatively quickly and efficiently.

B. Judicial and Procedural Economy

In terms of achieving judicial and procedural economy, what has been said above in relation to both cases can be reiterated. In the challenging circumstances of *Buncefield*—involving over one hundred groups of claimants—the judges and legal teams collaborated and cooperated as much as possible in order to save costs. They responded to the need for creativity and efficiency. Flexible procedures were adopted in order to process the complex litigation and the encouragement of direct negotiation proactively achieved the aim of settlement. Overall, the litigation exhibited great efficiency and cost savings, which were particularly encouraged by the Court. The time taken to resolve the entire litigation is impressive especially given that all of the actions remained separate and not formally joined within a coordinated structure. The *Corby* litigation, through the use of the GLO, which is appropriate in the case of a homogenous group of individual claimants where specific issues were generic and common to all the claimants, also demonstrated admirable efficiency. By using a GLO, individual claimants succeeded in overcoming the prohibitive issues that can be encountered in environmental mass harm litigation, in particular difficulties in dealing with technical scientific evidence and proving causation, as well as the exorbitant cost that such litigation can entail. The GLO was ideally suited to the circumstances of the case and achieved the benchmarks of judicial economy and procedural efficiency. Both mechanisms, when viewed from the standpoint of claimants and defendants, succeeded in avoiding re-litigation and delivered finality for all.

C. Fairness

This objective requires that all parties receive equal and fair treatment. This entails trying to achieve a balance between the rights of individuals and the interests of the group in endeavouring to litigate the action effectively. Both processes involving the use of case management and the GLO, by definition, require the compromise of individual participation rights and procedural autonomy to some degree. In *Buncefield*, all of the actions remained separate, and owing to the fact that the varying injuries and issues such as causation could not be resolved collectively, settlement was a priority. In *Buncefield*, the innovative case management approach resulted in flexibility and proactive achievement of settlement, which yielded great cost and time savings, among other advantages, to claimants, which far outweighed any curtailment of their individual autonomy. The settlements that the claimants achieved were the result of direct negotiations, so individualism was maintained in this regard and enabled compensation to be tailored to each claimant. Once claims were settled, they were sent on for assessment of quantum. It is remarkable that all claims were eventually settled. While individual claimants may not have had the same degree of freedom in negotiating matters such as instructing lawyers or influencing pleadings, and they may not have the degree of involvement in settlement that they may have otherwise experienced under individual litigation, the advantages of having their claims resolved efficiently and relatively swiftly far outweighed these disadvantages. As observed by Mulheron, 'any class litigation will starkly lower individualism in litigation'. This is a necessary evil in order to participate in multi-party litigation.[149] In *Corby*, the individuals still maintained their own claims but their actions were grouped together to deal with the technical requirements, such as proving causation. The claimants also maintained a degree of autonomy in agreeing their financial settlement with the defendants. It is clear from both *Corby* and *Buncefield* that the loss of individualism in that litigation had little importance compared to the alternative, prohibitive difficulties of individual litigation. Such issues include those of cost and risk, or of no litigation at all, compared with the advantages of group treatment and the achievement of settlement.

In terms of proportionality, it has been recognised that MPA litigation necessarily entails some compromise on behalf of individual rights in achieving the greater good overall.[150] If the principle of proportionality is applied to a cost-benefit analysis of both MPA cases in hand here, it seems that in each case the interests of individuals still fared well and that the cost to class members did not outweigh the benefit to class members. In *Buncefield*, were it not for the creative, pragmatic approach to costs and other such difficulties adopted by the Court and achieved by reaching settlements, the claimants would have been in a much more difficult situation. Similarly, in *Corby*, the Court's resources were applied in the most efficient way in order to deal with the common issues, such as causation, and to overcome the challenges of using complex scientific evidence. By dealing with these issues collectively as a group, the claimants achieved great 'strength in numbers' that enabled them to achieve settlement.

[149] See Mulheron analysis of this objective in ch 3: R Mulheron, *The Class Action in Common Law Legal Systems—A Comparative Perspective* (Hart Publishing, 2004) 62.

[150] See the discussion in ch 3 on proportionality.

D. Predictability

Corby avoided procedural uncertainty because it followed prescribed GLO procedures from an early stage and because, at the outset, the judge established the terms governing the litigation.[151] This was despite the risk that invoking a GLO can involve a degree of uncertainty, depending on which of two approaches are used.[152] While the individual claimants still maintained their own claims, the judgment given on the generic group issues facilitated the achievement of speedy settlements for all of them. Although *Buncefield* was a more creative ad hoc procedure, because the nature of the case so demanded, the fact that a flexible but understandable management approach was adopted in such a complex case greatly assisted both claimants and defendants. The only unpredictable element that had a negative impact was the costs arrangements, which became very complicated. This could have been organised at the outset if a GLO had been used.

E. Deterrence

This benchmark is relevant to the *Buncefield* case because this litigation was the result of clear design, maintenance, operational and behavioural failings. The use of MPAs in this type of scenario may perhaps influence future behaviour or deter by encouraging the observation of safety measures and procedures to minimise the potential harm that can result from such incidents, as well as penalising morally reprehensible behaviour. Similarly, in *Corby* there was negligent handling of the contaminated soil by the defendants that allegedly resulted in the personal injuries. There was a clear failure to adhere to proper standards of care by the defendants and it was held that this mismanagement of the toxic waste could have been the cause of the birth deformities. The victims in this case were innocent, compared with the negligent behaviour of the defendants. The GLO ruling and subsequent settlements provided deterrence of such behaviour in the future, both by the defendant and of others. Here, because the group harm was very significant and particularly obvious as it was established collectively, the aim of deterrence was achieved especially effectively. The dubious activity by the defendants was punished by the findings and settlements, thus satisfying the important aim of behaviour control. Clearly, the collective treatment of the claimants imposed much greater pressure than if such cases had been taken by the victims as individuals, who may have been confounded by the difficulties facing them in such litigation. The achievement of deterrence and behaviour modification in individual litigation is naturally much less than in litigation involving multiple claimants.

F. Compensation

Both the case management approach of *Buncefield* and the GLO mechanism approach of *Corby* arguably improved the availability of compensation to victims. By dealing with issues of quantum separately, the amount was tailored to each of the victims' cases (although

[151] Part 19 of the CPR, discussed previously, governs GLOs.
[152] Whether it is that of the test case or that of the generic issues.

in *Corby* the exact amounts cannot be known, because of the confidentiality surrounding the settlement). Financial compensation, as the traditional remedy for the types of harm exhibited in these cases, appears to have provided the claimants with substantive justice as much as was possible in the circumstances. *Corby* demonstrates corrective justice grounds for such compensation, due to the morally reprehensible negligent behaviour of the defendants in that case, compared with *Buncefield*, which was more concerned with achieving restorative justice for the victims of the harm.

In addition to the objectives discussed above, scientific uncertainties are incrementally being addressed and are helping to resolve earlier difficulties of environmental mass harm litigation. Two examples are: (1) the REACH legislation, previously discussed, which is creating a body of knowledge and information on the human impacts of chemicals; and (2) judicial changes to rules on causation, for example, in the *Fairchild* decision.[153] Efficiency is important. Both of the case studies of the GLO and case management approaches evidence all of the benchmarks being achieved. Another solution is that where a government does not enforce its own regulations, *qui tam* actions—which are private actions brought on behalf of government agencies—should be allowed.[154]

In summary, both MPA approaches seem to have provided adequate compensation for victims. The proceedings overall in both cases would appear to satisfy the deterrence, enforcement and behaviour modification requirements. In terms of procedural fairness and equality, both procedures dealt with victims in a way that would meet these aims. Finally, although the proceedings took some time, *Buncefield* in particular was a protracted case, the outcome of both cases demonstrate the great efficiency and economies of scale that group litigation can afford.

Traditionally, tort law and lawyers have been devoted to dealing with individuals. However, as seen, modern disasters that affect large numbers make this approach impossible, yet courts try to devise effective remedies for the victims. In terms of justice, fair treatment should include the right to be heard in court and for individuals to have equal access to the court system. However, the growth in population and in court caseloads makes this increasingly difficult. It is still essential that a court be concerned with individuals even if this is through mass processing of cases using devices such as MPAs. Paradoxically, sometimes mass treatment, either through courts or administrative agencies, can yield a more effective individual remedy. This can be achieved for example by certifying classes of litigants who could not afford to bring individual cases and through the use of other innovative procedures developed in the mass tort context, such as ADR. There are of course problems of mass toxic tort litigation where improvements could be made. These include issues such as jurisdictional, scientific, substantive and administrative challenges. This is because mass treatment differs from traditional one-claimant-one-defendant cases.

[153] *Fairchild v Glenhaven Funeral Services* [2002] 3 WLR 89 (HL).

[154] This term is Latin for 'who as well', a lawsuit brought by a private citizen (popularly called a 'whistle blower') against a person or company who is believed to have violated the law in the performance of a contract with the government or in violation of a government regulation, when there is a statute which provides for a penalty for such violations. *Qui tam* suits are brought for 'the government as well as the claimant'. In a *qui tam* action the claimant (the person bringing the suit) will be entitled to a percentage of the recovery of the penalty (which may include large amounts for breach of contract) as a reward for exposing the wrongdoing and recovering funds for the government. Sometimes the federal or state government will intervene and become a party to the suit in order to guarantee success and be part of any negotiations and conduct of the case. This type of action is generally based on significant violations that involve fraudulent or criminal acts, and not technical violations and/or errors.

Questions may need be addressed to explain the pros and cons of systems that allow the government to prosecute companies that damage the environment (as seen in Spain) versus systems that allow private victims to seek compensatory damages against the government (as seen in Sweden and the US) but it is beyond the scope of this study to explore this areas. As discussed in the chapters dealing with varying jurisdictions, the US has recently seen the decline of US class actions[155] and also, from the case studies above, it is evident that the GLO is not being taken up England and Wales to the extent that may have been expected. Where mass harm litigation arises, it presents many logistical challenges. It is clear that a combination of solutions is required to provide collective redress for mass harm and that MPAs provide an important role in the range of remedies required to achieve collective redress for mass harm. There is a clear need for managerial mechanisms such as MPAs or techniques of case management to respond to this need.

[155] This was discussed in ch 5 detailing US collective redress in the US. eg Robert Klonoff describes how, in recent years, the US courts have dramatically restrained the ability to bring class action lawsuits. See further R Klonoff, 'The Decline of Class Actions' (2013) 90 *Wash UL Rev* 729.

9

EU Collective Redress

1. Litigation Landscape

There has been much debate in the European Commission about how best to address collective redress in the EU in order to deal with mass harm and about whether a collective action or some other approach is appropriate for Member States.[1] Having examined a selection of common law jurisdictions' treatment of collective redress, we now have a broad background against which to evaluate MPAs and their use as a method of such redress. What is becoming clear from this examination is that litigation through MPAs is only one of a suite of possible remedies for mass harm, and therefore for collective redress. Other remedies lie in public enforcement, regulatory law and Alternative Dispute Resolution (ADR). In terms of the EU, it is important to remember that its raison d'être is the creation of the internal market and maintaining competitiveness, particularly by enhancing competition and consumer protection. It is essential to recognise that European traditions do not include the American approach of 'private enforcement', but are based on the primacy of public enforcement.[2] The EU uses regulatory law and public enforcement as its principal tools to protect these core objectives. Options for EU collective redress mechanisms must be tailored to reflect the reality of the different enforcement approaches between the US and EU.

This chapter will explore the history of EU collective redress policy and then some of the collective redress options being used in several Member States will be examined, as these reflect the emerging evidence that MPA litigation is not necessarily the best solution for mass harm redress. Other solutions, particularly of an ADR nature, are proving to be a very effective and possibly preferable approach in Europe as well as in the common law jurisdictions explored. For a long time there was no clear EU consensus on what method of enforcement is the best solution to incidents of mass harm, as the history of EU collective redress policy indicates. In June 2013, the European Commission published its policy on

[1] See s 2 of this chapter detailing the evolution of EU collective redress policy and also ch 3 on the MPA objectives which further explains this. This approach is seen eg in the Consultation Paper (EC) for 'Discussion on the Follow-up to the Green Paper on Consumer Collective Redress' COM(2008) 794, 15, as well as in the expert study by J Stuyck and others, *Commission Study on Alternative Means of Consumer Redress other than Redress Through Ordinary Judicial Proceedings* (Catholic University of Leuven, 2007). For further detail, see C Hodges, *The Reform of Class and Representative Actions in European Legal Systems: A New Framework for Collective Redress in Europe* (Hart Publishing, 2008).

[2] See C Hodges, 'European Union Legislation' in D Hensler, C Hodges and M Tulibacka, *The Globalisation of Class Actions* (2009) 622 The Annals of the American Academy of Political and Social Science 2009 81.

collective redress. This comprised a set of three documents. These were a Recommendation[3] and an accompanying Communication[4] on collective redress in Member States, alongside a proposal for a Directive[5] on rules governing actions for damages under national law for infringements of EU competition law. These will be discussed in detail in this chapter. In essence, the European collective redress debate questions:

> Whether private damages claims should be enlisted as supplementary mechanisms for regulatory enforcement and whether it is possible to balance civil procedures and funding systems for multiple claims to avoid excessive litigation and cost.[6]

What becomes clear from the analysis of the history of EU collective redress is that there is no single solution to the problems that mass harm presents, as it appears that remedies lie in a combination of techniques, including ADR.[7] The Commission's proposals, however, do not seem to recognise this more nuanced need for a combination of techniques and, while they recognise the need for solutions such as mediation, they advocate the introduction of a collective action mechanism as a key tool for enabling collective redress. As this discussion will show, such a solution is not a 'silver bullet' that will ensure effective mass harm redress but the use of collective actions may aid the management of mass harm cases.

2. Evolution of European Collective Redress Policy

A. Consumer Law Collective Redress

As explained in the exploration of EU collective redress in chapter three, the EU has struggled for a long time to reach a conclusion on consumer collective redress[8] but in the last few years has made considerable progress in achieving this end. A large body of legislation has been adopted for consumer protection over the past 30 years[9] and a Regulation on consumer protection cooperation has created a network of public enforcement authorities.[10] Also, EU policy advocates that Member States provide consumer representative procedures and some limited consumer protection instruments have been created to provide this.[11]

[3] Commission (EC) Recommendation of 11 June 2013 on Common Principles for Injunctive and Compensatory Collective Redress Mechanisms in the Member States concerning violations of rights granted under Union Law (2013/396/EU). The legal basis for this Recommendation is Art 292 of the Treaty on the Functioning of the European Union (TFEU).

[4] Commission (EC) Communication 'Towards a European Horizontal Framework for Collective Redress' COM(2013) 401/2.

[5] Commission (EC), 'Proposal for a Directive on Anti-trust Damages Actions' COM(2013) 404.

[6] Hodges, 'European Union Legislation' (n 2) 82.

[7] C Hodges, 'Collective Redress: A Breakthrough or Damp Squibb? (2014) 37 *J Consum Policy* 72.

[8] For an overview, see http://ec.europa.eu/consumers/redress_cons/collective_redress_en.htm.

[9] Examples include the Directive on misleading advertising, Directive 84/450/EEC, 1984 OJ L 250 Art 4.1. Under this legislation most Member States have provided for consumer associations to bring actions. Also Directive 93/13/EEC, Art 7, on unfair contract terms. 1993 OJ L 095. Both of these Directives were subsequently codified in the Directive on unfair business-to-consumer commercial practices (UCP)—Directive 2005/29/EC, 2005 OJ L 149, Art 4.

[10] Regulation 2006/2004, Arts 4.2 and 8.3.

[11] eg Directive (EC) 2009/22 of the European Parliament and of the Council of 23 April 2009 on Injunctions for the Protection of Consumers' Interests, 2009 OJ L 110/30 and Regulation (EC) 2006/2004 of the European Parliament and of the Council of 27 October 2004 on Consumer Protection Cooperation, 2004 OJ L 634/1.

EU policy also encourages Member States to improve access to justice for consumers and small businesses.[12] Such action usually occurs through consumer organisations that bring cases on behalf of consumer interests.[13] All of these developments have led to expectations that the consumer rights being created would be enforced.[14] Until recently, remedies have been limited to declaratory or injunctive relief but there are increasing calls, especially from consumers, to provide for US style monetary collective actions. The Commission had been cautious in its progress in deciding whether a private collective action-type mechanism is appropriate, and as seen in the chapter three, a number of EU collective redress criteria have emerged from these developments.

In 2008, DG SANCO carried out a consultation on benchmarks[15] against which options for collective redress could be evaluated and it published a Green Paper on Consumer Collective Redress in November 2008.[16] A key aim of the Green Paper was to identify the level of demand for collective redress and the problems with existing techniques in various Member States. Once this was identified, then various options among the techniques could be determined. This was a scoping exercise based on an analysis of various collective redress mechanisms in Member States. The Green Paper was also accompanied by a questions and answers document from the Commission that concluded:[17]

> Studies ... have shown that there is no easy answer to the problem. All the current redress systems have their strengths and weaknesses and no single mechanism is ideal for all types of claims.[18]

Commission opinion at this time acknowledged that 'there is a problem with consumer redress in general and with settling large scale consumer complaints in particular'.[19] In response to this problem, it appeared that the Commission, crucially, had decided to distance itself from the US enforcement approach, as it recognised the difference between the US private enforcement and the traditional EU public enforcement and regulatory approach, as reflected in the Member States. It implied that, for this reason, a different European form of collective private action would be designed instead of the US style class action and concluded that:

> US style class action is not envisaged. EU legal systems are very different from the US legal system, which is the result of a 'toxic cocktail'—a combination of several elements (punitive damages,

[12] eg to provide adequate legal aid (see Directive 2002/8 (EC) of the Council of 27 January 2003 to improve access to justice in cross-border disputes by establishing minimum common rules relating to legal aid for such disputes, 2003 OJ L 26/41).

[13] Many Member States already have similar mechanisms in their national law; see eg Commission (EC), 'Access of Consumers to Justice and the Settlement of Consumer Disputes in the Single Market' (Green Paper) COM(93) 576, 64 noted that of the then 12 Member States, 8 gave consumer organisations a right to bring claims for the protection of the collective interests of consumers. One of these (Belgium) permitted such actions to be undertaken by both consumer organisations and by an administrative authority, and 3 other States protected consumer collective interests through an independent administrative authority (the Office of Fair Trading in the UK, the Consumer Ombudsman in Denmark and the Director of Consumer Affairs in Ireland).

[14] Hodges, 'Collective Redress' (n 7) 68. This article gives detailed analysis of the evolution of consumer collective redress policy in the EU.

[15] See http://ec.europa.eu/consumers/redress_cons/collective_redress_en.htm#Benchmarks. There was criticism that the benchmarks used were based on the assumption that the only remedy was a judicial solution. The Commission privately accepted this criticism; see further C Hodges, 'Towards Parameters for EU Civil Justice Systems' in S Vogenauer and C Hodges (eds), *Civil Justice Systems in Europe: Implications for Choice of Forum and Choice of Contract Law* (Hart Publishing, 2014).

[16] Commission (EC), 'Consumer Collective Redress' (Green Paper) COM(2008) 794.

[17] Questions and Answers Document (MEMO/08/741, 27 November 2008).

[18] Ibid 3.

[19] Commissioner Kuneva, 27 November 2008.

> contingency fees, opt-out...). This combination should not be introduced in Europe. Different safeguards including loser pays principles are built into existing national collective redress schemes in Europe. All the Green Paper options, and in particular a possible EU collective procedure, reflect EU legal traditions. The Commission seeks to encourage a competitiveness culture e.g. where businesses, which play by the rules, can realize their competitive advantages, not a litigation culture.[20]

In order to refine the options in the Green Paper, DG SANCO issued a further consultation paper in 2009[21] and held a public hearing. The responses to these were enlightening because they indicated that none of the Green Paper options was considered to be adequate to achieve the twin EU policy aims of providing effective mass consumer redress and protecting the competitiveness of the internal market. Instead, a consensus emerged that a combination of several techniques was the best solution, declaring that:

> In the light of the consultation to the Green Paper three main elements seem able to address various aspects of the problem: collective ADR, combined with a judicial collective redress scheme as a 'stick', and a strengthening of consumer protection authorities. Among the non-legislative instruments, the internal complaint-handling scheme and a standard model for collective ADR seem to be best placed. The following options group some of these various elements[22]

It then set out elements of these three pillars, individually and in combination. DG SANCO has tried to adopt this three-pillar policy approach for consumer protection and to develop procedures for consumer ADR. This was ground-breaking as this was the first time that a multi-faceted approach to collective redress was advocated by the Commission, recognising that the solution to mass harm lies at several levels using a combination of techniques. As a consequence of this, and other developments in relation to ADR,[23] EU consumer law is now enforced by a combination of public authorities, self-regulatory or co-regulatory bodies, private enforcement through litigation, and also through consumer ADR bodies.[24]

In October 2010, the Commission issued a Joint information note, proposed by the EU Commissioners for Consumer Policy, Justice and Competition in collaboration, appropriately named 'Time to Act' as it truly had become time for the Commission to address holistically the matter of collective redress.[25] DG SANCO continued exploring different routes to resolving commercial disputes based on the use of ADR and issued its consultation paper on ADR in January 2011 noting that ADR had not yet reached its full potential.[26] Meanwhile, in parallel developments, the European Parliament decided to undertake its own review of collective redress and published a 2012 report on collective redress that noted 'efforts by the US Supreme Court to limit frivolous litigation and abuse of the US class action system' and highlighted that Europe 'must refrain from introducing a US-style

[20] European Commission (EC) DG SANCO, MEMO/08/741, 4

[21] Available at: http://ec.europa.eu/consumers/redress_cons/docs/consultation_paper2009.pdf.

[22] Consultation Paper (EC) for 'Discussion on the Follow-up to the Green Paper on Consumer Collective Redress' (n 1).

[23] Such as Directive 2013/11/EU of the European Parliament and of the Council of 21 May 2013 on alternative dispute resolution for consumer disputes and amending Regulation (EC) No 2006/2004 and Directive 2009/22/EC (Directive on Consumer ADR) OJ L 165.

[24] Hodges (n 7) 70.

[25] SEC(2010) 1192 (5 October 2010). This was based on the Commission's Work Programme 2010 'Time to Act' (COM(2010) 135 final (31 March 2010)).

[26] Commission (EC), Consultation paper on the use of Alternative Dispute Resolution as a means to resolve disputes related to commercial transactions and practices in the European Union (January 2011).

class action system or any system which does not respect European legal traditions'.[27] In 2012, the European Parliament adopted its resolution, 'Towards a Coherent European Approach to Collective Redress',[28] in which it called for:

> Any proposal in the field of collective redress to take the form of a horizontal framework including a common set of principles providing uniform access to justice via collective redress within the EU and specifically but not exclusively dealing with the infringement of consumers' rights.[29]

It noted that public enforcement is 'essential' for competition law and that DG SANCO's 2008 study showed that collective redress mechanisms in the Member States had 'not generated disproportionate economic consequences'.[30] It highlighted the need for safeguards to avoid abuse of collective redress and unmeritorious claims.[31] The Parliament's opinion shows that it acknowledged the crucial difference between European and US approaches to enforcement and, while it was supportive of the concept of a horizontal framework of national procedural laws for collective actions to avoid fragmentation, it underlined 'the need to take due account of the legal traditions and legal orders of the individual Member States'.[32] It asked the Commission 'to examine thoroughly the appropriate legal basis for any measure in the field of collective redress'.[33] It was conclusive, 'that in the event that it is decided a Union scheme of collective redress is needed and desirable'[34] that any such proposal should be in the form of a horizontal framework including a common set of principles that would provide uniform access to justice via collective redress within Europe, not just for infringement of consumer rights.[35] This thorough approach is reinforced by the results of empirical studies, which further underlined the need for new mechanisms and raised the question of whether litigation could ever be an effective answer to such problems in a European context.[36] The need for alternatives to the US litigation approach was clear from the opinion of both the European Parliament and DG SANCO. A further indication of the will to move away from the US approach during these EU debates was a very significant change in the terminology used in general, from using the term 'class actions', which was suggestive of litigation procedures, to achieving 'collective redress'. This might be understood as being indicative of the Commission's apprehension about adopting

[27] European Parliament Resolution of 2 February 2012 'Towards a Coherent European Approach to Collective Redress' 2011/2089(INI), para 2.

[28] Ibid.

[29] Ibid paras 15 and 16.

[30] Ibid para 6.

[31] The safeguards included points on standing, using only the opt-in principle, maintaining a 'loser pays' principle and not including third-party funding; Resolution (n 27) para 20.

[32] Hodges (n 7) 73. citing the Resolution (n 27) paras 15 and 16.

[33] Resolution (n 27) para 8.

[34] Ibid para 15.

[35] Ibid.

[36] An important study on private enforcement of competition law in the EU that gave important empirical data on this type of litigation spanning over more than a decade was the *AHRC Research Project on EU Competition Law: Comparative Enforcement and Collective Redress in the EU 1999–2012*, led by Professor B Rodger of Strathclyde University, available at: www.clcpecreu.co.uk; results were reported at a conference in London in September 2012. Findings included: that far more private enforcement cases have been brought than were thought to have existed in all large Member States; speed of response to competition infringements is of paramount importance, therefore injunctions are far more important than delayed damages actions. Also, there have been hardly any small value mass consumer claims based on competition law in Member States. There are varied reasons for this. This study was cited by Hodges (n 7) 72.

US style class actions and that the Commission was open to the possibility that there may be ways of achieving collective redress other than by the use of class actions as these were not the appropriate solution. It has been suggested that the term 'collective redress', which is the output objective, was later deliberately used instead of 'collective action' to cloud the fact that only one particular mechanism was being referred to.[37] Since the change of approach evident in the new consumer ADR policy, there has been reduced pressure for litigation mechanisms, so this shows that the three-pillar solution is very much alive and effective, which is very promising for consumers in need of redress for mass harm. There has not been as much improvement in public enforcement of consumer law yet, but, having identified that there are shortcomings,[38] the Commission aims to enhance national enforcement and to improve cross-border enforcement. It also intends to become more involved in providing this itself.[39] There are, of course, divergences between Member States and private enforcement mechanisms have not yet been harmonised.[40] This ADR approach eventually began to find favour in competition law, but the new policy advocating the introduction of collective actions and damages actions under the proposed Directive[41] for competition damages does not tally with an ADR approach, so how effectively this will work cannot be evidenced for some time.

B. Competition Law Collective Redress

In the US, private enforcement of competition law predominates over public enforcement. EU competition law, in a polar opposite approach to this, operates through public enforcement, with public authorities dominating in this role almost to the exclusion of private enforcement until recently.[42] However, in what appears to be a move towards private enforcement, the Commission's 2013 proposals advocate the introduction of damages for breaches of competition law.[43]

The evolution of EU competition law policy was obviously concurrent with the changes in EU consumer policy that we have examined. The first signs that the Commission had begun to move away from the public enforcement approach to competition law was in December 2005 when it published a Green Paper on damages for breaches of competition law,[44] in order to assist with EU policy of increasing regulatory enforcement of competition

[37] Ibid 74.

[38] Report from the Commission (EC) to the European Parliament, the Council and the European and Economic Social Committee of March 14, 2013: *First Report on the Application of Directive 2005/29/EC of the European Parliament and of the Council of 11 May 2005 Concerning Unfair Business-to-Consumer Commercial Practices in the Internal Market and Amending Council Directive 84/450, Directives 97/7/EC, 98/27/EC and 2002/65/EC of the European Parliament and of the Council and Regulation (EC) No 2006/2004 of the European Parliament and of the Council ('Unfair Commercial Practices Directive')*; COM(2013) 139 Final March 2013.

[39] Communication from the Commission to the European Parliament, The Council and the European Economic and Social Committee, 'On the Application of the Unfair Commercial Practices Directive Achieving a High Level of Protection—Building Trust in the Internal Market' (March 2013).

[40] The only harmonisation so far is the cooperation network for public authorities and early steps towards a 'creative' consumer ADR network; Hodges (n 7) 70.

[41] Directive Proposal (n 5) 404.

[42] The EU approach is demonstrated by the Modernisation Regulation, Regulation (EC) 1/2003, which decentralised enforcement and devolved power to national competition authorities, with no reference to private enforcement; Hodges (n 7) 70.

[43] Directive Proposal (n 5) 404.

[44] Commission (EC) on damages for breaches of competition law (Green Paper) COM(2005) 672.

law.[45] Extensive debate about these proposals resulted in the White Paper of 2008 that explored multiple reforms to enable private damages claims, particularly through a collective procedure.[46] Its proposals included two collective redress procedures for aggregating damages claims for competition breaches.[47] DG COMP then began work on a draft Directive that included proposals for collective actions to be introduced in order for private parties to claim damages for infringements of competition law but this was abandoned for reasons that included the inconsistent approach of the Commission to collective actions in the areas of competition and consumer redress.[48] In 2010, in order to resolve this and make progress on a united solution, President Barroso instructed his Commissioners for Justice, Competition and Consumer Affairs to collaborate on the drafting of a unified policy for collective redress.[49]

It might at this point be useful to recall that during the time of the Green and White Papers, as we have seen in the history of EU consumer policy, there was a lot of criticism of US class actions and litigation was discredited as the sole solution to mass harm redress. Strong academic opinion in the Stuyck Report[50] recommended alternative means to consumer redress other than through judicial proceedings. A key concern for the introduction of such methods was how could undertakings be urged or eventually obliged to engage in voluntary or supervised ADR. For consumer redress, as we have seen, this could be achieved using the combination of enhanced regulatory procedures and ADR as enforced by a combination of public authorities, self-regulatory or co-regulatory bodies, private enforcement through litigation and, increasingly, through consumer ADR bodies. There were also discussions on possible solutions, especially the development of realistic policy for competition enforcement that would integrate private and public consequences.[51] In these debates, once again the difference between the US private enforcement approach and that of the EU public enforcement approach was underlined when it was highlighted that the:

> Phenomenon of class actions in the USA is an integral function of its distinctive legal architecture and policy on emphasizing public enforcement, whereas EU architecture maintains strong public enforcement, certainly for competition enforcement[52]

[45] Ibid; Commission Staff Working Paper: 'Annex to the Commission (EC) Damages for breach of the EC antitrust rules (Green Paper)' SEC(2005) 1732.

[46] It included proposals as to whether an opt-in or opt-out model should be adopted and whether punitive damages should be permitted; Commission (EC), 'Damages actions for breach of EC antitrust rules' (White Paper) COM(2008) 165; Commission Staff Working Paper accompanying the White Paper on damages actions for breach of the EC antitrust rules, SEC(2008)404 'Making antitrust damages actions more effective in the EU: welfare impact and potential scenarios', final report submitted to the Commission on 21 December 2007.

[47] First, 'representative actions', brought by qualified entities, such as consumer organisations and State authorities, on behalf of identified or identifiable victims; and secondly, 'group actions', an opt-in collective private action damages claim that could be brought by 2 or more individuals, whereby they could merge their individual claims into a single action. See Commission (EC) on damages actions for breach of the EC antitrust rules (n 46).

[48] Hodges (n 7) 72.

[49] *Towards a Coherent European Approach to Collective Redress: Next Steps.* Joint information note by Vice-President Viviane Reading, Vice-President Joaquin Almunia and Commissioner John Dalli (5 October 2010).

[50] Stuyck and others, *Commission Study on Alternative Means of Consumer Redress other than Redress Through Ordinary Judicial Proceedings* (n 1) included reports on the variety of alternative means of consumer redress mechanisms from all EU Member States as well as the US, Canada and Australia. This highlighted the important growth in ADR mechanisms, stemming from a desire to avoid the costs and delays of litigation processes, which resulted in the adoption of new techniques involving ADR and ombudsman mechanisms.

[51] Hodges (n 7) 73.

[52] F Cafaggi and HW Micklitz (eds), *New Frontiers of Consumer Protection. The Interplay between Private and Public Enforcement* (Intersentia, 2009); and C Hodges, 'Objectives, Mechanisms and Policy Choices in Collective Enforcement and Redress' in J Steele and W van Boom (eds), *Mass Justice* (Edward Elgar, 2011).

Member States had also not been enamoured with the concept of the White Paper's proposals.[53] In light of all this strong opinion it is bizarre that DG COMP did not concur and that it instead decided to continue along the collective action and collective redress route.[54] This will be discussed further in section 4 dealing with the Commission's 2013 policy proposals.

3. EU Experience of Collective Redress and ADR in Member States

According to the principle of subsidiarity[55] the EU is under an obligation to respect Member States' national systems. This principle recognises that although the EU's aim is to establish an area of freedom, justice and security, it must respect the different legal systems of the Member States. Therefore, the experience of Member States is clearly key in informing the development of EU policy. For this reason it is important to examine this experience in order to help us understand why EU policy developed in the way that it has. As we have seen, an early informer of Commission policy was the Stuyck Report empirical study.[56] It showed that evidence does not demonstrate any unanimity about the cost-benefit justification of collective actions,[57] that potential advantages may be propounded, but so can risks and disadvantages,[58] as is particularly shown in the literature on US class actions.[59] We have seen ADR and various other methods of enforcement through public law and regulation already mentioned as viable alternatives to litigation. The reasons why a wider, holistic approach would be the most sensible way for the EU to proceed with collective redress are two-fold: first, because of the fundamental difference between the US and EU enforcement 'architecture' and legal traditions; secondly, because of this empirical evidence and support for the use of ADR and other techniques.

[53] J Kortmann and C Swaak, 'The EC White Paper on Antitrust Damage Actions: Why the Member States are (Right to be) Less than Enthusiastic' (2009) 30(7) *Eur Competition L Rev* 340–51.

[54] One of the reasons that DG COMP expressed for encouraging collective actions and damages was that it did not wish to have to oversee the payment of damages in addition to its role of imposing fines because it did not have the resources to do.

[55] TFEU, Art 67(1) states that the Union shall constitute an area of freedom, security and justice with respect for fundamental rights and the different legal systems and the traditions of the Member States.

[56] Stuyck and others (n 1).

[57] Hodges (n 2) 82 cites, as an example, the significant precedent in the case of the French consumer organisation UFC Que Choisir? It invested €500,000 in a damages case for overcharging against mobile phone operators but only 12,500 consumers (0.6%) opted to join and bring claims.

[58] Stuyck and others (n 1) identified, eg, a significant concern for consumers of the potential for one party to achieve additional advantages at the expense of another, especially in the case of legal counsel: para 377. For business, there is the concern about unmeritorious claims, pressure on businesses to settle even bad claims, as well as the risk of bankruptcy. The report claims that mechanisms can be provided to prevent unmeritorious claims, such as having judges assess the claims at an early stage. It later notes that in Sweden, a judge applies a cost-efficiency test at an early stage, and Australia requires that the award should exceed the costs: para 393. It dismisses the bankruptcy risk, citing it is business' failure to adhere to proper standards of conduct that drives bankruptcy, and no bankruptcies having occurred in Canada: para 378. For the legal system, the report dismisses the risk that courts would be overwhelmed, as this has not happened in Sweden, Canada or Australia. The report does not, however, note the crucial influence of local funding systems and cost rules on the incidence of claims, as cited by Hodges (n 2) 82.

[59] It noted that in 2004, 31.7% of federal class actions were civil rights cases, and 20.3% were securities actions.

DG SANCO has been pioneering in the Commission in its endorsement of an ADR approach. In a 2009 study for DG SANCO, 750 national ADR systems in the EU were identified, which have compliance rates by businesses averaging 99 per cent.[60] This was brought to life with DG SANCO's 'three-pillar' approach as shown in its 2009 Green Paper and follow-on consultation[61] and it also advocated that ADR techniques had yet to reach their full potential.[62] The European Parliament has been supportive of this concept also, highlighting the need for alternatives to the US litigation approach.[63] The empirical evidence and studies showed that an ADR and three-pillar approach was reducing the pressure on litigation mechanisms and that the most efficient way of dealing with mass harm was through alternative methods to judicial proceedings.[64] Also, as we have seen, a subtle change in the terminology being used had occurred, moving away from that of collective action and towards collective redress. Coupled with this evidence was the collaboration between the three DGs—DG COMP, DG SANCO and DG JUST—in an effort to adopt a unified and holistic approach to collective redress. In addition to this, a Directive was adopted in 2013 that obliges Member States to provide full ADR facilities within two years and requires businesses to comply with ADR schemes.[65] There has also been the introduction of a pan-EU online dispute resolution (ODR) facility to promote the resolution of national and cross-border ADR disputes.[66] All of these signs strongly indicate that efforts were being made at EU level to keep collective redress out of the courts where possible. Let us explore the ADR evidence further by examining its use in Member State and EU policy, to see where it has been working in practice 'on the ground'.

Debate in EU Member States about facilitating collective actions for damages has heightened during the past decade and a half. By 2007, 16 of the then 27 EU Member States had collective redress schemes that allowed for damages: Austria, Bulgaria, Denmark, Finland, France, Germany, Greece, Hungary, Italy, Lithuania, the Netherlands, Poland, Portugal, Spain, Sweden and England and Wales. These procedures vary greatly and have different results.[67] Evidence shows that, despite these mechanisms, there has been low

[60] Civic Consulting, *Study on the Use of Alternative Dispute Resolution in the European Union* (2009). According to this the numbers were Germany (247), Italy (129), UK (43) and France (35). The study said that ADR is more relevant in Belgium, UK, Spain, Sweden, Austria, Ireland, Netherland and Denmark than elsewhere. The highest number of cases for any individual scheme was the UK with the FOS often dealing with over 100,000 per annum—most other large schemes deal with 5,000 to 20,000 per annum. The total number of cases in the EU in 2008 was 530,000, increased from 410,000 in 2006. (As cited by Hodges (n 7) 70.) Subsequent research, however, showed that the number of substantial ADR bodies was far lower and that some were dealing with large numbers of cases and mass issues; see C Hodges, 'A Market-Based Competition Enforcement Policy' (2011) 22(3) *Eur Bus L Rev* 261–91; C Hodges, 'European Competition Enforcement Policy: Integrating Restitution and Behaviour Control' (2011) *World Competition* 385–96.

[61] eg Commission (EC), 'Consumer Collective Redress' (Green Paper) (n 16); Consultation Paper for 'Discussion on the Follow-up to the Green Paper on Consumer Collective Redress' (n 1).

[62] Consultation Paper on the use of Alternative Dispute Resolution as a means to resolve disputes related to commercial transactions and practices in the European Union (n 26).

[63] Resolution (n 27).

[64] Stuyck and others (n 1); C Hodges, *The Reform of Class and Representative Actions in European Legal Systems* (n 1). As cited by Hodges (n 7) 72.

[65] Directive on Consumer ADR (n 23).

[66] Regulation (EU) no 524/2013 of the European Parliament and of the Council of 21 May 2013 on online dispute resolution for consumer disputes (Regulation on Consumer ODR), 1 OJ No. L165.

[67] Stuyck and others (n 1).

usage of collective procedures in most Member States.[68] Studies and consultations by the Commission show that:

> The vast majority of the existing collective redress mechanisms tend to have some elements that work and some that do not. Almost all existing collective redress mechanisms have some added value compared to individual judicial redress and alternative dispute resolution schemes. But their efficiency and effectiveness could be improved. The mechanisms have been applied in relatively few cases.[69]

In terms of Member State collective redress mechanisms generally, most approaches are the antithesis of the US private enforcement of public law approach. This is perhaps because of a fear that policymakers have that private enforcement will only reach a significant level of activity if it is encouraged by considerable financial incentives and that these are associated with 'excess and abuse'.[70] This is generally the reason why most European States do not have opt-out class actions. It is also a factor in why decisions on liability and quantum are not made by juries, nor are there high success fees for legal advisers. High damages are influenced by the possible availability of vast punitive damages, which, even if they are rarely awarded, have an inflationary effect on settlements.[71] When we look at examples of the various collective redress mechanisms in some of these Member States in practice, we can get an idea of why so few class action cases are occurring, although there are of course different reasons for this in each Member State. A fundamental reason is because better alternative options to litigation exist and are now operating well, particularly consumer ADR, with some States having effectively adopted new regulatory powers.[72] This compounds the European approach of consciously discouraging litigation and also preferring public to private enforcement—the opposite of the US approach. However, both public and private enforcement exist throughout the EU. There is also a question of difference in litigation cultures. Overall, policymakers are questioning whether litigation is the best mechanism for the resolution of mass torts or whether other tools, broadly termed ADR and regulatory techniques, would be faster, more economical and better at controlling misbehaviour, particularly that of a corporate nature. Obviously, a further reason is that some jurisdictions' national rules on costs and funding create obstacles to mass litigation.[73] Examining the legal systems of the Member States, the majority of these use the 'loser pays costs' rule.[74] Also most EU Member States prohibit contingency fees and do not have juries or punitive damages in civil cases. Some EU countries have been innovative in encouraging public authorities to participate in delivering collective redress by way of private compensation in several ways. One way is through a public authority being empowered to bring a collective damages claim on behalf of multiple consumers, as evidenced in Denmark,

[68] Commission (EC), 'Consumer Collective Redress' (Green Paper) (n 16) para 12.
[69] Ibid.
[70] Hodges (n 2) 82.
[71] Ibid.
[72] Hodges (n 7) 81.
[73] Such as the 'loser pays' rules on costs and restrictions on obtaining funding. Although there are changes being seen in some jurisdictions such as those seen when the UK Government announced in March 2011 the introduction of contingency fees and qualified one way cost shifting for personal injury cases: Ministry of Justice, *Reforming Civil Litigation Funding and Costs in England and Wales—Implementation of Lord Justice Jackson's Recommendations: The Government Response* (2011)
[74] C Hodges, S Vogenauer and M Tulibacka, 'Costs and Funding of Civil Litigation: A Comparative Study' (2009) Oxford Legal Studies Research Paper No 55, available at: http://papers.ssrn.com/sol3/papers.cfm?abstract_id=1511714##.

Sweden, Norway and Finland. While private individuals or consumer associations may have the power to take damages claims, the costs and loser pays rule are prohibitive, making action by public authorities preferable.[75]

Throughout Europe, experience reflects low usage of collective actions. The evidence shows that class cases are slow, contrasting poorly with the faster, more efficient, less expensive solutions that can be achieved through the use of tools such as consumer ADR and regulatory schemes.[76] As a result, ADR and other techniques have filled the role of collective redress in many EU Member States. There are various examples of different collective redress systems in Europe. Several EU Member States have had class action procedures for a number of years and there is empirical evidence of their experience and it is worth a brief review of some examples.[77] While Spain has had a class action mechanism since 2000, this has only been used a few times with consumers instead taking their claims to a nationwide ADR system of arbitration and sectoral ombudsmen.[78] While the Nordic States of Norway, Sweden, Denmark and Finland have class action procedures, these seem to have been used very little. The reason for this is the existence of well-established, comprehensive consumer ADR schemes, as a result of which consumers hardly ever use the courts.[79] Germany has a very efficient civil justice procedure that has existed for a long time and which allows multiple similar claims to be processed together.[80] It also has legal expenses insurance and the German courts often deal with multiple individual claims. It would appear that German courts only encounter problems with mass litigation when there are vast numbers of victims involved, such as the *Deutsche Telekom* litigation, which involved claims by 17,000 investors. This litigation was an attempt to imitate a US class action that had resulted in the creation of a settlement fund of US$120 million. After over a decade, the German litigation eventually failed because it was held that there had been no underlying misrepresentation by Deutsche Telekom in its prospectus.[81] The massive numbers of claimants involved resulted in a litigation crisis, as a result of which, in 2005, a test case procedure was created under the German Act on Model Case Proceedings in the Capital Markets (KapMuG).[82]

[75] As seen in the England and Wales with the GLO as well as in Denmark, Sweden and Norway.

[76] Hodges (n 7) 81.

[77] 'Global Class Actions' Conference (Oxford) 2007.

[78] eg the Catalunian telecom and energy ombudsmen.

[79] C Hodges, I Benohrand and N Creutzfeldt-Banda, *Consumer ADR in Europe* (Hart Publishing, 2012).

[80] See J Langbein, 'The German Advantage in Civil Procedure' (1985) 52(4) *U Chicago L Rev* 823.

[81] This example was cited by Hodges (n 7) 80. Hodges also questions why the matter of whether there had been a misstatement was not posed through regulatory investigation.

[82] Kapitalanleger-Musterverfahrensgesetz [KapMuG] [Capital Markets Model Case Act] 2 October 2011, Elektronischer Bundesanzeiger [eBAnz] (Ger). An English translation is available at: www.bmj.de/cln_102/SharedDocs/Downloads/DE/pdfs/KapMuG_english.html. See M Bälz and F Blobel, 'Collective Litigation German Style: The Act on Model Proceedings in Capital Market Disputes' in E Gottschalk and others (eds), *Conflict of Laws in a Globalized World* (Cambridge University Press, 2007) 126, 135–38; P Gottwald, *On the Extension of Collective Legal Protection in German* (2007) 26 *Civ Just Q* 484, 492–94; H Micklitz and A Stadler, 'The Development of Collective Legal Actions in Europe, Especially in German Civil Procedure' (2006) 17 *Eur Bus L Rev* 1473, 1485–88; M Stürner, 'Model Case Proceedings in the Capital Markets: Tentative Steps Towards Group Litigation in Germany' (2007) 26 *Civ Just Q* 250, 252–53. Under this legislation, where a multitude of individual cases arise from similar facts, cases are suspended while a test case is decided by a higher court and then the remaining cases are resolved, taking into account the result of the test case. It is a type of opt-in procedure. An advantage to this is that the limitation period is suspended pending the outcome of the model case proceedings. However, neither the model case decision nor a settlement is binding on the class members that have registered their claims. Once the model case is decided, they can initiate a civil action. Finally, the law allows settlement to be reached between the model claimant and the defendant and for this to be approved by the court. This settlement is only binding on class members that have initiated proceedings.

The fact that the *Deutsche Telekom* litigation eventually failed in Germany does not instil confidence in the efficacy of US settlements or the need in Europe for behaviour modification through litigation.[83] Ombudsmen and other ADR bodies have also become popular in Germany recently, which shows that Germany too is moving towards ADR. In some circumstances specific ADR schemes can be devised such as the ombudsman and compensation scheme created following the Deutsche Bahn disaster in 1998.[84]

Several EU Member States have ADR systems for mass incidents. The Netherlands, for example, has the 2005 Dutch Collective Settlements Act, *Wet Collectieve Af-wikkeling Massaschade*, which provides for settlement-only class actions.[85] This provides that a group representing victims of a mass harm may try to reach a settlement with the wrongdoer. Class members can opt out if they disagree with the settlement; otherwise they are bound by it. Once a settlement has been agreed then the Dutch Court of Appeal in Amsterdam must then approve it. This has enabled many mass settlements and it also demonstrates a strong culture of non-judicial dispute resolution, enabled by a large network of sectoral dispute resolution boards. In Belgium, there are innovative consumer ADR procedures, which operate through Belmed, its official website. It has also dealt with all its mass harm cases by allowing private parties to 'piggy-back' on a criminal prosecution through the *partie civile* procedure, which requires the court to pay them compensation following the court decision.[86] We have seen in England and Wales how most early MPA attempts failed even though legal aid and the loser pays rule helped to enable these cases.[87] We have seen in the analysis of the English and Welsh system, that there has been resistance there to any type of collective action mechanism except for competition law.[88] Instead, there is a policy to include all three pillars—a regulatory power, ADR and collective actions—when dealing with mass harms.[89] Since the GLO's introduction in 1999 it has become more difficult to get legal aid and the loser pays rule is now commonly applied. As a result, there were hardly any mass harm cases being taken until the recent banking litigation. While legal aid was removed in 2013, the introduction of contingency fees, also known as damages-based agreements (DBAs), and qualified one-way cost shifting (QOCS) for personal injuries claims may encourage more mass claims by alleviating some of the financial risk for plaintiffs.[90] There are, however, many alternatives to litigation through a wide network of ombudsmen and ADR schemes

[83] Hodges (n 7) 80.

[84] This was set up by the German federal railway to deal with victims of the high-speed ICE train disaster at Eschede in 1998, in which 101 passengers died.

[85] The procedure is described in Arts 7:900–7:910 of the Burgerluk Wetboek [BW] [Dutch Civil Code] (Neth) and Arts 1013–1018 of the Wetboek van Burgerluke Rechtsvordering [Rv] [Dutch Judicial Code] (Neth). See further I Tzankova and D Lunsingh Scheurleer, 'The Netherlands' (2009) 622 *Annals Am Acad Pol & Soc Sci* 149. The complete version of this report is available at: http://globalclassactions.stanford.edu/content/class-actions-netherlands. See also J Fleming and J Kuster, 'The Netherlands' in P Karlsgodt (ed), *World Class Actions, A Guide to Group and Representative Actions Around the Globe* (Oxford University Press, 2012) 286; and M van der Heijden, 'Class Actions' in J van Erp and P van Vliet (eds), *Netherlands Reports to the Eighteenth International Congress of Comparative Law* (2010) 197.

[86] S Voet, 'Public Enforcement and A(O) DR as Mechanisms for Resolving Mass Problems: A Belgian Perspective' in C Hodges and A Stadler (eds), *Resolving Mass Disputes: ADR and Settlement of Mass Claims* (Edward Elgar, 2013).

[87] C Hodges, *Multi-Party Actions* (Oxford University Press 2001).

[88] BIS, *Consultation on Civil Enforcement Remedies: Consultation on Extending the Range of Remedies Available to Public Enforcers of Consumer Law* (2012).

[89] BIS, *Private Actions in Competition Law: A Consultation on Options for Reform—Government Response* (2013).

[90] eg in product liability, personal injury and medical negligence claims; Hodges (n 7) 80.

and regulators now have a duty to deliver redress.[91] Furthermore, enforcement policies adopted by regulatory bodies such as the Environment Agency have included this aim,[92] as have the addition of specific regulatory powers to deliver redress, restoration[93] or consumer redress schemes.[94] ADR has become part of court procedures in the past 10 years and we have seen the introduction of other consumer ADR arrangements that are expected to grow even further.[95] Evidence shows that in Sweden, Denmark, Finland, the Netherlands, Spain, Portugal, Italy, and to an increasing extent in England and Wales, consumers hardly ever use the courts; instead they use the ADR system.[96] By way of example, the Financial Services Ombudsman in England and Wales uses procedures to identify mass issues and brings these to the attention of the regulator so that a combined approach can be used to stop the infringements, achieving fast redress behavioural compliance.[97]

France did not have collective action procedures until very recently.[98] It has just introduced legislation, the French Law on Consumer Protection,[99] to provide for consumer and competition group actions and compensation that will follow on from decisions of the French or EU competition authorities. Only national consumer associations have standing and they can act in cases where consumers have suffered similar harm caused by the same defendant.[100] It also provides for mediation and any settlement must be court approved. Moreover, the provisions on collective actions are in line with the European Commission's adoption of a proposed Directive on damages actions for breaches of EU competition law, aimed at encouraging the use of private enforcement. It is the first Member State to have adopted legislation based on these initiatives.

While some Member States have been enthusiastic about introducing collective procedures, such as Norway,[101] Italy[102] and Poland,[103] their use in practice has been

[91] Since 2011, as a result of the introduction of the Regulatory Enforcement and Sanctions Act 2008; Legislative and Regulatory Reform Act 2006, s 23; Regulators Compliance Code, rev 2013. This has been successful at assisting consumers to achieve redress.

[92] A discussed in ch 4.

[93] eg the Environmental Civil Sanctions (England) Order 2010.

[94] Financial Services and Markets Act 2000, s 404F.

[95] Hodges, 'A Market-Based Competition Enforcement Policy' (n 60). The largest ADR entity deals with 1.2m enquiries annually, which led to 260,000 claims according to the Annual Review 2011–12 (Financial Ombudsman Service, 2012).

[96] Hodges (n 7) 85.

[97] Ibid.

[98] V Magnier, 'France' (2009) 622 *Annals Am Acad Pol & Soc Sci* 114. The complete version of this report is available at: http://globalclassactions.stanford.edu/content/class-actions-group-litigation-other-forms-collective-litigation-protocol-national-reporters. See also E Poisson and C Fléchet, 'France' in Karlsgodt, *World Class Actions* (n 85) 323.

[99] The French Law on Consumer Protection, Law no 2014-344 entered into force on 17 March 2014. This is also known as the 'Hamon Law'. Among the major changes, the legislation introduces class actions for damages resulting from anti-competitive practices implemented by undertakings.

[100] As a result of the sale of goods and/or supply of services or a breach of French or EU competition law.

[101] Norway has seen the greatest class action activity of any of the Nordic States, with 38 cases started from 2008 to the end of 2011. This may possibly because the court may decide to apply opt-out instead of opt-in, according to A Nordby, Danish Presidency, 'Copenhagen Conference on Collective Redress in a European Perspective' (Copenhagen, 22–23 March 2012) cited by Hodges (n 7) 80.

[102] Italy introduced class actions in 2010, following the adoption of Law of 12 December 2007 No 224, Art 2, para 446, and a considerable number of claims have since been filed but many, approximately 50%, were not certified.

[103] Class action procedures were introduced in Poland in 2010 with many cases following, approx 60 actions in 2 years, although many failed to be certified. In Hodges' opinion the class action procedure there has highlighted rather than solved underlying problems with the civil justice system; Hodges (n 7) 80.

inhibited by the ability of plaintiffs to meet certification requirements in many cases.[104] As well as indicating the low usage and success of the MPA systems in EU Member States, there is evidence that most Member States did not introduce collective actions to improve access to justice but that, instead, often the reason for their introduction was to give a mechanism to judges to enable them to manage multiple similar claims. This highlights the unifying theme of management running through MPA mechanisms and can be seen in the examples of Member State experience mentioned in chapter three on the MPA objectives. Spain needed a procedure to deal with the large-scale harm caused by a contaminated oil scandal. Germany had to manage the massive *Deutsche Telekom* litigation. England and Wales were faced with numerous large-scale product liability cases, a phenomenon described as 'simply one of managerial need, rather than enhancing access to justice or market health'.[105] This reality might be understood to reflect that the optimum collective redress solution lies in avoiding the courts and invoking alternative techniques through ADR, public enforcement and enhanced regulatory powers. Where a collective mechanism is needed, it seems to be effective only if invoked for logistical reasons. Perhaps this then is the answer for both EU policy and for other jurisdictions worldwide—a collective management tool rather than purely a litigation mechanism. It is up to each legal system to decide whether to achieve this through a collective action or other form of MPA. This is because in many cases, as we have seen, the underlying reason for the use of MPA procedures appears to be simply as a result of managerial need.

4. EU Commission's Collective Redress Policy Proposals 2013

Having examined the evolution of collective redress policy in the EU and also looked at the empirical evidence of the use of collective redress mechanisms in EU Member States, we have a good background against which to assess how collective redress can best be achieved going forward. From this examination, it is becoming clear that litigation is not the preferred means of ensuring mass harm redress and that the future for dispute resolution lies in invoking other mechanisms such as ADR. It is useful to address how the recent European Commission collective redress mechanisms measure up in light of this and against the objectives of MPAs, particularly as the Commission highlighted its own objectives in setting out its policy.

First, before looking at the Commission's policy proposals, it is important to raise a fundamental question about the implementation of EU collective redress policy and whether the EU institutions have competence to introduce harmonising legislation specifically for consumer protection or competition enforcement rather than as a general rule of law.[106] In answering this question it is clear that 'the creation of a unified system of civil dispute resolution presents considerable technical and political challenges and it will take a long

[104] It has been suggested that this may be reflective of either a 'valiant crusading zeal and the satisfactory operation of the certification safeguard by the courts, or, on the other hand, evidence of a worryingly aggressive compensation culture that needs strenuous control'; Hodges (n 7) 81.

[105] Ibid 82.

[106] Hodges (n 2) 82.

time'.[107] The involvement of DG JUST in the collective redress proposals became necessary because, if these are to operate through some form of collective action, then measures of civil procedure will be required. DG JUST ultimately aims to create a single civil justice system with harmonised procedures for all Member States and therefore this DG's involvement in the collective redress developments is necessary in order to assist with common policy for Member States. In terms of harmonising civil justice systems and procedures within the EU, early steps were taken in the 1990s. Several harmonising measures now exist within litigation systems, for example, the developments towards a European Judicial Network in civil and commercial matters, EJ-NET, and the Community framework to enable judicial cooperation in civil matters,[108] as well as the Brussels Regulation[109] As part of this harmonisation process, the EU aims to create a system for private enforcement and civil procedure. As we have seen, both the Commission and the European Parliament have examined the various techniques being used for collective redress in Member States in order to deliver a system that will enhance access to justice and collective redress in three areas of EU harmonisation, in particular: consumer protection, competition law enforcement and civil justice systems. The evolution of EU collective redress policy indicates that the Commission has been encouraging the introduction of collective actions in the areas of consumer and competition law for quite some time. DG SANCO has been doing so because of the need that it perceives to protect consumers and DG COMP wishes to provide for payment of competition damages though collective actions. DG JUST has joined this movement in order to help with the harmonisation of civil procedure. Taking the European Parliament's resolution into account in their deliberations, the consultations between three DGs—DG SANCO, DG COMP and DG JUST—culminated in the adoption of three policy documents in June 2013, when the European Commission eventually released its policy on collective redress, including a package of measures to facilitate providing for private damages. These three documents comprise the following:

First, a Commission Communication,[110] which reports on the main views expressed in the Commission's 2011 public consultation on collective redress and explains the Commission's position on a range of central issues on the topic, particularly following the European Parliament Resolution in 2012.[111] It also provides guidance for national courts on quantifying harm resulting from competition law infringements. The second document is a Commission Recommendation[112] and this sets out the Commission's actual policy on collective redress. The Recommendation advocates that all Member States should implement a collective action mechanism within two years. It advises that this mechanism is especially needed in the areas where EU law grants rights to companies and citizens: consumer protection, competition, protection of personal data, financial services legislation and investor protection, and environmental protection.[113] The aim behind this is not to harmonise the

[107] Hodges (n 1).

[108] Council Regulation (EC) 742/2002 of 25 April 2002 establishing a general Community framework of activities to facilitate the implementation of judicial cooperation in civil matters, [2002] OJ L 115/1.

[109] Council Regulation (EC) No 44/201 of 22 December 2000 on jurisdiction, recognition and enforcement of judgments in civil and commercial matters OJ L 12.

[110] Communication (n 4).

[111] Resolution (n 27).

[112] Recommendation (n 3).

[113] See Aarhus Convention, Art 9(3)–(5).

legal systems of Member States but to give some non-binding, common principles that Member States ought to take into account when creating collective redress mechanisms. By doing so, the Commission aims to improve access to justice, to curb illegal activity and to make it possible for those who suffer mass harm to get compensation, while also avoiding abusive litigation by providing appropriate procedural safeguards.[114] The third document is a proposal for a Directive on competition damages actions under national law for infringements of competition law.[115] Both the Recommendation and this Directive aim to work together as mechanisms to be used to resolve breaches of EU competition law and so deal with competition actions.

The Commission's proposals and their inherent objectives have previously been examined in chapter three, so this section will endeavour to avoid repetition. The proposals for collective redress that this package contains adhere to many of the characteristics and safeguards that the Parliament advocated in its resolution.[116] While the aim of the measures is clearly to enhance access to justice this must be compatible with EU's economic aim. Also, it is important to assess how the Commission's collective redress proposals will measure up against the reality of how existing collective redress mechanisms operate in EU Member States.

A. The Communication

In outlining its MPA objectives, the Commission's Communication was very mindful of the features required of collective redress mechanisms. It highlighted particularly the need for safeguards, both to protect against abuse and to take account of the variations among the collective redress mechanisms seen in Member States as well as their general civil and procedural rules. In detailing the measures necessary in order to take account of the diversity of EU Member States and of the lessons to be learnt from their various collective redress mechanisms, it lists the safeguards required by the Commission. First, collective actions are only to be permitted once certain admissibility requirements are satisfied. As for standing, in order to ensure that the representative entity is genuinely acting in the best interests of the group that it represents, certain requirements as set out in the Recommendation must be met in order to qualify for this. In terms of what type of model for collective action is to be used, an 'opt-in' model is preferred, and those Member States that already have 'opt-out' mechanisms must demonstrate that this is 'duly justified by reasons of sound administration of justice'. Furthermore, potential claimants must be provided with adequate information.[117] All of these requirements tally with the MPA objectives of judicial and procedural economy, predictability and fairness (in particular the objective of non-abuse).

The Communication crucially acknowledged the important role of public enforcement in collective redress.[118] It emphasised that in certain areas, specifically those of competition, environment and data protection, public enforcement plays a major role and that this

[114] Recommendation (n 3) Art 1.

[115] Directive Proposal (n 5) 404. An Impact Assessment Report that accompanies the proposal is available at: http://ec.europa.eu/competition/antitrust/actionsdamages/impact_assessment_en.pdf.

[116] Resolution (n 27).

[117] Communication (n 4) para 3.

[118] Ibid paras 12–13.

must not be jeopardised by litigation being commenced before the conclusion of the public investigation. In order to achieve this, it is provided that, in areas where a public authority has the power to decide that EU law has been violated, private collective redress actions should be stayed until the authority's proceedings have been concluded. The Commission proposed that public access to documents belonging to the public authority be restricted and that limitation rules be suspended in order to achieve this. In relation to damages, so as to discourage the risk of abuse, the Commission stated that punitive damages should not be permitted. As for ADR, this should be encouraged but remain voluntary although judges should not be prohibited from encouraging parties to seek a consensual solution,[119] and where a consensual solution is achieved, the legality of this outcome should be confirmed by court.[120]

B. The Recommendation

This sets out a number of common European principles that national collective redress systems should respect. First, it recommends that Member States should have a collective redress system that allows private individuals and entities to obtain court orders to deliver 'injunctive relief; where their rights granted by EU law have been infringed, and for the payment of damages through compensation where a large number of persons or entities have been harmed by the same illegal practice.[121] This highlights the MPA objectives of access to justice, compensation and deterrence. For both injunctive and compensatory collective redress, the Recommendation provides that only public authorities,[122] officially designated representative bodies and bodies certified on an ad hoc basis by a national court or national authority for a particular representative action, will have standing to bring a representative action.[123] There are eligibility characteristics that must be met by such bodies.[124] This resonates with the MPA objective of fairness, especially that of non-abuse. Also the class representative should be able to distribute information about an alleged mass harm situation and his intention to seek an injunction to stop this violation, if it involves rights granted under EU law, and his objective to pursue an action for damages.[125]

In order to create an efficient and just system, Member States should ensure that the collective redress procedures are fair, equitable, timely and not prohibitively expensive.[126]

[119] This already occurs for mediation in cross-border disputes, where, under Art 5 of Directive (EC) 2008/52/EC on certain aspects of mediation in civil and commercial matters, courts hearing disputes may invite the parties to try mediation in an effort to resolve the dispute.

[120] Recommendation (n 3) point 30.

[121] Ibid Point 1.

[122] Ibid Art 7.

[123] Ibid Arts 4 and 6.

[124] First, in order to ensure that class representatives are not motivated by personal gain, bodies certified must be of a non-profit making nature. Also, there must be a direct relationship between the body's main objectives and the rights granted under EU law that are allegedly being violated and in respect of which the action is being taken. Finally, they must have sufficient capacity in terms of resources and expertise in order to be able to represent multiple claimants and to act in their best interest.

[125] Recommendation (n 3) Art 10. The methods for dissemination should take into account the particular circumstances of the mass harm situation concerned, the freedom of expression, the right to information and the right to protection of the reputation or the goodwill of a defendant before its responsibility for the alleged violation or harm is established by the final judgment of the court (Art 11).

[126] Ibid Point 2.

These aims reflect the MPA objectives of judicial and procedural economy and fairness. The injunctive collective redress provisions of the Recommendation provide that, in order to prevent any further harm, injunctive collective redress actions should be dealt as quickly as possible and, where possible, summarily.[127] Member States should also provide sanctions to be imposed on defendants in order to ensure compliance with the injunctive order.[128] This underlines the aim of the MPA objective of deterrence. As early as possible in the litigation, the judge should confirm the admissibility of the collective action.[129] The Recommendation's compensatory collective redress provisions provide that these should be primarily provided on an opt-in basis.[130] Class members may leave or join the class at any time before final judgment is made or the case is settled.[131] These provisions reflect the MPA objective of judicial and procedural economy and fairness. Parties to the dispute should be encouraged to settle the dispute out of court.[132] Collective ADR should also be taken into account[133] and any collective settlement must be court-approved;[134] again, these provisions are in the interests of the MPA objective of fairness, particularly that of non- abuse. Contingency fees[135] and punitive damages[136] are both prohibited by the Commission, underlining its MPA objectives of fairness and non-abuse. The Recommendation also deals with collective follow-on actions.

In terms of the funding of a collective redress procedure, the Recommendation obliges the plaintiff to clarify to the court the source of funding for the legal action at the beginning of the action.[137] While third-party funding is not expressly prohibited, it states that if the action is being financed in this way the court can stay the proceedings in certain circumstances.[138] This reflects the MPA objectives of fairness and non-abuse in order to facilitate transparency and to ensure there is no conflict of interests. Therefore, it should only be permitted once certain conditions are met because, in the Commission's view, 'an inappropriate system of third-party financing runs the risk of stimulating abusive litigation or litigation that does little to serve the best interests of litigants'. It stated that the judge in collective litigation should have the central role and should effectively manage the case and

[127] Art 19.

[128] Ibid Art 20. This should include the payments of a fixed amount for each day's delay or any other amount provided for in national legislation.

[129] Ibid Arts 8–9.

[130] Ibid Art 21. Opt-out collective actions are possible by law or court order, but this should be justified by reasons of sound administration of justice.

[131] Ibid Arts 22 and 23—as long as this does not undermine the sound administration of justice.

[132] This should be possible at both the pre-trial stage and during the trial according to Art 25. This should be done taking into account the Mediation Directive (Directive (EC) 2008/52, of the European Parliament and of the Council of 21 May 2008 on certain aspects of mediation in civil and commercial matters, 2008 OJ L 136.

[133] Recommendation (n 3) Art 26.

[134] Ibid Art 28.

[135] Ibid Arts 29 and 30. Art 29 prescribes that the Member States should ensure that the lawyers' remuneration and the method by which it is calculated do not create any incentive to litigation that is unnecessary from the point of view of the interest of any of the parties. If, in exceptional cases, contingency fees are allowed, Member States should provide for appropriate national regulation of those fees in collective redress cases, taking into account the right to full compensation of the class members.

[136] Ibid Art 31.

[137] Ibid Art 13.

[138] According to Art 15 this will occur if (1) there is a conflict of interest between the third party and the plaintiff and its members; (2) the third party has insufficient resources in order to meet its financial commitments to the plaintiff; or (3) if the plaintiff has insufficient resources to meet any adverse costs should the collective redress procedure fail.

be vigilant against any possible abuses.[139] This would appear to suggest that the collective action had an important managerial feature. Also, there are restrictions on the behaviour of the third party.[140] Finally, and crucially, the 'loser pays' rule applies to collective redress actions.[141] Again these requirements echo the MPA objectives of fairness and judicial and procedural economy.

C. Proposed Directive on Competition Damages

The proposed Directive relates to national damages claims for breaches of Articles 101 or 102 of the Treaty on the Functioning of the European Union and seeks to ensure a common approach across Member States. DG COMP's underlying aim was to propose a collective action for competition damages but, bizarrely, the proposed Directive does not mention collective action at all. There were several reasons for this, most importantly, the three DGs were mindful that a proposal for collective actions, particularly on a horizontal basis, would not be supported by the Member States, and so instead, as a 'political solution', the Commission decided to merely generally address numerous technical issues relating to competition damages that needed to be resolved.[142] The only reference in the proposals to collective action is in the Recommendation, which says that Members States should implement a collective action procedure for all cases within two years.[143] A very important new departure is that, in stark contrast to the US system, the new EU approach to competition law collective redress, as detailed in the proposal for the Directive, does not rely on private litigation to achieve deterrence and punishment. Instead, in a crucial step forward in addressing the approach suited to EU collective redress, it acknowledges the important role that is played by competition authorities in handling violations of competition law. The Directive seeks to optimise the interaction between public and private enforcement of competition law; to minimise discrepancies between rules applicable to antitrust damages actions in Member States; and to ensure that victims of infringements of EU competition law can obtain full compensation for the harm they have suffered. These aims reflect the MPA objectives of compensation and deterrence.

Collective actions for competition cases have been a particular concern for the EU since the European Court of Justice decision in the *Courage* case in 2001.[144] In 2008, the

[139] Recommendation (n 3) Point 4.

[140] Art 16 prohibits the third party from (1) seeking to influence procedural decisions of the plaintiff, including on settlements; (2) providing financing for a collective action against a defendant who is a competitor of the fund provider or against a defendant on whom the fund provider is dependent; and (3) charging excessive interest on the funds provided.

[141] Art 13.

[142] Such as a requirement that courts cannot take decisions contrary to authorities' infringement decisions, limitation periods, joint and several liability, the passing-on defence, a rule on indirect purchases, and a rebuttable presumption that infringements cause harm; Hodges (n 7) 75.

[143] Ibid. In reality, the Commission will assess within 4 years whether the proposal of further legislative measures is necessary to reinforce the horizontal measures and will also assess 'its impact on access to justice, on the right to obtain compensation, on the need to prevent abusive litigation and on the functioning of the single market, the Economy of the EU and consumer trust'.

[144] Case C-453/99 *Courage Ltd v Bernard Crehan* [2001] ECR I-6297. The ECJ established that private actions for damages also apply to breaches of EU competition law by private individuals. See also Cases C-295/04 to C-298/04 *Manfredi v Lloyd Adriatico Assicurazioni SpA* [2006] ECR I-6619.

Commission issued a *White Paper on Damages Actions for Breach of EC Antitrust Rules.*[145] This recommended allowing the participation of victims in group actions and that these would be led by recognised consumer groups. The Directive's main aim is to provide for full and fair compensation once such an infringement has been found and sanctioned by such authorities. Overall, this Directive takes a position similar to the Recommendation.

When viewed as a whole, these documents show clearly that the Commission is mindful of the differences between the US and EU approaches to enforcement. It is respectful of the role of public law and regulation in the EU. However, in a bold move, it seems that the European Commission policy, following years of scepticism, is now endorsing initiatives to provide a framework for collective redress. The mechanisms that this espouses appear to be a supplementary tool to enable compensation and deterrence and so are complementary to existing enforcement tools. Obviously, how effective this framework will be in terms of the amount of litigation and the degree of abuse that will result will depend on how they are implemented in Member State law and the sectors in which the proposed collective action is used.

5. Safeguards

In terms of evaluating the safeguards that the Commission has proposed in its collective redress policy, it is important to assess how these will fare when weighed against the practicalities of implementing these procedures in Member States. It is argued that the claim by the Commission that its safeguards create a strong barrier against abuse cannot be sustained.[146] First, the EU rules on subsidiarity[147] mean that in reality it will not possible for Member States to wholly comply with the safeguards outlined and the exemptions that they provide. Furthermore, if it is left to each Member State to introduce safeguards, because of the varying national contexts, the extent to which these are observed will determine whether or not the safeguards encourage litigation and how effective they are at discouraging abuse. There is already considerable variation in how safeguards operate in Member States, for example differences in contingency fees rules[148] and many States permit conditional or success fees. Overall, complex issues such as funding and costs vary hugely between jurisdictions, so it is impossible to propose a 'one size fits all' approach. Secondly, the Recommendation contains too many exemptions, for example: contingency fees should not be permitted but may be exceptionally, if regulated;[149] procedures should be opt-in but may be opt-out where 'justified by reasons of sound administration of justice';[150] the loser should pay the costs but subject to conditions of national law.[151] Hodges' expert opinion states that, following closer inspection, it is clear that what the Commission asserts to be a

[145] See http://ec.europa.eu/competition/antitrust/actionsdamages/documents.html.

[146] Hodges (n 7) 78.

[147] TFEU, Art 67(1).

[148] These are permitted in Denmark, England and Wales, and Lithuania. Also, it is effectively impossible to prohibit contingency fees or third-party funding, because the use of an intermediary sidesteps this; Hodges (n 7) 79.

[149] Recommendation (n 30) para 30.

[150] Ibid para 21.

[151] Ibid para 13.

pro forma list of safeguards turns out to be a 'flaky, permeable and porous wall, with little stability' and he confirms that it is 'certainly premature to talk of a definitive EU model for a collective action'.[152] Member States will continue to have their varying litigation methods and the introduction of new collective action mechanisms could possibly fuel other abuses such as forum-shopping.

6. Environment

In terms of how the environment fares in the evolution of collective redress policy, it seems to be very much part of the Commission's enforcement vision to include it. This was first seen in 2010 when the Commissioners for Justice, Competition and Consumer Affairs were requested to collaborate on the drafting of a unified policy for collective redress.[153] As part of this process, they consulted other Commissioners, including the Environment Commissioner. It was debated how collective action might be appropriate for environmental law enforcement. This is conceptually very difficult to achieve because EU legislation is based on the polluter pays principle and provides for enforcement by public authorities, not enforcement by private parties, or private damages, as these are governed by national law. In attempting to elaborate some non- binding, common principles that Member States ought to take into account when creating collective redress mechanisms, the 2013 Commission Recommendation advocates that all Member States should have a collective redress mechanism in the areas where EU law grants rights to companies and citizens including environmental protection. As stated at the outset of the proposals, their aim is not to harmonise the legal systems of Member States, but the Commission aims to improve access to justice, to curb illegal activity and to make it possible for those who suffer mass harm to get compensation. The horizontal approach recommended by the Commission was also requested by the European Parliament in order to avoid 'inconsistencies between the different Commission initiatives on collective redress, a fact which points to the need for a more coherent system'.[154] Public enforcement clearly prevails in enforcement of competition, environmental and data protection law.[155] The Communication did, however, acknowledge this important role of public enforcement in collective redress, so this reflects the reality of environmental enforcement. It emphasised that in certain areas, specifically including environment, public enforcement plays a major role and that this must not be jeopardised by litigation being commenced before the conclusion of the public investigation. In its Communication, the Commission said that 'collective redress is a procedural tool that can be relevant for EU policies in other areas other than competition or consumer protection. Good examples are financial services, environmental protection'.[156] Perhaps if the mechanism to be used for environmental collective redress is more of a managerial

[152] Hodges (n 7) 79.

[153] *Towards a Coherent European Approach to Collective Redress: Next Steps* (n 49).

[154] Communication (n 4) para 1.3.

[155] F Bignmai, 'Cooperative Legalism and the Non-Americanization of European Regulatory Styles: The Case of Data Privacy' (2011) 59(2) *Am J Comp L* 411–61.

[156] Communication (n 4) para 1.3.

tool rather than a collective action this will allow it will enable judges and claimants to overcome the logistical challenges of dealing with environmental mass harm claims and to avail of the advantages that the clustering of such claims can yield. This ought to be possible despite the reality that in the EU environmental law is largely a matter for public rather than private enforcement.

7. Conclusions on European Collective Redress Outlook

From the examination of EU Member States' experience, litigation does not seem to be the preferable solution to achieving effective collective redress. There are not many mass cases being taken in the EU due to inherent funding and costs issues as well as the length of time such cases can take. It is evident that Member States have not generally introduced horizontal collective actions but that they have instead deliberately restricted them to specific areas such as consumer protection.[157] One of the key reasons for this is because Member States, in many areas, do not use litigation as the main tool for resolving mass disputes; instead, they use other mechanisms such as ADR and regulation to achieve collective solutions.[158] Hodges suggests that Member States do not appear to wish to alter the internal balance of their legal systems by switching to litigation for all types of claims.[159] As the Swedish experience shows, more claims would be made against governments and private parties if this were to occur. The Recommendation's suggestion of a horizontal collective action is not in keeping with most Member States' legal traditions and would be a bold step towards converting the balance in national legal systems on public and private enforcement firmly towards the latter.[160] At EU level, political opinion in Europe has firmly rejected the US class actions model for fear of its perceived adverse effects, ranging from excessive litigation and exorbitant costs[161] to excessive pressure on defendants to settle regardless of merit, resulting in a profound resistance to privatising dispute resolution. This opinion seems to have prevailed despite indications by American experts that such allegations may be mythical and are empirically unclear.[162] While European enforcement has previously largely been through public law, both public and private enforcement mechanisms exist. However changes are being seen which indicate a move away from the traditional perception that public bodies enforce regulation and that compensation is claimed in private litigation; instead, we are seeing how regulators can achieve behaviour control and deliver restitution

[157] Hodges (n 1).

[158] Hodges (n 7) 85.

[159] Ibid.

[160] D Kelemen, 'Eurolegalism. *The Transformation of Law and Regulation in the European Union* (Harvard University Press, Boston 2011) as cited by Hodges (n 7) 88.

[161] In a study of US class actions by D Hensler, B Dombey-Moore, B Giddens, J Gross, E Moller and N Pace, *Class Action Dilemmas. Pursuing Public Goals for Private Gain* (RAND Institute for Civil Justice, 2000) it was discovered that class action lawyers in the US received significant fees from between half a million dollars to $75m in successful suits and that hourly fees ranged from $320 to $2,000.

[162] See D Hensler, 'The Globalisation of Class Actions: An Overview' in Hensler, Hodges and Tulibacka, *The Globalisation of Class Actions* (n 2); Hensler and others, *Class Action Dilemmas* (n 161); D Hensler, 'Third-Party Financing of Class Action Litigation in the United States: Will the Sky Fall?' (2014) 63 *De Paul L Rev* 1101.

to individuals very quickly and inexpensively.[163] ADR and related techniques are growing in popularity throughout Europe as a more efficient and accessible route to collective redress. A logistical challenge that emerges is how mechanisms for delivering compensation and deterrence can integrate the elements of ADR, regulators and courts into a model for a civil justice system that can deal with both individual and mass disputes in an economical and efficient way. Evidence shows that if public authorities use a regulatory redress power, it can be possible to agree on sanctioning and damages aspects of a claim during the public investigation stage.[164] If a country can effectively integrate its regulation and dispute resolution systems then a very efficient and effective system can be achieved. Such an approach would bridge the divide between public and private law as well as that of common law and civil law, but Hodges propounds that Europe needs to first address the question of what balance it desires between public and private enforcement. He suggests that if the Member States' national courts are viewed as a laboratory within which different techniques can be tried out, within the broad framework, then this provides an exciting future for dispute resolution.[165] The EU Communication stated a fundamental point that:

> Collective damages actions should aim to secure compensation of damage that is found to be caused by an infringement. The punishment and deterrence functions should be exercised by public enforcement. There is no need for EU initiatives on collective redress to go beyond the goal of compensation.[166]

The Recommendation added to this recognition of the primacy of public law enforcement by stating that where a public authority is empowered to make decisions on a breach of EU, collective actions should only commence after any public proceedings have been concluded.[167] The EU model, however, ought to encourage non-judicial resolution through ADR and try new ways of combining public and private mechanisms to deliver this. The Commission has failed to take a holistic view of enforcement and options such as giving public authorities powers of regulatory redress. In evaluating the Commission's proposals, while the collective action it proposes should be able to resolve large numbers of individual claims for compensation of harm and it is adequate to ensure legally certain and fair outcomes, it is unlikely to promote procedural economy and highly unlikely to resolve claims in a timely manner.[168] While it does provide some strong safeguards against abusive litigation, it has not managed to avoid economic incentives to bringing speculative claims but these measures will limit them.[169] While the Commission's new proposals in some way acknowledge the role played by public enforcement and ADR, its reliance on the introduction of a collective redress procedure is trying to push a metaphorical square public enforcement peg into a private litigational round hole. Perhaps if these proposals contained more of a managerial tool to help deal with mass claims rather than purely as a collective action procedure then it may help to ease the difficulties often encountered when dealing with such claims.

[163] The UK has a model for all types of collective redress, especially consumer collective redress, which comprises three pillars, combining *ex ante* and *ex post* techniques; MoJ, 'Government's Response to the Civil Justice Council's Report: "Improving Access to Justice through Collective Actions"' (2009).

[164] Hodges (n 7) 85.

[165] C Hodges, "Collective Redress in Europe: The New Model" (2010) 29 *Civil J Q* 370, 22.

[166] Communication (n 4) para 3.1.

[167] Recommendation (n 3) para 33.

[168] Hodges (n 7) 87.

[169] Ibid.

10

Collective Redress for Mass Harm in Ireland

This chapter examines the prospects for mass harm in Ireland, a common law jurisdiction that does not yet have an effective mechanism for multi-party litigation. This is despite recommendations by the Irish Law Reform Commission (LRC), Ireland's principal public body for the investigation of law reform, for the introduction of a new litigation procedure in the form of a multi-party action.[1] It examines the alternative methods of litigation that have been used by courts in cases where a MPA mechanism would have had an obvious role. The implications of this approach for access to justice in Ireland are evaluated and discussed in light of the LRC Report recommendations. In conclusion, it evaluates what the future may hold for multi-party litigation and access to environmental justice in light of domestic, European and international developments in this area. The example of environmental mass harm illustrates some of the practical aspects of this procedural lacuna.

1. Litigation Landscape

As explained in this research, MPAs, by enabling victims of mass harm to combine their legal actions, can be a key tool in achieving the overall objectives set out in this study. They can enable litigants to overcome many of the impediments facing citizens who take legal actions individually.[2] Ireland, also a common law jurisdiction, is still somewhat at sea procedurally between the class action mechanisms seen in the US and the emerging group litigation approach in England and Wales. This is because Ireland, at present, has no formal statutory or court rules for MPAs, so neither multi-party nor specifically collective action

[1] The Law Reform Commission was established by the Law Reform Commission Act 1975 as an independent statutory body whose main aim is to keep the law under review and to make practical proposals for its reform. It has published over 100 documents containing proposals for law reform which are available online at www.lawreform.ie. The LRC usually publishes in 2 stages: first, a Consultation Paper and then a Report. This occurred with the Multi-Party Litigation recommendations. The Consultation Paper is intended to form the basis for discussion and its recommendations, conclusions and suggestions are therefore provisional. The LRC *Consultation Paper on Multi-Party Litigation* was published in 2003 and its *Report on Multi-Party Litigation* was published in 2005.

[2] eg problems associated with funding and standing. See for further detail, A Ryall, 'Delivering the Rule of Environmental Law in Ireland: Where Do we Go from here?' in S Kingston (ed), *European Perspectives on Environmental Law and Governance* (Routledge, 2013).

This also explores international conventions such as Aarhus (The United Nation Convention on Access to Information, Public Participation in Decision-making and Access to Justice in Environmental Matters) and highlights the need for access to justice as a key facet of the aim of improving environmental governance in Europe.

is yet permitted, save for very limited representative actions. These possibilities are rarely invoked because they are of such restricted use. This fact distinguishes Ireland from other common law jurisdictions with MPA mechanisms and appears to be a gap in the Irish legal framework. Under the existing statutory framework MPAs seem to be actively discouraged. Ireland does not yet have a mechanism for MPAs as such. Instead, occasionally the courts use a confusing array of alternative methods in cases where MPAs would have played an obvious role. In recent years there have been a number of cases of mass harm, including contaminated blood products, army deafness and asbestos-related ill health. Such cases usually draw widespread public interest due to the nature of their claims, the scale of the potential class or the prospect of State liability. Normally, however, owing to the lack of an appropriate mechanism, those with cases potentially suited to an MPA must pursue them in another way. Great injustices and inefficiencies have resulted from these improvisations.

2. The Irish Approach: No MPAs

The LRC has recognised the procedural gap that results from the absence of MPAs. In a major study in 2005, it explored the prospects for MPAs in Ireland and has recommended their introduction.[3] The key recommendations of this pivotal report are described further below. Despite the LRC recommendations, there have not yet been any such legislative proposals for change in Ireland. This raises a number of questions. It is possible to speculate that there are policy reasons for the lack of MPAs. It seems that there is almost a de facto prohibition on such mechanisms, because of the lack of a procedure providing for them and because of the presence of rules that effectively prohibit them, including for example the prohibition on damages awards for representative actions.[4] Despite the LRC's recommendations for MPAs in mass tort and personal injury litigation—an area where the State has been and is likely to be a regular defendant—the State has been very slow to introduce a MPA system.[5] Irish policymakers may be exercising caution for fear of opening apocryphal litigation floodgates by having a full-blown collective action procedure, bringing with it the risks that some have alleged this mechanism can unleash where such procedure is abused and is not accompanied by adequate controls.[6] Perhaps there is a concern regarding competitiveness or attractiveness as a location for foreign investors wishing to set up business in Ireland. However, the MPA procedure, as recommended by the LRC, is designed to minimise such risks.

Irish Supreme Court Judge Denham, when launching the LRC Report in 2005, commented that:

> It is probable that the less well off, those disadvantaged in our society, would be the main beneficiaries of a new procedure enabling multi-party action … It is no easy task- the challenge is

[3] Irish Law Reform Commission, *Report on Multi-party Litigation* (LRC 76-2005).

[4] There is no explicit reason for this prohibition; it is likely to discourage the taking of such actions to achieve a monetary award. Remedies are limited to injunctive or declaratory relief. The bar on the bringing of representative actions in tort currently exists in ord 6, r 10 of the Circuit Court Rules 2001.

[5] L Broderick, 'Class Actions—Opting In or Out of the Bandwagon' (Accountancy Ireland Archive, 2005).

[6] A Miller, 'Of Frankenstein Monsters and Shining Knights: Myth, Reality and the "Class Action Problem"' (1979) 92 *Harv L Rev* 664 (outlining these problems while defending class actions and asserting that the problems are overstated).

> to find a just balance in multi-party litigation between procedural efficiency and fairness. The Law Reform Commission has met this challenge successfully. Implementation of this Report would bring us a step closer to succeeding in this task.[7]

In these words, Mrs Justice Denham identified the *raisons d'être* of the MPA. She highlighted three of the key benefits that they are designed to achieve: access to justice; procedural efficiency; and fairness. Ireland's lack of MPAs cannot be explored in a vacuum and the situation here must be examined in light of these objectives. This contribution examines the limited arrangements currently available in Ireland to see to what extent they meet these three requirements.

A. Overview of Current Irish Mechanisms for Dealing with Mass Harm

Multi-party litigation can arise in a variety of situations that can be broadly categorised as follows.

i. Public Actions

This denotes a category of actions whereby certain public officials are empowered to institute litigation on behalf of a wide group of affected individuals. For example, regulatory bodies (or a given regulator) and the Director of Public Prosecutions (DPP) may institute public actions for the prosecution of regulatory offences, such as those in the financial sector.[8] Another example is that the Attorney General may sue on behalf of the public and bodies such as NGOs using section 6 of the Ministers and Secretaries Act 1924 for the assertion of public rights.[9] In the environmental context, one might include prosecutions or other enforcement action taken by the Environmental Protection Agency within this category.

ii. Organisation Actions

It may be possible for certain organisations to institute proceedings that could otherwise be taken by a number of individuals. Such organisations are often public interest groups or pressure groups that are deemed to have a sufficient interest in the case to qualify for standing. In this way an action by an appropriate organisation could effectively dispose of multiple potential individual cases.[10] However, the issue of *locus standi* could operate as an obstacle and also the possibility of damages does not exist, as only declaratory or injunctive relief may be given. This may be a deterrent to such actions being used in environment-related cases (although, in the case of actions to enforce the environmental impact assessment (EIA) Directive or the integrated pollution prevention and control

[7] Ibid.

[8] See also the jurisdictions of the Competition Authority and the Director of Consumer Affairs to institute proceedings on behalf of consumers.

[9] eg the case of *Attorney General (SPUC) v Open Door Counselling Ltd* [1988] IR 593 (this case was taken by the Attorney General on behalf of the Society for the Protection of the Unborn Child to challenge the distribution in Ireland by Open Door Counselling of information on abortion services abroad).

[10] An example of this is the case of *Irish Penal Reform Trust v Minister for Justice, Equality and Law Reform* [2005] IEHC 305.

(IPPC Directive) the fact that environmental NGOs enjoy automatic standing avoids some of these difficulties).[11]

iii. Litigation Avoidance

Occasionally it may be best to deal with a group of individual actions together in a way that avoids litigation and to facilitate a remedy in a more sensitive and efficient way, particularly where a question of public interest is involved. An obvious example of this is the special mechanisms such as statutory no-fault compensation schemes that deal with mass cases of personal injury (for example, injuries arising from infected blood products supplied by State bodies,[12] and injuries suffered by those who had been in residential institutional care).[13] In situations of serious injury or widespread mismanagement, usually for which there is some State accountability, there have been cases in which a public inquiry is necessitated, for example the recently established State inquiry into banking malpractice. The aim of a public inquiry is to determine facts relating to a particular incident or series of incidents of public interest and to ascertain whether a wrong has been committed against society or the public interest. Its aim is *not* to deliver judgment on legal rights. Depending on the results of such inquiry this may lead to claims for compensation by victims or their relatives, such as occurred with the Hepatitis C Tribunal and the Institutional Redress Board under the no-fault compensation schemes discussed above.

Other methods of litigation avoidance, which have been used particularly in consumer actions, include the use of ADR. In the US, ADR has recently been endorsed in the US Supreme Court's decision in *AT&T Mobility LLC v Concepcion*.[14] In this case, the Court invalidated a Californian law that attempted to limit contract arbitration clauses considered unfair to consumers. The Court held that if there is an arbitration clause in a contract, parties must be held to that. If this approach is followed in other courts and jurisdictions, this will strengthen the use of ADR as an alternative to class action litigation. This decision would appear to indicate that in the consumer field there has been a major shift to arbitration and class arbitration.

This research has also explored how prevention through regulation may be another method of potentially avoiding litigation. While the function of regulation in the domain of multi-party litigation may not be immediately obvious, the influence of effective regulatory mechanisms will often function to prevent the wrong arising in the first place and therefore preclude the need for any type of multi-party litigation.[15] Regulation often relates to areas in which there is great potential for multiple parties, for example consumer regulation and the safety of pharmaceutical products. In such circumstances, regulation plays an essential role in multi-party litigation. There is an important background role played by certain Irish regulatory and standards agencies in this area: the Office of the Director of

[11] Council Directive 85/337/EEC on the assessment of effects of certain public and private projects on the environment, (EIA Directive) OJ L 175 1985 or Directive 2008/1/EC of the European Parliament and of the Council of 15 January 2008 concerning integrated pollution prevention and control (the IPPC Directive), OJ L 24, 2008. See Directive (EC) 2003/35 OJ 2002 L 156/17, amending the EIA Directive to implement the Aarhus Convention.

[12] See Hepatitis C Compensation Tribunal Act 1997 (No 34/1997).

[13] See Residential Institutions Redress Act 2002 (No 13/2002).

[14] *AT&T Mobility v Concepcion*, 563 US Reports, 27 April 2011.

[15] LRC Report (n 3).

Consumer Affairs and the Irish Medicines Board, for example, are particularly active and effective. Also, the State Claims Agency is charged with the function of identifying risks that could lead to future claims against public bodies. It is empowered to liaise with these bodies to ensure that these foreseeable risks are managed and controlled appropriately. In this way it carries out an important preventative role. This Agency was established as a direct result of the State's largest litigation experience, the army deafness claims (discussed below).[16] In the environmental context, the Department of the Environment, Community and Local Government carries out this regulatory role in conjunction with the Environmental Protection Agency (EPA) and local authorities.

iv. EU Initiatives

Several EU instruments, for example those provided for consumer protection, permit a nominated competent authority (in Ireland's case, the Director of Consumer Affairs) to initiate proceedings on behalf of consumers.[17]

v. Private Actions

This is the main focus of this chapter and refers to procedures that enable a group of individuals to institute proceedings to deal with that group collectively. Unlike the public action or organisation action, in private litigation the decision to pursue an action rests solely with the group of individuals. As mentioned at the outset, Ireland has a confusing array of mechanisms that have occasionally been used for cases of mass harm. These are rarely invoked and are private multi-party procedures that currently fall short of MPAs. They comprise the following four mechanisms.

First, there are *representative actions*. Irish courts have taken a very restrictive attitude towards these: they are permitted in very limited circumstances in which parties have the same interest and where certain prerequisites are met.[18] They cannot be used for tort claims[19] and it is not possible to get damages. It is not possible to get legal aid for these cases. This type of representative action is a long way from the US class action procedure.

Secondly, there is the tool of *joinder*. This is a process whereby the court can simply join additional litigants to an action where it is necessary in the interests of justice and in this way it can hear related cases together. The joinder system is used regularly to combine actions involving two or more parties and can, on occasion, broaden to actions involving many parties.[20]

[16] Ibid for further detail.

[17] See eg Council Directive (EC) 93/13/EEC of 5 April 1993 on unfair terms in consumer contracts OJ 1993 L 95/29.

[18] This 'same interest' has been examined in representative proceedings in other common law jurisdictions, such as those in England and Wales.

[19] Ord 6, r 10 of the Circuit Court Rules 2001 expressly excludes representative actions founded on tort. No further explanation can be found of why this is so but this was also stated by the Supreme Court in *Moore v Attorney General (No 2)* [1930] IR 471.

[20] See eg *Abrahamson v Law Society* [1996] 1 IR 403 (Law students challenged the Law Society's decision to deny them exemption from the entrance examination to the Law Society. Their individual actions were combined in a single action before the High Court as the plaintiffs were a defined group with identical claims for declaratory and injunctive relief, represented by one legal team.)

Thirdly, there is the tool of *consolidation*. This is an alternative to a joinder. It occurs where the court rules that disputes must be tried or consolidated together by a plaintiff uniting several causes of action in the same proceedings.[21] This rule further provides that where such causes of action cannot be tried together conveniently, the court may order separate trials or make such other order as may be necessary or expedient to dispose of the matters.[22] Where a plaintiff does not take steps to unite several causes of action in the same proceedings, matters pending in the High Court may be consolidated by order of the court on the application of any party and regardless of whether or not all the parties consent to the order.[23] Aside from the provisions in the Rules, the court has an inherent jurisdiction to order that cases be heard simultaneously.[24] The difference between joinder and consolidation is that consolidation does *not* involve making all the claimants parties to a single set of proceedings. Instead, the plaintiff litigates the consolidated claims on the premise that he represents the other litigants. Any judgment is deemed to be binding on the other litigants (the plaintiffs in the parallel proceedings, with which his claim has been consolidated). In this way consolidation resembles the representative action and is a less flexible system for managing large class claims.

Fourthly, *test cases* are a commonly used mechanism. These are currently used in Ireland as the favoured means of dealing with mass harm litigation. Quite often a plaintiff proceeds on an individual basis. The test case establishes a benchmark and, while subsequent actions by other litigants are not bound by the result, the test case outcome gives an indicator of the outcome of future litigation both in terms of formal precedent and the similarity of subsequent proceedings.[25] This is uncomplicated where the test case pronounces an administrative or legislative action unconstitutional,[26] but is less straightforward where an individual assessment of damages is necessary. Test cases were used to deal with the many army deafness claims taken against the State and also in private actions.[27] These are unduly costly and result in procedural inefficiencies as well as unnecessary duplication, as illustrated in the examples discussed further below.

vi. Other Discrete Areas

Certain specific provisions under Irish law provide for representative proceedings to be brought under the law relating to trusts and estates and derivative actions on behalf of shareholders in company law and in relation to fatality claims.

[21] Ord 18, r 1 of the Irish Rules of the Superior Courts (RSC) provides that a plaintiff may unite several causes of action together in the same proceedings.

[22] RSC, Ord 18, r 1 provides that where it appears to the court that causes of action are such that they cannot all be conveniently disposed of together, the court may order any of such causes of action to be excluded and consequential amendments to be made to such order as to costs may be just.

[23] RSC, Ord 4, r 6; *Duffy v News Group Newspapers Ltd* [1992] 2 IR 369.

[24] *O'Neill v Ryanair Ltd* [1992] 1 IR 160.

[25] G Whyte, *Social Inclusion and the Legal System* (Institute of Public Administration, 2002) 104.

[26] See G Hogan and G Whyte, *Kelly: Irish Constitution* (4th edn, Butterworths, 2003) 487–97 (such a declaration nullifies the impugned act or legislation in all situations including those where litigation is pending).

[27] See eg *Gough v Neary* [2003] 3 IR 92, [2003] IESC 39 (successful negligence claim against an obstetrician for an unnecessary hysterectomy during childbirth, in advance of a further 65 similar cases pending against him).

B. Cases Exemplifying the Problems of Mass Harm Litigation in Ireland

The following cases are a clear illustration of what occurs when some of the above private action procedures are used and there is no appropriate multi-party procedure. They support the contention that by proceeding on the basis of such fragmented and piecemeal procedures, access to justice is impeded, and gross procedural inefficiencies and procedural unfairness result. They fall far short of the three objectives of MPAs identified by Mrs Justice Denham above.

i. Social Welfare Equality Cases

An early example is the two cases of *Cotter and McDermott v Minister for Social Welfare and Attorney General.*[28] These resulted from the failure by Ireland to implement the 1978 Directive on Equal Treatment in Social Welfare.[29] The two cases were test cases for 11,200 married women who instituted proceedings, out of a total 69,000 who had been disadvantaged by this failure. The State settled these two cases along with another 2,700 without admission of liability. However, this ignored approximately 8,500 claims initiated as well as the remaining 58,000 married women who had not yet initiated proceedings. This was followed by the case of *Tate v Minister for Social Welfare* involving 70 of these women, in which Miss Justice Carroll ruled in the High Court that they too were entitled to relief.[30] This decision resulted in the Government announcing that the required payments would be made to the entire group of 69,000 women, with this amount totalling £265 million including interest.

ii. Army Deafness Claims

The army deafness litigation is the best example of multiple, similar claims over a period of 13 years, resulting from hundreds of individual army deafness cases. Claims of hearing loss were brought by serving and former members of the Defence Forces. It was found that the Defence Forces, and consequently the State, were liable for negligence in failure to prevent noise-induced hearing loss of serving and former members of the Defence Forces. The

[28] Case 286/85 *Cotter and McDermott v Minister for Social Welfare (No 1)* [1987] ECR 1453 and Case 377/89 *Cotter and McDermott v Minister for Social Welfare (No 2)* [1991] 1 ECR 1155. These cases arose from the fact that until 1986 Ireland's social welfare policy had discriminated against married women. Married men were the automatic recipients of child benefit and received higher rates of welfare payment based on a presumption that their wives were dependent on them. For married women to receive these payments, they had to prove that their spouses were incapable of supporting themselves. In 1984, a Directive obliged Ireland to remove these practices of sex discrimination, but it did not do so until 1986. The Free Legal Advice Centre (FLAC) (a pro bono NGO) took a case arguing the entitlement of married women to back-payments during the 2-year period when Ireland's discriminatory policy was in breach of EU law. Their victory had far-reaching consequences, making it possible for 69,000 women to claim their entitlement.

[29] Council Directive (EC) 79/7/EEC of 19 December 1978 on the progressive implementation of the principle of equal treatment for men and women in matters of social security OJ 1979 L 6/24.

[30] [1995] 1 IR 418.

State's alleged negligence resulted in approximately 14,650 soldiers claiming partial or total loss of hearing.[31]

iii. Pyrite Construction Dispute

In 2011, the Irish High Court finished hearing a case that had been running for over two years against the Irish construction industry with claims of more than €100 million. These claims were brought by 550 homeowners who had purchased houses that developed structural faults, due to the use of pyrite infill during construction. This was the longest running case in the history of the Commercial Court and one of the most expensive court cases in the history of the State. The plaintiffs took separate actions and the same lawyers did not represent them all. The action was settled when a €25.5 million repair fund was agreed. This case typifies the problems inherent in the current procedure whereby plaintiffs must initiate separate and individual claims seeking damages particular to his or her situation. The cost, delay and wasteful inefficiencies of this system are self-evident and work only to the advantage of lawyers, whose fees are mounting as long as the litigation continues.

While these examples are not necessarily environment-related, they suggest that it is in the interests of the State, in the interests of litigants, and in the interests of justice to embrace some form of MPA procedure to avoid the anomalous situations illustrated above. Cases where environmental harm is suffered by numerous victims and caused by an identifiable defendant or group of defendants are an obvious further example of where an MPA procedure would be of great assistance. Such a procedure would enhance access to justice and help surmount prohibitive obstacles such as the high litigation costs faced by individuals. These constitute gaps in Ireland's current litigation system, which arguably falls short in this respect of that of other EU Member States, particularly when viewed in light of the requirements of the Aarhus Convention.

3. Particular Difficulties with Multi-party Litigation in Ireland

Ireland does not have a very high level of private civil litigation because legal costs can be prohibitive. The issue of lawyers' fees is controversial in Ireland. There have been recent recommendations for reform in this area from Ireland's Competition Authority and further reform is envisaged in the pending Legal Services Regulation Bill 2011, by formalising an obligation for lawyers to outline costs to clients in advance.[32] Funding cases is a crucial area, and one with which litigants often have difficulty dealing. Owing to the failure of the Irish authorities to invest public resources in facilitating private civil litigation, the question of funding is a factor not only in relation to the issue of access to justice but also to considerations of fairness and the efficiency of the civil court system. Recognising that funding is so central, it is useful to look at key elements related to this issue.

[31] So far the total cost of the litigation for final claims amount to a cost of €278m, of which €184.5m comprises awards or settlements and €94m was paid by the State in legal costs. The overall cost borne by the Irish taxpayer has been €300m.

[32] No 58/2011.

A. Legal Aid

Ireland does not have a comprehensive and effective system for civil legal aid as it is limited to means-tested parties in family law and some limited civil litigation matters.[33] In theory, it is possible, under the guidelines for civil legal aid, to get funding for personal injury litigation where the criteria for assistance are met.[34] However, the means testing level set under the financial eligibility requirement test that applies to the funding available to the Legal Aid Board has meant that any such application would almost certainly fail. As a result, a body of so-called Middle Income Not Eligible for Legal Aid (MINELA) has developed in Ireland, and even those fulfilling the financial criteria for civil legal aid are very unlikely to succeed in securing it unless their case falls within a limited number of categories, notably family law and asylum law.[35] Environmental law areas fall outside these categories, although, arguably, it is an area that requires civil legal aid as parties who wish to bring actions are often acting in the public interest and not just on their own behalf. As such, the tradition of civil legal aid is significantly less generous and efficient than might be presumed. The Irish civil legal aid scheme specifically excludes test cases and MPAs of any sort, so it is not available for representative actions.[36]

In order to avoid the risk of ruinously expensive legal costs, litigants commonly proceed by using the device of 'men of straw'[37] for challenges under the Planning Acts and in common law and nuisance. There is a very limited additional funding scheme for those not eligible for civil or criminal legal aid called the Attorney General's Scheme, but this is not applicable to most civil legal cases.[38] Perhaps the Civil Legal Aid Act 1995 should be amended to allow funding of some of the improvised mechanisms of MPAs, for example representative actions, even if only on grounds of efficiency. The LRC recommended in its 2005 *Report on Multi-party Litigation* that this Act be amended to make provision for the funding of an otherwise eligible group member for his proportion of an eventual costs order. As for other litigants who are not eligible for civil legal aid, it seems that in order to avoid costs their best option remains to await a similar case, to be used as a test case, where litigants are willing to proceed despite lack of legal aid funding.

[33] For detail please see the section on Civil Legal Aid on the website for the Legal Aid Board at www.legalaidboard.ie.

[34] The Civil Legal Aid Act 1995 (No 32/1995) does not expressly exclude personal injury litigation.

[35] MINELA is a term coined under the civil legal aid system in England and Wales.

[36] The Civil Legal Aid Act 1995, s 28(9)(a)(ix) specifically excludes legal aid for 'matters as respects which the application for legal aid is made by or on behalf of a person who is a member and acting on behalf of a group of persons having the same interests in the proceedings concerned'.

[37] Those with extremely limited financial means, hence, no assets to risk losing if costs are awarded against them. It is possible to speculate that the more relaxed approach of the Irish courts to the proprietary interest requirement for *locus standi* in nuisance actions is a tacit recognition of the 'man of straw' plaintiff.

[38] For details of this please see the section on the Attorney General's Scheme at www.attorneygeneral.ie/ This Scheme provides payment for legal representation in certain types of legal cases not covered by the civil legal aid or criminal legal aid schemes. It is an *ex gratia* scheme set up with funds available from the Oireachtas. The Chief State Solicitor's Office administers application the Scheme. It generally covers: certain types of judicial review (relating to criminal matters); bail applications; extraditions including European Arrest Warrant applications; and *habeas corpus*.

B. Insurance

Litigation insurance is not generally available in Ireland. 'Before-the-event' (BTE) insurance is very uncommon in jurisdictions where, as a rule, costs follow the event and it is unheard of that anybody would take on 'after-the-event' insurance. If BTE legal expense insurance were to become widespread in this jurisdiction, this could act as a potential means of financing MPA litigation.

C. Costs Follow the Event

Finally, but crucially, costs generally follow the event, which means that the award will be made in favour of the successful party. Accordingly, the loser of a case usually has to pay the entire amount of the costs, which is a double financial burden, having to meet both sets of costs in the action. However, this is at the discretion of the presiding judge and is not a statutory requirement. The main problem with this serious litigation risk is that of having to meet the other side's costs as well as one's own. If MPAs were to be introduced there would have to be changes to how costs are currently decided. Furthermore, it should be noted that the standard rule that costs follow the event does not apply for certain environmental cases.[39]

D. Conditional Fee Arrangements (CFAs)

In Ireland it is illegal for barristers and solicitors to charge contingency fees based on a percentage or proportion of any award or settlement for a case, despite this being a common practice in other common law jurisdictions.[40] However there are occasions on which lawyers agree to represent clients on the basis of CFAs, which is permitted and is a common method of deferred payment for legal services, including in environmental cases.[41]

E. Advertising and the Irish Legal Profession

In relation to advertising, solicitors are allowed to advertise but there are severe restrictions, for instance advertising in respect of personal injury claims.[42] This would appear to suggest

[39] As discussed more fully by Ryall, 'Delivering the Rule of Environmental Law in Ireland' (n 2).

[40] Code of Conduct of the Bar of Ireland, s 12.1(e): 'Barristers may not accept instructions on condition that payment will be subsequently fixed as a percentage or other proportion of the amount awarded'.

[41] This label though is potentially misleading and must be explained further. Where costs follow the event, this term suggests that where the client is unsuccessful in the action, the solicitor will absorb the fees and if no damages are awarded then there is no fee. However, in fact, these agreements do not insulate the client from costs in the event that their case is unsuccessful. Instead, they merely defer the payment of these costs until the close of the action. This means that the client does not have to pay for representation at the beginning of the litigation, but the solicitor can later pursue the client for these costs as they remain as a debt due between the client and solicitor, although the solicitor may decide against the pursuit of these costs, which is often the case.

[42] The Solicitors Advertising Regulations 2002, SI 518/2002, were introduced pursuant to s 4 of the Solicitors (Amendment) Act 2002 (No 19/2002), which preserves the right of a solicitor to advertise, but severely restricts personal injuries advertising.

that such restrictions on advertising could certainly impact on solicitors running MPAs. However, notification of potential litigants does not pose too difficult a challenge in Ireland, owing to the small size of the jurisdiction.

4. Irish Law Reform Commission Report on Multi-party Litigation 2005—A Closer Look

As discussed above, this report followed on from the publication by the Commission in 2003 of a Consultation Paper on multi-party litigation.[43] The report focuses on the potential for reform of private multi-party litigation which, to date in Ireland, is usually proceeded by way of test cases. A comparative review of selected multi-party procedures from a variety of jurisdictions as well as current Irish arrangements for multi-party litigation was undertaken to inform this report. As already noted, the LRC concluded that, to date, ad hoc arrangements have been used to deal with the demands of multi-party litigation and that a more structured approach should be available in the form of the MPA. The LRC stated that its proposals for multi-party litigation are not to be considered as replacements for existing procedures, particularly the test case, but rather as providing an alternative procedure where this is more appropriate. Despite this recommendation, MPAs have yet to be introduced by the legislature.

The LRC recommended that any reform in this area should be based on principles of procedural fairness, efficiency and access to justice. Again, this anchors any reform in this area to the three objectives of MPAs identified by Mrs Justice Denham. In particular, the LRC recommended that there should be active case management by the courts, which is in keeping with the general trend in the reform of civil procedure such as those in the Woolf reform recommendations. This report was welcomed by the Free Legal Advice Centre, an Irish pro bono legal service, as well as by several senior members of the judiciary.[44]

The LRC Report recommended, inter alia:

— the introduction of a completely new procedure to be called a Multi-Party Action (MPA). The MPA would operate as a flexible tool to deal collectively with cases that are sufficiently similar, to be introduced by way of the Irish Rules of Court, where common issues among the individual actions are involved;
— the MPA procedure should operate on the basis of an opt-in system whereby individual litigants will be included in the group only where they decide to join the group action. This is very different, for instance, from the Canadian class action procedure in which individuals are deemed to be part of the class unless they opt out;
— MPAs would require certification by a court before they could become established;

[43] Irish Law Reform Commission, *Consultation Paper on Multi-Party Litigation* (LRC CP 25-2003)14.

[44] See www.flac.ie/download/pdf/dec04_lrc_class_actions.pdf. FLAC enthusiastically welcomed the Commission's recommendation to introduce MPAs, on the basis that to do so can only strengthen public interest litigation and increase access to justice. In particular, it notes the necessity of amending the Civil Legal Aid Act 1995 to allow for legal aid in representative actions. It emphasises that the objective of increasing access to justice should underpin all decisions taken in relation to the specifics of the procedure, including those relating to costs.

- — the court would certify the MPA only where it was considered to offer a fair and efficient means of resolving the common issues involved;
- — the court would establish an MPA Register containing a list of the cases in the MPA;
- — the court would, where appropriate, select lead cases to go forward as representative of those in the group;
- — the court would set a general cut-off date for entry into the MPA;
- — a single legal representative would be agreed by the MPA members or nominated by the court to deal with the common issues arising in the MPA;
- — the cost associated with the MPA would be spread among its members in equal measure; and
- — where an individual member of the MPA would have been eligible as an individual litigant for civil legal aid, they should continue to be eligible for aid to the extent of their share of the costs under an MPA and they will receive funding for this from the Irish Legal Aid Board.[45]

The LRC drafted an amendment to the Irish Rules of the Superior Courts to provide for the introduction of MPAs and also drafted an amendment bill to provide for civil legal aid for MPAs for those eligible for legal aid funding. The report's recommendations include the distinction between general issues in common and subsidiary issues (that individuals may wish to pursue otherwise) and also how to include small claims.[46] The LRC recommended that costs should be shared equally among a group so, in this way, it did not find a solution to the general problem of funding identified earlier in this chapter. It did, however, address the civil legal aid aspect of this barrier, by providing eligibility requirements for this aid for those who would otherwise qualify for civil legal aid and drafting amendments to provide for this in the Rules of Court. The Government has yet to adopt these recommendations by legislation. To date, no changes have been made to the Rules of Court. As mentioned earlier, it was predicted that, in circumstances where the State has been and is likely to be a regular defendant, it is likely that the State will be slow to introduce a MPA system.

5. Evaluation of Irish Mass Harm Mechanisms and MPA Objectives

In the absence of formal MPA Rules in Ireland, while it is still possible to use existing key mechanisms in combination to provide an alternative framework for MPAs, the resulting improvisation falls short of delivering the procedural justice contained in the aims of the MPA objectives. The LRC Report advocated that principles for reform in this area should ensure procedural fairness and practicality, procedural efficiency and access to justice.[47] The discussion below will concentrate on these three areas. Overall, the LRC supported the objectives for multi-party litigation procedure advocated by Hodges in his discussion of

[45] See further details at: www.legalaidboard.ie/lab/publishing.nsf/Content/Civil_Legal_Aid.

[46] Note Ireland already has a small claims court for disputes up to a value of €2,000, such as those involving consumers, which parties can take without the need to engage a lawyer.

[47] LRC Report (n 3).

Group Litigation Orders (GLOs) and the need for 'managerial mechanisms' that can enable procedural justice.[48]

A. Access to Justice

In discussing access to justice, the LRC stated that this has traditionally formed a central rationale behind the introduction of multi-party procedures. Under individual litigation (or within the test case model used in Ireland), costs are calculated for the entirety of the case on an individual level. With this approach, the potential exposure to costs orders may present a real disincentive to the institution of proceedings in the first place.[49] By contrast, where the cost of litigating the generic issue is calculated on the basis of a single incident and divided among a group of members, there will be substantial savings to be made at an individual level.[50] While considering access to justice as a laudable principle, the LRC was, however, wary to avoid inferring unrealistic guarantees from its status as a constitutional slogan.[51] The Irish Constitution holds the rule of law as a core concept of Ireland's legal system. It provides that everyone is subject to the law and its constitutional structure provides for the right of access to the courts and of access to justice. There has been much discussion recently about the high cost of litigation. One concern expressed was that not only those on legal aid and those of considerable financial means should have access, but that many litigants who potentially fall between these two categories should have access as well. The Irish Supreme Court recognised the constitutional right of access to the courts in the case of *McAuley v Minister for Posts and Telegraphs*. In that case, Mr Justice Kenny J held:

> [t]hat there is a right to have recourse to the High Court to defend and vindicate a legal right and that it is one of the personal rights of the citizen included in the general guarantee in Article 40.3, seems to me to be a necessary inference from Article 34.3.1 of the Constitution ... if the High Court has this full original jurisdiction ... it must follow that the citizens have a right to have recourse to that Court[52]

The LRC stated, however, that this constitutional right of access, recognised in *McCauley*, has never been considered absolute. It has operated, to date, to prevent unreasonable impediments being placed in the way of individuals wishing to litigate. The LRC qualified this by adding that this did not mean that a clear and unrestricted path needed to be provided for the litigant, as certain obstacles are necessary in the interest of the smooth operation of the judicial process and for the vindication of the rights of the other parties to the litigation.[53] It illustrated this point by reference to an example of a court striking out

[48] Ibid 1.53, 19, citing C Hodges, *Multi-Party Actions* (Oxford University Press, 2001) 68, ch 5 [11].

[49] See the discussion by the LRC on deferred payment of fees, the limitations of civil legal aid and legal expenses in LRC Report (n 3) ch 3.

[50] Ibid 20.

[51] Ibid.

[52] [1966] IR 345. In *State (McCormack) v Curran*, Finlay CJ stated that '[t]he right of access to the courts, stated in its broadest fashion, is the right to initiate litigation in the courts' (1987) ILRM 225; see also *Murphy v Greene* [1990] 2 IR 566 (McCarthy J).

[53] LRC Report (n 3) 20.

an action as frivolous or out of time.[54] In the LRC's opinion, so long as these impediments are not unreasonable, they are compatible with the constitutional principle of access to the courts. It viewed the issue of access to justice in the context of multi-party litigation in light of this backdrop and considered that a careful balance between the avoidance of undue impediments to legitimate litigation and the filtration from the system of frivolous actions is required.[55] Access to justice itself, therefore, does not seem to have been the primary objective of the LRC. While savings will be made on an individual basis as a result of the consolidation of the group action, naturally there remains an element of risk and potential financial exposure that exists in all litigation. Despite this, the LRC propounded that savings resulting from the efficiencies of multi-party procedures ensure that meaningful access to justice will be strengthened.[56] The LRC was mindful of developments in case management of litigation generally and the reforms recommended in England and Wales which intended to reduce the cost of such litigation by such means as the use of judicial management.[57]

In the opinion of Justice McGuinness, former President of the LRC, the Irish methods of dealing with multiple cases have led to some 'appalling situations because of the lack of multi-party actions' such as the army deafness litigation.[58] Ireland has had its access to justice record condemned previously in several landmark cases in the European Court of Human Rights. Probably the most significant example of this is the historic judgment in *Airey v Ireland*[59] where the court declared that the right of access to justice must not be 'theoretical and illusory' but 'practical and effective'.[60] Such issues have also arisen in the ECJ.[61] Notably, as discussed, the English Supreme Court made an order for reference in *R (Edwards and Pallikaropoulos) v Environment Agency and DEFRA*, the first case in which that court has had to consider the relationship between Article 9 of the Aarhus Convention, which requires that environmental litigation not be 'prohibitively expensive', and the normal rule under English (and Irish) civil procedure that an unsuccessful judicial review claimant should pay the respondent's costs.[62] The appellant argued in that case that for her to pay the respondents' costs would render the litigation prohibitively expensive.[63]

[54] The Statute of Limitations aims to strike the appropriate balance between the right to litigate, the interests of certainty and protection against outdated, historical claims.

[55] LRC Report (n 3) 21.

[56] Ibid.

[57] In 2 reports on civil procedure in the mid-1990s by Lord Woolf (see Lord Woolf, *Access to Justice Interim Report* (1995) and Lord Woolf, *Access to Justice Final Report* (1996)), which led to the enactment of the UK Civil Procedure Act 1997 and the Civil Procedure Rules 1998 (CPR).

[58] Hon Catherine McGuinness, former President of the Irish Law Reform Commission (Address to the 'Globalisation of Class Actions' Conference, Oxford University, December 2007).

[59] (1979) 2 EHRR 305.

[60] Ibid 314.

[61] As discussed by Ryall (n 2).

[62] *R (Edwards and Pallikaropoulos) v Environment Agency and DEFRA* [2010] UKSC 57. The Supreme Court had rejected Mrs Pallikaropoulos' application for a Protective Costs Order in advance of her appeal on the basis that, inter alia, insufficient information had been provided as to her financial means to conclude that the proceedings would be 'prohibitively expensive' for her. She nonetheless proceeded with her appeal. When it was dismissed, the Supreme Court ordered that she pay the respondents' costs (totalling around £88,000).

[63] [2010] UKSC 57.

B. Judicial and Procedural Economy

Procedural efficiency relates to savings that may be made without impacting on the central issue of procedural fairness and practicality, as discussed below. This efficiency should affect each individual within the group. An example given by the LRC is that of defendant liability and the ways in which multi-party treatment may save costs. This resembles the 'economies of scale' factors discussed by Woolf. The LRC recognised that it is a challenge for litigation to find an appropriate balance between procedural efficiency and broad procedural fairness.[64] It opined that, ideally, a multi-party procedure should render the system as efficient for the collective group as the demands for individual fairness will allow.

In terms of procedural efficiency, this was recognised by the LRC as one of the key principles for reform in this area. It would appear that case management is an essential element of any State's legal system as it enhances the service provided to the public and minimises inefficiencies. Case management is only a recent phenomenon in the Irish legal system and has been emerging since the mid-1990s. As there has been a surge in the volume of litigation since that period there is a clear need to develop efficiency. This increase in volume of work has been matched by the increased complexity of cases in this period. There has also been an increase in similar case litigation. The need for private MPAs is an obvious corollary in order to ensure the fundamental right of access to justice. A rare example of case management was seen in some of the Irish asbestos litigation.

C. Fairness

The LRC acknowledged that the need for procedural fairness is the core element in any multi-party litigation. In its view, any multi-party procedure should facilitate and not hinder the resolution of individual actions. It recommended that, while a single procedural structure under the management of a designated judge may be capable of dealing with the multi-party action, it is important to divide the various elements of a case into convenient categories that lend themselves to collective resolution. Procedural fairness is also important from the perspective of the defendant and the LRC recommended that this should entail transparency in terms of the future potential scope of the litigation and result in an appropriate reduction in associated costs.

The need for procedural fairness is a core element in any reform of multi-party litigation, as detailed by the LRC in its 2005 MPA Report.[65] Further, Article 6 of the European Convention on Human Rights requires protection of the right to a fair trial. In criminal cases and in cases to determine civil rights, Article 6 protects the right to a public hearing before an independent and impartial tribunal within a reasonable time, among other requirements. According to the LRC, as the boundaries of the procedure will be dictated by the individual cases within the collective group, a multi-party procedure should facilitate the resolution of individual actions.

[64] LRC Report (n 3) 18.
[65] Ibid.

D. Predictability, Deterrence and Compensation

From this discussion on Irish collective redress it would appear that the achievement of the additional MPA objectives of predictability, deterrence and compensation are compromised by the lack of MPA mechanism. These objectives have been examined in detail in chapter three and so will not be repeated in detail here. Suffice it to say that, without formal MPA procedures, those involved in mass harm litigation face huge unpredictability of outcome when they have to improvise with alternative procedures, such as test cases, in order to seek a remedy. Similarly, without MPA procedures, victims of mass harm may encounter difficulties in seeking to be awarded compensation by the courts for harm suffered. Compensation tribunals and redress schemes are of course among alternative routes to such compensation. It is important to note however, that, as discussed in chapter three, flexibility—and case management—can detract from predictability, and this is not acceptable in some legal systems (notably civil law). It would appear that the LRC may have recommended the introduction of a multi-party action procedure partly because its recommended procedure would encourage Irish civil procedure towards case management. Finally, as previously discussed, MPAs can play an important role in deterrence and enforcement. Without MPA procedures, the objective of deterrence may be harder to achieve.

6. Environmental Enforcement in Ireland

As the environment is a diffuse interest, it does not fit naturally within the framework that is traditionally recognised by the law for the protection of individual rights. Ireland's environmental law enforcement landscape is currently lacking in several areas in relation to both the formal and informal enforcement mechanisms available to citizens. In both law and practice, private individuals and NGOs are inclined to have a secondary role in the regulation of environmental matters, as compared to public authorities. There is considerable acknowledgement by the Irish legislature that individuals or groups can have an interest in the environment, despite the more prominent role played by the regulatory authorities in this area and the adjustments that have been made to deal with problems of legal standing and cost. Existing tools for citizen enforcement are, however, hampered by issues of accessibility and cost.

7. What May Lie Ahead

A. Developments in England and Wales

Perhaps pressure is building in Ireland because its closest neighbour, England and Wales, has introduced a mechanism to aid multi-party access to justice. Developments there are likely to be watched very closely in Ireland, particularly those surrounding the Group Litigation Order and the 2013 announcement of the introduction of collective actions for competition law infringements. Also, some recent cases examined in chapter eight on English collective redress demonstrate the courts there taking an innovative approach to such cases and not necessarily relying on the GLO. More recently however, as discussed in chapter eight, few group actions, let alone toxic tort claims, have been successfully initiated in the UK[66] given the complexity of evidence and the consequent costs of funding the action.[67] It should be noted that the LRC's report is in line with the Woolf reforms, so there is a broad consensus regarding the requirements of justice in civil litigation. Ireland may be belatedly following in the footsteps of the English legal system if it does proceed with (some of) the LRC's recommendations, taking the advice of the Woolf Report's primary recommendation for introduction of case management and also new provisions for multi-party litigation. However, as stated previously, it is quite possible that the State may find itself the defendant in such multi-party litigation and so it may remain averse to its introduction, particularly in the current economic climate.

B. Aarhus and Human Rights

The Irish legal landscape may well be forced to change as Ireland formally incorporated the European Convention on Human Rights into its legal system in 2003.[68] As noted above, Article 6 of the Convention provides for the right to a fair trial. Current legal mechanisms for mass harm arguably do not provide this. Furthermore, as Ireland was the last EU Member State to ratify the Aarhus Convention, questions of access to justice may well be raised by this lack of legal mechanism.

In examining the Aarhus Convention's implications, it is notable that the Aarhus Convention Compliance Committee (the ACCC) has handed down findings that the UK Government is making it too expensive for environmental campaigners to take cases through the English courts.[69] This statement could open the door to new rules in relation to legal costs and community groups wishing to take cases to the English and Welsh courts. Under the Convention, which was ratified by the UK in 2005, the UK Government is obliged to give rights and to remove financial barriers for citizens who wish to mount legal challenges. The ACCC found that the UK was failing to ensure court proceedings were not prohibitively expensive and that measures were required to overcome the financial barriers to accessing justice in environmental matters. These issues, as previously discussed in chapter eight on England and Wales, have also arisen in the ECJ, such as in the recent referral from the UK Supreme Court in the *Edwards* case.[70]

[66] See R Mulheron, 'Reform of Collective Redress in England and Wales: A Perspective of Need' (2008) Research Paper prepared for the Civil Justice Council of England and Wales.

[67] Since the introduction of the GLOs in 2000, although it has been possible for numerous claimants to pursue a group litigation action when there are common or closely related issues of fact and law, there are just 69 such actions listed on Her Majesty's Court Service website for 2010—about 7 each year—across all types of claim. According to Mulheron, the second highest category of these actions was environmental claims at 15%; Mulheron, 'Reform of Collective Redress in England and Wales' (n 66).

[68] European Convention of Human Rights Act 2003 (No 20/2003).

[69] ACCC/C/2008/33.

[70] *R (Edwards and Pallikaropoulos) v Environment Agency and DEFRA* (n 62).

While Aarhus relates to environmental matters specifically, the culture of procedural rights stemming from its requirements might well inform developments in terms of general litigation. The environmental arena as often been a trailblazer for the emergence of such procedural rights. Ireland provides an example of where the introduction of rules on freedom of access to environmental information, introduced to transpose a 1990 Directive on access to environmental information, preceded the introduction of a more general Freedom of Information Act,[71] which did not come into effect until 1997.[72] This example of a culture relating to procedural rights could inform the development of rules for general civil litigation.

C. EU Initiatives

In June 2013, as discussed in chapter nine on EU collective redress, the European Commission published its policy on collective redress. Ultimately, Ireland may have no choice but to be persuaded by these EU developments that may help finally make up its mind on MPAs. With such decisive moves at European level at this point Ireland may not have the luxury of waiting any longer and may be forced to row in with the EU approach.

8. Conclusions

The debate continues on whether MPA type procedures should be adopted in Ireland, including in environmental cases. As demonstrated, the Irish legal system currently does not provide a viable mechanism for multi-party litigation. Despite this void, multi-plaintiff personal injury litigation is not alien to Ireland. The army deafness cases and the current banking inquiry following the recent banking system collapse are examples of mass harm straining to find redress within existing, albeit deficient, litigation mechanisms. The asbestos litigation and pyrite litigation are early examples of environmental-type mass harm being litigated in Ireland, but it is only a matter of time before other such mass environmental harm matters will need to be litigated on a large scale level in Ireland.

In recommending the introduction of a multi-party procedure in the form of an MPA, the LRC's 2005 Report set out a scheme providing for a fair and efficient procedure to be executed under judicial supervision. As discussed, there are many advantages to such a procedural mechanism, including the reduction of the cost of litigating an issue and the overall cost of achieving a resolution. Further, scarce court resources could be used more efficiently. By avoiding repetitious court hearings and clogging up the already overburdened court system, the MPA would ultimately result in the saving of legal costs to all involved. Finally and most importantly, access to justice will be available to many who would otherwise have been excluded. It is obvious that the existing system of principally using test cases is ineffective. While it does militate against speculative claims, and ensures a full and fair

[71] Freedom of Information Act (No 13/1997).

[72] Directive (EC) 90/313/EEC OJ 1990 L 158/56 provided for access to environmental information. This Directive had been implemented in Ireland by means of various statutory instruments made in 1993, 1996 and 1998.

hearing to genuine claims, it is inefficient and results in what Mrs Justice McGuinness of the Irish Supreme Court termed 'appalling situations' because of the lack of MPAs.[73] It is not user-friendly and needs to go further to provide access to justice for all. Also urgently in need of adjustment in order to facilitate access to justice are the Irish costs and civil legal aid systems, although some reform may be provided in relation to costs if the pending Legal Services Regulation Bill 2011 is passed.[74] A key conclusion for Ireland for Ireland, however, would appear to be that, as a common law country, it may be unwise to adopt a collective action procedure without having case management and one or more very experienced judges who could conduct and control such litigation effectively, and one whose decisions were not regularly appealed. How realistic such a possibility is remains to be seen.

Furthermore, the impediment to access to justice in Ireland as a result of the lack of an effective procedural mass harm mechanism affects Ireland's ability to potentially comply with the Aarhus Convention. The availability of MPAs is crucial in the context of the overall EU environmental governance debate in terms of increasing access to justice more broadly for citizens, as well as all of the MPA objectives identified in this research. This state of flux is not particular to Ireland. Irish commentators will watch with great interest changes that are emerging in the US, England and Wales and at EU level. In the meantime, it seems without doubt that the time has come for Ireland to finally get in on the multi-party action, as without it there is a severe lacuna in the mechanisms for mass harm redress in Ireland.

[73] Hon Catherine McGuinness, former President of the Irish Law Reform Commission (Address to the 'Globalisation of Class Actions' Conference, Oxford University, December 2007).

[74] The Committee Stage of the promulgation of this Bill passed this legislation on 11 July 2014. The Report Stage before the Dail has yet to commence. According to the Department of Justice, the Enactment was expected to occur at some stage in early 2015 but is still outstanding.

11

Conclusion

This study commenced by exploring the phenomenon of mass harm. As we have seen, mass harm clearly presents many challenges. Collective redress tries to resolve the challenge of how a remedy for such harm may be sought. This research examines MPAs in particular as one of the mechanisms that may be used to achieve collective redress. Without some form of effective MPA, it is evident that there cannot be procedural justice and so MPAs play an important role in helping to deliver this. The role of MPAs is a topic of much debate in many common law jurisdictions. In this research it is assumed that there is damage that could be rectified by MPAs. Empirical evidence is required to establish this, however, and to clarify how many cases are not brought that could be brought, as well as determining how many cases are brought individually that could be handled more cheaply and quickly by MPA. A common theme that emerges from an examination of MPA procedures in the jurisdictions studied is that of the need for effective management of mass harm collective redress. This is essentially the overarching reason behind the need for MPA procedures.

The most obvious benefits of MPAs are that they present advantages in terms of access to justice, reduced and shared costs, as well as procedural efficiency. MPAs, however, are not without their difficulties. There is much evidence of this, as seen in the practical experience of the selected common law jurisdictions examined. Lord Woolf was cognisant of the inherent difficulties with multi-party procedures and that this mechanism was 'not a panacea but merely the next step forward in … hammering out ways of managing the unmanageable'. Despite these difficulties, there is still a huge need for mechanisms to deliver procedural justice. Examples of this need are manifold. The Irish Law Reform Commission (LRC) Report highlighted the need for procedural fairness as a core element in any multi-party litigation and cited Hodges' call for a 'managerial mechanism to move forward resolution of all the individual claims'.[1] There was strong emphasis in the LRC's approach on judicial case management of litigation, as recommended by the Committee on Court Practice and Procedure in 2003. The Civil Justice Council of England and Wales (CJC) Report echoed the reference by Lord Woolf and the LRC to access to justice as being one of the three key principles that should underpin a system of collective redress and espoused several principles reflecting Woolf's commitment to procedural justice now being as important as substantive justice, which guided the CJC to recommend collective redress reform.

In order to evaluate various MPA mechanisms, this research created an analytical framework of MPA objectives against which the effectiveness of MPAs could be assessed. These were used as touchstones against which to assess the various MPA mechanisms in the common law jurisdictions examined. It is clear that the collective nature of MPAs may assist

[1] C Hodges, *Multi-Party Actions* (Oxford University Press, 2001) 68 ch 5 [11].

plaintiffs to overcome difficulties in taking legal action because their greater combined resources may enable them to 'pool their resources' and deal with these challenges collectively. It explores how, paradoxically, it is possible that mass treatment, whether by judges or other bodies helping with collective redress, can sometimes achieve a more effective remedy for individuals either through court or by using other procedures that are evolving for the resolution of mass torts context, such as Alternative Dispute Resolution (ADR) and ombudsmen. MPAs can also aid enforcement. The difference between private and public enforcement must be highlighted to understand the roles that MPAs can play. In the US, MPA mechanisms are used as a form of 'private attorney general'. In Europe, enforcement is predominantly provided by public agencies and compensation may be pursued in some circumstances by way of a private action through some form of MPA.

The comparative examination of the selected common law jurisdictions helps to inform the understanding of how MPAs can operate in practice. The US MPA experience teaches broad lessons about MPA litigation. Extensive MPA litigation there is a necessarily intended result of US private enforcement policy. The criticism of US class actions, its side-effects of conflicts of interests and the resultant alleged widespread abuses are attributable to this.[2] There is also, however, a strong counter-argument that such 'abuse' criticism is unwarranted.[3] Some commentators credit class actions with a mission to provide 'ready, meaningful justice for the relatively disempowered in contemporary "massified" societies'.[4] Furthermore, there is an argument that class actions and other procedures for group litigation offer the potential for improving social welfare by generating economic benefits that exceed their costs, but that this potential has not been fully realised to date.[5] There is no easy answer to this debate. It is important to note that, as this research has shown, it can be increasingly difficult to get certification in the US and also that in the consumer field there has been a major shift towards arbitration and class arbitration. Notwithstanding this, the US experience of collective redress teaches invaluable lessons about the use of MPA and their effects. There appears to be a strong argument that they can assist with the management of mass harm.

Canada and Australia, outside of the US, are the two most notable jurisdictions that have adopted legislative changes to facilitate mass harm through collective action procedures for cases of mass torts. Kalajdzic states that class action is justified in Canada by its tripartite aim to promote judicial economy, to ensure behaviour modification and to increase access to justice.[6] It has been shown that although it is a procedural device, it is one with enormous potential to effect political, financial and social consequences.[7] The reform of class action procedure in Canada resulting from the Class Proceedings Act 1992 has enhanced procedures. As explained by the Supreme Court of Canada, this has enabled it to overcome

[2] eg defendants being blackmailed into settling weak cases and lawyers sometimes receiving comparatively more compensation than their clients.

[3] D Hensler, 'Third-Party Financing of Class Action Litigation in the United States: Will the Sky Fall?' (2014) 63 *De Paul L Rev* 1101.

[4] F Valdes, 'Procedure, Policy and Power: Class Actions and Social Justice in Historical and Comparative Perspective' (2008) 24 *Ga St UL Rev* 627, 648.

[5] See G Miller, 'Group Litigation in the Enforcement of Tort Law' in J Arden (ed), *Research Handbook on the Economics of Torts* (Edward Elgar, 2013) 262.

[6] J Kalajdzic (ed), *Accessing Justice, Appraising Class Actions, Ten Years After Dutton, Hollick & Rumley* (Lexis Nexis, 2011) 6.

[7] Ibid.

'procedural complexities ... to ensure that the courts had a procedural rule sufficiently refined to allow them to deal efficiently ... with the increasingly complicated cases of the modern era'.[8] This appears to support the view that Canadian class actions, as a form of MPA mechanism, have delivered enhanced procedural efficiency enabling better management of mass harm litigation. In summary of representative proceedings in Australia, they are now an established an important part of its legal landscape. This growth is as a result of several factors including Federal Government support for such proceedings, as well as third-party funding, increasingly plaintiff-friendly representative proceedings laws and the growth of plaintiff representative proceedings law practices. The inbuilt safeguards in the Australian system however, have helped to avoid what some feared would be an 'explosion' of class action suits. Notwithstanding this, as stated earlier, Australia has become the most likely jurisdiction in which a corporation will face significant MPA litigation, outside of the US. This is because of the relative ease with which such proceedings can be commenced in Australia and has led to actions being commenced in a wide variety of circumstances. It is important to remember that in Australia, the requirement that third-party funders need to have contracts with all group members so as to recover their fee, and the need to exclude 'free riders' and hence maximise the group membership, has led to a *reversal* of the initial opt-out model into a de facto opt-in model. This has really big implications. The Australian experience shows how MPA use can grow hugely if there is demand and therefore it is crucial that safeguards against abuse are included in any such mechanism.

While there is no fully-fledged collective action system in England and Wales yet, British courts have commented with regret on the absence of such mechanism in their own unaided efforts to structure alternative procedural techniques for mass tort claims.[9] Such comment, however, may have been more of an invitation than a plea for a mechanism, since the courts made up a procedure themselves, which was subsequently put into the rules by Lord Woolf. Also, successive governments have considered but largely rejected the introduction of such a mechanism: recent policy has been that the sectoral approach should be adopted, and the only sector in which a collective action has been mooted by government is that of competition law, where it forms only one part of a 'three pillar' policy. It is notable that many commentators focus only on the competition collective action element of this and omit the point that it is (almost certainly) a 'last resort' pathway, and that the new regulator's power is intended to be the first path. Unusually, the competition sector has no specific structure for ADR representation, but ADR is still encouraged, and practice is likely to evolve. Representative actions, group litigation and creative case management have helped in some way to fill this procedural void but the use of the GLO has not been invoked as much as might have been expected. In terms of the usage of the GLO, the outcome for claimants' success has been mixed, as often the legal costs far outweigh the damages and it seems that GLOs are not being used frequently in practice. In practice, it would appear that case management has been used more often as an alternative. We can perceive from this that perhaps MPAs are not being used as much as was expected and that the alternative routes to collective redress are taking their place so that litigation is becoming an option of last resort.

[8] *Hollick v Metropolitan Toronto (Municipality)* (2001) SCC 68, 205 DLR (4th) 19 (SCC) [14].

[9] eg *Nash v Eli Lilly* [1993] 4 All ER 383, 409J (CA), where it was stated that 'There may well be a strong case for legislative action to provide a jurisdictional structure for the collation and resolution of mass product liability claims, particularly in the pharmaceutical field'. See further J Fleming, 'Mass Torts' (1994) 42 *Am J Comp L* 508.

Instead of litigation mechanisms, alternative routes of enforcement have been pursued with success, indicating that collective redress can be achieved in ways other than through the use of aggregate litigation. It does appear that in some circumstances, mass harm cases present logistical difficulties and that there is a need for managerial mechanisms to help surmount these challenges. The *Corby* and *Buncefield* case studies illustrate the advantages that can be conferred by the use of management mechanisms such as MPAs or case management techniques. This is discussed in detail also in section four of chapter three, which highlights the importance of management techniques in cases of mass harm. It is important to compare cases in which some predictability is given by having a clear procedure with those in which managerial flexibility is important, as exemplified by *Corby* and *Buncefield*. Like the US trend towards MDL noted previously, the GLO is located firmly within a matrix of judicial case management. *Buncefield* demonstrates that, in at least some circumstances, a flexible case management power is all that is required to deal with litigation. It is important to note, however, that flexibility—and case management—detract from predictability, and this is not acceptable in some legal systems (notably civil law). Overall, there are important lessons to be learnt about MPA litigation from the experience of the common law jurisdictions. It is evident that in suitable cases, such procedures have the potential to increase the efficiency of litigation, enhance enforcement and compensate victims of mass harm. While this potential is not always realised, MPA litigation, despite its shortcomings, can offer managerial assistance in cases of mass harm. What is becoming clear from this is that there is a strong need for a managerial tool to ease the difficulties of dealing with mass harm cases.

As we have seen, the US class action is the original class action model. It has certain distinguishing features, such as incentives and few barriers—for claimants and intermediaries to bring actions. In contrast, such incentive and barrier features are not found—and a positively different balance is favoured—in the EU. The European perception of the US class action system seems to be that it encourages excess and abuse. From the explanation of the US enforcement architecture compared with that of the EU, it is clear that Europe takes a polar opposite standpoint to that of the US. The reasons why the US and EU adopt these different policies towards litigation are a function of the political balance that is adopted by a State between public and private enforcement and there are political considerations that underlie the difference in choice, such as whether private enforcement is desired as a form of regulation. This choice has political implications; for example, a preference for public enforcement requires a regulatory system and structures that can support this approach. As we have seen from the protracted debate in this area, a balance must be achieved at both EU level and within Member States about how enforcement policy is to be divided between private and public actors. This will dictate how collective redress mechanisms can be used in legal systems. EU jurisdictions provide for both public and private enforcement. European Member State experience shows, however, that collective actions are falling out of favour and that, instead, ADR and other emerging innovative collective redress techniques are being used. It appears that achieving collective redress through alternatives to litigation, particularly the use of ombudsmen and ADR, is indicative of the future of EU collective redress. Such mechanisms avoid the difficulties inherent in the court process and can be arguably more efficient than traditional litigation and provide a less formal, less intimidating way of resolving disputes.[10] This appears to suggest that, in appropriate cases,

[10] F Iacobucci, 'What is Access to Justice in the Context of Class Actions' in Kalajdzic, *Accessing Justice* (n 6) 24.

collective redress may be more easily achieved outside of the courts, which may provide a more efficient, private and consequently, preferable solution. It would appear that the EU collective redress policy, by advocating a degree of case management and the use of collective actions as a last resort, where other enforcement mechanisms fail, recognises the need for mechanisms to manage mass harm litigation.

As demonstrated by the Irish experience of mass harm redress, it is evident that there are cases of mass harm occurring in that jurisdiction and that there is a need for an efficient procedural mechanism to manage this reality. The Irish experience indicates that owing to the lack of such mechanism, other methods have to be used by way of improvisation in order to actuate this. The appalling delay, cost and injustice evidenced by the experience of victims of Pyrite damage or Thalidomide, for example, show that this current practice is causing much difficulty. There are likely to be underlying policy reasons on the part of the legislature for Ireland's reticence in relation to adopting MPAs, despite the recommendations by the LRC that they should be introduced. One reason is likely to be the aim of discouraging large-scale litigation. Another reason is possibly to avoid the State being defendant in such action. The Swedish experience indicates that more claims are taken against governments as well as private parties if there are MPAs, so this is not an improbable risk.[11] The MPA experience from other jurisdictions illustrates the extent to which MPA procedural mechanisms can enhance procedural justice, in appropriate cases. This experience may inform the metaphysical question of whether Ireland ought to adopt an MPA mechanism to remedy the current procedural lacuna. It would appear that the Irish Law Reform Commission may have recommended the introduction of a multi-party action procedure partly because its recommended procedure would encourage Irish civil procedure towards case management. A key conclusion for Ireland, however, would appear to be that, as a common law country, it may be unwise to adopt a collective action procedure without having case management and one or more very experienced judges who could conduct and control such litigation effectively, and one whose decisions were not regularly appealed. How realistic such a possibility is remains to be seen.

A crucial factor in relation to access to justice through MPAs is the issue of funding. The specific funding challenges where they are discussed in the context of each jurisdiction and generally give further evidence of this.[12] For example, claims cannot be brought in the US without contingency fees and the fact that there is no cost shifting. This is also the case in Canada were it not for contingency fees, consortia of funders, costs only being enforceable against representative claimants, and the use of the device of 'men of straw' to defeat cost shifting.[13] In Australia, the difficulties of funding have largely been alleviated by the introduction of third-party funding, with representative plaintiffs being 'men of straw'. Historically, funding has been a very large stumbling block in England and Wales and an ongoing problem in Ireland due to the lack of legal aid. Overall, funding of MPAs is absolutely critical and is closely affected by the prevailing costs regime. Ultimately, private funding in a loser pays system that has no or limited legal aid can only be through lawyers (through contingency fees) or through other funding intermediaries (such as insurers or investors). So this research identifies that there is a policy choice between allowing funding

[11] C Hodges, 'Collective Redress: A Breakthrough or Damp Squibb? (2014) 37 *J Consum Policy* 86.
[12] See eg ch 4, s 2 B.
[13] See further ch 6, s 2.

by intermediaries and the risk that it will lead to conflicts of interest and the potential threat of abuse that is too great. If MPAs are to be encouraged, then liberal funding conditions must exist but then abuse must be expected and safeguards will be necessary to prevent it. If there are too many safeguards then the MPA mechanism will be restricted. Hodges believes that it is not possible to calibrate safeguards so as to have just enough access to justice and not too much abuse.[14] For this reason, it would appear that Gidi's opinion that 'class actions can succeed in the absence of discovery, contingency fees, the American cost rule, an entrepreneurial bar, and powerful and active judges, at least as effectively as can traditional individual litigation' is clearly misplaced.[15] So this dilemma is a real 'catch 22'. Ultimately, the US has decided that it is in favour of private enforcement, but the EU does not prioritise private enforcement, and uses it in a much more restricted role, certainly in relation to 'deterrence' (ie regulation), so this explains the difference between the opposing US and EU positions. Australia and Canada have clearly chosen to follow the US model. For these reasons, it would appear that funding and costs rules are far more important than detailed procedural aspects. We must be cognisant of the fact that in Australia, the requirement that third-party funders need to have contracts with all group members so as to recover their fee, and the need to exclude 'free riders' and hence maximise the group membership, has led to a *reversal* of the initial opt-out model into a de facto opt-in model.

The expert studies examined in this research suggest that access to justice is the key goal of MPAs. It would appear that traditional national civil justice systems are not designed to provide effective access to justice for mass harm events. Cappelletti saw access to justice evolving in three successive, but overlapping, 'waves' to accommodate mass claims: State funding (legal aid); introduction of class or collective action procedures; and mediation and ADR techniques for collective redress.[16] The evolution of civil justice in the European context seems to be seeing those three stages of evolution.[17] If so, increasingly, ADR may appear to be supplanting class actions as a remedy.

The types of claim for which MPAs may be sought vary broadly and as this research shows, can comprise harm in the following areas: consumer, competition, financial services, securities, communications, property disputes, environmental, claims against government and personal injuries. MPAs do not always assist in all of these claims. For example, as the US experience has found, some claims inherently involve individual issues (such as representations and reliance in mis-selling cases, or individual causation and extent of damage in personal injury cases), so a collective approach is not necessarily of assistance in such cases. Certain types of claims have been found by experience not to fit MPAs well. An example of this is the lack of success in Canada in certifying health claims and therefore environmental health claims.[18] That experience repeats that of the US class action, that where individual issues predominate, aggregation is of little help in achieving judicial economy. Individual issues predominate in many personal injuries cases, for example, the need to deal with

[14] Hodges, 'Collective Redress' (n 11) 72.

[15] A Gidi, 'Class Actions in Brazil—A Model for Civil Law Countries' (2003) 51 *Am J Comp L* 322.

[16] R Money-Kryle, 'The Origins and Roles of Class Action Laws across the World: What Types of Problem do they Deal with, and what Safeguards do they Have?' ('Building Effective Markets—the Role of an Integrated Legal System' Conference, Zurich, January 2013).

[17] Ibid.

[18] As courts remain reluctant to certify health-related environmental issues because of the importance of individual issues; see further ch 6, s 4.

individual causation, and quantum (even if of a defective drug or procedure). Similarly, investor cases may require individual reliance on a misrepresentation to be proved. Similarly, it is important to clarify how management techniques may be 'dispositive', as asserted by Hodges. By that, he was asserting that a generic inquiry could not be dispositive of cases that involved significant elements of individual facts. It would appear that English judges generally agreed, as they do not like to preside over broad preliminary product liability claims, for example that a drug might be dangerous, if there would be a need for extensive later analysis of the merits of individual cases, some of which turned out not to have good individual merits. From the various types of disaster identified in this research, such as single-event, serial/creeping injuries and toxic damage, it appears that Fleming's conclusion about collective treatment of such mass harm is correct.[19] The first category, first (single events) poses least problems to traditional tort remedies. In most cases, causation is straightforward and contributory negligence is seldom a factor. For these reasons, it is easy to consolidate claims as they all concern the same operative facts. The second category (creeping disasters), he asserts, is vastly more challenging to legal process. In addition to the hurdles in the first category, there are added issues of causation (including possibly multiple causes), as well as possible consumer misuse of the product and often latency of injuries. These require individualised handling for each separate claimant, which does not facilitate aggregative resolution. The third category (toxic or environmental torts) is beleaguered by even more problems.[20] It would appear that mass tort actions also are not effective for similar reasons.

Environmental mass harm is one area in which mass harm presents particular difficulties for claimants seeking collective redress. The use of MPAs as mechanisms to help to overcome these difficulties was assessed. Large environmental and toxic tort cases entail challenges for litigants and judges alike due to the complexity and cost of technical evidence. Environmental mass harm presents typical examples of circumstances in which the handling of multiple claims can give rise to common or related issues of fact or law and the clustering of such claims strengthens individual claims. The collective treatment of environmental mass harm cases may alleviate some of these difficulties. As both *Corby* and *Buncefield* showed, claimants in mass environmental harm cases can benefit from efficient case management. This may be through the use of GLO or creative case management, particularly for fact management.[21] *Corby*, for example, demonstrated how the obstacles of mass harm litigation that may confound individuals could sometimes be overcome as part of a group action. There the claimants were able to overcome difficulties inherent in dealing with technical scientific evidence, such as trying to establish causation, individually. Instead, by dealing with such issues collectively, a GLO produced an efficient result and yet the individuals still maintained their own claims, though actions were grouped together for technical requirements. A GLO seems best suited to a multi-party toxic tort action where similar injuries have occurred. Case management was seen in *Buncefield* and

[19] Fleming, 'Mass Torts' (n 9) 508.

[20] Difficulties encountered in environmental mass harm and toxic torts are discussed in ch 4.

[21] Fact management in group actions is one complexity, as is the assessment of quantum for loss of amenity. In cases such as these there can be hundreds of individual cases which all raise the same issues. Fact management is therefore complex but crucial. The challenge is to ensure that the claims are assessed efficiently, economically and proportionately: J Thornton, 'Group Actions for Private Nuisance: Fact Management and Assessing Quantum for Loss of Amenity' *e-law* November 2012. See: www.lexology.com

proved a preferable solution where varying injuries occur and issues such as causation cannot easily be resolved collectively.

It would appear that the best solution in order to try to achieve MPA objectives for mass environmental harm is to have the widest range of possible legal remedies in order to deter pollution, to compensate harm and to protect the environment. There are of course problems of mass toxic tort litigation where improvements could be made, as mass treatment differs from traditional adversarial cases.[22] It would appear that the findings for environmental mass harm seem to be very different from other mass harms. As this discussion has shown, environmental mass harm has various complexities and peculiarities that render it difficult for individuals to benefit from MPA treatment, as compared to other areas of mass harm (such as mass harm resulting in 'scattered damages', consumer mass harm, competition law infringements) that lend themselves to resolution through collective treatment. As for solutions that MPAs may offer for environmental mass harm, the evidence would appear to suggest the conclusion that MPAs might be a largely illusory tool for remedying such harm. It has been demonstrated, for example, that MPAs for mass environmental harm are of limited use in Canada as they are unlikely to be certified there. In Europe it is a plausible conclusion that the MPA looks like it may not be the most suitable route to collective redress for mass environmental harm. Overall however, while mass litigation is not necessarily the solution to environmental mass harm claims, it would appear that environmental mass harm could benefit from the managerial advantages that MPAs can confer.

It appears that MPAs still have their place in the litigation landscape and can, in fact, be required to assist with the management of mass harm litigation. If such a mechanism is to be in the form of a collective action it will require inbuilt safeguards to protect against abuse. In terms of safeguards that should be adopted, we can learn from other common law jurisdictions and their experience of the need for prerequisites such as superiority, commonality and adequacy of representation. As for notice, this should be required for collective action procedures. Whether procedures should be opt-in or opt-out will depend on the circumstances, but both should be possible.[23] Ideally, standing should be reserved for associations or government agencies, so that individuals need not be involved in financing a collective action. Also, as contingency fees tend create a risk of conflicts of interest because they invest lawyers with a personal stake in the result of the litigation, the best way to avoid this is to prohibit such arrangements. Overall, MPAs ought to give judges strong managerial powers to deal with these actions, to help them deal with whatever the circumstances of the case may require.

Collective actions alone are an outdated approach for dealing with the problem of mass harm and they are clearly not the most efficient route to justice. Therefore collective actions are not a silver bullet that can be used by the masses to achieve collective redress. The role

[22] For scientific, substantive and administrative reasons.

[23] Group litigation presumes a definite decision to litigate: N Andrews, 'Multi-Party Proceedings in England: Representative and Group Actions' (2001) 11 *Duke Int'l & Comp L* 249, 260. This is in clear contrast to class actions, which usually contain opt-out mechanisms and also in contrast to representative actions, which do not require any decision by those being represented.

of judges is to clarify the law and to deliver justice. It is clear that in some cases they need assistance from managerial mechanisms to help them to deal with multiple cases. However, the courts are not the only forum in which to resolve legal disputes and the collective redress sphere includes preferable alternatives that can take various guises including ADR and ombudsmen. A modern, holistic approach is required to achieve collective redress for mass harm from a range of solutions. Collective actions or some managerial form of MPA certainly has its place within this range. The successful use of MPA and ADR mechanisms in EU Member States, in appropriate circumstances, is indicative of their suitability as routes to achieving collective redress and that they still have a role in helping to deliver this.

From this evaluation, the merits and demerits of the various forms of MPAs are clear. If mass claims occur in the legal system, however, judges do need managerial mechanisms to deal with them effectively. For this reason where MPAs are required, they should be possible. They should, however, only be available where there is requirement for such a mechanism because, as we have seen in the US, there are negative aspects to using MPAs as the main means of enforcement. Litigation is not the only way of delivering collective redress, as evidenced by the discussion surrounding EU collective redress policy and EU Member State evidence. In summary, it seems that MPA litigation is necessary as a remedy of last resort to deal with mass harm where other techniques fail to deliver collective redress and where there is therefore no alternative to the courts. This conclusion is provisional, however, as it can only be supported by an analysis of data on costs, duration and outcomes in a comparison of all available models (various forms of ADR, regulatory powers and so on). This conclusion is therefore a possibility, that would need to be established through a wider comparative analysis requires that is far beyond what this work can tackle. The optimum way of achieving collective redress requires an integrated model comprising a combination of tools including regulation, ADR, courts, ombudsmen, among others. This would prevent abuse and allow the key aspects of justice to be delivered in an efficient and accessible way, including the achievement of the MPA objectives identified in this study. Hopefully this is what the new EU collective redress policy will achieve in practice, but until it is implemented in Member States in practice, there is no evidence of how effective this collective redress policy will be.

APPENDIX: FEDERAL RULES OF CIVIL PROCEDURE 2016 EDITION

Rule 23—Class Actions

(a) **Prerequisites.** One or more members of a class may sue or be sued as representative parties on behalf of all members only if:

(1) the class is so numerous that joinder of all members is impracticable;
(2) there are questions of law or fact common to the class;
(3) the claims or defenses of the representative parties are typical of the claims or defenses of the class; and
(4) the representative parties will fairly and adequately protect the interests of the class.

(b) **Types of Class Actions.** A class action may be maintained if Rule 23(a) is satisfied and if:

(1) prosecuting separate actions by or against individual class members would create a risk of:
 (A) inconsistent or varying adjudications with respect to individual class members that would establish incompatible standards of conduct for the party opposing the class; or
 (B) adjudications with respect to individual class members that, as a practical matter, would be dispositive of the interests of the other members not parties to the individual adjudications or would substantially impair or impede their ability to protect their interests;
(2) the party opposing the class has acted or refused to act on grounds that apply generally to the class, so that final injunctive relief or corresponding declaratory relief is appropriate respecting the class as a whole; or
(3) the court finds that the questions of law or fact common to class members predominate over any questions affecting only individual members, and that a class action is superior to other available methods for fairly and efficiently adjudicating the controversy. The matters pertinent to these findings include:
 (A) the class members' interests in individually controlling the prosecution or defense of separate actions;
 (B) the extent and nature of any litigation concerning the controversy already begun by or against class members;
 (C) the desirability or undesirability of concentrating the litigation of the claims in the particular forum; and
 (D) the likely difficulties in managing a class action.

(c) **Certification Order; Notice to Class Members; Judgment; Issues Classes; Subclasses.**

(1) Certification Order.
  (A) *Time to Issue.* At an early practicable time after a person sues or is sued as a class representative, the court must determine by order whether to certify the action as a class action.
  (B) *Defining the Class; Appointing Class Counsel.* An order that certifies a class action must define the class and the class claims, issues, or defenses, and must appoint class counsel under Rule 23(g).
  (C) *Altering or Amending the Order.* An order that grants or denies class certification may be altered or amended before final judgment.
(2) Notice.
  (A) *For (b)(1) or (b)(2) Classes.* For any class certified under Rule 23(b)(1) or (b)(2), the court may direct appropriate notice to the class.
  (B) *For (b)(3) Classes.* For any class certified under Rule 23(b)(3), the court must direct to class members the best notice that is practicable under the circumstances, including individual notice to all members who can be identified through reasonable effort. The notice must clearly and concisely state in plain, easily understood language:
    (i) the nature of the action;
    (ii) the definition of the class certified;
    (iii) the class claims, issues, or defenses;
    (iv) that a class member may enter an appearance through an attorney if the member so desires;
    (v) that the court will exclude from the class any member who requests exclusion;
    (vi) the time and manner for requesting exclusion; and
    (vii) the binding effect of a class judgment on members under Rule 23(c)(3).
(3) *Judgment.* Whether or not favorable to the class, the judgment in a class action must:
  (A) for any class certified under Rule 23(b)(1) or (b)(2), include and describe those whom the court finds to be class members; and
  (B) for any class certified under Rule 23(b)(3), include and specify or describe those to whom the Rule 23(c)(2) notice was directed, who have not requested exclusion, and whom the court finds to be class members.
(4) *Particular Issues.* When appropriate, an action may be brought or maintained as a class action with respect to particular issues.
(5) *Subclasses.* When appropriate, a class may be divided into subclasses that are each treated as a class under this rule.

(d) Conducting the Action.

(1) *In General.* In conducting an action under this rule, the court may issue orders that:
  (A) determine the course of proceedings or prescribe measures to prevent undue repetition or complication in presenting evidence or argument;
  (B) require—to protect class members and fairly conduct the action—giving appropriate notice to some or all class members of:
    (i) any step in the action;

(ii) the proposed extent of the judgment; or
(iii) the members' opportunity to signify whether they consider the representation fair and adequate, to intervene and present claims or defenses, or to otherwise come into the action;

(C) impose conditions on the representative parties or on intervenors;
(D) require that the pleadings be amended to eliminate allegations about representation of absent persons and that the action proceed accordingly; or
(E) deal with similar procedural matters.

(2) *Combining and Amending Orders.* An order under Rule 23(d)(1) may be altered or amended from time to time and may be combined with an order under Rule 16.

(e) **Settlement, Voluntary Dismissal, or Compromise**. The claims, issues, or defenses of a certified class may be settled, voluntarily dismissed, or compromised only with the court's approval. The following procedures apply to a proposed settlement, voluntary dismissal, or compromise:

(1) The court must direct notice in a reasonable manner to all class members who would be bound by the proposal.
(2) If the proposal would bind class members, the court may approve it only after a hearing and on finding that it is fair, reasonable, and adequate.
(3) The parties seeking approval must file a statement identifying any agreement made in connection with the proposal.
(4) If the class action was previously certified under Rule 23(b)(3), the court may refuse to approve a settlement unless it affords a new opportunity to request exclusion to individual class members who had an earlier opportunity to request exclusion but did not do so.
(5) Any class member may object to the proposal if it requires court approval under this subdivision (e); the objection may be withdrawn only with the court's approval.

(f) **Appeals**. A court of appeals may permit an appeal from an order granting or denying class-action certification under this rule if a petition for permission to appeal is filed with the circuit clerk within 14 days after the order is entered. An appeal does not stay proceedings in the district court unless the district judge or the court of appeals so orders.

(g) **Class Counsel**.

(1) *Appointing Class Counsel.* Unless a statute provides otherwise, a court that certifies a class must appoint class counsel. In appointing class counsel, the court:

(A) must consider:

(i) the work counsel has done in identifying or investigating potential claims in the action;
(ii) counsel's experience in handling class actions, other complex litigation, and the types of claims asserted in the action;
(iii) counsel's knowledge of the applicable law; and
(iv) the resources that counsel will commit to representing the class;

(B) may consider any other matter pertinent to counsel's ability to fairly and adequately represent the interests of the class;

(C) may order potential class counsel to provide information on any subject pertinent to the appointment and to propose terms for attorney's fees and nontaxable costs;
(D) may include in the appointing order provisions about the award of attorney's fees or nontaxable costs under Rule 23(h); and
(E) may make further orders in connection with the appointment.

(2) *Standard for Appointing Class Counsel.* When one applicant seeks appointment as class counsel, the court may appoint that applicant only if the applicant is adequate under Rule 23(g)(1) and (4). If more than one adequate applicant seeks appointment, the court must appoint the applicant best able to represent the interests of the class.
(3) *Interim Counsel.* The court may designate interim counsel to act on behalf of a putative class before determining whether to certify the action as a class action.
(4) *Duty of Class Counsel.* Class counsel must fairly and adequately represent the interests of the class.

(h) **Attorney's Fees and Nontaxable Costs.** In a certified class action, the court may award reasonable attorney's fees and nontaxable costs that are authorized by law or by the parties' agreement. The following procedures apply:

(1) A claim for an award must be made by motion under Rule 54(d)(2), subject to the provisions of this subdivision (h), at a time the court sets. Notice of the motion must be served on all parties and, for motions by class counsel, directed to class members in a reasonable manner.
(2) A class member, or a party from whom payment is sought, may object to the motion.
(3) The court may hold a hearing and must find the facts and state its legal conclusions under Rule 52(a).
(4) The court may refer issues related to the amount of the award to a special master or a magistrate judge, as provided in Rule 54(d)(2)(D).

(As amended Feb. 28, 1966, eff. July 1, 1966; Mar. 2, 1987, eff. Aug. 1, 1987; Apr. 24, 1998, eff. Dec. 1, 1998; Mar. 27, 2003, eff. Dec. 1, 2003; Apr. 30, 2007, eff. Dec. 1, 2007; Mar. 26, 2009, eff. Dec. 1, 2009.)

BIBLIOGRAPHY

Agyeman J and Evans B, 'Just Sustainability: the Emerging Discourse of Environmental Justice in Britain' (2004)170 No. 2 *The Geographical Journal* 155.

Alberta Law Reform Institute Report 'Report on Class Actions, Final Report No 85, Dec 2000' (AltaLRI Report).

Alkadamani R, 'The Beginnings of "Class Actions"?' (1992) 8 *Australian Bar Review* 271.

Allens *Focus*, 'High Court Gives Green Light to Litigation Funding' (August 2006).

——, Yet Another Tick for Litigation Funding' (October 2009).

Andrews N, 'Multi-Party Proceedings in England: Representative and Group Actions' (2001) 11 *Duke Journal of International & Comparative Law* 249.

Arden J (ed), *Research Handbook on the Economics of Torts* (Edward Elgar, 2013).

Ashford N, *Crisis in the Workplace: Occupational Disease and Injury* Report to the Ford Foundation (1976).

Australian Law Reform Commission (ALRC), *Managing Justice* (Rep No 89, 1994) 7.90.

Ayers I and Braithwaite J, *Responsive Regulation* (Oxford University Press, 2002).

Backhaus J, Cassonne A and Ramello G (eds), *The Law of Economics and Class Actions in Europe: Lessons from America* (Edward Elgar, 2005).

Baert K and Guindon A, 'Class Proceedings in Ontario: the Growing Risk of Adverse Costs Awards Against Representative Plaintiffs' (Paper presented at the 5th Annual Symposium on Class Actions, Toronto, April 2008).

Baker R and Markoff M, 'By-Products Liability: Using Common Law Private Actions To Clean Up Hazardous Waste Sites' (1986) 10 *Harvard Environmental Law Review* 99.

Balen P, Cartwright F and Dickens H, 'Group Actions in a Product Liability Context' [1994] 140 *Consumer Law Journal* 1999.

Bälz M and Blobel F, 'Collective Litigation German Style: The Act on Model Proceedings in Capital Market Disputes' in E Gottschalk and others (eds), *Conflict of Laws in a Globalized World* (Cambridge University Press, 2007).

Barling G, 'Collective Redress for Breach of Competition Law: A Case for Reform?' (2011) 10 *Competition Law Journal* 5–20.

Barnes D and Conley J, *Statistical Evidence in Litigation* (Little, Brown and Co, 1986, supp 1989).

Bernstein A, 'Formed by Thalidomide: Mass Torts as a False Cure for Toxic Exposure' (1997) 97 *Columbia Law Review* 7.

Bernstein D, 'Getting to Causation in Toxic Tort Cases' (2008) 74 *Brooklyn Law Review* 1.

Bernstein R, 'Judicial Economy and Class Actions' (1978) 4 *Journal of Legal Studies* 349.

Betts J, *Mass Toxic Tort Litigation and Class Action Rule Reform in the United States* (Bepress Legal Series, 2003).

Bignmai F, 'Cooperative Legalism and the Non-Americanization of European Regulatory Styles: The Case of Data Privacy' (2011) 59 *American Journal of Comparative Law* 411.

Bogart W, 'Questioning Litigation's Role—Courts and Class Actions in Canada' (1986) 62 *Indiana Law Journal* 665.

——, Kalajdzic J and Matthews I, *Class Actions in Canada: A National Procedure in a Multi-Jurisdictional Society?* (A report prepared for 'The Globalisation of Class Actions' Conference, Oxford University, December 2007).

Boston G and Madden, S, *Law of Environmental and Toxic Tort Cases: Cases, Materials and Problems* (West Academic Publishing Boston, 2005).
Branch W, *Class Actions in Canada* (Canada Law Book, 2007).
Broderick L, 'Class Actions—Opting In or Out of the Bandwagon' (Accountancy Ireland Archive, 2005).
Bullard R, *Dumping in Dixie: Race, Class and Environmental Quality* (Westview Press, 2000).
Bullard R and Wright B, 'The Quest for Environmental Equity: Mobilizing the Black Community for Social Change' (1990) 3 *Race, Poverty and Env't* 5–16.
Burke T, *Lawyers, Lawsuits and Legal Rights* (University of California Press, 2002).
Cafaggi F and Micklitz HW (eds), *New Frontiers of Consumer Protection. The Interplay between Private and Public Enforcement* (Intersentia, 2009).
—— and Muir Watt H (eds), *The Regulatory Function of European Private Law* (Edward Elgar, 2009).
Camp J and Matthews S, 'Actions Brought Under the Class Proceedings Act, RSBC, 1995, c 50' in CLE Society of BC, *Torts—1998 Update* (1998) 23.
Cappelletti M, 'Social and Political Aspects of Civil Procedure—Reforms and Trends in Western and Eastern Europe' (1971) 69 *Michigan Law Review* 847.
Caruana J, Morabito J and Morabito V, 'Turning the Spotlight on Class Representatives—Empirical Insights from Down Under' (2012) 30 *Windsor Ybk of Access to Justice* 1–38.
Cashman P, *Class Action Law and Practice* (Federation Press, 2007).
Civic Consulting, *Study on the Use of Alternative Dispute Resolution in the European Union* (2009).
Civil Justice Council of England and Wales, *Improving Access to Justice through Collective Actions: Developing a More Efficient and Effective Procedure for Collective Actions* (2008).
Coffee J, 'Class Wars: The Dilemma of the Mass Tort Class Action' (1995) 95 *Columbia Law Review* 1343.
——, 'Reforming the Securities Class Action: An Essay on Deterrence and its Implementation' (2006) 106 *Columbia Law Review* 1534.
Colopy J, 'The Road Less Travelled: Pursuing Environmental Justice Through Title VI of the Civil Rights Act' (1994) 13 *Stanford Environmental Law Journal* 125–89.
Commoner B, 'The Hazards of Risk Assessment' (1989) 14 *Columbia Journal of Environmental Law.* 365–66.
Commission (EC), 'Access of Consumers to Justice and the Settlement of Consumer Disputes in the Single Market' (Green Paper) COM(93) 576.
Commission (EC), 'Damages Actions for Breach of the EC Antitrust Rules' (Green Paper) COM(2005) 672.
Commission (EC), 'Consumer Collective Redress' (Green Paper) COM(2008) 794.
Commission (EC), 'Damages Actions for Breach of the EC Antitrust Rules' (White Paper) COM(2008) 165.
Commission (EC), 'Consultation Paper for Discussion on the Follow-up to the Green Paper on Consumer Collective Redress' 2009 COM(2008) 794.
——, 'Consultation Paper on the Use of Alternative Dispute Resolution as a Means to Resolve Disputes Related to Commercial Transactions and Practices in the European Union' (2011).
Commission (EC), 'Proposal for a Directive on Anti-trust Damages Actions' COM(2013) 404.
——, Communication 'Towards a European Horizontal Framework for Collective Redress' COM(2013) 401/2.
—— Recommendation of 11 June 2013 on Common Principles for Injunctive and Compensatory Collective Redress Mechanisms in the Member States concerning violations of rights granted under Union Law (2013/396/EU).
The Competent Authority, *Buncefield: Why Did it Happen? The Underlying Causes of the Explosion and Fire at the Buncefield Oil Storage Depot, Hemel Hempstead, Hertfordshire on 11 December 2005* (2011).

Coonan G 'Public Interest Law and the Irish Legal System: All Crass and No Class' (2002) 5 *Trinity College Law Review* 44.
Cooper E, 'The (Cloudy) Future of Class Actions' (1998) 40 *Arizona Law Review* 923.
——, 'Class Action Advice in the Form of Questions' (2001) 11 *Duke Journal of Comparative and International Law* 223.
Crant R, 'The Nature of Regulatory Choices' (1978) 33 *Food Drug Cosmetic Law Journal* 413.
Dam K, 'Class Actions: Efficiency, Compensation, Deterrence and Conflict of Interest' (1975) 4 *Journal of Legal Studies* 47.
Davis M, 'Occupational Hazards and Black Workers' (1977) 6 (5) *Urban Health* 16.
——, 'Towards the Proper Role for Mass Tort Class Actions' (1998) 77 *Oregon Law Review* 157.
Department of Business, Innovation and Skills, *Consultation on Civil Enforcement Remedies: Consultation on Extending the Range of Remedies Available to Public Enforcers of Consumer Law* (2012).
Department of Constitutional Affairs, *Tackling the 'Compensation Culture': Government Response to Better Regulation Task Force Report 'Better Routes to Redress'* (2005).
——, *Private Actions in Competition Law: A Consultation on Options for Reform—Government Response* (2013).
De Sadeleer N, *Access to Environmental Matters and the Role of NGOs* (Europa Law Publishing, 2005).
Dreyfuss R, 'Class Action Judgment Enforcement in Italy: Procedural "Due Process" Requirements' (2002) 19 *Tulane Journal of International and Comparative Law* 5.
Ebesson J and Okawa JP, *Environmental Law and Justice in Context* (Cambridge University Press, 2009).
Elliot D, 'The Future of Toxic Torts: Of Chemophobia, Risk as a Compensable Injury and Hybrid Compensation Systems' (1988) 25 *Houston Law Review* 781.
Environmental Protection Agency, *Environmental Equity: Reducing Risk for All Communities* (1992).
European Justice Forum, 'Lessons from the United States, Australia and the United Kingdom' (EJF: 2006).
European Parliament, 'Towards a Coherent European Approach to Collective Redress' Resolution of 2 February 2012, 2011/2089(INI).
Ewald W, 'Comparative Jurisprudence II: The Logic of Legal Transplants' (1995) 43 *American Journal of Comparative Law* 489–510.
Farber D, *Eco-Pragmatism: Making Sensible Environmental Decisions in an Uncertain World* (University of Chicago Press, 1999).
Farhang S, *The Litigation State: Public Regulation and Private Lawsuits in the US* (Princeton University Press, 2010).
Faure M, 'Environmental Liability' in *Tort Law and Economics*, 1 *Encyclopedia of Law and Economics* (2nd edn, Edward Elgar Publishing 2009).
——, *Tort Law and Economics* (Edward Elgar, 2009).
The Federal Judicial Center, *Preliminary Report on Time Study Class Action Cases* (1995).
——, *An Empirical Study of Class Actions in Four Federal District Courts: Final Report to the Advisory Committee on Civil Rules* (1996).
Fleming J, 'Mass Torts' (1994) 42 *American Journal of Comparative Law* 508.
—— and Kuster J, 'The Netherlands' in P Karlsgodt (ed), *World Class Actions, A Guide to Group and Representative Actions Around the Globe* (Oxford University Press, 2012).
Financial Times, 'The Toxic Time Bomb Exploding Throughout the Corporate World' (9 September 2002).
Finn S, 'In a Class All its Own: The Advent of the Modern Class Action and Its Changing Legal and Social Mission' (2005) 2 *Canadian Class Action Review* 333.
Fiss O, 'The Political Theory of the Class Action' (1996) 53 *Washington & Lee Law Review* 21, 25.

Galanter M, 'Why the "Haves" Come Out Ahead: Speculations on the Limits of Legal Change' (1974) 9 *Law & Society Review* 95.

Galligan T, 'Deterrence: The Legitimate Function of the Public Tort' (2001) 58 *Washington and Lee Law Review* 1019.

Garth B, Nagel I and Plager S, 'The Institution of the Private Attorney General: Perspectives from an Empirical Study of Class Action Litigation' (1988) 61 *Southern California Law Review* 353.

Gibbons S, 'Group Litigation, Class Actions and Lord Woolf's Three Objectives—A Critical Analysis' (2008) 27 *Civil Justice Quarterly* 208.

Gidi A, 'Class Actions in Brazil—A Model for Civil Law Countries' (2003) 51 *American Journal of Comparative Law* 311.

Ginsberg W and Weiss L, 'Common Law Liability for Toxic Torts: A Phantom Remedy' (1981) 9 *Hofstra Law Review* 859.

Gordon Levine A, *Love Canal: Science, Politics and People* (Heath, 1982).

Gottwald P, 'On the Extension of Collective Legal Protection in German' (2007) 26 *Civil Justice Quarterly* 484.

Grave D and Adams K, *Class Actions in Australia* (Lawbook Co, 2005).

Gunningham N, Kagan R and Thornton D, 'Shades of Green—Business, Regulation and Environment' (Stanford University Press, 2003).

The Hampton Report, 'Reducing Administrative Burdens: Effective Inspection and Enforcement' (HM, Treasury 2005).

Harbour L and others, 'Class Actions: An American Perspective' in C Hodges, *Multi-Party Actions* (Oxford University Press, 2001).

Hardberger A, 'Life Liberty, and the Pursuit of Water: Evaluating Water as a Human Right and the Duties and Obligations it Creates' (2005) 4 *Northwestern Journal of International Human Rights* 342.

Harlow C, *Understanding Tort Law* (Thomson Sweet and Maxwell, 2005).

——, 'Global Administrative Law: the Quest for Principles and Values' (2006) 17(1) *European Journal of International Law* 187.

—— and Rawlings R, *Pressure through Tort Law* (Routledge, 1992).

Harmon Wilson S, 'Public Law Litigation and Public International Law in the US' *The US Justice System: An Encyclopedia* (ABC-Clio, 2011)

Hawkes L, 'Parens Patriae and the Union Carbide Case' (1998) 21 *Cornell International Law Journal* 181.

Hay B and Rosenberg D, '"Sweetheart" and "Blackmail" Settlements in Class Actions: Reality and Remedy' (2000) 75 *Notre Dame L Rev* 1377.

Hedley S, 'Group Personal Injury Litigation and Public Opinion' (1994) 14 *Legal Studies* 70, 73.

Heffernan L, 'Comparative Common Law Approaches to Multi-Party Litigation: The American Class Action Procedure' (2003) 25 *Dublin University Law Journal* 15.

Hensler D, 'Revisiting the Monster: New Myths and Realities of Class Action and Other Large Scale Litigation' (2001) 11 *Duke Journal of Comparative and International Law* 179.

——, 'Has the Fat Lady Sung? The Future of Mass Toxic Torts' (2007) 26 *Review of Litigation* 883.

——, 'The Socio-Economics of Mass Torts: What We Know, Don't Know and Should Know' in J Arden (ed), *Research Handbook on the Economics of Torts* (Edward Elgar, 2013).

——, 'Third-Party Financing of Class Action Litigation in the United States: Will the Sky Fall?' (2014) 63 *De Paul Law Review* 1101.

—— and Peterson M, 'Understanding Mass Personal Injury Litigation: A Socio-Legal Analysis' (1993) 59 *Brooklyn Law Review* 961.

—— and others, *Class Action Dilemmas: Pursuing Private Goals for Public Gain* (RAND Institute, 2000).

——, Hodges C and Tulibacka M (eds), *The Globalization of Class Actions*, (2009) 622 The Annals of the American Academy of Political and Social Science.
——, Dombey-Moore B, Giddens B, Gross J, Moller E and Pace N, *Class Action Dilemmas. Pursuing Public Goals for Private Gain* (RAND Institute for Civil Justice, 2000).
Higgins A and Zuckerman A, 'Class Actions in England? Efficacy, Autonomy and Proportionality in Collective Redress' (2013) University of Oxford Legal Research Paper Series.
Hodges C, *Multi-Party Actions* (Oxford University Press, 2001).
——, 'Multi-Party Actions: A European Approach' (2001) 11 *Duke Journal of Comparative and International Law* 349.
——, 'Nordic Compensation Schemes for Drug Injuries' (2006) 29 *Journal of Consumer Policy* 142.
——, *The Reform of Class and Representative Actions in European Legal Systems: A New Framework for Collective Redress in Europe* (Hart Publishing, 2008).
——, 'European Union Legislation' in D Hensler, C Hodges and M Tulibacka, *The Globalization of Class Actions* (2009) 622 The Annals of the American Academy of Political and Social Science 82.
——, 'Collective Redress in Europe: The New Model' (2010) 7 *Civil Justice Quarterly* 370.
——, 'A Market-Based Competition Enforcement Policy' (2011) 22(3) *European Business Law Review* 261.
——, 'European Competition Enforcement Policy: Integrating Restitution and Behaviour Control' (2011) *World Competition* 385.
——, 'Objectives, Mechanisms and Policy Choices in Collective Enforcement and Redress' in J Steele and W van Boom (eds), *Mass Justice* (Edward Elgar, 2011).
——, 'Collective Redress: A Breakthrough or Damp Squibb? (2014) 37 *Journal of Consumer Policy* 70.
——, 'Towards Parameters for EU Civil Justice Systems' in S Vogenauer and C Hodges (eds), *Civil Justice Systems in Europe: Implications for Choice of Forum and Choice of Contract Law* (Hart Publishing, 2014).
——, *Law and Corporate Behaviour: Integrating Theories of Regulation, Enforcement, Compliance and Ethics* (Hart Publishing, forthcoming).
——, Vogenauer S and Tulibacka M, 'Costs and Funding of Civil Litigation: A Comparative Study' (2009) Oxford Legal Studies Research Paper No 55.
——, Benohr I and Creutzfeldt-Banda N, *Consumer ADR in Europe* (Hart Publishing, 2012).
—— and Stadler A (eds), *Resolving Mass Disputes: ADR and Settlement of Mass Claims* (Edward Elgar, 2013).
—— and Stadler A, *ADR and Settlement of Mass Claims* (Edward Elgar, 2014).
—— and Vogenauer S (eds), *Civil Justice Systems in Europe: Implications for Choice of Forum and Choice of Contract Law* (Hart Publishing, 2014).
Hogan G and Whyte G, *Kelly: The Irish Constitution* (4th edn, Butterworths, 2003).
Hogg P, *Constitutional Law of Canada* (5th edn, Thomson Canada Limited 2007).
Hurwitz W, 'An Analysis of Common Law and Statutory Remedies for Hazardous Waste Injuries' (1980) 12 *Rutgers Law Review* 117.
——, 'Environmental Health: An Analysis of Available and Proposed Remedies for Victims of Toxic Waste Contamination' (1981) 7 *American Journal of Law & Medicine* 61.
Iacobucci F, 'What is Access to Justice in the Context of Class Actions' in J Kalajdzic (ed), *Accessing Justice, Appraising Class Actions: Ten Years after Dutton Hollick and Rumley* (LexisNexis, 2011) 20.
Irish Law Reform Commission, *Consultation Paper on Multi-Party Litigation* (LRC CP 25-2003).
——, *Report on Multi-party Litigation* (LRC 76-2005).
Jackson R, *Review of Civil Litigation Costs: Final Report* (December 2010).
James F and others, *Civil Procedure* (5th edn, Foundation Press, 2001).
Jewell T and Steele J, *Law in Environmental Decision-making: National, European, and International Perspectives* (Clarendon Press, 1998).

Jones C, 'Disorderly and Unfair: The Weird Present and Uncertain Future of "Full Faith and Credit" in Inter-jurisdictional Class Actions (Paper presented to the 4th Annual Symposium on Class Actions, Toronto, 26–27 April 2007) [unpublished].

Kahn-Freund O, 'On Uses and Misuses of Comparative Law' (1974) 37 *Modern Law Review* 1–27.

Kalajdzic J, 'Accessing Justice' ('Class Actions' Conference, University of Windsor, Canada, March 2011).

—— (ed), *Accessing Justice, Appraising Class Actions: Ten Years after Dutton Hollick and Rumley* (LexisNexis, 2011).

——, *Access to Justice for the Masses? A Critical and Empirical Analysis of Class Actions* (UBC Press, forthcoming).

——, Bogart W and Matthews I in D Hensler, C Hodges and M Tulibacka (eds), *The Globalization of Class Actions* (2009) 622 The Annals of the American Academy of Political and Social Science 41.

Kalven H and Rosenfield M, 'The Contemporary Function of the Class Suit' (1941) *University of Chicago Law Review* 684.

Kanner A, 'Emerging Conceptions of Latent Personal Injuries in Toxic Tort Litigation' (1987) 18 *Rutgers Law Journal* 343.

——, 'Future Trends in Toxic Tort Litigation' (1989) 20 *Rutgers Law Journal* 667.

——, 'Medical Monitoring: State and Federal Perspectives' (1989) 2 *Tulane Environmental Law Journal* 1.

——, 'Ruminations on Trial by Jury: An Essay in Honor of Judge Robert S. Vance' (1990) 5 *Toxics Law Reporter* (BNA) 415.

——, *Environmental and Toxic Tort Trials* (Lexis-Nexis, 1991, and supp 1997).

——, 'Environmental Justice, Torts and Causation' (1995) 34 *Washburn Law Journal* 505.

——, 'Rebuilding America' (1995) 20 *National Association of Environmental Professionals News* 17.

——, 'Rethinking Superfund' (1995) 20 *National Association of Environmental Professionals News* 19.

——, 'The Politics of Toxic Tort Law' (1997) 2 *Widener Law Symposium Journal* 163.

——, 'Toxic Tort Litigation in a Regulatory World' (2002) 41 *Washburn Law Journal* 535.

——, 'Equity in Toxic Tort Litigation: Unjust Enrichment and the Poor' (2004) 26 *Law and Policy* 209.

——, *Environmental and Toxic Tort Trials* (2nd edn, Lexis Nexis, 2005).

—— and Trevor E, 'Federal Expansion of State Statute of Limitations in Hazardous Materials Cases' (1988) 29 *The Barrister* 34.

Kaplan B, 'A Prefatory Note to "The Class Action—A Symposium,"' (1969) 10 *BC Indust & Comm L Rev* 497.

Kelemen D, 'Eurolegalism. *The Transformation of Law and Regulation in the European Union* (Harvard University Press, Boston 2011).

Kellam J, 'Toxic Torts' (1998) 8 *Australian Product Liability Reporter* 161.

—— and Stuart Clark S, 'Multi-Party Actions in Australia' in C Hodges, *Multi-Party Actions* (Oxford University Press, 2001) 269.

King G, Koehane G and Verba R, 'The Importance of Research Design in Political Science Designing Social Inquiry: Scientific Inference in Qualitative Research' (1995) 89 *The American Political Science Review* 475–81.

Kingsbury B, 'The Concept of "Law" in Global Administrative Law' (2009) 20(1) *European Journal of International Law* 23.

——, Krisch N, Stewart R and Wiener J, 'Global Governance as Administration—National and Transnational Approaches to Global Administrative Law' (2005) 68(3) and (4) *Law and Contemporary Problems* 1.

Kingston S, *European Perspectives on Environmental Law and Policy* (Routledge, 2012).

——, 'Mind the Gap: Difficulties in Enforcement and the Continuing Promise of EU Environmental Law' in S Kingston (ed), *European Perspectives on Environmental Law and Governance* (Routledge, 2013) 147.

Kleefeld J, 'Class Actions as Alternative Dispute Resolution' (2001) 39 *Osgoode Hall Law Journal* 817.
Klonoff R, 'The Decline of Class Actions' (2013) 90 *Washington University Law Review* 729.
Knorr M, 'Environmental Injustice: Inequities between Empirical Data and Federal, State Legislative and Judicial Responses' (1997) 6 *University of Baltimore Journal of Environmental Law* 71.
Koch H, 'Non-Class Group Litigation under EU and German Law' (2001) 11 *Duke Journal of Comparative & International Law* 255.
Kortmann J and Swaak C, 'The EC White Paper on Antitrust Damage Actions: Why the Member States are (Right to be) Less than Enthusiastic' (2009) 30(7) *European Competition Law Review* 340.
Kramer L, *Environmental Law and Justice in Context* (Cambridge University Press, 2009).
LaMarca G, 'Market Share Liability, Industry-Wide Liability, Alternative Liability and Concert of Action: Modern Legal Concepts Preserving Liability for Defective but Unidentifiable Products' (1981) 31 *Drake L Rev* 61.
Langbein J, 'The German Advantage in Civil Procedure' (1985) 52(4) *University of Chicago Law Review* 823.
Law Reform Committee of South Australia, *Report Relating to Class Actions* (Rep no 36, 1977).
Lennox D, 'Building a Class' (2001) 24 *Advocates' Quarterly* 377.
Lennox S, 'Toxic Torts: Now a Reality in Ireland' (1997)15 *Irish Law Times* 236.
Lindblom H in D Hensler, C Hodges and M Tulibacka, *The Globalization of Class Actions* (2009) 622 The Annals of the American Academy of Political and Social Science 231.
Lindbloom P and Watson G, 'Complex Litigation—A Comparative Perspective: a "Two-edged Sword"' (1993) 12 *Civil Justice Quarterly* 33.
Lucas K, Walker G, Eames M, Fay H and Poustie M, 'Environment and Social Justice' (2004) *Rapid Research and Evidence Review* Policy Studies Institute.
Macrory R, *Regulatory Justice: Sanctioning in a post-Hampton World; Regulatory Justice: Making Sanctions Effective* (HM Treasury, 2006).
Magnier V, 'France' (2009) 622 *Annals of the American Academy of Political and Social Science* 114.
Majone G, *Regulating Europe* (Routledge, 1996).
Manitoba Civil Justice Litigation Committee, *Civil Justice Review Task Force Report* (1996).
Markesinis B, *Foreign Law and Comparative Methodology* (Hart Publishing, 1997).
——, *Always on the Same Path* (Hart Publishing, 2001) 306.
McGuinness Justice C, Address to the 'Globalisation of Class Actions' Conference, Oxford University (12–14 December 2007).
McIntyre O, 'Liability for Asbestos-related Illness: Redefining the Rules on "Toxic Torts"' (20050) 4 *Judicial Studies Institute Journal196.*
——, 'The Test for Causation in Relation to "Indivisible Environmental Diseases": Fairchild v Glenhaven Funeral Services Ltd' (2003) 10(2) *Irish Planning and Environmental Law Journal* 32.
Micklitz H and Stadler A, 'The Development of Collective Legal Actions in Europe, Especially in German Civil Procedure' (2006) 17 *European Business Law Review* 1473, 1485.
Miller A, 'Of Frankenstein Monsters and Shining Knights: Myth, Reality, and the "Class Action Problem"' (1979) 92 *Harvard Law Review* 664.
Miller G, 'Some Thoughts on Australian Class Actions in Light of the American Experience' in the Hon Justice KE Lindgren (ed), *Investor Class Actions* (Ross Parsons Centre of Commercial, Corporate and Taxation Law, 2009).
——, 'Group Litigation in the Enforcement of Tort Law' in J Arden (ed), *Research Handbook on the Economics of Torts* (Edward Elgar, 2013) 262.
Money-Kyrle R, 'The Origins and Roles of Class Action Laws across the World: What Types of Problem do they Deal with, and What Safeguards do they Have?' ('Building Effective Markets—the Role of an Integrated Legal System' Conference, Zurich, January 2013).
——, *Collective Actions—A Comparative Study* (Hart Publishing, 2015).

Morabito V, 'Group Litigation in Australia—"Desperately Seeking" Effective Class Action Regimes' (National Report for Australia prepared for the 'Globalisation of Class Actions' Conference, Oxford University, December 2007).

——, 'Class Actions, Group Litigation and Other Forms of Collective Litigation: National Report Australia'. 622 The Annals of the American Academy of Political and Social Science (March 2009) 320–32.

—— 'An Empirical Study of Australia's Class Action Regimes—First Report: Class Action Facts and Figures'(Department of Business Law and Taxation, Monash University, December 2009)

——, 'Australasia' in D Hensler, C Hodges and M Tulibacka (eds), *The Globalization of Class Actions* (2009) 622 The Annals of the American Academy of Political and Social Science 320.

——, 'Opt In or Opt Out? A Class Dilemma for New Zealand' (2011) 24 *New Zealand Universities Law* Review 421.

——, 'Clashing Classes Down Under—Evaluating Australia's Competing Class Actions through Empirical and Comparative Perspectives' (2012) 27 *Connecticut Journal of International Law* 245.

——, 'An Empirical Study of Appeals by Class Members in Australia's Federal Class Actions' (2013) 42 *Common Law World Review* 240.

—— and Caruana J, 'Australian Unions—The Unknown Class Action Protagonists' (2011) 30 *Civil Justice Quarterly* 382.

—— and Caruana J, 'Can Class Action Regimes Operate Satisfactorily without a Certification Device? Empirical Insights from the Federal Court of Australia' (2013) 61(3) *American Journal of Comparative Law* 579.

—— and Waye V, 'Reining in Litigation Entrepreneurs—A New Zealand Proposal' [2011] 2 *New Zealand Law Review* 323.

Mulheron R, *The Class Action in Common Law Legal Systems—A Comparative Perspective* (Hart Publishing, 2004).

——, 'From Representative Rule to Class Action: Steps Rather than Leaps' (2005) 24 *Civil Justice Quarterly* 424.

——, 'Reform of Collective Redress in England: A Perspective of Need' (2008) Research Paper for Submission to the Civil Justice Council.

——, 'A Missed Gem of an Opportunity for the Representative Rule' [2012] 23 *European Business Law Review* 49–60.

——, 'Cultural Dimensions of Group Litigation' ('International Association of Procedural Law' Conference, Moscow, 2012).

Newberg H and Conte A, *Newberg on Class Actions* (3rd edn, McGraw-Hill Inc, 1992).

Noonan J, *Persons and Masks of the Law: Cordozo, Holmes and Wythe as Makers of the Mask* (Farrar, Strauss & Giroux, 1976).

Nordby A, Danish Presidency, 'Copenhagen Conference on Collective Redress in a European Perspective' (Copenhagen, 22–23 March 2012).

Northrop S, 'Exporting Environmental Justice by Importing Claimants: the Suitability and Feasibility of Globalization of Mass Tort Class Actions' (2006) 18 *Georgetown International Environmental Law Review* 779.

Ontario Law Reform Commission, *Report on Class Actions*, vols 1, 2 and 3 (Toronto, Canada, Ministry of the Attorney General, 1982).

Osofsky H, 'Learning from Environmental Justice: a New Model for International Environmental Rights' (2005) 24 *Stanford Environmental Law Journal* 71.

Pace N, 'Group and Aggregate Litigation in the United States' in D Hensler, C Hodges and M Tulibacka (eds), *The Globalization of Class Actions* (2009) 622 The Annals of the American Academy of Political and Social Science.

——, Carroll S, Vogelsang I and Zakaras L, *Insurance Class Actions in the United States* (RAND Corporation, 2007).

—— and Rubenstein W, 'How Transparent are Class Action Outcomes? Empirical Research on the Availability of Class Action Claims Data' (2008) RAND Working Paper Series.

Pellegrini Grinover A, 'Brazil' in D Hensler, C Hodges and M Tulibacka, *The Globalization of Class Actions* (2009) 622 The Annals of the American Academy of Political and Social Science 63.

Peysner J, 'Access to Justice in Multi-party Actions' in P O'Dell and C Willett (eds), *Global Governance and the Quest for Civil Society* vol 3 (Hart Publishing, 2008).

Phair R, 'Resolving the "Choice-of-Law Problem" in Rule 23(b) (3) Nationwide Class Actions' (2000) 67 *University of Chicago L Rev* 835.

Poisson E and Fléchet C, 'France' in P Karlsgodt (ed), *World Class Actions, A Guide to Group and Representative Actions Around the Globe* (Oxford University Press, 2012).

Poltak C, 'Ontario and Her Sisters: Should Full Faith and Credit Apply to the National Class' (2006) 3 *The Canadian Class Action Review* 437.

Potts D and Rivlin S, 'Proposed Rule Change to Federal Civil Procedure May Introduce New Challenges in Environmental Class Action Litigation' (2003) 27 *Harvard Environmental Law Review.*

Prestage J and McKee G, 'Class Actions in the Common Law Provinces of Canada' in C Hodges, *Multi Party Actions* (Oxford University Press, 2001).

Prichard J, 'Class Action Reform: Some General Comments' (1984) 9 *Canadian Business Law Journal* 309.

Priest G, 'The Invention of Enterprise Liability: A Critical History of the Intellectual Foundations of Modern Tort Law' (1985) 14 *J Legal Stud* 461, 462.

Puxon, 'Comment' (1996) 7 *Med L Rev* 229.

Rawls J, *A Theory of Justice* (Oxford University Press, 1972).

Redish M, *Wholesale Justice: Constitutional Democracy and the Problem of the Class Action Lawsuit* (Stanford Law Books, 2009).

—— and Berlow C, 'The Class Action as Political Theory' (2007) 85 *Washington University Law Review* 753.

Resnik J, 'Managerial Judges' (1982) 96 *Harvard Law Review* 374.

Richards D, *The Moral Criticism of Law* (Dickinson-Wadsworth, 1977).

Robinson G and Abraham K, 'Collective Justice in Tort Law' (1992) 78 *Virginia Law Review* 1481.

Romano C, 'International Dispute Settlement' (2007) *Oxford Handbook of International Environmental Law* Loyola-LA Legal Studies Paper No 2007-14.

Rosenberg D, 'The Causal Connection in Mass Exposure Cases: A "Public Law" Vision of the Tort System' (1984) 97 *Harvard Law Review* 849.

——, 'Decoupling Deterrence and Compensation Functions in Mass Tort Class Actions For Future Loss' (2002) 88 *Virginia Law Review* 1871.

——, 'Mandatory-Litigation Class Action: The Only Option for Mass Tort Cases' (2002) 115 *Harvard Law Review* 831.

Roth R, 'Mass Tort Malignancy: In the Search for a Cure, Courts Should Continue to Certify Mandatory, Settlement-Only Class Actions' (1999) 79 *Boston University Law Review* 577.

Rowe T, 'A Distant Mirror: The Bill of Peace in Early American Mass Torts' (1997) 39 *Arizona Law Review* 711.

——, 'Debates over Group Litigation in a Comparative Perspective: What Can We Learn From Each Other?'(2001) 11 *Duke Journal of Comparative Group Litigation and International Law* 157.

Ryall A, 'Delivering the Rule of Environmental Law in Ireland: Where Do we Go from here?' in S Kingston (ed), *European Perspectives on Environmental Law and Governance* (Routledge, 2013).

Saiman C, 'Faith in Legal Doctrine: An Anglo-American Comparison' ('Obligations V: Rights and Private Law' Conference, University of Oxford, July 2010).

Schlossberg D, *Defining Environmental Justice: Theories, Movements and Nature* (Oxford University Press, 2007).

Schwartz G, 'Mixed Theories of Tort Law: Affirming both Deterrence and Corrective Justice' (1997) 75 *Texas Law Review* 1801.
Scott C and Black J, *Cranston's Consumers and the Law* (3rd edn, Butterworths, 2000).
Scottish Law Commission, *Multi-Party Actions* (Rep no 154, 1996).
Seltzer R, 'Punitive Damages in Mass Tort Litigation: Addressing the Problems of Fairness, Efficiency and Control' (1983) LII *Fordham Law Review* 37.
Seymour J, 'Representative Procedures and the Future of Multi-Party Actions' (1999) 62 *Modern Law Review* 564.
Shapo M, 'Tort Law and Environmental Law Risk' (1991) 14 *Pace Environmental Law Review* 531.
Shavell S, *Economic Analysis of Accident Law* (Harvard University Press, 1987).
Shelton D, 'Human Rights, and Environmental Rights, and the Right to the Environment' (1991) 28 *Stanford Journal of International Law* 103.
——, 'Environmental Justice in the Postmodern World' in K Bosselmann, and B Richardson (eds) *Environmental Justice and Market Mechanisms: Key Challenges for Environmental Law and Policy* (Kluwer Law International, 1999) 23.
——, 'Environmental Rights' in P Alston (ed), *Peoples' Rights* (Oxford University Press, 2001) 214.
Sherman E, 'The Class Action Fairness Act 2005' (2006) 80 *Tulane Law Review* 1593.
Sherman E, 'Group Litigation under Foreign Legal Systems: Variations and Alternatives to American Class Actions' (2002) 52 *DePaul L Rev* 401.
Sokolow M, 'Hazardous Waste Liability and Compensation: Old Solutions, New Solutions, No Solutions' (1982) 14 *Connecticut Law Review* 307.
Sorabji J, 'The Hidden Class action in English Civil Procedure' (2009) 28 *Civil Justice Q* 498
Spence D, *Enforcement of Environmental Law: The Case for Reform* (Law Reform Committee of the Law Society of Ireland, 2007).
Spence S, 'Looking Back … In a Collective Way: A Short History of Class Action Law' (2002) 11 *ABA Business Law 6.*
Steele J, 'Remedies and Remediation: Foundational Issues in Environmental Liability' (1995) 58 *Modern Law Review* 615–36.
——, 'Participation and Deliberation in Environmental Law: Exploring a Problem-solving Approach' *Oxford Journal of Legal Studies* (Oxford University Press, 2001) 415–22.
—— and Van Boom W (eds), *Mass Justice: Challenges of Representation and Distribution* (Edward Elgar, 2011).
Stuart Clark S and Harris C, 'Multi-Plaintiff Litigation in Australia: A Comparative Perspective' (2001) 11 *Duke Journal of Comparative & International Law* 289.
Stürner M, 'Model Case Proceedings in the Capital Markets: Tentative Steps Towards Group Litigation in Germany' (2007) 26 *Civil Justice Quarterly* 250.
Stuyck J and others, *Commission Study on Alternative Means of Consumer Redress other than Redress through Ordinary Judicial Proceedings* (Catholic University of Leuven, 2007).
Sutts, Stosberg LLP 'Vioxx National Class Action Canada', available at: www.vioxxnationalclassaction.com.
Thornton J, 'Group Actions for Private Nuisance: Fact Management and Assessing Quantum for Loss of Amenity' *e-law* November 2012, See: www.lexology.com.
Tiller E and Cross F, 'What is Legal Doctrine?'(2007) 100 *Northwestern University Law Review* 517.
Toffolon-Weiss M and Roberts J, 'Toxic Torts, Public Interest Law, and Environmental Justice: Evidence from Louisiana' (2004) 26 *Law & Policy* 259.
Trebilcock M, *A Study on Consumer Misleading and Unfair Trade Practices* (Information Canada, 1976) 270.
Tur R, 'Litigation and the Consumer Interest: The Class Action and Beyond' (1982) 2 *Legal Studies* 135.

Tzankova I and Lunsingh Scheurleer D, 'The Netherlands' (2009) 622 *Annals Am Acad Pol & Soc Sci* 149.
UNECE Convention on Access to Information, Public Participation in Decision-Making and Access to Justice in Environmental Matters, 38 ILM (1999) 517 (Aarhus, 25 June 1998).
Valdes F, 'Procedure, Policy and Power: Class Actions and Social Justice in Historical and Comparative Perspective' (2008) 24 *Ga St UL Rev* 627, 648.
Van der Heijde M, 'Class Actions' in J van Erp and P van Vliet (eds), *Netherlands Reports to the Eighteenth International Congress of Comparative Law* (2010) 197.
The Victoria Law Reform Commission (VLRC), *Civil Justice Review Draft Proposals* (Melbourne, Australia, 2007).
Voet S, 'Public Enforcement and A(O) DR as Mechanisms for Resolving Mass Problems: A Belgian Perspective' in C Hodges and A Stadler (eds), *Resolving Mass Disputes: ADR and Settlement of Mass Claims* (Edward Elgar, 2013).
Walker G, *Environmental Justice: Concepts, Evidence, and Politics* (Routledge, 2012).
Watson A, *Legal Transplants: An Approach to Comparative Law* (University of Georgia Press, 1974).
——, 'Legal Transplants and Law Reform' (1976) 92 *Law Quarterly Review* 79.
Watson G, 'Class Actions: The Canadian Experience' (2001) 11 *Duke Journal of Comparative & International Law* 269.
Waye V and Morabito V, 'Collective Forms of Consumer Redress: Financial Ombudsman Service Case Study' (2012) 12 *Journal of Corporate Law Studies* 1.
Weddle D, 'Settlement Class Actions and "Mere Exposure" Future Claimants: Problems in Mass Toxic Tort Liability' (1998) 47 *Drake Law Review* 113.
Weiner W and Szyndrowski D, 'The Class Action, from the English Bill of Peace to Federal Rule of Civil Procedure 23: Is there a Common Thread?'(1987) 8 *Whittier Law Review* 935.
Weinstein J, *Individual Justice in Mass Torts Litigation* (Northwestern University Press, 1995).
Willging T, Hooper L and Niemic J, *Empirical Study of Class Actions I Four Federal District Courts: Final Report to the Advisory Committee on Civil Rules* (1996).
Williams M, 'The History of Daubert and its Effects on Toxic Tort Class Action' (2003) 22 *The Review of Litigation* 181.
Woolf Lord, *Access to Justice Interim Report* (1995).
——, *Access to Justice: Final Report* (1996).
Whyte G, *Social Inclusion and the Legal System* (Institute of Public Administration, 2002).
Winkler, Justice, 'Advocacy in Class Proceedings Litigation' (2000) 19 *Advocates' Society Journal* 6.
Woolley D and others, *Environmental Law* (Oxford University Press, 2000).
Yeazell S, 'From Group Litigation to Class Action, Pt 2' (1980) 27 *University of California Los Angeles Law Review* 1067.
——, *From Medieval Group Litigation to The Modern Class Action* (Yale University Press, 1987).
Zander M (ed), *What's Wrong with the Law* (British Broadcasting Corporation, 1970).
Zuckerman A, *Justice in Crisis: Comparative Dimensions of Civil Procedure* (Oxford University Press, 1999).
——, *Zuckerman on Civil Procedure* (Sweet & Maxwell, 2006).

INDEX

www.ingramcontent.com/pod-product-compliance
Ingram Content Group UK Ltd.
Pitfield, Milton Keynes, MK11 3LW, UK
UKHW050944290926
15470UKWH00005B/1617

9 781509 905294